D0214289

# AFRICAN AMERICAN SLAVE NARRATIVES

# AFRICAN AMERICAN SLAVE NARRATIVES

## AN ANTHOLOGY
## VOLUME I

Edited by Sterling Lecater Bland, Jr.

GREENWOOD PRESS
Westport, Connecticut • London

**Library of Congress Cataloging-in-Publication Data**

African American slave narratives : an anthology / Sterling Lecater Bland, Jr.
p. cm.
Includes bibliographical references and index.
ISBN 0-313-31168-4 (set : alk. paper)–ISBN 0-313-31716-X (v. 1 : alk. paper)–ISBN 0-313-31717-8 (v. 2 : alk. paper)–ISBN 0-313-31718-6 (v. 3 : alk. paper)
1. Slaves–United States–Biography. 2. Slaves–United States–Social conditions. 3. Afro-Americans–Biography. 4. Slaves' writings, American. I. Bland, Sterling Lecater, date–
E444.A23 2001
973'.0496073'00922–dc21 00-042228
[B]

British Library Cataloguing in Publication Data is available.



Library of Congress Catalog Card Number: 00-042228
ISBN: 0-313-31168-4 (set)
0-313-31716-X (Vol. I)
0-313-31717-8 (Vol. II)
0-313-31718-6 (Vol. III)

First published in 2001

Greenwood Press, 88 Post Road West, Westport, CT 06881
An imprint of Greenwood Publishing Group, Inc.
www.greenwood.com

Printed in the United States of America

The paper used in this book complies with the Permanent Paper Standard issued by the National Information Standards Organization (Z39.48–1984).

10 9 8 7 6 5 4 3 2 1

For Freddie Belk, one who believed
19 January 1904–20 February 2000

Behold, God is my salvation; I will trust, and not be afraid: for the Lord Jehovah is my strength and my song; he also is become my salvation.
–Isaiah 12:2

[The fugitive slaves] encounter a whole Iliad of woes, not in plundering and enslaving others, but in recovering for themselves those rights which they have been deprived from birth. Or if the Iliad should be thought not to present a parallel case, we know not where one who wished to write a modern Odyssey could find a better subject than in the adventures of a fugitive slave. What a combination of qualities and deeds and sufferings most fitted to attract human sympathy in each particular case!

–Ephraim Peabody, "Narrative of Fugitive Slaves"
(*Christian Examiner*, July 1949)

Thou shalt not deliver unto his master the servant which is escaped from his master unto thee: He shall dwell with thee, even among you, in that place which he shall choose in one of thy gates, where it liketh him best: thou shalt not oppress him.

–Deuteronomy 23:15–16

# CONTENTS

# PREFACE

> [W]hen we get a little farther from the conflict, some brave and truth-loving man, with all the facts before him . . . will gather from here and there the scattered fragments . . . and give those who shall come after us an impartial history of this the grandest moral conflict of the century. [For] Truth is patient and time is just.
>
> –Frederick Douglass, 1891

Like many others, I was first introduced to the power of African American slave narrative writing by reading the *Narrative of the Life of Frederick Douglass* (1845). Several years ago, as I began research on fugitive slave narratives, the influential subgenre of African American slave narrative writing, it became increasingly clear that there are many other voices besides Douglass's that contribute to the tradition of which Douglass's *Narrative* is such an exemplary part. This anthology represents my attempt to offer some of those lesser-known voices in the context of the social and political circumstances that contributed to their composition and widespread influence. This volume is not conceived as an encyclopedic recitation of the approximately seventy fugitive slave narratives produced as books in the three decades preceding the Civil War. Instead, this is an attempt to use a selection of these narrative works as a starting point for discussing the ways African American writing and American culture influenced and ultimately grew out of each other. I have chosen the writings I have because they, in and of themselves, provide a certain level of nuance and because they provide an avenue for encountering a variety of literary and cultural subjects.

These narratives each convey a genuine sense of the ways these writers used language, structured their writing, and chose which aspects of their lives to present and extrapolate into deeper significance regarding themselves as individuals and the relationship of that individual self to the collective. Taken together, these narratives articulate thoughts and feelings that have an aesthetic beauty as well as a practical relevance to the lives of their writers and their audience.

This literature is also representative of the interconnectedness that exists among cultures. African American antebellum writing focuses mainly on the issue of slavery. It primarily addresses this issue in terms of actual experiences of physical bondage. It also expresses this issue from a spiritual perspective that emphasizes a spiritual journey from sin to redemption. It is the experience of slavery and the literature that experience produced that contribute to the feelings of double consciousness that W.E.B. Du Bois describes in *The Souls of Black Folk* (1903). Slavery undoubtedly altered western culture and the ways that culture perceived and expressed itself. These narratives document and expand the discussion surrounding these writings and their relation to a variety of cultural, political, social, and class-based conditions. Slave narrative writing incorporates, directly and indirectly, its African origins while also addressing the ways it simultaneously influenced and was influenced by the cultures with which it interacted.

My greatest acknowledgments for this anthology are to those who contributed to its initial conception and subsequent compilation. I am grateful to Kenneth Silverman, who first encouraged me to undertake this project as my interest in slave narrative writing was developing. I am especially thankful to the general and humanities reference librarians at Firestone Library (Princeton University) and at Alexander Library, Mabel Smith Douglass Library, and Dana Library (Rutgers University) who made it possible for me to identify and locate the wide variety of materials I required to complete this project. I am particularly grateful to Mary George and Emily Belcher at Firestone Library for patiently offering assistance, guidance, and direction. I owe special debts of gratitude to George Butler and Frank Saunders at Greenwood Press for their generous support and enthusiastic collaboration.

The community I have experienced while teaching and writing at Rutgers University in Newark, New Jersey, has made my work both enjoyable and intellectually stimulating. I am particularly grateful to Fran Bartkowski, Barbara Foley, Gabriel Miller, and Clement Price for being welcoming, encouraging about my work, and generous with their help. I would especially like to acknowledge the students who participated in the undergraduate "Introduction to African American Literature" classes I taught during the fall and spring semesters of 1996 and 1997 and the graduate seminar, "African American

Novel," I taught during the spring semester of 1997. Their interest in African American literature and their sense of intellectual curiosity made my own explorations into finding ways to examine slave narrative writing fun, challenging, and exciting.

During the years in which the ideas for this book were formulated, given shape, and revised, I benefited from the stimulus, inspiration, and vision of teachers, fellow students, colleagues, friends, family, and acquaintances far too numerous to name. Several, however, deserve specific mention: David Carroll, Isabelle Kaminski, Marilyn Campbell, Jane Low, Alessandra Bocco, Jennifer Manlowe, Eileen Reilly, Julie Armstrong, Jacqueline Ivens, Laurie Altman, Carolyn Fox, Edward Murray, Scott Murray, and Janice Bland.

My deepest thanks and acknowledgment continue to go to my parents, Ula and Sterling Bland, Sr., for their unceasing love and constant encouragement. This book is lovingly dedicated to the memory of my grandmother, Freddie Belk.

In bringing these narratives together for this volume, I have attempted, as much as possible, to avoid modernizing or trying to make consistent various styles of capitalization, grammar, spelling, and punctuation. Unless there are obvious areas of confusion for contemporary readers, I have retained these elements as they were used in the original texts. I have, however, silently corrected obvious errors. The texts of the narratives included here are presented in their entirety and are not abridged or condensed in any way.

# INTRODUCTION

## Bearing Witness: The Fugitive Slave Narrative and Its Traditions

> This fugitive slave literature is destined to be a powerful lever. We have the most profound conviction of its potency. We see in it the easy and infallible means of abolitionizing the free States. Argument provokes argument, reason is met by sophistry. But narratives of slaves go right to the hearts of men.
>
> –Boston *Chronotype*, quoted in *Anti Slavery Bugle*, November 3, 1849

This anthology presents a selection of the narratives produced by African American ex-slaves between roughly 1830 and 1865. With the notable exceptions of Nat Turner, who was tried and hanged for organizing a slave rebellion in Southampton, Virginia, and James Mars, who was born in Connecticut and lived his entire life in the North, these slaves had all escaped southern bondage.[1] They were writing, often with the encouragement of abolitionist sponsorship, firsthand accounts of their lives as slaves, their personal (and often spiritual) development, their desire for freedom, and their subsequent escape. Like the experiences they contain, African American fugitive slave narratives represent the kinds of tensions involved in trying to bring together disparate thoughts and experiences within the borders of what is fundamentally a generic literary form. The narratives these writers produced are illuminating in terms of what they say, what they refrain from saying, and the varying techniques used to achieve their intended results.

The popularity of the nineteenth-century fugitive slave narrative as a genre was based on a number of circumstances. These included the complex interrelationship between the increasing influence of abolitionist activity, the increasing political debate about slavery, the public desire to read about the experiences of slaves, and an increasing interest in the first-person accounts of the effects of slavery on individuals.

## THE AFRICAN PRESENCE IN NORTH AMERICA

There are no easy ways to draw connections between slave narrative writing and the social, political, and cultural elements that contributed to the development of the genre. What is clear, however, is that any examination of slave narrative writing necessarily requires some inspection of those factors.[2] A great deal has been made of the twenty Africans who were brought by the European settlers who arrived in Jamestown, Virginia in 1619. But scholars like Leo Wiener in his pioneering study *Africa and the Discovery of America* and Ivan Van Sertima in his book *They Came Before Columbus* compile evidence from archaeology, linguistics, sculpture, weaving styles for cloth, burial conventions, evidence of similar worship customs, and ship-building practices to make a strong case for the presence of Africans in the Americas before the arrival of European explorers. Others see the African presence in closer proximity to European expansion into the Americas.

In any case, the important point that should be made is that the earliest Africans in the Americas were not slaves–most were explorers. Estevanico (1500?–1539) accompanied the Spanish explorers Panfilo de Narvaez and Alvar Nunez Cabeza de Vaca on their travels to the American southwest.[3] Even the twenty Africans who landed in Jamestown in 1619 were considered indentured servants rather than slaves. Indentureship meant that after fulfilling their contract, usually seven years, they were free to actively pursue a livelihood, purchase land, and generally live as free citizens.

This all changed over the next half-century. The system of indentured servitude was gradually eliminated for blacks as well as whites. Instead, by the mid-seventeenth century, most procedures were changed to specify that all Africans (including those currently in the colonies and those who would arrive in the future) would live as slaves for their entire lives, rather than for the duration of a contractually specified amount of time. A number of factors contributed to the expansion of the African slave trade in the Americas, including the quickly expanding rice, tobacco, cotton, and indigo economy in the southern colonies; the rise of the planter class; the institution of laws allowing Africans to be considered property; intellectual arguments endorsing ideas of African inferiority; and a complicity in the Atlantic slave trade that involved, among others, the British colonies, Great Britain, Spain, Portugal, and the Dutch. Even an area like New England, which did not make extensive use of slave labor, economically benefited from the slave trade because of its involvement in the shipping industry.

## THE ENSLAVEMENT OF AFRICANS AND THE NEW NATION

The amount of human loss resulting from the Atlantic slave trade is astounding. When the earliest Europeans ventured into the areas on the western coast of Africa that are now known as Senegal, Ivory Coast, Ghana, and Nigeria, they encountered what they saw as a thriving slave trade between numerous African nations and Arab traders to the north. That practice was substantially expanded when slaves were provided to the British colonies. The most conservative estimates suggest that between the sixteenth century and the nineteenth century, anywhere from ten to twenty million Africans survived middle passage and arrived in the Americas. This is only a small portion of the total number of Africans who were shipped from Africa. It is estimated that fifty percent of all Africans who were sent from Africa perished in transit and never arrived in the Americas.[4]

As the colonies expanded, they found themselves involved in a number of military conflicts with the French and with Native Americans, and eventually in the Revolutionary War with the British. African Americans participated in all military conflicts. There was continuous concern, however, especially in the South, about blacks, slaves and freemen alike carrying weapons. During the Revolutionary War, for instance, Georgia and South Carolina even went so far as to refuse to allow slaves to bear arms at all. As the war continued, northern colonies desperate for support often enlisted southern slaves in what were initially non-combat assignments that frequently became combat assignments. After the war, about 5,000 of the slaves who participated were granted their emancipation.

When the framers of the Constitution sought to draft a document that would effectively combine power among a group of colonies that often had competing self-interests, the issue of African American representation became crucial to that delicate balance of power. In 1790, for instance, there were 757,208 African Americans in the United States. African Americans accounted for nineteen percent of the entire American population. The African American population, however, was primarily confined to the South. Of the African American population, 697,681 were slaves; only 59,527 were free.[5] In an effort to avoid giving slaveholding states a disproportionate amount of power in the House of Representatives, the framers of the Constitution eventually settled on the well-known compromise that minimized the presence of African Americans: "Representatives and direct Taxes shall be apportioned among the several States which may be included within this Union, according to their respective Numbers, which shall be determined by adding to the whole Number of free Persons, including those bound to Service for a Term of Years, and excluding Indians not taxed, three fifths of all other Persons" (Article I, section 2). The Constitution sanctioned the continuation of the Atlantic slave trade until at least 1808: "The Migration or Importation of such Persons as any of the States now existing shall think proper to admit, shall not be prohibited by the Congress prior to the Year one thousand eight hundred and eight, but a tax or duty may be imposed on such Importation, not exceeding ten dollars for each Person" (Article I, section 9). The Constitution was ratified in 1788. The national discussion about slavery was simply postponed, not resolved.

## SLAVERY AND REGIONAL SELF-INTEREST

The country expanded rapidly during the twenty-year interim between the ratification of the Constitution in 1788 and the abolition of the African Slave Trade in 1808. Historians traditionally cite Eli Whitney's invention of the cotton gin in 1793 as the turning point in the establishment of cotton as the South's primary cash crop. This, to some extent, is true. But the cotton gin should be seen in a larger context of industrialization that included the invention of a cotton spinning machine by Samuel Slater in 1790, development of assembly line factory production techniques, and John Fitch's construction of the steamboat in 1790. The cotton spinning machine, the factory system, mass production, and cheap, efficient transportation made cotton a tremendously profitable crop. These technological advancements energized the strength of the southern economy.[6]

The expansion of cotton production was directly proportional to the increase in the southern slave population. In 1800, the South produced roughly 100,000 bales with a slave population of approximately 850,000. By 1860, the South produced about 3,750,000 bales of cotton with a slave population of 4,000,000. Profits per acre soared, as did the prices of slaves. Between 1802 and 1860, the average price of a field hand rose from approximately $600.00 to over $1,800.00. The relationship between the increasing numbers of slave laborers and their prices indicates the immense profitability of cotton.[7] But this profitability, which bolstered America's economic presence in the world, also meant that the issue of slavery, the importance of which had declined in the years immediately following the Revolutionary War, was revived.

Between the Revolutionary War and the early part of the nineteenth century, the issue of how finally to resolve the "Negro problem" turned to the possibility of colonization. Proponents of colonization suggested that black Americans could either be removed to the western parts of the North American continent or be returned to Africa. For some black Americans, immigrating to areas in Africa like the newly formed Republic of Liberia was a viable option. For the majority of black Americans, however, colonization simply meant that they would be deported to lives of even greater uncertainty. It is worth noting that while the lives of southern blacks were sharply defined by the hardships of chattel slavery, the lives of blacks in the North were also defined by economic hardship, legal constraint, the inability to vote, and other forms of racial discrimination.

The conditions of blacks throughout the country created an environment in which black insurrection was a constant possibility. Among many others, organized uprisings were led by Toussaint L'Ouverture in Santo Domingo, or what is now known as Haiti (1793–1801), Gabriel Prosser in Richmond, Virginia (1800), Denmark Vesey in Charleston, South Carolina (1822), and Nat Turner in Southampton, Virginia (1831). With the exception of the Santo Domingo revolution, most of the other insurrections resulted in the capture and eventual execution of their organizers.[8] Though the uprisings themselves were often contained relatively quickly, their effects were often substantial. Repressive measures were taken with the objective of making it difficult for blacks to communicate and organize. Especially in the South, increasingly restrictive legislation ("slave codes") made education and peaceful congregation illegal for blacks. Travel for slaves and free blacks throughout the South was closely monitored. Contact between blacks was sharply limited and bearing arms or engaging in certain kinds of occupations without white consent was prohibited.

## NATIONAL EXPANSION, ABOLITIONISM, AND THE SOUTH'S "PECULIAR INSTITUTION"

The country grew at a tremendous rate in the years between the ratification of the Constitution and 1820. The population grew from four million to 9.6 million, the economy continued to expand, and Manifest Destiny pushed the frontier further and further west. Issues like tariff laws and the establishment of a national banking system were some of the important debates that engaged all sections of the country.

No issue, though, was continuously more divisive than the issue of slavery. Congressional debate did not address the moral aspects of slavery. Slavery was discussed as a political issue that was largely based on the economic concerns of particular sections of the country. It was therefore defined by what amounted to little more than sectionalized, partisan political concerns and solutions. One of those solutions, the Missouri Compromise of 1820, sidestepped any substantial discussion about slavery by focusing instead on maintaining the fragile balance of power that existed within the Union. The compromise called for Maine to be granted statehood on March 15, 1820. Missouri entered the Union as a slave state on August 10, 1821. The balance of slave and free states between the twenty-four states in the Union remained equal. In addition, all western areas north of Missouri's southern boundary would in the future be considered free territory. The western areas south of that boundary would in the future be considered slave territory.

Though the Missouri Compromise of 1820 was unsatisfactory to many, it served the purpose of temporarily averting attention from resolving what to do about slavery in territories that, in the future, might possibly seek statehood. That tenuous accord was not seriously threatened again until 1849, when California sought to enter the Union as a free state. (As in other instances, California's position was economic rather than humanitarian. The 1849 Gold Rush had brought thousands to the region in hopes of quickly making their fortunes. Slaves, as well as Mexican immigrants, were viewed as providing unwanted competition to white gold seekers.) Henry Clay, a senator from Kentucky, understood that California needed to be admitted to the Union as a free state. He was also keenly aware that the South would require some kind of reparation. His proposal was heralded as an opportunity for the country finally to resolve virtually all of the ongoing sectional disagreements about slavery. Among the numerous terms of his proposal, California would be allowed to enter the Union as a free state, the District of Columbia would eliminate slave trading (though not the actual institution of slavery itself), and the federal government would revise and significantly strengthen enforcement of the Fugitive Slave Act of 1793. Fugitive slaves who were captured would not be allowed to testify on their own behalf and would be returned to the South without the due process of a trial. Citizens were required under the terms of the act to report all fugitives and faced legal punishment for aiding their escape. As with the Missouri Compromise of 1820, this compromise only temporarily maintained the Union's delicate balance of power. This balance finally collapsed in February 1860 when the Alabama legislature voted to leave the Union if Abraham Lincoln, the Republican candidate for president, won the upcoming election. By mid-1861, South Carolina, Mississippi, Florida, Alabama, Georgia, Louisiana, Texas, Virginia, Arkansas, North Carolina, and Tennessee had all voted to secede. They formed the Confederate States of America, elected Jefferson Davis as their interim president, and began commandeering federal property throughout the South. Under President Lincoln's orders, federal troops eventually retaliated in an effort to reunify the nation.[9]

## STYLISTIC CHANGES

The slave narrative as it developed out of this climate represents the ways former-slave writers were willing to adapt prevailing narrative forms to their needs. Simultaneously, however, they undercut the very notion of a "traditional" form by co-opting these forms for distinctly non-traditional uses. The eighteenth-century slave narrative form was strongly shaped by the literary conventions from which it drew. These stylistic techniques, while certainly popular throughout the eighteenth and early third of the nineteenth centuries, were endowed with a certain amount of urgency as political differences began to escalate and the role of the slave narrator became co-opted by the growth of the New England abolitionist movement. These changes initiated shifts in the ways slave narrators were encouraged to present their work as well as the ways their audiences received their work. With the publication of popular slave narratives that went through multiple printings and were translated into several languages, the slave narrative became fairly well established as a genre of narrative writing that had the potential to attract a large audience. But as political pressures in the North intensified to persuade the South to bring about the end of slavery, the objectives of the slave narratives sought more directly to address the antislavery impulse.

Eighteenth-century narratives were often framed in terms of their spiritual and adventurous components. Many of the most influential eighteenth-century narrative writers were Afro-British. The most well-known examples of their writing include *A Narrative of the Uncommon Sufferings and Surprising Deliverance of Briton Hammon, a Negro Man* (1760), *A Narrative of the Most Remarkable Particulars in the Life of James Albert Ukawsaw Gronniosaw, an African Prince* (1770), *A Narrative of the Lord's Wonderful Dealings with John Marrant, a Black* (1785), Ottobah Cugoano's *Thoughts and Sentiments on the Evil and Wicked Traffic of Slavery and Commerce of the Human Species* (1787), and *The Interesting Narrative of the Life of Olaudah Equiano, or Gustavus Vassa, The African* (1791). But the fundamental issues addressed were issues of bondage and freedom. The injustices attached to involuntary bondage were vigorously assailed on moral, religious, and social grounds, but it was on the enormous unjustness of the slave trade that these narrators eventually focused their attention.

Presumably, the distinctions made between the abolition of the Atlantic slave trade and the abolition of slavery itself reflected a belief on the part of blacks as well as whites that ending the slave trade would effectively bring an end to slavery itself.[10] The objective of bringing about the end of the slave trade to the United States through legislation was accomplished in 1808 when President Thomas Jefferson signed into law the African Slave Trade Act. (This act simply ended the practice of importing slaves from Africa. The trading of slaves who were already within the United States remained legal until President Lincoln issued the Emancipation Proclamation in 1863.) If slaves were no longer traded as human chattel, the thinking went, the slave system would eventually moderate itself and die out. During the first two decades of the nineteenth century, the attention the public had given to the slave issue was redirected to other social concerns. Largely owing to their popularity, slave narratives continued to be written and published after the African Slave Trade Act: *The Blind American Slave or Memoirs of Boyrereau Brincho* (1810); *Account of Life, Experience, Travels, and Gospel Labours of George White, an African, Written by Himself and Revised by a Friend* (1810); *The Life, History, and Unparalleled Sufferings of John Jea, The African Preacher* (1815); *The Negro Servant: An Authentic Narrative of a Young Negro, Showing How He Was Made a Slave in Africa, and Carried to Jamaica, Where He Was Sold to a Captain in His Majesty's Navy, and Taken to America, Where He Became a Christian, and Afterwards Brought to England and Baptised* (1815); *Incidents in the Life of Solomon Bayley* (published in North America in 1820 and in London in 1825); *Life of William Grimes, the Runaway Slave* (1824); and *Life and Adventures of Robert Voorhis, the Hermit of Massachusetts, Who Has Lived Fourteen Years in a Case, Secluded from Human Society. Comprising an Account of His Birth, Parentage, Sufferings, and Providential Escape from Unjust and Cruel Bondage in Early Life—and His Reasons for Be-*

*coming a Recluse. Taken from his own mouth by Henry Trumbull, and published for his benefit* (1829). As many of the titles suggest, the emphasis continued to be on adventure and religious conversion.

The renewed interest of white Americans in the abolitionist cause during the late 1820s and early 1830s sparked an abolitionist need for first-person accounts of slavery and its effects. The abolitionists saw slave narratives as an instrument that could be used to sway public opinion in their favor. Slaves were eagerly approached by abolitionists and encouraged to write their narratives. Public demand for more narratives greatly increased. The triangularity of this relationship helped fuse antebellum black writing with prevailing sociopolitical conditions. One of the fundamental shifts specific to blacks was that direct connections to Africa began to disappear. Eighteenth-century writers like James Albert Ukawsaw Gronniosaw and Olaudah Equiano provided first-person accounts of the narrator's African experiences.[11] The experiences recounted in their narratives were very much a function of their recollections of their lives in Africa. But the African-born freeman who expressed his independence by attempting to gain control over his financial, spiritual, and social affairs was gradually replaced by the fugitive slave narrator who coupled explicit examples of physical violence and psychological abuse with candid objections to the morality of self-professed Christians who allowed the system to continue. Fugitive slave narrators no longer relied on extended philosophical examinations of slavery and were instead encouraged, by abolitionists and their reading public, to highlight the most lurid and sensational accounts of their lives. The abolition of slavery, rather than simply the eradication of the slave trade, became the primary focus. In order to achieve that goal, the slave narrative adjusted to accommodate.[12]

## THE ERASURE OF ORIGINS

Eighteenth-century slave narratives were an indirect product of Enlightened thinking, emphasizing fundamental, individual freedoms—whether religious, intellectual, political, or social. These influences became considerably more focused and concentrated on the institution of slavery in the 1830s. For blacks, the shift from African origins to farm- and plantation-based origins brought with it a subtle but important shift in the kinds of stock episodes that comprised the narratives. Though both eighteenth- and nineteenth-century narratives often began with details concerning the birth of the narrator, the nineteenth-century narrative moved on to specific descriptions of slavery. Eighteenth-century narrators like Equiano, Gronniosaw, and Cugoano presented the idealized African experiences of its narrators and then contrasted the order and humanity of Africa with the inhumane brutality of European culture. Nautical adventures involving danger, excitement, and a certain amount of autonomy for the eighteenth-century narrator were replaced with nineteenth-century accounts of farms and plantations, in which the names of savage slaveholders were given and individual personalities were described. Slavery was no longer presented as a large, impersonal issue, but rather as a situation in which one group of individuals unjustly enslaved another group of individuals.

Even as slave narratives shifted their perspective from shipboard adventures and Native American captivities, they still possessed many elements that would endear them to a large reading audience. They described sympathetic characters who were mistreated by cruel, heartless male and female slaveholders. The slaves were distinctly exotic and wondrously strange to their readership. Plots were moved forward by the excitement of slaves' plans for escape and their eventual arrival in a free state. Slave narratives drew on the kind of episodic structure that was so prevalent in the historical novels of writers like James Fenimore Cooper and William Gilmore Simms, as well as the kind of sentimental writings that regularly appeared in magazines like *North American Review, Graham's*, and the *Southern Literary Messenger.*

While slave narratives benefited from the attention given them by abolitionists, they also owed a portion of their increasing popularity to larger cultural changes within the United States, like national literacy, an expanding reading public, and improvements in printing procedures. The number of magazines, for instance, rapidly grew from the five magazines published in the United States in 1794 to about 100 in 1825, and eventually reached more than 500 by 1865. Improvements in the postal system allowed for the timely dispersal of periodic reading material to ever-increasing areas. The expansion of the penny press, through newspapers like the *New York Herald* and the *New York Sun*, offered mass circulation.[13]

## POLITICAL ENTRENCHMENT AND INCREASING IDEOLOGICAL DISCORD

Nineteenth-century slave experiences were shaped by the close interaction on farms and plantations of slaves with masters and overseers. Slaves were forced to participate in a system in desperate need of inexpensive labor, but a system nonetheless seriously threatened by abolitionist pressures from without and the fear of slave revolt from within. By the 1820s, the abolitionist movement was slowly beginning to gather momentum. In 1820, John Quincy Adams wrote in his diary his belief that slavery was "the great and foul stain upon the North American Union," and that slavery would undoubtedly be the question upon which the future existence of the Union would be decided.[14]

Though Adams chose only to express these sentiments privately, others like Benjamin Lundy, who edited a Baltimore newspaper called *The Genius of Universal Emancipation*, publicly called for the federal government to involve itself in influencing the South to abolish slavery. Lundy's assistant, William Lloyd

Garrison, was more confrontational in his stance against slavery and rejected the use of political methods to achieve his ends. Instead, he frequently burned the Constitution at public lectures as a gesture indicating the institutionalized bias of the government against willingly enacting legislation that would bring about the end of slavery. Garrison's incendiary speeches were not always well received by others who felt threatened by their implied violence.[15]

Though relatively small in number, Garrison's followers had a strong effect on the abolitionist debate. His ideas about the need to bring about full equality for blacks rather than simply the need for abolitionists to "free" blacks was also important in shaping the abolitionist agenda. As the South galvanized itself to the growing northern objection to slavery, it also became more sensitive and reactive to slave insurrection and the threat of slave insurrection. Southerners reacted quickly and violently to any hint of slave revolt. The threat of slave revolt, for instance, was quickly extinguished when rumors revealed the insurrection planned by Denmark Vesey in 1822. In retaliation, southerners killed thirty-seven slaves and deported another thirty. Although there was no actual uprising, even the *threat* of rebellion was enough to bring about this kind of reaction.

Actual rebellions were treated with equal severity.[16] After a slave revolt in Louisiana, sixteen blacks were captured and killed. Their heads were placed on poles along the Mississippi River in an attempt to intimidate others who may have considered formulating similar plans. The famous Nat Turner rebellion in Southampton, Virginia, in 1831 became seen as one of the more dramatic examples of the dangers for southerners of slave revolts. At least fifty-five white people were killed before control was eventually regained. The effects of the rebellion were felt throughout the South. Runaway slaves were relentlessly tracked and southern states made it increasingly difficult for slaveowners to free their slaves.[17]

From this perspective, the patterns leading to the development of an organized abolitionist movement are fairly clear. The very institution of slavery itself formed the basis for slave unrest and raised the potential for slave revolt. Slave revolt became a fundamental way of expressing a desire for freedom and a willingness to fight and die for it. White abolitionism was built upon what was essentially black abolitionism or, more precisely, a sustained revolutionary conflict. The abolitionist movement was initiated by blacks and appropriated by non-blacks who were troubled, on moral and religious grounds, by the thought of southern denial of human rights. This non-black abolitionist movement was as troubling to pro-slavery advocates as actual slave uprisings.[18] Abolitionists were perceived as being outside troublemakers who did not fully understand the facts of the matter. The assertion that abolitionism was very much a function of slave discontent did not appear in most literature of the white abolitionist movement. But the fact that slaves did indeed revolt indicates that slaves did not readily accept their subordinate position.

The increased scrutiny and draconian restrictions placed upon slaves as a result of pressures by abolitionists and the possibility of slave revolts caused many slaves to view escape as their only hope for survival.[19] The internalization of the escape motif became the primary structuring device of most slave narratives.[20] Nineteenth-century slave narratives were placed in a position in which they had to present as a sympathetic character a slave who may have been forced to lie, steal, and use other deceptions in order to gain his or her freedom. This is a rhetorical continuation of the Du Boisian notion of African American double-consciousness that eighteenth-century narrators earlier encountered. In a paper delivered to the American Negro Academy in March of 1897, W.E.B. Du Bois noted that "No Negro who has given earnest thought to the situation of his people in America has failed, at some time in his life, to find himself at these crossroads, has failed to ask himself at some time: what, after all, am I? Am I an American or am I a Negro? Can I be both? Or is it my duty to cease to be a Negro as soon as possible and be an American?"[21] Though Du Bois is speaking particularly about the difficulty of reconciling a nationalistic American identity with a collective black identity, this impediment also sits at the root of African American slave narrative writing. Slave narrative writers were deeply aware of their positions as Americans who contributed, under the harshest conditions, to the development of the country. But because of the conditions in which they lived, blacks were also acutely conscious of their alienation from a complete involvement with the country they were helping to create. Virtually all slave narratives seek, at some level, to explore the disparity between blackness and cultural, political, social, spiritual, and economic assimilation.

## ABOLITIONIST EXPANSION AND ITS APPROPRIATION OF THE EX-SLAVE'S VOICE

The expansion of the abolitionist agenda had a profound effect on the production and distribution of slave writings because the publication of slave narratives was seen to have a large impact on swaying public opinion. As the number of abolitionist societies grew in New England, so too did the publications they produced. A host of publications routinely included slave narratives: *The Abolitionist; or record of the New England Anti-slavery Society; The African Observer; American and Foreign Anti-slavery Society; The American Anti-slavery Almanac; American Convention for Promoting the Abolition of Slavery, and Improving the Condition of the African Race; Anti-slavery Examiner; Anti-slavery Record; Anti-slavery Reporter; Anti-slavery Tracts; The Argus; Christian Examiner; The Emancipator; The Genius of Universal Emancipation; Herald of Freedom; Journal of Negro History; The Liberator; The Liberty Bell; Quarterly Anti-slavery Magazine; Putnams's Magazine; Slave's Friend; National Enquirer; Observer.* Ex-slaves were increasingly encouraged to tell their stories both as public orations and as written narratives. The oral, performative component of the narrative is especially significant. It is probable that by initially presenting their experiences as an oral presentation, slave narrators were able to gauge and revise the effectiveness of various combinations of experience before composing the written version of the narrative.

The abolitionist movement can be seen as one of the many reform movements that existed in the United States during the pre–Civil War era, including the temperance movement, the creation of utopian communities, and the women's rights movement.[22] The atmosphere that was created by the antislavery movement also permeated other movements seeking civil rights. It was a political movement that, among other things, enabled black writers to find avenues to literary expression that they otherwise would not have found. But as instrumental as the antislavery movement was to the literary expression of black experience, it should also be underscored that the directions of the antislavery movement were very much influenced by the involvement of blacks as well as whites. The movement came to be identified with the cause of white, New England liberals, but that cause grew directly out of the enslavement of blacks and their individual and collective reactions to that enslavement. In an individual response to their captivity, slaves ran away and sought to find ways in which they could buy their freedom. In a collective response, slaves planned insurrections, arranged networks though which other slaves could escape to the North, organized antislavery groups, and published antislavery pamphlets. All of this activity preceded the white abolitionist groups that developed during the 1820s and 1830s. Though overshadowed by white activists, blacks, as the people most directly affected by the successes and failures of the antislavery movement, remained involved and were acutely instrumental in its success.

In 1830, there were about fifty black abolitionist societies in existence and actively working to bring an end to slavery.[23] After 1830, these groups grew in size and influence by associating themselves with white abolitionist groups. White abolitionist groups found it very beneficial to the advancement of their cause to be able to present black speakers who would be willing to speak at their meetings and provide firsthand examples of the experiences of being enslaved.[24] These oratorical accounts were rendered in a way that was intended to arouse a certain amount of sympathy and support from the audience.

These speeches did not require a great deal of artistry. What was important was the heartfelt expression of experiences. Given the nature of these lectures, there was less of an emphasis on a full and complete oral history and more interest given to the incidents in the life that were most vivid and moving for the audience. Indeed, if the speaker was too polished in his or her delivery, the audience would begin to doubt that the speaker had ever been a slave. The written narratives often grew out of these lectures and primarily adhered to similar rules. The narratives were episodic in structure and contained vivid descriptions of beatings. Narrators noted when they began to feel the beginnings of a desire to escape and discussed the plotting of the escape (and possibly false starts at making that escape), the eventual escape itself, the creation of a new life in free territory, and reflections on slavery and its effects on both blacks and whites.

## RELIGION

Black writing was as deeply shaped by the intersection of abolition and religion as it was by various social, cultural, and individual imperatives. The religious influences on the black experience in America have their basis in Africa and in the transferal of those influences to the status of blacks in America.[25] In a literary sense, these religious influences recur throughout the structures and themes of the narratives. But religion was also a fundamental component of abolitionism. Religion was used both to defend slavery and to argue for its elimination. Slaveholders and slaves each professed a deep sense of religiosity, though clearly the outward manifestation of the lessons they absorbed were fundamentally different.

In attempting to renovate the fundamental ways in which the country viewed and responded to issues concerning race, black and white abolitionists also created a climate that questioned the traditional ways religion itself was practiced. Abolitionists believed that their campaign against slavery demanded that they create a very humanized picture of the slave while simultaneously depicting a starkly inhuman system that encouraged the unfair subjugation of one human by another. Abolitionists sought to sway public opinion by gathering the most persuasive accounts of slavery they could muster.

> The fugitive slave literature is destined to be a powerful lever. We have the most profound conviction of its potency. We see in it the easy and infallible means of abolitionizing the free states. Argument provokes argument, reason is met by sophistry. But narratives of slaves go right to the hearts of men. . . . Stir up honest men's souls with such a book, and they won't set much by disclaimers; they won't be squeamish how radically they vote against a system which surpasses any hell which theology has ever been able to conjure up.[26]

The abolitionist goal was to persuade northerners of the intrinsic iniquity of the slave system. Southerners could not be targeted as a potential audience for antislavery activity. The South realized the injustice of slavery but knew that its entire economic system revolved around the availability of large quantities of slave labor. Since northerners did not directly profit from slavery, they could be persuaded on the basis of emotional and moral reasoning.[27]

Clearly, slavery was not abolished solely on the basis of slave narratives. But for abolitionist sponsors, these narratives achieved the goal they sought to achieve: Slave narratives created a climate in which the victims of slavery were humanized and presented as sympathetic figures simply seeking the freedom they deserved. This placed an undue stress on the narrators. They were simultaneously forced to present themselves as individual characters, as representatives of their race, and as embodiments of the injustices visited upon the race. If whites could earlier have claimed a certain amount of ignorance regarding the kinds of exploitation African slaves faced, fugitive slaves graphically presented examples of the nature of the exploitation as well as the physical and mental abuses that accompanied that exploitation. Southerners, however, were under no illusions regarding their need for slaves and the inevitability of a system that demanded a large, unskilled labor pool to run the system.

> Nay, supposing that we were all convinced, and thought of slavery precisely as you do, at what ear of "Moral suasion" do you imagine you could prevail on us to give up a thousand millions of dollars in the value of our slaves, and a thousand millions of dollars more in the depreciation of our lands, in consequence of the want of laborers to cultivate them?[28]

## "WHAT IF I AM A WOMAN?": WOMEN, RELIGION, AND THE ANTISLAVERY MOVEMENT

The questioning of American religious practice through abolitionist activity was especially evident in the thoughts of organized antislavery women and the reactions to their work. For many women who involved themselves in the antislavery movement during the 1830s and 1840s, the stand against slavery and racism indicated a more central evangelically-based belief that social change could be used to bring a moral redemption to American culture.[29] Though they needed to present their ideas in a public platform, women faced the constrictions of the private, domestic sphere within which they were supposed to operate. Maria W. Stewart, a black antislavery activist living in Boston, argued in 1831 that blacks should enjoy the same rights as whites, and that blacks themselves needed to stand up and assert those rights: "All the nations of the earth are crying out for Liberty and Equality. Away, away with tyranny and oppression! And shall Afric's [*sic*] sons be silent any longer?"[30] Though she acknowledged societal difference in attitudes toward women working in the public arena, it was the responsibility of women as much as men to respond: "What if I am a woman? . . . God at this eventful period" has "raise[d] up . . . females to strive, by their example both in public and private to assist" in the social and political progress of African Americans.[31]

Stewart was the first American woman, black or white, in recorded American history to speak publicly about black civil rights and women's rights. Her message, both in lectures and political writings, challenged her listeners, most often black, to organize against slavery in the South and racism in the North. Her language and many of the themes she used relied heavily on the language and allusion of the Old Testament, especially Jeremiah and Lamentations, as well as the prophets Isaiah and Ezekiel. She frequently turned to the book of Revelation, possibly because of its emphasis on written language and on the final, catastrophic war of good and evil, and because of its didactically prophetic nature. But her position as a woman speaking before audiences of men and women (or "promiscuous" audiences, as they were called) is especially striking. She relied on biblical precedent to support her work: "The spirit of God came before me and I spake before many . . . reflecting on what I had said, I felt ashamed. . . . And something said within my breast 'press forward, I will be with thee.' And my heart made this reply, 'Lord, if thou wilt be with me, then I will speak for thee as long as I live.' "[32]

Other female antislavery activists indicated a similar religious basis to their political actions. The *Ninth Annual Report of the Boston Female Anti-Slavery Society* notes that its members chose publicly to oppose slavery "After deep thought, careful examination, and fervent prayer for divine direction."[33] The *Proceedings of the Anti-Slavery Convention of American Women . . . 1837* argues, using biblical precedent, for the importance of women's involvement in political issues:

> When the Lord led out his chosen people like a flock into the wilderness, from the house of bondage, was it not a woman whom He sent before them with Moses and Aaron? . . . And was not the deliverance of Israel from Egyptian bondage a political concern? Did it not shake the throne of the Pharaohs, desolate the land of Egypt, and strike terror into the stubborn hearts of subtle politicians? Miriam then interfered with the political concerns of Egypt; and we doubt not, had the monarch been permitted to lay his hand upon the sister of Moses, she would have suffered as a leader in this daring attempt to lead out her sisters from the house of bondage.[34]

But ironically, these comments arguing for a public presence for women in the antislavery movement and employing a deep awareness of evangelical doctrine caused hostile reactions outside antislavery organizations as well as division within. Though women saw an evangelical foundation for their actions, religious leaders often found their thoughts and activities threatening.

In an article published in *The Liberator* on September 1, 1837, entitled "Appeal of Clerical Abolitionists on Anti-Slavery Measures," several notable Boston ministers wrote to express their belief that women were actually using the overthrow of "slavery to overthrow government, civil and domestic, the Sabbath and the church and ministry." This was the beginning of a major division in the antislavery agenda. One of the primary issues of conflict was the question of how women could best be involved. Garrison urged his followers to accept women as full members, which they did. But in reaction to the decision by the Massachusetts Anti-Slavery Society and the New England Anti-Slavery Society to accept women members, religious-based groups decided to establish the Massachusetts Abolition Society, which would exclude women members. This intersection of religion and the abolitionist movement defined the direction of the abolitionist agenda and certainly delineated the ways in which the abolitionist movement influenced the development of slave narrative writing and the forms (male-centered and adventure-oriented) that writing was encouraged to take.

In terms of these elements and the production of women's slave narratives, it is also important to note that women were sought out proportionately less than men to tell their stories on abolitionist platforms. This is partially a function of the bias against women speaking in public and partially because of the nineteenth-century emphasis on women being domestic and submissive. It should come as no surprise that initially, the loudest criticism of women serving as public speakers came from those who were made most uncomfortable by what they saw as threats to their authority.[35]

## THE SAMENESS OF THE NARRATIVES

Structurally and thematically, there is an overwhelming sameness throughout slave narrative writing. This sameness became increasingly rigid over the course of the eighteenth-century until the involvement of the abolitionist movement securely codified this style of black writing through the Civil War. Among other conventions, the basic outlines of the narratives usually include on the title page the assertion that the narrative was either written by the slave or dictated to some friend who did the actual writing. Before the beginning of the actual narrative, there are usually a series of introductions or prefaces that serve as testimonials to the character of the narrator and the accuracy of the narrative. This introductory material is customarily written by white abolitionist supporters or white editors and authors who served as literary benefactors to the slave writer. The functions of these prefaces are to emphasize the fundamental truth of the narrative to follow, the connections between the preface writer and the narrative writer, and the fact that the narrative understates rather than overstates the effects of the slave system.

The narratives themselves tend to open at the beginning of the narrator's life, with a short discussion of what facts the narrator actually knows about his or her birth. These customarily do not include precise information about the date of birth, but are usually very specific in designating the geographic location of the birth. Parentage is frequently an issue with the slave narrator. As often as not, there is a question of parentage that suggests the possibility of a white ancestor. Having established basic facts concerning the narrator, the narrative tends to shift to external conditions. Central to these conditions are the heartless slaveowner and the precarious nature of the slave's existence. Descriptions of the slave auction served to show the uncertain nature of the lives of slaves. Christianity, or at least the Christianity professed by most slaveholders, was routinely shown to be of little help to the slave. Indeed, the slaveholders claiming Christian faith were characteristically described as being especially malicious.

There are a number of other recurrent elements in the fugitive slave narrative genre. They include accounts of the restrictions and obstacles that slaves faced in obtaining an education and learning to read and write; descriptions and summaries of the efforts of others to escape to freedom; successful and unsuccessful attempts on the part of the narrator to escape; final thoughts on slavery and the toll it takes on both the slaveholder and the enslaved; and supplementary material following the conclusion of the narrative (like more letters from supporters or other endorsements) that serves as a kind of framing counterpoint to the material preceding the narrative.[36]

What becomes clear from even a cursory look at several narratives is that all of this structural apparatus leaves very little room for the voice of the narrator to come through. The narratives virtually all look outward to the reality of slavery in hopes of addressing the reading audience and encouraging it to express its political strength in expectation of bringing an end to slavery. The lives of the narrators became secondary to the political issues at hand. Though central to the narrative, their lives more than anything illustrate what slavery was and what slavery was about. The detail the reader gets is formulaic and not overly revealing of the personal thoughts and desires of the narrator. The only interior life discussed by the narrator is the life directly related to slavery and its abolition. At heart, this was the single, guiding principle behind virtually all fugitive slave narrative writing. Their literary sponsors sought to use a well-defined genre to serve a particular, well-defined political agenda. Everyone involved with the narratives–including narrators themselves, their sponsors, and their intended audience–understood the objectives the narratives sought to accomplish. It is inevitable that most of the narratives bear striking similarities to each other.[37]

## THE RECONSTRUCTIVE VOICE

Having argued for the deeply formulaic nature of the slave narrative as a genre, it is also worth noting that the kind of reconstructive voice that appears at the beginning of the narrative is also a fairly stock ingredient in the American autobiographical form of the early to mid-nineteenth century. Narrators created a place for themselves in the minds of their readers by associating themselves with any number of geographic and familial coordinates. The primary difference, of course, between the narratives of former slaves and the autobiographies of white writers is that white writers were likely to spend more time remarking on why they chose to write their autobiographies and considerably less time commenting on the nature and circumstances surrounding their birth. For the ex-slave writer, the purpose of the narrative was fairly clear, since writers wanted to write about the slave system and bring about its collapse. Though the *why* of the autobiography was fairly unchanging, the *who* of the autobiography differed. The reader is paradoxically denied access to any particularities because these are the details that are most often shadowy and indistinct.

Black narratives play off the expectations initiated by white autobiographies because black narratives are not able to present the kinds of details the white autobiographer was able to draw upon to identify himself or herself. Black autobiography became distinct from white autobiography in the fundamental inability of the ex-slave to write his or her autobiography using the features common to white autobiography. Parentage is unclear or sketchy. At best, it goes back only as far as a grandparent. Brothers and sisters often do not share a common father so the idea of a family name is useless. Perhaps this is one of the reasons why a recurring component of the slave narrative involves taking a new last name once the slave achieves relative freedom. Since the last name did not signify an intrinsic connection to any kind of conventional familial structure, former slaves felt free to change their last name to correspond with their newly-won freedom. In losing this customary method of gaining the reader's attention, black narrators were forced to find other ways to engage the reader's interest.[38] So, while the black narrator adopted the narrative form, he or she relinquished any claim on the conventions intrinsic to that form.

Former slaves were very aware that their audience was largely white. They were acutely alert to the fact that their readers might not find their portrayals of their captivity or their captors particularly barbarous or horrific. This seems to be one of the primary reasons for the kinds of authenticating documents supplied by whites at the beginning and the end of the narrative. Because of the source of the narrative, slave narratives required white corroboration in order to achieve any kind of resonance with readers. This layer of validation was particular to black autobiography written for a white audience, since white narratives of Native American captivities or explorations of inhospitable places around the world seldom used these same kinds of framing devices to add a patina of legitimacy.[39]

The ways in which the narratives may be read is very much a function of the relationship that was constructed between the author, the author's experiences, and the intended audience. Black writers interpreted for whites, by way of various levels of mediation, the experiences of blacks. One way they did this was to focus the readers' attention outside of the usual parameters of their existence. At the most literal level, this was done by directing the audience's attention to a specific geographic region. At a more figurative level, the successive experiences of the narrator, eventually leading to a decision to seek freedom followed by episodic accounts of the escape, serve to displace the reader from a comfortable, isolated emotional space.[40]

Slave narrators used various strategies to approach their audience, but this approach was always a function of the writer's conception of the audience and the kind of response the writer sought to rouse. Writers like Lunsford Lane, James W. C. Pennington, and Josiah Henson try to show their audience that slaves are essentially hardworking, honest, and spiritual people who were driven to lie, cheat, and steal by the extremity of the conditions in which they lived. Slave narrators were engaged in a fierce struggle for the right to create themselves rhetorically, but first they had to revise some of their audience's negative perceptions about black life.

In framing my discussion of the slave narrative in the way I have, my intention is to argue for a view that sees them, from their very beginning, as triangular narratives whose meanings are a function of the relationship that was rhetorically developed between the writer of the narrative, the mediators who facilitated the production of the narrative and served as its gatekeepers, and the intended audience. Implicit within this configuration are elements of religion. These aspects are reflected in explicit Christian references and influences as well as in the implicit structuring of the narrative. The life of the fugitive slave is depicted as being a literal journey to freedom that involves the same kind of escape from physical oppression that the soul experiences in its attempts to free itself from the spiritual tyranny of sin. The narrative depicts a similar movement from bondage to freedom.

But the influences that bound the slave writer as closely to form and structure as slaveholders bound the slave to the plantation were abolitionists and their political agenda. The development of the abolitionist political agenda offered slaves a literal and figurative platform for widespread expression of their experiences within the framework of a literature offering clearly defined didactic patterns. But these patterns of self-expression were ultimately as limiting as they were freeing. As with the physical movement from slavery to freedom or the movement from south to north—where slaves often realized that they had traded one kind of oppression for another—so, too, did the literary articulation of their experiences ultimately become limiting.

Though the slave's narrative was closely controlled, it is important to note that it was one of several forms, including the novel, the essay, and poetry, that black writers actively chose to use. The writers like Douglass, Pennington, and Brown who went on to explore other literary outlets were well aware of the limitations as well as the possibilities of the slave narrative genre. Virtually all writings by fugitive slaves seek to establish a didactic purpose. Their writings move with a sense of direction and political purpose that is reflected in work by succeeding black writers. This cultural and political commitment eventually reached a similar pinnacle of political involvement in the black writings of the 1960s.[41]

## THE LITERARY LEGACY OF THE NARRATIVES

The legacy of the narratives is as much a function of social and political conditions as the narratives themselves. As the narratives of former slaves suggested, racial awareness was inexorably fused with the desire for freedom and autonomy. For the slave writer, these elements were rendered in physical and, to a somewhat lesser extent, spiritual terms. Subsequent African American writers rendered these desires in broader cultural and political terms. In the generation or so following the end of the Civil War, African American writers like Elizabeth Keckley in *Behind the Scenes: Thirty Years a Slave and Four Years in the White House* (1868) and, probably most famously, Booker T. Washington in *Up from Slavery* (1901) continued overtly to use the slave narrative form.

The realities of slavery and its effects were acknowledged, but now, however, the emphasis shifted away from descriptions of past oppression and toward an awareness of the possibilities for the future.

The New Negro Renaissance that occurred during the 1920s opened a creative dialogue between black poets, novelists, playwrights, musicians, visual artists, and intellectuals and their African American and African pasts. Anthologies like the *Book of American Negro Poetry* (1922), which was compiled by James Weldon Johnson, and *The New Negro* (1925), compiled by Alain Locke, sought to clarify and describe the vast web of cultural and literary traditions that linked a large and increasingly disparate body of African American writing. One of the difficulties inherent in an examination of the slave narrative is that the relationship of the individual to the genre is particularly diffuse. The technique that used individual identity in the service of a collective presence ultimately produced stories and narrative voices that mistakenly gave the impression of a single, unique, homogeneous identity. Twentieth-century writing based on the foundation of fugitive slave narrative writing refutes this essentialized view of African American culture and experience. The past in general (and slavery in particular) was seen as a pastiche of many stories, each equally valid. Out of the increased awareness of the explicit relationship between the past and the present, mid-twentieth-century works like Richard Wright's autobiography *Black Boy* (1945), Chester Himes's *If He Hollers Let Him Go* (1945), Ralph Ellison's *Invisible Man* (1952), Claude Brown's *Manchild in the Promised Land* (1965), *The Autobiography of Malcolm X* (1965), and Eldridge Cleaver's *Soul on Ice* (1968) used the first-person narrative voice as a way of examining racial interaction.

In many ways, Alex Haley's book *Roots* (1976) and its subsequent television miniseries offered, in a popularized, easily accessible manner, some indication of the sweep and influence of slavery as an ongoing presence in the fabric of contemporary American culture. Novels like Octavia Butler's *Kindred* (1979), Toni Morrison's *Beloved* (1987), Sherley Anne Williams's *Dessa Rose* (1986), and Charles Johnson's *Middle Passage* (1989), as well as films like the adaptation of *Beloved* (1998) and Steven Spielberg's *Amistad* (1997) all seek to use the imaginative process to reinterpret and ultimately revise the slave experience and its narrative form in ways that assert its continuing influence and relevance in contemporary American culture.[42] By situating slavery within an increasingly globalized context, contemporary artists and thinkers are seeing the slave experience as something much larger than a "peculiar institution" simply inflicted upon Africans and their descendants. In this enlarged context of examination, slavery is an integral thread running throughout the fabric of western culture. The global framework of contemporary evaluations of slavery returns slavery to the fundamental points by writers like Ottobah Cugoano and Olaudah Equiano articulated several centuries earlier: Slavery was a blight on all of western culture. It ultimately infected everyone it touched and continues to have individual and collective literary and cultural legacies.

## NOTES

1. Fabricant, "Thomas R. Gray and William Styron," 332–61; Oates, *The Fires of Jubilee*; Sundquist, *To Wake the Nations*; Greenberg, ed., *The Confessions of Nat Turner and Related Documents.*

2. This extremely abbreviated summary of American history is drawn from a number of sources including: Blum, et al., *The National Experience*; Burner, et al., *The American People*; Current, et al., *American History*; Estell, *African America*; Garraty, *The American Nation*; Garraty, *A Short History of the American Nation, Volume I;* Jones, *The Limits of Liberty*; Kelley, *The Shaping of the American Past*; Nash, *Retracing the Past*; Norton, et al., *A People and a Nation*; Unger, *These United States.*

3. Estevanico, also called Esteban, was a black slave from Morocco. He became one of the first explorers of the American southwest. He originally arrived in North America as a servant to explorers who landed in 1528 in what is now Tampa Bay, Florida. During their explorations, Estevanico was captured by Native Americans in what is now Texas. During his captivity, Estevanico was told about the Seven Cities of Cibola, which were said to be made of gold. Estevanico eventually escaped and guided explorers into what is now Arizona and New Mexico. He was killed by Zuni. Estell, *African America*, 1; Terrell, *Estevanico the Black*, 49–55, 109–39, and *Search for the Seven Cities*, 24–47.

4. Estell, *African America*, 4–5.

5. Estell, *African America*, 10–11; Rice, *The Rise and Fall of Black Slavery*, 63–101.

6. Garraty, *A Short History of the American Nation, Volume I*, 143–44.

7. Garraty, *A Short History of the American Nation, Volume I*, 143–44, 146–49; Bancroft, *Slave Trading in the Old South*, 19–44.

8. Egerton, "The Scenes Which Are Acted in St. Domingo," 41–64.

9. Potter, *Lincoln and His Party in the Secession Crisis*, 45–74; Cox, *Lincoln and Black Freedom*, 3–43.

10. Foster, *Witnessing Slavery*, 51–52.

11. Starling, *The Slave Narrative*, 59; Foster, *Witnessing Slavery*, 52–53; Costanzo, *Surprising Narrative*, 41–90, 109–13.

12. Foster, *Witnessing Slavery*, 148; Yellin, *The Intricate Knot*, 166; Andrews, *To Tell a Free Story*, 61–96.

13. McMichael, ed., *Anthology of American Literature, Volume I*, 550.

14. Garraty, *A Short History of the American Nation, Volume I*, 184–86. See also Joyner, "A Single Southern Culture: Cultural Interaction in the Old South," 3–22; Genovese, *Roll, Jordan, Roll*, 3–158.

15. Garraty, *A Short History of the American Nation, Volume I*, 184–85; Mayer, *All on Fire*, 3–70, 213–99, 333–481; Lowance, *Against Slavery*, 92–130.

16. Carroll, *Slave Insurrections in the United States 1800–1865*; 47–82, 83–117, 129–44.

17. Garraty, *A Short History of the American Nation, Volume I*, 221–22.

18. Faust, ed., *The Ideology of Slavery*, 1–20.

19. Franklin and Schweninger, *Runaway Slaves*, 209–33. See also Blockson, *The Underground Railroad*, esp. 23–155, 163–209.

20. Hedin, "The American Slave Narrative: The Justification of the Picaro," 635–36; Starling, *The Slave Narrative*, 29–33.

21. Quoted in Early, ed., *Lure and Loathing*, xix.

22. Filler, *The Crusade Against Slavery, 1830–1860*, 28–47.

23. Magdol, *The Antislavery Rank and File*, 3–14, 43–51, 61–99; Perry, *Radical Abolitionism*, 92–128; Filler, *The Crusade Against Slavery, 1830–1860*, 10–27; Rice, *The Rise and Fall of Black Slavery*, 305–52.

24. Garraty, *A Short History of the American Nation, Volume I*, 184–85; Harrold, *The Abolitionists and the South, 1831–1861*, 26–63.

25. Raboteau, *Slave Religion*, 211–88, 290–318.

26. Quoted in Nichols, *Many Thousand Gone*, 178. See also Harrold, *The Abolitionists and the South, 1831–1861*, 84–106.

27. McKivigan, *The War against Proslavery Religion*, 18–35, 56–73; Mathews, *Slavery and Methodism*, 113–245; Strong, *Perfectionist Politics*, 44–65; Soderlund, *Quakers and Slavery*, 15–31, 173–87.

28. Nichols, *Many Thousand Gone*, 180; also quoted in Aptheker, *Essays in the History of the American Negro*, 137.

29. Morton, ed., *Discovering the Women in Slavery*, 1–26. See also Fleischner, *Mastering Slavery*, 11–32.

30. Loewenberg and Bogin, eds., *Black Women in Nineteenth-Century Life*, 186. Also quoted in Yellin and Van Horne, eds., *The Abolitionist Sisterhood*, 4.

31. Loewenberg and Bogin, eds., *Black Women in Nineteenth-Century Life*, 198, 199. Also quoted in Yellin and Van Horne, eds., *The Abolitionist Sisterhood*, 4.

32. Quoted in Richardson, ed., *Maria Stewart*, 19.

33. Boston Female Anti-Slavery Society, "Ten Years of Experience," published as *Ninth Annual Report of the Boston Female Anti-Slavery Society. Presented October 12, 1842*, 8; Hansen, *Strained Sisterhood*, 13–28, 64–92.

34. *Proceedings of the Anti-Slavery Convention of American Women, May 9th, 10th, 11th, 12th 1837*, 10–11.

35. Foster, *Witnessing Slavery*, 58–59; Stetson, "Studying Slavery: Some Literary and Pedagogical Considerations on the Black Female Slave," 83; Braxton, *Black Women Writing Autobiography*, 1989; White, *Ar'n't I a Woman?* 62–90.

36. Olney, " 'I Was Born,' " 152–54.

37. Olney, " 'I Was Born,' " 152–54.

38. Olney, " 'I Was Born,' " 153–56; Andrews, *To Tell a Free Story*, 27–29.

39. Andrews, *To Tell a Free Story*, 26; Gates, Jr., *Figures in Black*, 89.

40. Bruss, *Autobiographical Acts*, 23; Swindells, *The Uses of Autobiography*, 1–30, 89–97.

41. Butterfield, *Black Autobiography in America*, 23–31; Stepto, *From Behind the Veil*, 3–31; Huggins, *Black Odyssey*, 114–53, 203–42.

42. Stepto, *From Behind the Veil*, 32–194; Van Deburg, *Slavery and Race in American Popular Culture*, 25–49, 67–129.

# 1

# NAT TURNER (1800–1831)

## THE CONFESSIONS OF NAT TURNER

In 1831, Southampton, Virginia was a small county that was inhabited by approximately 16,000 people, including whites, a relatively high proportion of free blacks, and slaves.[1] Southampton County is in the southeastern portion of Virginia, near the North Carolina border. Though slavery had been a fixture in the South since the seventeenth century, there had never been a sustained slave insurrection. In 1790, there was a large-scale uprising on the island of Santo Domingo. The rebellion overthrew French control and established Haiti, the first independent black republic in the New World.[2]

In 1800, the year Nat Turner was born, Gabriel Prosser formed plans in Richmond, Virginia, for blacks to revolt on the belief that the ideals of life, liberty, and the pursuit of happiness contained in the Declaration of Independence should apply to blacks as well as whites. Though Prosser's plans were entirely confined to Richmond, Virginia, authorities promptly responded by activating the state militia and arresting Gabriel Prosser and about thirty-four of his followers. All were eventually tried and sentenced to death by hanging. Though no whites were killed and Prosser's plans were stopped before they began, the question remained about whether or not large-scale black revolution, similar to what had occurred on Santo Domingo, where some 60,000 people died, could ever occur in the American South.

That question was emphatically answered during August 21 through August 23, 1831, when Nat Turner and a small group of collaborators (initially a group of six that expanded to possibly as many as fifty or sixty) carried on an insurrection in Southampton that resulted in the deaths of at least fifty-five white people. Most of Turner's group was captured by August 23, though

Turner himself remained at large before being captured around noon on October 30, 1831.

While *The Confessions of Nat Turner* is only one of several accounts of the insurrection that were published at the time, it emerged, almost from its initial publication, as the most influential. In the days following his capture, Nat Turner was asked by Thomas R. Gray, a white southern lawyer and slaveholder, to provide a firsthand account of his actions and the motives propelling those actions. Though Gray entitled the resulting document a "confession," it is not an actual transcript of Turner's trial. It was dictated to Gray, who then wrote, edited, and commented upon it in his introduction, in his conclusion, and at various places throughout the narrative. While Turner's control of the narrative is clearly compromised by Gray's close involvement with it and by some disparity between the narrative and official court documents, its details are largely corroborated by unrelated, contemporaneous documentation.

The full extent of Gray's editorial involvement with Turner's story is unclear. What is abundantly clear, however, is that neither voice can fully exist as a freestanding, authorized voice on its own. Each voice needs the limiting and defining qualities of the other for its own existence and significance. Gray furthermore needed the hysteria created by Turner's insurrection in order to sell the booklet itself. The compressed time frame of composition (Gray interviewed Turner on November 1–3, 1831, he acquired a copyright on November 10, Turner was hanged on November 11, and the booklet was published in Baltimore less than two weeks later) closely coincides with the fact that Gray's financial fortunes were quickly diminishing from the relative prosperity he enjoyed in 1829, when he had twenty-one slaves and eight hundred acres of land, to the single horse he reported as property just three years later.[3]

Turner's vision of revolution both encompassed and transcended physical enslavement. For Turner, slavery in the South served as the basis for his holy war. He saw himself as a prophet in the lineage of Christ. His narrative suggests that he saw his childhood intelligence and prophetic visions as evidence of that fact. Several events in Turner's life contribute to his outlook: the agreement by both blacks and whites that from childhood Turner was intelligent and would be dissatisfied as a slave; his father's escape to the North; and his literacy, religious visions, status as a lay preacher, and intense sense of mission. Most emphatically, Turner's narrative indicates the ways in which the religious rhetoric used by slaveholders as a means of control and justification of the slave system could be inverted and used as a justification for violent revolution and social change. Turner's story has served as the inspiration for a number of fictional accounts, including *The Old Dominion; or, The Southampton Massacre* (1856) by G[eorge] P[ayne] R[ainsford] James; *Dred: A Tale of the Great Dismal Swamp together with Anti-slavery Tales and papers, and Life in Florida after the War* (1856) by Harriet Beecher Stowe; *Homoselle* (1881) by Mary Spear Tiernan; *Their Shadows Before: A Story of the Southampton Insurrection* (1899) by Pauline Carrington [Rust] Bouve; *Ol' Prophet Nat* (1967) by Daniel Panger; *The Confes-*

*sions of Nat Turner* (1967) by William Styron; and *Dessa Rose* (1986) by Sherley Anne Williams.

*The Confessions of Nat Turner* reprinted here is from the original edition of the booklet published by Thomas R. Gray in 1831.

## FURTHER READING

William L. Andrews, "Inter(racial)textuality in Nineteenth-Century Southern Narrative" (1991); William L. Andrews, *To Tell a Free Story* (1986); Herbert Aptheker, *American Negro Slave Revolts* (1983); Herbert Aptheker, *Nat Turner's Slave Rebellion* (1966); Douglas Barzelay and Robert Sussman, "William Styron on *The Confessions of Nat Turner*" (1968); Sterling Lecater Bland, Jr., *Voices of the Fugitives* (2000); John Henrik Clarke, ed., *William Styron's Nat Turner* (1968); Douglas R. Egerton, *Gabriel's Revolution* (1993); Douglas R. Egerton, "The Scenes Which Are Acted in St. Domingo" (1999); Daniel S. Fabricant, "Thomas R. Gray and William Styron: Finally, a Critical Look at the 1831 *Confessions of Nat Turner*" (1993); Eric Foner, ed., *Nat Turner* (1971); Alison Goodyear Freehling, *Drift Toward Dissolution* (1982); Eugene D. Genovese, *From Rebellion to Revolution* (1979); Eugene D. Genovese, *Roll, Jordan, Roll* (1974); Kenneth S. Greenberg, ed., *The Confessions of Nat Turner and Related Documents* (1996); Seymour L. Gross and Eileen Bender, "History, Politics, and Literature: The Myth of Nat Turner" (1971); Vincent Harding, *There Is a River* (1981); Vincent Harding, "You've Taken My Nat and Gone" (1995); Peter Kolchin, *Unfree Labor* (1987); Lawrence W. Levine, *Black Culture and Black Consciousness* (1977); Stephen B. Oates, *The Fires of Jubilee* (1975); Thomas C. Parramore, *Southampton County, Virginia* (1978); Albert J. Raboteau, *Slave Religion* (1978); Mechal Sobel, *Trabelin' On* (1988); Marion Wilson Starling, *The Slave Narrative* (1988); Albert E. Stone, *The Return of Nat Turner* (1992); William Styron, *The Confessions of Nat Turner* (1967); Eric J. Sundquist, *To Wake the Nations* (1993); David E. Swift, *Black Prophets of Justice* (1989); Henry Irving Tragle, *The Southampton Slave Revolt of 1831* (1971); James L. W. West III, *Conversations with William Styron* (1985); Deborah Gray White, *Ar'n't I a Woman? Female Slaves in the Plantation South* (1985); Peter H. Wood, "Nat Turner: The Unknown Slave as Visionary Leader" (1988).

# THE CONFESSIONS of NAT TURNER, The Leader of the Late INSURRECTION IN SOUTHAMPTON, VA.

As fully and voluntarily made to
THOMAS R. GRAY,

In the prison where he was confined, and acknowledged by him to be such when read before the Court of Southampton; with the certificate, under seal of the Court, convened at Jerusalem,[4] Nov. 5, 1831, for his trial.

Also, An Authentic
ACCOUNT OF THE WHOLE INSURRECTION.
With Lists Of The Whites Who Were Murdered.
And Of The Negroes Brought Before The Court Of Southampton, And There Sentenced, &.

Baltimore:
PUBLISHED BY THOMAS R. GRAY.
Lucas & Deaver, print.
1831.

## DISTRICT OF COLUMBIA, TO WIT

*Be it remembered,* That on this tenth day of November, Anno Domini, eighteen hundred and thirty-one, Thomas R. Gray[5] of the said District, deposited in this office the title of a book, which is in the words as following:

"The Confessions of Nat Turner, the leader of the late insurrection in Southampton, Virginia, as fully and voluntarily made to Thomas R. Gray, in the prison where he was confined, and acknowledged by him to be such when read before the Court of Southampton; with the certificate, under seal, of the Court convened at Jerusalem, November 5, 1831, for his trial. Also, an authentic account of the whole insurrection, with lists of the whites who were murdered, and of the negroes brought before the Court of Southampton, and there sentenced, &. the right whereof he claims as proprietor, in conformity with an Act of Congress, entitled "An act to amend the several acts respecting Copy Rights."

(Seal.)

EDMUND J. LEE, Clerk of the District.

In testimony that the above is a true copy, from the record of the District Court for the District of Columbia, I, Edmund J. Lee, the Clerk thereof, have hereunto set my hand and affixed the seal of my office, this 10th day of November, 1831.

EDMUND J. LEE, C.D.C.

## TO THE PUBLIC

The late insurrection in Southampton has greatly excited the public mind, and led to a thousand idle, exaggerated and mischievous reports.[6] It is the first instance in our history of an open rebellion of the slaves, and attended with such atrocious circumstances of cruelty and destruction, as could not fail to leave a deep impression, not only upon the minds of the community where this fearful tragedy was wrought, but throughout every portion of our country, in which this population is to be found. Public curiosity has been on the stretch to understand the origin and progress of this dreadful conspiracy, and the motives which influence its diabolical actors. The insurgent slaves had all been destroyed, or apprehended, tried and executed, (with the exception of the leader,) without revealing any thing at all satisfactory, as to the motives which governed them, or the means by which they expected to accomplish their object. Every thing connected with the sad affair was wrapt in mystery, until Nat Turner, the leader of this ferocious band, whose name has resounded throughout our widely extended empire, was captured. This "great Bandit" was taken by a single individual, in a cave near the residence of his late owner, on Sunday, the thirtieth of October, without attempting to make the slightest resistance, and on the following day safely lodged in the jail of the County. His captor was Benjamin Phipps, armed with a shot gun well charged. Nat's only weapon was a small light sword which he immediately surrendered, and begged that his life might be spared. Since his confinement, by permission of the Jailor, I have had ready access to him, and finding that he was willing to make a full and free confession of the origin, progress and consummation of the insurrectory movements of the slaves of which he was the contriver and head; I determined for the gratification of public curiosity to commit his statements to writing, and publish them, with little or no variation, from his own words. That this is a faithful record of his confessions, the annexed certificate of the County Court of Southampton, will attest. They certainly bear one stamp of truth and sincerity. He makes no attempt (as all the other insurgents who were examined did,) to exculpate himself, but frankly acknowledges his full participation in all the guilt of the transaction. He was not only the contriver of the conspiracy, but gave the first blow towards its execution.

It will thus appear, that whilst every thing upon the surface of society wore a calm and peaceful aspect; whilst not one note of preparation was heard to warn the devoted inhabitants of woe and death, a gloomy fanatic was revolving in the recesses of his own dark, bewildered, and overwrought mind, schemes of indiscriminate massacre to the whites. Schemes too fearfully executed as far as his fiendish band proceeded in their desolating march. No cry for mercy penetrated their flinty bosoms. No acts of remembered kindness made the least impression upon these remorseless murderers. Men, women and children, from hoary age to helpless infancy were involved in the same cruel fate. Never did a band of savages do their work of death more unsparingly. Apprehension for their own personal safety seems to have been the only principle of restraint in the whole course of their bloody proceedings. And it is not the least remarkable feature in this horrid transaction, that a band actuated by such hellish purposes, should have resisted so feebly, when met by the whites in arms. Desperation alone, one would think, might have led to greater efforts. More than twenty of them attacked Dr. Blunt's house on Tuesday morning, a little before day-break, defended by two men and three boys. They fled precipitately at the first fire; and their future plans of mischief, were entirely disconcerted and broken up. Escaping thence, each individual sought his own safety either in concealment, or by returning home, with the hope that his participation might escape detection, and all were shot down in the course of a few days, or captured and brought to trial and punishment. Nat has survived all his followers, and the gallows will speedily close his career. His own account of the conspiracy is submitted to the public, without comment. It reads an awful, and it is hoped, a useful lesson, as to the operations of a mind like his, endeavoring to grapple with things beyond its reach. How it first became bewildered and confounded, and finally corrupted and led to the conception and perpetration of the most atrocious and heart-rending deeds. It is calculated also to demonstrate the policy of our laws in restraint of this class of our population, and to induce all those entrusted with their execution, as well as our citizens generally, to see that they are strictly and rigidly enforced. Each particular community should look to its own safety, whilst the general guardians of the laws, keep a watchful eye over all. If Nat's statements can be relied on, the insurrection in this county was entirely local, and his designs confided but to a few, and these in his immediate vicinity. It was not instigated by motives of revenge or sudden anger, but the results of long deliberation, and a settled purpose of mind. The offspring of gloomy fanaticism, acting upon materials but too well prepared for such impressions. It will be long remembered in the annals of our country, and many a mother as she presses her infant darling to her bosom, will shudder at the recollection of Nat Turner, and his band of ferocious miscreants.

Believing the following narrative, by removing doubts and conjectures from the public mind which otherwise must have remained, would give general satisfaction, it is respectfully submitted to the public by their ob't serv't,

T. R. GRAY.

Jerusalem, Southampton, Va. Nov. 5, 1831.

We the undersigned, members of the Court convened at Jerusalem, on Saturday, the 5th day of Nov. 1831, for the trial of Nat, *alias* Nat Turner, a negro slave, late the property of Putnam Moore,[7] deceased, do hereby certify, that the confessions of Nat, to Thomas R. Gray, was read to him in our presence, and that Nat acknowledged the same to be full, free, and voluntary; and that furthermore, when called upon by the presiding Magistrate of the Court, to state if he had any thing to say, why sentence of death should not be passed upon him, replied he had nothing further than he had communicated to Mr. Gray. Given under our hands and seals at Jerusalem, this 5th day of November, 1831.

JEREMIAH COBB, [Seal.]
THOMAS PRETLOW, [Seal.]
JAMES W. PARKER [Seal.]
CARR BOWERS, [Seal.]
SAMUEL B. HINES, [Seal.]
ORRIS A. BROWNE, [Seal.]

State of Virginia, Southampton County, to wit:

I, James Rochelle, Clerk of the County Court of Southampton in the State of Virginia, do hereby certify, that Jeremiah Cobb, Thomas Pretlow, James W. Parker, Carr Bowers, Samuel B. Hines, and Orris A. Browne, esqr's are acting Justices of the Peace, in and for the County aforesaid, and were members of the Court which convened at Jerusalem, on Saturday the 5th day of November, 1831, for the trial of Nat *alias* Nat Turner, a negro slave, late the property of Putnam Moore, deceased, who was tried and convicted, as an insurgent in the late insurrection in the county of Southampton aforesaid, and that full faith and credit are due, and ought to be given to their acts as Justices of the peace aforesaid.

[Seal.]

In testimony whereof, I have hereunto set my hand and caused the seal of the Court aforesaid, to be affixed this 5th day of November, 1831

JAMES ROCHELLE, C.S.C.C.

## CONFESSION

Agreeable to his own appointment, on the evening he was committed to prison, with permission of the jailer, I visited NAT on Tuesday the 1st November, when, without being questioned at all, he commenced his narrative in the following words:–

SIR,–You have asked me to give a history of the motives which induced me to undertake the late insurrection,[8] as you call it–To do so I must go back to the days of my infancy, and even before I was born. I was thirty-one years of age the 2nd of October last, and born the property of Benj. Turner, of this county. In my childhood a circumstance occurred which made an indelible impression on my mind, and laid the ground work of that enthusiasm, which has terminated so fatally to many, both white and black, and for which I am about to atone at the gallows. It is here necessary to relate this circumstance–trifling as it may seem, it was the commencement of that belief which has grown with time, and even now, sir, in this dungeon, helpless and forsaken as I am, I cannot divest myself of. Being at play with other children, when three or four years old, I was telling them something, which my mother overhearing, said it had happened before I was born–I stuck to my story, however, and related somethings which went, in her opinion, to confirm it–others being called on were greatly astonished, knowing that these things had happened, and caused them to say in my hearing, I surely would be a prophet, as the Lord had shewn me things that had happened before my birth. And my father and mother strengthened me in this my first impression, saying in my presence, I was intended for some great purpose, which they had always thought from certain marks on my head and breast–[a parcel of excrescences which I believe are not at all uncommon, particularly among negroes, as I have seen several with the same. In this case he has either cut them off or they have nearly disappeared]–My grandmother, who was very religious, and to whom I was much attached–my master, who belonged to the church, and other religious persons who visited the house, and whom I often saw at prayers, noticing the singularity of my manners, I suppose, and my uncommon intelligence for a child, remarked I had too much sense to be raised, and if I was, I would never be of any service to any one as a slave–To a mind like mine, restless, inquisitive and observant of every thing that was passing, it is easy to suppose that religion was the subject to which it would be directed, and although this subject principally occupied my thoughts—there was nothing that I saw or heard of to which my attention was not directed—The manner in which I learned to read and write, not only had great influence on my own mind, as I acquired it with the most perfect ease, so much so, that I have no recollection whatever of learning the alphabet—but to the astonishment of the family, one day, when a book was shewn to me to keep me from crying, I began spelling the names of different objects—this was a source of wonder to all in the neighborhood, particularly the blacks—and this learning was constantly improved at all opportunities—when I got large enough to go to work, while employed, I was reflecting on many things that would present themselves to my imagination, and whenever an opportunity occurred of looking at a book, when the school children were getting their lessons, I would find many things that the fertility of my own imagination had depicted to me before; all my time, not devoted to my master's service, was spent either in prayer, or in making experiments in casting different things in moulds made of earth, in attempting to make paper, gun-powder, and many other experiments, that although I could not perfect, yet convinced me of its practicablity if I had the means.* I was not addicted to stealing in my youth, nor have ever been—Yet such was the confidence of the negroes in the neighborhood, even at this early period of my life, in my superior judgment, that they would often carry me with them when they were going on any roguery, to plan for them. Growing up among them, with this confidence in my superior judgment, and when this, in their opinions, was perfected by Divine inspiration, from the circumstances already alluded to in my infancy, and which belief was ever afterwards zealously inculcated by the austerity of my life and manners, which became the subject of remark by white and black.—Having soon discovered to be great, I must appear so, and therefore studiously avoided mixing in society, and wrapped myself in mystery, devoting my time to fasting and prayer—By this time, having arrived to man's estate,[9] and hearing the scriptures commented on at meetings, I was struck with that particular passage which says: "Seek ye the kingdom of Heaven and all things shall be added unto you."[10] I reflected much on this passage, and prayed daily for light on this subject—As I was praying one day at my plough, the spirit spoke to me, saying "Seek ye the kingdom of Heaven and all things shall be added unto you." *Question*—what do you mean by the Spirit. *Ans.* The Spirit that spoke to the prophets in former days—and I was greatly astonished, and for two years prayed continually, whenever my duty would permit—and then again I had the same revelation, which fully confirmed me in the impression that I was ordained for some great purpose in the hands of the Almighty. Several years rolled round, in which many events occurred to strengthen me in this my belief. At this time I reverted in my mind to the remarks made of me in my childhood, and the things that had been shewn

*When questioned as to the manner of manufacturing those different articles, he was found well informed on the subject.

me–and as it had been said of me in my childhood by those by whom I had been taught to pray, both white and black, and in whom I had the greatest confidence, that I had too much sense to be raised, and if I was, I would never be of any use to any one as a slave. Now finding I had arrived to man's estate, and was a slave, and these revelations being made known to me, I began to direct my attention to this great object, to fulfil the purpose for which, by this time, I felt assured I was intended. Knowing the influence I had obtained over the minds of my fellow servants, (not by the means of conjuring and such like tricks–for to them I always spoke of such things with contempt) but by the communion of the Spirit whose revelations I often communicated to them, and they believed and said my wisdom came from God. I now began to prepare them for my purpose, by telling them something was about to happen that would terminate in fulfilling the great promise that had been made to me–About this time I was placed under an overseer, from whom I ranaway–and after remaining in the woods thirty days, I returned, to the astonishment of the negroes on the plantation, who thought I had made my escape to some other part of the country, as my father had done before. But the reason of my return was, that the Spirit appeared to me and said I had my wishes directed to the things of this world, and not to the kingdom of Heaven, and that I should return to the service of my earthly master–"For he who knoweth his Master's will, and doeth it not, shall be beaten with many stripes, and thus have I chastened you."[11] And the negroes found fault, and murmurred against me, saying that if they had my sense they would not serve any master in the world. And about this time I had a vision–and I saw white spirits and black spirits engaged in battle, and the sun was darkened–the thunder rolled in the Heavens, and blood flowed in streams–and I heard a voice saying, "Such is your luck, such you are called to see, and let it come rough or smooth, you must surely bare it. I now withdrew myself as much as my situation would permit, from the intercourse of my fellow servants, for the avowed purpose of serving the Spirit more fully–and it appeared to me, and reminded me of the things it had already shown me, and that it would then reveal to me the knowledge of the elements, the revolution of the planets, the operation of tides, and changes of the seasons. After this revelation in the year of 1825, and the knowledge of the elements being made known to me, I sought more than ever to obtain true holiness before the great day of judgment should appear, and then I began to receive the true knowledge of faith. And from the first steps of righteousness until the last, was I made perfect; and the Holy Ghost was with me, and said, "Behold me as I stand in the Heavens"–and I looked and saw the forms of men in different attitudes–and there were lights in the sky to which the children of darkness gave other names than what they really were–for they were the lights of the Savior's hands, stretched forth from east to west, even as they were extended on the cross on Calvary for the redemption of sinners. And I wondered greatly at these miracles, and prayed to be informed of a certainty of the meaning thereof–and shortly afterwards, while laboring in the field, I discovered drops of blood on the corn as though it were dew from heaven—and I communicated it to many, both white and black, in the neighborhood—and I then found on the leaves in the woods hieroglyphic characters, and numbers, with the forms of men in different attitudes, portrayed in blood, and representing the figures I had seen before in the heavens. And now the Holy Ghost had revealed itself to me, and made plain the miracles it had shown me—For as the blood of Christ had been shed on this earth, and had ascended to heaven for the salvation of sinners, and was now returning to earth again in the form of dew—and as the leaves on the trees bore the impression of the figures I had seen in the heavens, it was plain to me that the Savior was about to lay down the yoke he had borne for the sins of men, and the great day of judgment was at hand. About this time I told these things to a white man, (Etheldred T. Brantley) on whom it had a wonderful effect—and he ceased from his wickedness, and was attacked immediately with a cutaneous eruption, and blood oozed from the pores of his skin, and after praying and fasting nine days, he was healed, and the Spirit appeared to me again, and said, as the Savior had been baptised so should we be also—and when the white people would not let us be baptised by the church, we went down into the water together, in the sight of many who reviled us, and were baptised by the Spirit—After this I rejoiced greatly, and gave thanks to God. And on the 12th of May, 1828, I heard a loud noise in the heavens, and the Spirit instantly appeared to me and said the Serpent was loosened, and Christ had laid down the yoke he had borne for the sins of men, and that I should take it on and fight against the Serpent, for the time was fast approaching when the first should be last and the last should be first.[12] *Ques.* Do you not find yourself mistaken now? *Ans.* Was not Christ crucified? And by signs in the heavens that it would make known to me when I should commence the great work—and until the first sign appeared, I should conceal it from the knowledge of men—And on the appearance of the sign, (the eclipse of the sun last February) I should arise and prepare myself, and slay my enemies with their own weapons. And immediately on the sign appearing in the heavens, the seal was removed from my lips, and I communicated the great work laid out for me to do, to four in whom I had the greatest confidence, (Henry, Hark, Nelson, and Sam)—It was intended by us to have begun the work of death on the 4th July last—Many were the plans formed and rejected by us, and it affected my mind to such a degree, that I fell sick, and the time passed without our coming to any determination how to commence—Still forming new schemes and rejecting them, when the sign appeared again, which determined me not to wait longer.

Since the commencement of 1830, I had been living with Mr. Joseph Travis, who was to me a kind master, and placed the greatest confidence in me; in fact, I had no cause to complain of his treatment to me. On Saturday evening, the 20th of August, it was agreed between Henry, Hark and myself, to prepare a dinner the next day for the men we expected, and then to concert a plan, as we had not yet determined on any. Hark, on the following morning, brought a pig, and Henry brandy, and being joined by Sam, Nelson, Will and Jack, they prepared in the woods a dinner, where, about three o'clock, I joined them.

*Q.* Why were you so backward in joining them.

*A.* The same reason that had caused me not to mix with them for years before.

I saluted them on coming up, and asked Will how came he there, he answered, his life was worth no more than others, and his liberty as dear to him. I asked him if he thought to obtain it? He said he would, or lose his life. This was enough to put him in full confidence. Jack, I knew, was only a tool in the hands of Hark, it was quickly agreed we should commence at home (Mr. J. Travis') on that night, and until we had armed and equipped ourselves, and gathered sufficient force, neither age nor sex was to be spared,[13] (which was invariably adhered to). We remained at the feast, until about two hours in the night, when we went to the house and found Austin; they all went to the cider press and drank, except myself. On returning to the house, Hark went to the door with an axe, for the purpose of breaking it open, as we knew we were strong enough to murder the family, if they were awaked by the noise; but reflecting that it might create an alarm in the neighborhood, we determined to enter the house secretly, and murder them whilst sleeping. Hark got a ladder and set it against the chimney, on which I ascended, and hoisting a window, entered and came down stairs, unbarred the door, and removed the guns from their places. It was then observed that I must spill the first blood. On which, armed with a hatchet, and accompanied by Will, I entered my master's chamber, it being dark, I could not give a death blow, the hatchet glanced from his head, he sprang from the bed and called his wife, it was his last word, Will laid him dead, with a blow of his axe, and Mrs. Travis shared the same fate, as she lay in bed. The murder of this family, five in number, was the work of a moment, not one of them awoke; there was a little infant sleeping in a cradle, that was forgotten, until we had left the house and gone some distance, when Henry and Will returned and killed it; we got here, four guns that would shoot, and several old muskets, with a pound or two of powder. We remained some time at the barn, where we paraded; I formed them in a line as soldiers, and after carrying them through all the manoeuvres I was master of marched them off to Mr. Salathul Francis', about six hundred yards distant. Sam and Will went to the door and knocked. Mr. Francis asked who was there, Sam replied it was him, and he had a letter for him, on which he got up and came to the door; they immediately seized him, and dragging him out a little from the door, he was dispatched by repeated blows on the head; there was no other white person in the family. We started from there for Mrs. Reese's, maintaining the most perfect silence on our march, where finding the door unlocked, we entered, and murdered Mrs. Reese in her bed, while sleeping; her son awoke, but it was only to sleep the sleep of death, he had only time to say who is that, and he was no more. From Mrs. Reese's we went to Mrs. Turner's, a mile distant, which we reached about sunrise, on Monday morning. Henry, Austin, and Sam, went to the still, where, finding Mr. Peebles, Austin shot him, and the rest of us went to the house; as we approached, the family discovered us, and shut the door. Vain hope! Will, with one stroke of his axe, opened it, and we entered and found Mrs. Turner and Mrs. Newsome in the middle of a room, almost frightened to death. Will immediately killed Mrs. Turner, with one blow of his axe. I took Mrs. Newsome by the hand, and with the sword I had when I was apprehended, I struck her several blows over the head, but not being able to kill her, as the sword was dull. Will turning around and discovering it, despatched her also. A general destruction of property and search for money and ammunition, always succeeded the murders. By this time my company amounted to fifteen, and nine men mounted, who started for Mrs. Whitehead's, (the other six were to go through a by way to Mr. Bryant's, and rejoin us at Mrs. Whitehead's,) as we approached the house we discovered Mr. Richard Whitehead standing in the cotton patch, near the lane fence; we called him over into the lane, and Will, the executioner, was near at hand, with his fatal axe, to send him to an untimely grave. As we pushed on to the house, I discovered some one run round the garden, and thinking it was some of the white family, I pursued them, but finding it was a servant girl belonging to the house, I returned to commence the work of death, but they whom I left, had not been idle; all the family were already murdered, but Mrs. Whitehead and her daughter Margaret. As I came round to the door I saw Will pulling Mrs. Whitehead out of the house, and at the step he nearly severed her head from her body, with his broad axe. Miss Margaret, when I discovered her, had concealed herself in the corner, formed by the projection of cellar cap from the house; on my approach she fled, but was soon overtaken, and after repeated blows with a sword, I killed her by a blow on the head, with a fence rail. By this time, the six who had gone by Mr. Bryant's, rejoined us, and informed me they had done the work of death assigned them. We again divided, part going to Mr. Richard Porter's, and from thence to Nathaniel Francis', the others to Mr. Howell Harris', and Mr. T. Doyles. On my reaching Mr. Porter's, he had escaped with his family. I understood there, that the alarm had already spread, and I immediately returned to bring up those sent to Mr. Doyles, and Mr. Howell Harris'; the party I left going on to Mr. Francis', having told them I would join them in that neighborhood. I met these sent to Mr. Doyles' and Mr. Harris' returning, having met Mr. Doyle on the road and killed him; and learning from some who joined them, that Mr. Harris was from home, I immediately pursued the course taken by the party gone on before; but knowing they would complete the work of death and pillage, at Mr. Francis' before I could get there, I went to Mr. Peter Edwards', expecting to find them there, but they had been here also. I then went to Mr. John T. Barrow's, they had been here and murdered him. I pursued on their track to Capt. Newit Harris', where I found the greater part mounted, and ready to start; the men now amounting to about forty, shouted and hurraed as I rode up, some were in the yard, loading their guns, others drinking. They said Captain Harris and his family had escaped, the property in the house they destroyed, robbing him of money and other valuables. I ordered them to mount and march instantly, this was about nine or ten o'clock, Monday morning. I proceeded to Mr. Levi Waller's, two or three miles distant. I took my station in the rear, and as it was my object to carry terror and devastation wherever we went, I placed fifteen or twenty of the best armed and most relied on, in front, who generally approached the houses as fast as their horses could run; this was for two purposes, to prevent escape and strike terror to the inhabitants–on this account I never got to the houses, after leaving Mrs. Whitehead's, until the murders were committed, except in one case. I sometimes got in sight in time to see the work of death completed, viewed the mangled bodies as they lay, in silent satisfaction, and immediately started in quest of other victims–Having murdered Mrs. Waller and ten children, we started for Mr. William Williams'–having killed him and two little boys that were there; while engaged in this, Mrs. Williams fled and got some distance from the house, but she was pursued, overtaken, and compelled to get up behind one of the company, who brought her back, and after showing her the mangled body of her lifeless husband, she was told to get down and lay by his side, where she was shot dead. I then started for Mr. Jacob Williams, where the family were murdered–Here he found a young man named Drury, who had come on business with Mr. Williams–he was pursued, overtaken and shot. Mrs. Vaughan was the next place we visited–and after murdering the family here, I determined on starting for Jerusalem–Our number amounted now to fifty or sixty, all mounted and armed with guns, axes, swords and clubs–On reaching Mr. James W. Parker's gate, immediately on the road leading to Jerusalem, and about three miles distant, it was proposed to me to call there, but I objected, as I knew he was gone to Jerusalem, and my object was to reach there as soon as possible; but some of the men having relations at Mr. Parker's it was agreed that they might call and get his people. I remained at the gate on the road, with seven or eight; the others going across the field to the house, about half a mile off. After waiting some time for them, I became impatient, and started to the house for them, and on our return we were met by a party of white when, who had pursued our blood-stained track, and who had fired on those at the gate, and dispersed them, which I knew nothing of, not having been at that time rejoined by any of them–Immediately on discovering the whites, I ordered my men to halt and form, as they appeared to be alarmed–The white men, eighteen in number, approached us in about one hundred yards, when one of them fired, (this was against the positive orders of Captain Alexander P. Peete, who commanded, and who had directed the men to reserve their fire until within thirty paces)–And I discovered about half of them retreating, I then ordered my men to fire and rush on them; the few remaining stood their ground until we approached within fifty yards, when they fired and retreated. We pursued and overtook some of them who we thought we left dead; (they were not killed) after pursuing them about two hundred yards, and rising a little hill, I discovered they were met by another party, and had halted, and were re-loading their guns, (this was a small party from Jerusalem who knew the negroes were in the field, and had just tied their horses to await their return to the road, knowing that Mr. Parker and family were in Jerusalem, but knew nothing of the party that had gone in with Captain Peete; on hearing the firing they immediately rushed to the spot and arrived just in time to arrest the progress of these barbarous villians, and save the lives of their friends and fellow citizens). Thinking that those who retreated first, and the party who fired on us at fifty or sixty yards distant, had all fallen back to meet others with ammunition. As I saw them reloading their guns, and more coming up than I saw at first, and several of my bravest men being wounded, the others became panick struck and squandered over the field; the white men pursued and fired on us several times. Hark had his horse shot under him, and I caught another for him as it was running by me; five or six of my men were wounded, but none left on the field; finding myself defeated here I instantly determined to go through a private way, and cross the Nottoway river at the Cypress Bridge, three miles below Jerusalem, and attack that place in the rear, as I expected they would look for me on the other road, and I had a great desire to get there to procure arms and ammunition. After going a short distance in this private way, accompanied by about twenty men, I overtook two or three who told me the others were dispersed in every direction. After trying in vain to collect a sufficient force to proceed to Jerusalem, I determined to return, as I was sure they would make back to their old neighborhood, where they would rejoin me, make new recruits, and come down again. On my way back, I called at Mrs. Thomas's, Mrs. Spencer's, and several other places, the white families having fled, we found no more victims to gratify our thirst for blood, we stopped at Majr. Ridley's quarter for the night, and being joined by four of his men, with the recruits made since my defeat, we mustered now about forty strong. After placing out sentinels, I laid down to sleep, but was quickly roused by a great racket; starting up, I found some mounted, and others in great confusion; one of the sentinels having given the alarm that we were about to be attacked, I ordered some to ride round and reconnoitre, and on their return the others being more alarmed, not knowing who they were, fled in different ways, so that I was reduced to about twenty again; with this I determined to attempt to recruit, and proceed on to rally in the neighborhood, I had left. Dr. Blunt's was the nearest house, which we reached just before day; on riding up the yard, Hark fired a gun. We expected Dr. Blunt and his family were at Maj. Ridley's, as I knew there was a company of men there; the gun was fired to ascertain if any of the family were at home; we were immediately fired upon and retreated, leaving several of my men. I do not know what became of them, as I never saw them afterwards. Pursuing our course back and coming in sight of Captain Harris', where we had been the day before, we discovered a party of white men at the house, on which all deserted me but two, (Jacob and Nat), we concealed ourselves in the woods until near night, when I sent them in search of Henry, Sam, Nelson, and Hark, and directed them to rally all they could, at the place we had had our dinner the Sunday before, where they would find me, and I accordingly returned there as soon as it was dark and remained until Wednesday evening, when discovering white men riding around the place as though they were looking for some one, and none of my men joining me, I concluded Jacob and Nat had been taken, and compelled to betray me. On this I gave up all hope for the present; and on Thursday night after having supplied myself with provisions from Mr. Travis's, I scratched a hole under a pile of fence rails in a field, where I concealed myself for six weeks, never leaving my hiding place but for a few minutes in the dead of night to get water which was very near; thinking by this time I could venture out, I began to go about in the night and eaves drop the houses in the neighborhood; pursuing this course for about a fortnight and gathering little or no intelligence, afraid of speaking to any human being, and returning every morning to my cave before the dawn of day. I know not how long I might have led this life, if accident had not betrayed me, a dog in the neighborhood passing by my hiding place one night while I was out, was attracted by some meat I had in my cave, and crawled in and stole it, and was coming out just as I returned. A few nights after, two negroes having started to go hunting with the same dog, and passed that way, the dog came again to the place, and having just gone out to walk about, discovered me and barked, on which thinking myself discovered, I spoke to them to beg concealment. On making myself known they fled from me. Knowing then they would betray me, I immediately left my hiding place, and was pursued almost incessantly until I was taken a fortnight afterwards by Mr. Benjamin Phipps, in a little hole I had dug out with my sword, for the purpose of concealment, under the top of a fallen tree. On Mr. Phipps' discovering the place of my concealment, he cocked his gun and aimed at me. I requested him not to shoot and I would give up, upon which he demanded my sword. I delivered it to him, and he brought me to prison. During the time I was pursued, I had many hair breadth escapes, which your time will not permit you to relate. I am here loaded with chains, and willing to suffer the fate that awaits me.

I here proceeded to make some inquiries of him, after assuring him of the certain death that awaited him, and that concealment would only bring destruction on the innocent as well as guilty, of his own color, if he knew of any extensive or concerted plan. His answer was, I do not. When I questioned him as to the insurrection in North Carolina happening about the same time, he denied any knowledge of it; and when I looked him in the face as though I would search his inmost thoughts, he replied, "I see sir, you doubt my word; but can you not think the same ideas, and strange appearances about this time in the heaven's might prompt others, as well as myself, to this undertaking." I now had much conversation with and asked him many questions, having forborne to do so previously, except in the cases noted in parenthesis; but during his statement, I had, unnoticed by him, taken notes as to some particular circumstances, and having the advantage of his statement before me in writing, on the evening of the third day that I had been with him, I began a cross examination, and found his statement corroborated by every circumstance coming within my own knowledge or the confessions of others who had been either killed or executed, and whom he had not seen nor had any knowledge since 22d of August last, he expressed himself fully satisfied as to the impracticability of his attempt. It has been said he was ignorant and cowardly, and that his object was to murder and rob for the purpose of obtaining money to make his escape. It is notorious, that he was never known to have a dollar in his life; to swear an oath, or drink a drop of spirits. As to his ignorance, he certainly never had the advantages of education, but he can read and write, (it was taught him by his parents,) and for natural intelligence and quickness of apprehension, is surpassed by few men I have ever seen. As to his being a coward, his reason as given for not resisting Mr. Phipps, shews the decision of his character. When he saw Mr. Phipps present his gun, he said he knew it was impossible for him to escape as the woods were full of men; he therefore thought it was better to surrender, and trust to fortune for his escape. He is a complete fanatic, or plays his part most admirably. On other subjects he possesses an uncommon share of intelligence, with a mind capable of attaining any thing; but warped and perverted by the influence of early impressions. He is below the ordinary stature, though strong and active, having the true negro face, every feature of which is strongly marked. I shall not attempt to describe the effect of his narrative, as told and commented on by himself, in the condemned hole of the prison. The calm, deliberate composure with which he spoke of his late deeds and intentions, the expression of his fiend-like face when excited by enthusiasm, still bearing the stains of the blood of helpless innocence about him; clothed with rags and covered with chains; yet daring to raise his manacled hands to heaven, with a spirit soaring above the attributes of man; I looked on him and my blood curdled in my veins.

I will not shock the feelings of humanity, nor wound afresh the bosoms of the disconsolate sufferers in this unparalleled and inhuman massacre, by detailing the deeds of their fiend-like barbarity. There were two or three who were in the power of these wretches, had they known it, and who escaped in the most providential manner. There were two whom they thought they left dead on the field at Mr. Parker's, but who were only stunned by the blows of their guns, as they did not take time to re-load when they charged on them. The escape of a little girl who went to school at Mr. Waller's, and where the children were collecting for that purpose, excited general sympathy. As their teacher had not arrived, they were at play in the yard, and seeing the negroes approach, she ran up on a dirt chimney, (such as are common to log houses,) and remained there unnoticed during the massacre of the eleven that were killed at this place. She remained on her hiding place till just before the arrival of a party, who were in pursuit of the murderers, when she came down and fled to a swamp, where, a mere child as she was, with the horrors of the late scene before her, she lay concealed until the next day, when seeing a party go up to the house, she came up, and on being asked how she escaped, replied with the utmost simplicity, "The Lord helped her." She was taken up behind a gentleman of the party, and returned to the arms of her weeping mother. Miss Whitehead concealed herself between the bed and the mat that supported it, while they murdered her sister in the same room, without discovering her. She was afterwards carried off, and concealed for protection by a slave of the family, who gave evidence against several of them on their trial. Mrs. Nathaniel Francis, while concealed in a closet heard their blows, and the shrieks of the victims of these ruthless savages; they then entered the closet, where she was concealed, and went out without discovering her. While in this hiding place, she heard two of her women in a quarrel about the division of her clothes. Mr. John T. Baron, discovering them approaching his house, told his wife to make her escape, and scorning to fly, fell fighting on his own threshold. After firing his rifle, he discharged his gun at them, and then broke it over the villain who first approached him, but he was overpowered, and slain. His bravery, however, saved from the hands of these monsters, his lovely and amiable wife, who will long lament a husband so deserving of her love. As directed by him, she attempted to escape through the garden, when she was caught and held by one of her servant girls, but another coming to her rescue, she fled to the woods, and concealed herself. Few indeed, were those who escaped their work of death. But fortunate for society, the hand of retributive justice has overtaken them; and not one that was known to be concerned has escaped.

## The Commonwealth, vs. Nat Turner

Charged with making insurrection, and plotting to take away the lives of divers free white persons, &c. on the 22d of August, 1831.

The court composed of ——, having met for the trial of Nat Turner, the prisoner was brought in and arraigned, and upon his arraignment pleaded *Not guilty*; saying to his counsel, that he did not feel so.

On the part of the Commonwealth, Levi Waller was introduced, who being sworn, deposed as follows: (*agreeably to Nat's own Confession.*) Col. Trezvant* was then introduced, who being sworn, narrated Nat's Confession to him, as follows: (*his Confession as given to Mr. Gray.*) The prisoner introduced no evidence, and the case was submitted without argument to the court, who having found him guilty, Jeremiah Cobb, Esq. Chairman, pronounced the sentence of the court, in the following words: Nat Turner! Stand up. Have you any thing to say why sentence of death should not be pronounced against you?

*The committing Magistrate.

*Ans.* I have not. I have made a full confession to Mr. Gray, and I have nothing more to say.

Attend then to the sentence of the Court. You have been arraigned and tried before this court, and convicted of one of the highest crimes in our criminal code. You have been convicted of plotting in cold blood, the indiscriminate destruction of men, of helpless women, and of infant children. The evidence before us leaves not a shadow of doubt, but that your hands were often imbrued in the blood of the innocent; and your own confession tells us that they were stained with the blood of a master; in your own language, "too indulgent." Could I stop here, your crime would be sufficiently aggravated. But the original contriver of a plan, deep and deadly, one that never can be effected, you managed so far to put it into execution, as to deprive us of many of our most valuable citizens; and this was done when they were asleep, and defenseless; under circumstances shocking to humanity. And while upon this part of the subject, I cannot but call your attention to the poor misguided wretches who have gone before you. They are not few in number–they were your bosom associates; and the blood of all cries aloud, and calls upon you, as the author of their misfortune. Yes! You forced them unprepared, from Time to Eternity. Borne down by this load of guilt, your only justification is, that you were led away by fanaticism. If this be true, from my soul I pity you; and while you have my sympathies, I am, nevertheless called upon to pass the sentence of the court. The time between this and your execution, will necessarily be very short; and your only hope must be in another world. The judgment of the court is, that you be taken hence to the jail from whence you came, thence to the place of execution, and on Friday next, between the hours of 10 A.M. and 2 P.M. be hung by the neck until you are dead! dead! dead! and may the Lord have mercy upon your soul.

### A list of persons murdered in the Insurrection, on the 21st and 22nd of August, 1831

Joseph Travers and wife and three children, Mrs. Elizabeth Turner, Hartwell Prebles, Sarah Newsome, Mrs. P. Reese and son William, Trajan Doyle, Henry Bryant and wife and child, and wife's mother, Mrs. Catharine Whitehead, son Richard and four daughters and grand-child, Salathiel Francis, Nathaniel Francis' overseer and two children, John T. Barrow, George Vaughan, Mrs. Levi Waller and ten children, William Williams, wife and two boys, Mrs. Caswell Worrell and child, Mrs. Rebecca Vaughan, Ann Eliza Vaughan, and son Arthur, Mrs. John K. Williams and child, Mrs. Jacob Williams and three children, and Edwin Drury–amounting to fifty-five.[14]

**A List of Negroes brought before the Court of Southampton, with their owners' names, and sentence**

| | | |
|---|---|---|
| Daniel, | Richard Porter, | Convicted. |
| Moses | J. T. Barrow, | do. |
| Tom, | Caty Whitehead, | Discharged. |
| Jack and Andrew, | Caty Whitehead | Con. and transported |
| Jacob, | Geo. H. Charlton, | Disch'd without trial. |
| Isaac, | Ditto, | Convi. and transported. |
| Jack, | Everett Bryant, | Discharged. |
| Nathan, | Benj. Blunt's estate, | Convicted. |
| Nathan, Tom, and | Nathaniel Francis, | Convicted and transported |
| Davy, (boys,) | Elizabeth Turner, | Convicted. |
| Davy, | Thomas Ridley, | Do. |
| Curtis, | Do. | Do. |
| Stephen, | Benjamin Edwards, | Convicted and transp'd. |
| Hardy and Isham, | Nathaniel Francis, | Convicted. |
| Sam, | Joseph Travis' estate. | Do. |
| Hark, | Do. | Do. and transported. |
| Moses, (a boy,) | Levi Waller, | Convicted. |
| Davy, | Jacob Williams, | Do. |
| Nelson, | Edm'd Turner's estate | Do. |
| Nat, | Wm. Reese's estate | Do. |
| Dred, | Nathaniel Francis, | Do. |
| Arnold, Artist, (free) | | Discharged. |
| Sam, | J. W. Parker, | Acquitted. |
| Ferry and Archer, | J. W. Parker, | Disch'd. without trial. |
| Jim, | William Vaughan, | Acquitted. |
| Bob, | Temperance Parker, | Do. |
| Davy, | Joseph Parker, | |
| Daniel, | Solomon D. Parker | Disch'd without trial. |
| Thomas Haithcock, (free,) | | Sent on for further trial. |
| Joe, | John C. Turner, | Convicted. |
| Lucy, | John T. Barrow, | Do. |
| Matt, | Thomas Ridley, | Acquitted. |
| Jim, | Richard Porter, | Do. |
| Exum Artes, (free,) | | Sent on for further trial. |

| | | |
|---|---|---|
| Joe, | Richard P. Briggs, | Disch'd without trial. |
| Bury Newsome, (free,) | | Sent on for further trial. |
| Stephen, | James Bell, | Acquitted. |
| Jim and Isaac, | Samuel Champion, | Convicted and trans'd. |
| Preston, | Hannah Williamson | Acquitted. |
| Frank, | Solomon D. Parker | Convi'd and transp'd. |
| Jack and Shadrach, | Nathaniel Simmons | Acquitted.[15] |
| Nelson, | Benj. Blunt's estate, | Do. |
| Sam, | Peter Edwards, | Convicted. |
| Archer, | Arthur G. Reese, | Acquitted. |
| Isham Turner, (free,) | | Sent on for further trial. |
| Nat Turner, | Putnam Moore, dec'd. | Convicted. |

## EDITORIAL NOTES TO *THE CONFESSIONS OF NAT TURNER*

1. According to the 1830 census, the total population of Southampton was 16,074, consisting of 6,573 free whites, 1,745 free blacks, and 7,756 slaves. See Tragle, *The Southampton Slave Revolt of 1831*, 15.

2. Egerton, "The Scenes Which Are Acted in St. Domingo," 41–64.

3. Fabricant, "Thomas R. Gray and William Styron," 339–40; Sundquist, *To Wake the Nations*, 46–47; Tragle, *The Southampton Slave Revolt of 1831*, 402–9.

4. In 1634, Virginia was divided into eight districts, or shires. One was called Warrasqyoyocke or Smith's Hundred. Its boundaries included the James River on the north and the North Carolina border to the south. In 1637, the name was changed to Isle of Wight Plantation. In 1749, the tract was separated into two parts, with the Blackwater River as the dividing line. While the upper portion remained Isle of Wight Plantation, the southern portion became known as Southampton County. A courthouse was built a few years later on the banks of the Nottoway River. The village that grew up in the vicinity became known as Jerusalem. It was incorporated by the state legislature as a town in 1888, and the name was changed to Courtland. See Tragle, *The Southampton Slave Revolt of 1831*, 13–14, 15.

5. Thomas Ruffin Gray, a lawyer and slaveholder, served as legal council for several of Turner's co-conspirators, though not for Turner himself. His decision to gain access to Turner and elicit his story is most likely some combination of his desire to perform the public service of explaining Turner's motives and to profit from public interest in the insurrection by publishing the firsthand account of its leader.

6. Newspapers like the *Richmond Enquirer*, the *Richmond Constitutional Whig*, and the *Norfolk American Beacon* sought to allay fears of widespread revolt but also insisted on the possibility of far-reaching insurrection and the need for vigilance. There was no indication in the adjacent counties in North Carolina that similar slave activity was planned. The newspapers incited hysteria, however, and many blacks, slave and free, were lynched, jailed, and otherwise harassed. See Tragle, *The Southampton Slave Revolt*

*of 1831*, 4–5; Elliot, "The Nat Turner Insurrection as Reported in the North Carolina Press," 1–18.

7. Nat Turner was initially owned by Benjamin Turner. Upon the death of his owner sometime around 1822, Nat Turner was purchased by Thomas Moore for his infant son, Putnam, who became Nat Turner's legal owner. At the time of the insurrection, Nat Turner was working for Moore's widow, who had remarried Joseph Travis.

8. Turner refutes Gray's use of the word "insurrection," as have subsequent authorities. "Insurrection" refers to an actual uprising against the government in open resistance. "Revolt" is generally seen as an uprising against a civil government (though it may also be directed toward a military government). A "rebellion" goes beyond an "insurrection" by actively seeking to overthrow the government. See Aptheker, *Nat Turner's Slave Rebellion*, 2 n.2; Tragle, *The Southampton Slave Revolt of 1831*, 21–22.

9. Referring to the attainment of a particular mental, physical, or material condition of life.

10. Luke 12:31, "But rather seek ye the kingdom of God; and all these things shall be added unto you."

11. Luke 12:47, "And that servant, which knew his lord's will, and prepared not himself, neither did according to his will, shall be beaten with many stripes."

12. Matthew 19:30, "But many that are first shall be last; and the last shall be first"; Matthew 20:16, "So the last shall be first, and the first last: for many be called, but few chosen"; Mark 10:31, "But many that are first shall be last; and the last first"; Luke 13:30, "And, behold, there are last which shall be first, and there are first which shall be last."

13. The conspirators planned indiscriminately to attack all white men, women, and children.

14. Fifty-five may be inaccurate. Fifty-seven is more commonly given and there are references to as many as sixty-four. This disparity may be caused by a number of children killed whose names are not included here. See Tragle, *The Southampton Slave Revolt of 1831*, 4.

15. Jack and Shadrach had their charges of "treason against the Commonwealth" dismissed by the Southampton County court on October 17, 1831. The court ruled that slaves could not be tried for treason. See Tragle, *The Southampton Slave Revolt of 1831*, 22.

# 2

# MOSES ROPER (1816?–?)

## A Narrative of the Adventures and Escape of Moses Roper

Moses Roper begins the introduction to his *Narrative* by writing "The determination of laying this little narrative before the public, did not arise from any desire to make myself conspicuous, but with the view of exposing the cruel system of slavery as will here be laid before my readers." As Roper indicates, the *Narrative* results from his desire to educate readers to the brutal realities of the slave system. In order to complete that education, Roper emphasizes the physical circumstances of the slave system as forcefully as he emphasizes that the facts of his descriptions can be documented and are objective: "But the facts related here do not come before the reader unsubstantiated by collateral evidence, nor highly coloured to the disadvantage of cruel task-masters." As Marion Wilson Starling observes, the ability to authenticate facts was not always the case with previous slave narratives, most notably *Slavery in the United States: A Narrative of the Life and Adventures of Charles Ball, a Black Man* (1836) and *Narrative of James Williams. An American slave; who was for several years a driver on a cotton plantation in Alabama* (1836).[1]

Moses Roper avoids many of the pitfalls of authentication by placing the focus of his narration on slavery. There are relatively few (if any) areas in which the reader is given access to Moses Roper's emotional responses to his experiences as a slave. In moments when the reader might expect judgment and bitterness, Roper regularly turns to a series of traditional Christian responses: "But I desire to express my entire resignation to the will of God"; "But if the all-wise disposer of all things should see fit to keep them still in suffering and bondage, it is a mercy to know, that he orders all things well, that he is still the judge of all the earth, and that under such dispensations of his providence, he is working out that which shall be most for the advantage of his creatures"; "It is far from my wish to attempt to degrade America in the eyes of Britons. I love her institutions in the Free States, her zeal for Christ; I bear no enmity even to the slave-holders, but regret their delusions, many I am aware are deeply sensible of the fault, but some I regret to say are not, and I could wish to open their eyes to their sin; may the period come, when God shall wipe off this deep stain from her constitution, and may America soon be *indeed* the land of the free."

According to his *Narrative*, Moses Roper was born in North Carolina. His mother was a biracial slave and his father a white slaveholder who eventually married the woman Roper's mother worked for. Roper was sold and traded several times before being sold at age thirteen or fourteen to Mr. Gooch, an especially cruel and brutal slaveholder who sought to break Roper's spirit and train Roper in the ways of field labor. Mr. Gooch's intense series of punishments only served to convince Roper of the need to escape. The descriptions of Roper's numerous escapes (and subsequent captures) are punctuated by the seemingly endless supply of tortures Mr. Gooch invents to use against Roper as punishment. After being briefly reunited with his mother and his siblings for the last time, Roper was captured and returned yet again to Mr. Gooch and his punishments. Mr. Gooch, finally tired of Roper's endless escapes, decided to sell him. Roper's experiences with a number of slave trader's eventually resulted in his successful escape to New York and New England before sailing in the fall of 1835 for England, where Roper married, found a community of supporters, and, finally, freedom.

Moses Roper creates a narrative that authoritatively depicts a sadistically cruel slaveholder (implicitly representative of all slaveholders) who relentlessly pursues and punishes all who attempt to escape his evil. Roper gives his readers an opportunity to observe and critique the slave system by giving a first-hand account that employs an objective distance, a moderate tone, and that minimizes rather than exaggerates examples of physical and psychological abuse.

The narrative reprinted here is from the fourth edition of *A Narrative of the Adventures and Escape of Moses Roper*. This edition was originally published in London, England, in 1840. The first edition of the narrative was published in 1838.

## FURTHER READING

William L. Andrews, *To Tell a Free Story* (1986); Marion Wilson Starling, *The Slave Narrative* (1988).

# A NARRATIVE
## OF THE
# ADVENTURES AND ESCAPE
## OF
# MOSES ROPER,
## FROM
# AMERICAN SLAVERY;
## WITH A PREFACE,
# BY THE REV. T. PRICE, D.D.

"By our sufferings since ye brought us
To the man-degrading mart;
All sustained by patience, taught us
Only by a broken heart."

FOURTH EDITION.

LONDON:
HARVEY AND DARTON, 55, GRACECHURCH STREET.
To be had also of G. WIGHTMAN, 24, Paternoster Row; WILLIAM BALL, Aldine Chambers, Paternoster Row; and at the BRITISH AND FOREIGN ANTI-SLAVERY OFFICE, 27, New Broad Street.

1840.

ENTERED AT STATIONER'S HALL.

LONDON:
JOHNSTON & BARRETT, Printers, 13,
Mark Lane.

## PREFACE

The following narrative was to have appeared under the auspices of The Rev. Dr. Morison, of Chelsea, whose generous exertions on behalf of Moses Roper have entitled him to the admiration and gratitude of every philanthropist. But the illness of the doctor having prevented him from reading the manuscript, I have been requested to supply his lack of service. To this request I assent reluctantly, as the narrative would have derived a fuller sanction and wider currency, had circumstances permitted the original purpose to be carried out. Moses Roper was introduced to Dr. Morison, by an eminent American abolitionist, in a letter, dated November 9th, 1835, in which honourable testimony is borne to his general character, and the soundness of his religious profession. "He has spent about ten days in my house," says Dr. Morison's correspondent, "I have watched him attentively, and have no doubt that he is an excellent young man, that he possesses uncommon intelligence, sincere piety, and a strong desire to preach the Gospel. He can tell you his own story better than any one else; and I believe, that if he should receive an education, he would be able to counteract the false and wicked misrepresentations of American slavery, which are made in your country by our Priests and Levites who visit you."

Dr. Morison, as might have been anticipated from his well-known character, heartily responded to the appeal of his American correspondent. He sent his letter to the Patriot Newspaper, remarking in his own communication to the Editor, "I have seen Moses Roper, the fugitive slave. He comes to this country, as you will perceive, well authenticated as to character and religious standing; and my anxiety is, that the means may forthwith be supplied by some of your generous readers, for placing him in some appropriate seminary for the improvement of his mind, that he may be trained for future usefulness in the church. His thirst for knowledge is great; and he may yet become a most important agent in liberating his country from the curse of slavery."

Moses Roper brought with him to this country several other testimonies, from persons residing in different parts of the States; but it is unnecessary to extend this Preface by quoting them. They all speak the same language, and bear unequivocal witness to his sobriety, intelligence, and honesty.

He is now in the land of freedom, and is earnestly desirous of availing himself of the advantages of his position. His great ambition is to be qualified for usefulness amongst his own people; and the progress he has already made, justifies the belief, that, if the means of education can be secured for a short time longer, he will be eminently qualified to instruct the children of Africa in the truths of the gospel of Christ. He has drawn up the following narrative, partly with the hope of being assisted in this legitimate object, and partly to engage the sympathies of our countrymen on behalf of his oppressed brethren. I trust that he will not be disappointed in either of these expectations, but that all the friends of humanity and religion among us, will cheerfully render him their aid, by promoting the circulation of his volume. Should this be done to the extent that is quite possible, the difficulties now lying in his way will be removed.

Of the narrative itself it is not necessary that I should say much. It is his own production, and carries with it internal evidence of truth. Some of its statements will probably startle those readers who are unacquainted with the details of the slave system; but no such feeling will be produced in any who are conversant with the practice of slavery, whether in America or our own colonies. There is no vice too loathsome—no passion too cruel or remorseless, to be engendered by this horrid system. It brutalizes all who administer it, and seeks to efface the likeness of God, stamped on the brow of its victims. It makes the former class demons, and reduces the latter to the level of brutes.

I could easily adduce from the records of our own slave system,[2] as well as from those of America, several instances of equal atrocity to any which Moses Roper has recorded. But this is unnecessary, and I shall therefore merely add, the unqualified expression of my own confidence in the truth of this narrative, and my strong recommendation of it to the patronage of the British Public.

THOMAS PRICE.

HACKNEY.

## INTRODUCTION

The determination of laying this little narrative before the public, did not arise from any desire to make myself conspicuous, but with the view of exposing the cruel system of slavery as will here be laid before my readers; from the urgent calls of nearly all the friends to whom I had related any part of the story, and also from the recommendation of anti-slavery meetings, which I have attended, through the suggestion of many warm friends of the cause of the oppressed.

The general narrative, I am aware, may seem to many of my readers, and especially to those who have not been before put in possession of the actual features of this accursed system, somewhat at variance with the dictates of humanity. But the facts related here do not come before the reader unsubstantiated by collateral evidence, nor highly coloured to the disadvantage of cruel task-masters.

My readers may be put in possession of facts respecting this system which equal in cruelty my own narrative, on an authority which may be investigated with the greatest satisfaction. Besides which, this little book will not be confined to a small circle of my own friends in London, or even in England. The slaveholder, the colonizationist, and even Mr. Gooch himself, will be able to obtain this document, and be at liberty to draw from it whatever they are honestly able, in order to set me down as the tool of a party. Yea, even friend Brechenridge, a gentleman known at Glasgow, will be able to possess this, and to draw from it all the forcible arguments on his own side, which in his wisdom, honesty, and candour, he may be able to adduce.

The earnest wish to lay this narrative before my friends as an impartial statement of facts, has led me to develope some part of my conduct, which I now deeply deplore. The ignorance in which the poor slaves are kept by their masters, preclude almost the possibility of their being alive to any moral duties.

With these remarks, I leave the statement before the public. May this little volume be the instrument of opening the eyes of the ignorant to the system–of convincing the wicked, cruel, and hardened slave-holder–and of befriending generally the cause of oppressed humanity.

LIBERTUS.
LONDON.

## CHAPTER I

**Birth-place of the Author.–The first time he was sold from his Mother, and passed through several other hands.**

I was born in North Carolina, in Caswell County, I am not able to tell in what year or month. What I shall now relate, is, what was told me by my mother and grandmother. A few months before I was born, my father married my mother's young mistress. As soon as my father's wife heard of my birth, she sent one of my mother's sisters to see whether I was white or black, and when my aunt had seen me, she returned back as soon as she could, and told her mistress that I was white, and resembled Mr. Roper very much. Mr. R.'s wife being not pleased with this report, she got a large club-stick and knife, and hastened to the place in which my mother was confined. She went into my mother's room with full intention to murder me with her knife and club, but as she was going to stick the knife into me, my grandmother happening to come in, caught the knife and saved my life. But as well as I can recollect from what my mother told me, my father sold her and myself, soon after her confinement. I cannot recollect anything that is worth notice till I was six or seven years old. My mother being half white, and my father a white man, I was at that time very white. Soon after I was six or seven years of age, my mother's old master died, that is, my father's wife's father. All his slaves had to be divided among the children.* I have mentioned before of my father disposing of me, I am not sure whether he exchanged me and my mother for another slave or not, but think it very likely he did exchange me with one of his wife's brothers or sisters, because I remember when my mother's old master died, I was living with my father's wife's brother-in-law, whose name was Mr. Durham. My mother was drawn with the other slaves.

*Slaves are usually a part of the marriage portion, but lent rather than given, to be returned to the estate at the decease of the father, in order that they may be divided equally among his children.

The way they divide their slaves is this: they write the names of different slaves on a small piece of paper, and put it into a box, and let them all draw. I think that Mr. Durham drew my mother, and Mr. Fowler drew me, so we were separated a considerable distance, I cannot say how far. My resembling my father so very much, and being whiter than the other slaves, caused me to be soon sold to what they call a negro trader, who took me to the Southern States of America, several hundred miles from my mother. As well as I can recollect, I was then about six years old. The trader, Mr. Mitchell, after travelling several hundred miles, and selling a good many of his slaves, found he could not sell me very well, (as I was so much whiter than the other slaves were) for he had been trying several months–left me with a Mr. Sneed, who kept a large boardinghouse, who took me to wait at table, and sell me if he could. I think I stayed with Mr. Sneed about a year, but he could not sell me. When Mr. Mitchell had sold his slaves, he went to the north, and brought up another drove, and returned to the south with them, and sent his son-in-law into Washington, in Georgia, after me, so he came and took me from Mr. Sneed, and met his father-in-law with me, in a town called Lancaster, with his drove of slaves. We stayed in Lancaster a week, because it was court week, and there were a great many people there, and it was a good opportunity for selling the slaves, and there he was enabled to sell me to a gentleman, Dr. Jones, who was both a Doctor and a Cotton Planter. He took me into his shop to beat up and to mix medicines, which was not a very hard employment, but I did not keep it long, as the Doctor soon sent me to his cotton plantation, that I might be burnt darker by the sun. He sent for me to be with a tailor to learn the trade, but all the journeymen being white men, Mr. Bryant, the tailor, did not let me work in the shop; I cannot say whether it was the prejudice of his journeymen, in not wanting me to sit in the shop with them, or whether Mr. Bryant wanted to keep me about the house to do the domestic work, instead of teaching me the trade. After several months, my master came to know how I got on with the trade: I am not able to tell Mr. Bryant's answer, but it was either that I could not learn, or that his journeymen were not willing that I should sit in the shop with them. I was only once in the shop all the time I was there, and then only for an hour or two, before his wife called me out to do some other work. So my master took me home, and as he was going to send a load of cotton to Camden, about forty miles distance, he sent me with the bales of cotton to be sold with it, where I was soon sold to a gentleman, named Allen, but Mr. Allen soon exchanged me for a female slave, to please his wife. The traders who bought me, were named Cooper and Lindsey, who took me for sale, but could not sell me, people objecting to my being rather white. They then took me to the city of Fayetteville, North Carolina, where he swopt me for a boy, that was blacker than me, to Mr. Smith, who lived several miles off.

I was with Mr. Smith nearly a year. I arrived at the first knowledge of my age when I lived with him. I was then between twelve and thirteen years old, it was when President Jackson[3] was elected the first time, and he has been President eight years, so I must be nearly twenty-one years of age. At this time I was quite a small boy, and was sold to Mr. Hodge, a negro trader. Here I began to enter into hardships.

## CHAPTER II

**The Author's being sold to Mr. J. Gooch.—The cruel treatment he both received and witnessed while on his estate.—Repeated attempts at running away.—Escapes to his mother after being absent from her about ten years.—Meets with his sister, whom he had never seen before, on the road, who conducted him to his mother.**

After travelling several hundred miles, Mr. Hodge sold me to Mr. Gooch, the Cotton Planter, Cashaw County, South Carolina, he purchased me at a town called Liberty Hill, about three miles from his home. As soon as he got home, he immediately put me on his cotton plantation to work, and put me under overseers, gave me allowance of meat and bread with the other slaves, which was not half enough for me to live upon, and very laborious work; here my heart was almost broke with grief at leaving my fellow-slaves. Mr. Gooch did not mind my grief, for he flogged me nearly every day, and very severely. Mr. Gooch bought me for his son-in-law, Mr. Hammans, about five miles from his residence. This man had but two slaves besides myself, he treated me very kindly for a week or two, but in summer, when cotton was ready to hoe, he gave me task work, connected with this department, which I could not get done, not having worked on cotton farms before. When I failed in my task he commenced flogging me, and set me to work without any shirt, in the cotton field, in a very hot sun, in the month of July. In August, Mr. Condell, his overseer, gave me a task at pulling fodder; having finished my task before night, I left the field, the rain came on which soaked the fodder, on discovering this, he threatened to flog me for not getting in the fodder before the rain came. This was the first time I attempted to run away, knowing that I should get a flogging. I was then between thirteen and fourteen years of age, I ran away to the woods half naked, I was caught by a slave-holder, who put me in Lancaster Gaol.[4] When they put slaves in gaol, they advertise for their masters to own them; but if the master does not claim his slave in six months, from the time of imprisonment, the slave is sold for gaol fees. When the slave runs away, the master always adopts a more rigorous system of flogging, this was the case in the present instance. After this, having determined from my youth to gain my freedom, I made several attempts, was caught, and got a severe flogging of 100 lashes, each time. Mr. Hammans was a very severe and cruel master, and his wife still worse, she used to tie me up and flog me while naked.

After Mr. Hammans saw that I was determined to die in the woods, and not live with him, he tried to obtain a piece to land from his father-in-law, Mr. Gooch; not having the means of purchasing it, he exchanged me for the land.

As soon as Mr. Gooch had possession of me again, knowing that I was averse to going back to him, he chained me by the neck to his chaise.[5] In this manner, he took me to his home at MacDaniel's Ferry, in the County of Chester, a distance of fifteen miles. After which, he put me into a swamp, to cut trees, the heaviest work, which men of twenty-five or thirty years of age have to do, I being but sixteen. Here I was on very short allowance of food, and having heavy work, was too weak to fulfil my tasks. For this, I got many severe floggings; and, after I had got my irons[6] off, I made another attempt at running away. He took my irons off, in the full anticipation that I could never get across the Catarba River, even when at liberty. On this, I procured a small Indian canoe, which was tied to a tree, and ultimately got across the river in it. I then wandered through the wilderness for several days without any food, and but a drop of water to allay my thirst, till I became so starved, that I was obliged to go to a house to beg for something to eat, when I was captured, and again imprisoned.

Mr. Gooch having heard of me through an advertisement, sent his son after me; he tied me up, and took me back to his father. Mr. Gooch then obtained the assistance of another slave-holder, and tied me up in his blacksmith's shop and gave me fifty lashes with a cow-hide. He then put a log chain, weighing twenty-five pounds, round my neck, and sent me into a field, into which he followed me with the cow-hide, intending to set his slaves to flog me again. Knowing this, and dreading to suffer again in this way, I gave him the slip, and got out of his sight, he having stopped to speak with the other slave-holder.

I got to a canal on the Catarba River, on the banks of which, and near to a lock,[7] I procured a stone and a piece of iron, with which I forced the ring off my chain, and got it off, and then crossed the river, and walked about twenty miles, when I fell in with a slave-holder, named Ballad, who had married the sister of Mr. Hammans. I knew that he was not so cruel as Mr. Gooch, and therefore, begged of him to buy me. Mr. Ballad, who was one of the best planters in the neighbourhood, said, that he was not able to buy me, and stated, that he was obliged to take me back to my master, on account of the heavy fine attaching to a man harbouring a slave. Mr. Ballad proceeded to take me back; as we came in sight of Mr. Gooch's, all the treatment that I had met with there, came forcibly upon my mind, the powerful influence of which is beyond description. On my knees, with tears in my eyes, with terror in my countenance, and fervency in all my features, I implored Mr. Ballad to buy me, but he again refused, and I was taken back to my dreaded and cruel master. Having reached Mr. Gooch's, he proceeded to punish me. This he did, by first tying my wrists together and placing them over the knees, he then put a stick through, under my knees and over my arms, and having thus secured my arms, he proceeded to flog me, and gave me 500 lashes on my bare back. This may appear incredible, but the marks which they left, at present remain on my body, a standing testimony to the truth of this statement of his severity. He then chained me down in a log-pen with a 40lbs. chain, and made me lie on the damp earth all night. In the morning, after his breakfast, he came to me, and without giving me any breakfast, tied me to a large heavy harrow,[8] which is usually drawn by a horse, and made me drag it to the cotton field for the horse to use in the field. Thus, the reader will see, that it was of no possible use to my master, to make me drag it to the field and not through it; his cruelty went so far, as actually to make me the slave of his horse, and thus to degrade me. He then flogged me again, and set me to work in the corn field the whole of that day, and at night, chained me down in the log-pen as before. The next morning, he took me to the cotton field, and gave me a third flogging, and set me to hoe cotton. At this time, I was dreadfully sore and weak with the repeated floggings and harsh treatment I had endured. He put me under a black man, with orders, that if I did not keep my row up in hoeing with this man, he was to flog me. The reader must recollect here, that not being used to this kind of work, having been a domestic slave, it was quite impossible for me to keep up with him, and, therefore, I was repeatedly flogged during the day.

Mr. Gooch had a female slave about eighteen years old, who also had been a domestic slave, and, through not being able to fulfil her task, had run away; which slave he was at this time punishing for that offence. On the third day, he chained me to this female slave, with a large chain of 40lbs.* weight round the neck. It was most harrowing to my feelings thus to be chained to a young female slave, for whom I would rather have suffered 100 lashes than she should have been thus treated; he kept me chained to her during the week, and repeatedly flogged us both, while thus chained together, and forced us to keep up with the other slaves, although retarded by the heavy weight of the log-chain.

Here again, words are insufficient to describe the misery which possessed both body and mind whilst under this treatment, and which was most dreadfully increased by the sympathy which I felt for my poor, degraded fellow-sufferer. On the Friday morning, I entreated my master to set me free from my chains, and promised him to do the task which was given me, and more, if possible, if he would desist from flogging me. This he refused to do until Saturday night, when he did set me free. This must rather be ascribed to his own interest in preserving me from death, as it was very evident I could no longer have survived under such treatment.

After this, though still determined in my own mind to escape, I stayed with him several months, during which, he frequently flogged me, but not so severely as before related. During this time, I had opportunity for recovering

*This was a chain that they used to draw logs with from the woods, when they clear their land.

my health, and using means to heal my wounds. My master's cruelty was not confined to me, it was his general conduct to all his slaves. I might relate many instances to substantiate this, but will confine myself to one or two. Mr. Gooch, it is proper to observe, was a member of a Baptist Church, called Black Jack Meeting House, in Cashaw county, which church I attended for several years, but was never inside. This is accounted for, by the fact, that the coloured population are not permitted to mix with the white population. In the Roman Catholic church no distinction is made. Mr. Gooch had a slave named Phil, who was a member of a Methodist church; this man was between seventy and eighty years of age; he was so feeble that he could not accomplish his tasks, for which his master used to chain him round the neck, and run him down a steep hill; this treatment he never relinquished to the time of his death. Another case, was that of a slave, named Peter, who, for not doing his task, he flogged nearly to death, and afterwards pulled out his pistol to shoot him, but his (Mr. Gooch's) daughter snatched the pistol from his hand. Another mode of punishment which this man adopted, was that of using iron horns, with bells, attached to the back of the slave's neck.

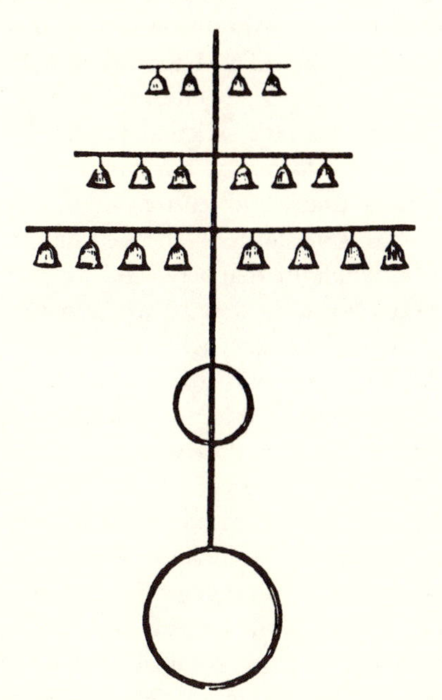

This instrument he used to prevent the negroes running away, being a very ponderous machine, several feet in height, and the cross pieces being two feet four, and six feet in length. This custom is generally adopted among the slaveholders in South Carolina, and some other slave States. One morning, about an hour before day break, I was going on an errand for my master; having proceeded about a quarter of a mile, I came up to a man, named King, (Mr.

Sumlin's overseer,) who had caught a young girl that had run away with the above machine on her. She had proceeded four miles from her station, with the intention of getting into the hands of a more humane master. She came up with this overseer nearly dead, and could get no farther; he immediately secured her, and took her back to her master, a Mr. Johnston.

Having been in the habit of going over many slave States with my master, I had good opportunities of witnessing the harsh treatment which was adopted by masters towards their slaves. As I have never read nor heard of anything connected with slavery, so cruel as what I have myself witnessed, it will be well to mention a case or two.

A large farmer, Colonel M'Quiller, in Cashaw county, South Carolina, was in the habit of driving nails into a hogshead,[9] so as to leave the point of the nail just protruding in the inside of the cask; into this, he used to put his slaves for punishment, and roll them down a very long and steep hill. I have heard from several slaves (though I had no means of ascertaining the truth of the statement) that in this way he killed six or seven of his slaves. This plan was first adopted by a Mr. Perry, who lived on the Catarba River, and has since been adopted by several planters. Another was, that of a young lad, who had been hired by Mr. Bell, a member of a Methodist church, to hoe three-quarters of an acre of cotton per day. Having been brought up as a domestic slave, he was not able to accomplish the task assigned to him. On the Saturday night, he left three or four rows to do on the Sunday; on the same night it rained very hard, by which the master could tell that he had done some of the rows on Sunday. On Monday, his master took and tied him up to a tree in the field, and kept him there the whole of that day, and flogged him at intervals. At night, when he was taken down, he was so weak that he could not get home, having a mile to go. Two white men, who were employed by Mr. Bell, put him on a horse, took him home, and threw him down on the kitchen floor, while they proceeded to their supper. In a little time, they heard some deep groans proceeding from the kitchen, they went to see him die; he had groaned his last. Thus, Mr. Bell flogged the poor boy, even to death; for what? for breaking the Sabbath, when he (his master) had set him a task, on Saturday, which it was not possible for him to do, and which, if he did not do no mercy would be extended towards him! So much for the regard of this Methodist for the observance of the Sabbath.* The general custom in this respect is, that if a man kills his own slave, no notice is taken of it by the civil functionaries; but if a man kills a slave, belonging to another master, he is compelled to pay the worth of the slave. In this case, a jury met, returned a verdict of "Wilful Murder" against this man, and ordered him to pay the value. Mr. Bell was unable to do this, but a Mr. Cunningham paid the debt, and took this Mr. Bell, with this recommendation for cruelty, to be his overseer.

*I am happy to find that the Methodists are quite a different people in England, and I hope that they will do all that they can to enlighten their slave-holding brethren in America.

It will be observed, that most of the cases here cited, are those in respect to males. Many instances, however, in respect to females, might be mentioned, but are too disgusting to appear in this narrative. The cases here brought forward are not rare, but the continued feature of slavery. But I must now follow up the narrative, as regards myself, in particular. I stayed with this master for several months, during which time we went on very well in general. In August, 1831, (this was my first acquaintance with any date;) I happened to hear a man mention this date, and, as it excited my curiosity, I asked what it meant, they told me it was the number of the year from the birth of Christ. On this date, August, 1831, some cows broke into a crib where the corn is kept, and ate a great deal. For this, his slaves were tied up, and received several floggings; but myself and another man, hearing the groans of those who were being flogged, stayed back in the field, and would not come up. Upon this, I thought to escape punishment. On the Monday morning, however, I heard my master flogging the other man who was in the field; he could not see me, it being a field of Indian corn, which grows to a great height. Being afraid that he would catch me, and dreading a flogging more than many others, I determined to run for it; and, after travelling forty miles, I arrived at the estate of Mr. Crawford, in North Carolina, Mecklinburgh county. Having formerly heard people talk about the Free States, I determined upon going thither, and, if possible, in my way to find out my poor mother, who was in slavery, several hundred miles from Chester; but the hope of doing the latter, was very faint, and, even if I did, it was not likely that she would know me, having been separated from her when between five and six years old.

The first night I slept in a barn, upon Mr. Crawford's estate, and, having overslept myself, was awoke by Mr. Crawford's overseer, upon which I was dreadfully frightened; he asked me, what I was doing there? I made no reply to him then; and he, making sure that he had secured a run-a-way slave, did not press me for an answer. On my way to his house, however, I made up the following story, which I told him in the presence of his wife;–I said that I had been bound to a very cruel master when I was a little boy, and that having been treated very badly, I wanted to get home to see my mother. This statement may appear to some to be untrue, but as I understood the word *bound*, I considered it to apply to my case, having been sold to him, and thereby bound to serve him; though still, I did rather hope that he would understand it, that I was bound when a boy, till twenty-one years of age. Though I was white at that time, he would not believe my story, on account of my hair being curly and woolly, which led him to conclude I was possessed of enslaved blood.[10] The overseer's wife, however, who seemed much interested in me, said she did not think I was of African origin, and that she had seen white men still darker than me; her persuasion prevailed; and, after the overseer had given me as much buttermilk as I could drink, and something to eat, which was very acceptable, having had nothing for two days, I set off for Charlotte, in North Carolina, the largest town in the county. I went on very quickly the whole of that day, fearful of being pursued. The trees were very thick on each side of the road, and only a few houses, at the distance of two or three miles apart; as I proceeded, I turned round in all directions to see if I was pursued, and if I caught a glimpse of any one coming along the road, I immediately rushed into the thickest part of the wood, to elude the grasp of what, I was afraid, might be my master. I went on in this way the whole day; at night, I came up with two waggons, they had been to market; the regular road waggons do not generally put up at inns, but encamp in the roads and fields. When I came to them, I told them the same story I had told Mr. Crawford's overseer, with the assurance that the statement would meet the same success. After they had heard me, they gave me something to eat, and also a lodging in the camp with them.

I then went on with them about five miles, and they agreed to take me with them as far as they went, if I would assist them. This I promised to do. In the morning, however, I was much frightened by one of the men putting several questions to me–we were then about three miles from Charlotte. When within a mile of that town, we stopped at a brook to water the horses; while stopping there I saw the men whispering, and fancying I overheard them say they would put me in Charlotte gaol when they got there, I made my escape into the woods, pretending to be looking after something till I got out of their sight. I then ran on as fast I could, but did not go through the town of Charlotte, as had been my intention, being a large town, I was fearful it might prove fatal to my escape. Here I was at a loss how to get on, as houses were not very distant from each other for nearly 200 miles.

While thinking what I should do, I observed some waggons before me, which I determined to keep behind, and never go nearer to them, than a quarter of a mile–in this way I travelled till I got to Salisbury. If I happened to meet any person on the road, I was afraid they would take me up, I asked them how far the waggons had got on before me? to make them suppose I belonged to the waggons. At night, I slept on the ground in the woods, some little distance from the waggons, but not near enough, to be seen by the men belonging to them. All this time, I had but little food, principally fruit, which I found on the road. On Thursday night, I got into Salisbury, having left Chester on the Monday morning preceding. After this, being afraid my master was in pursuit of me, I left the usual line of road, and took another direction, through Huntsville and Salem, principally through fields and woods; on my way to Caswell Court-House, a distance of nearly 200 miles from Salisbury,* I was stopped by a white man, to whom I told my old story, and again succeeded in my escape. I also came up with a small cart, driven by a poor man, who had been moving into some of the western territories, and was going back to Virginia, to move some more of his luggage. On this, I told him I was going

*The distance from Salisbury to Caswell Court-house is not so far, but I had to go a round about way.

the same way to Hilton, thirteen miles from Caswell Court-House, he took me up in his cart, and we went to the Red House, two miles from Hilton, the place where Mr. Mitchell took me from, when six years old, to go to the Southern States. This was a very providential circumstance, for it happened, that at the time I had to pass through Caswell Court-House, a fair or election was going on, which caused the place to be much crowded with people, and rendered it more dangerous for me to pass through.

At the Red House I left the cart, and wandered about a long time, not knowing which way to go and find my mother. After some time, I took the road leading over Ikeo Creek. I shortly came up with a little girl, about six years old, and asked her where she was going, she said, to her mother's, pointing to a house on a hill, about half a mile off. She had been to the overseer's house, and was returning to her mother. I then felt some emotions arising in my breast, which I cannot describe, but will be fully explained in the sequel.[11] I told her, that I was very thirsty, and would go with her to get something to drink. On our way, I asked her several questions, such as her name, that of her mother, she said her's was Maria, and her mother's Nancy. I inquired, if her mother had any more children? she said, five besides herself, and that they had been told, that one had been sold when a little boy. I then asked, the name of this child? she said it was Moses. These answers as we approached the house, led me nearer and nearer to the finding out the object of my pursuit, and of recognizing in the little girl, the person of my own sister.

## CHAPTER III

**An account of the Author's meeting with his mother, who did not know him, but was with her a very short time before he was taken by armed men, and imprisoned for 31 days, and then taken back to his master.**

At last, I got to my mother's house!! my mother was at home, I asked her, if she knew me? she said, no. Her master was having a house built just by, and the men were digging a well, she supposed, that I was one of the diggers. I told her, I knew her very well, and thought that if she looked at me a little, she would know me, but this had no effect. I then asked her, if she had any sons? she said, yes; but none so large as me, I then waited a few minutes, and narrated some circumstances to her, attending my being sold into slavery and how she grieved at my loss. Here the mother's feelings on that dire occasion, and which, a mother only can know, rushed to her mind: she saw her own son before her, for whom she had so often wept; and, in an instant, we were clasped in each other's arms, amidst the ardent interchange of caresses and tears of joy. Ten years had elapsed since I had seen my dear mother. My own feelings, and the circumstances attending my coming home, have often been brought to mind since, on a perusal of the 42nd, 43rd, 44th, and 45th chapters of Genesis.[12] What could picture my feelings so well, as I once more beheld the mother who had brought me into the world, and had nourished me, not with the anticipation of my being torn from her maternal care, when only six years old, to become the prey of a mercenary and blood-stained slave holder; I say, what picture so vivid in description of this part of my tale, as the 7th and 8th verses of the 42nd chapter of Genesis. "And Joseph saw his brethren, and he knew them, but made himself strange unto them. And Joseph knew his brethren, but they knew not him." After the first emotion of the mother, on recognizing her first-born had somewhat subsided, could the reader not fancy the little one, my sister, as she told her simple tale of meeting with me to her mother, how she would say, while the parent listened with intense interest; "The man asked me straitly of our state and our kindred, saying, is your father yet alive, and have ye another brother." Or, when at last, I could no longer refrain from making myself known, I say, I was ready to burst into a frenzy of joy. How applicable the 1st, 2nd, and 3rd verses of the 45th chapter, "Then Joseph could not refrain himself before all them that stood by him, and he wept aloud, and said unto his brethren, I am Joseph, doth my father still live." Then when the mother knew her son, when the brothers and sisters owned their brother; "he kissed all his brethren and wept over them, and after that his brethren talked with him," 15th verse. At night, my mother's husband, a blacksmith, belonging to Mr. Jefferson at the Red House, came home, he was surprised to see me with the family, not knowing who I was. He had been married to my mother, when I was a babe, and had always been very fond of me. After the same tale had been told him, and the same emotions filled his soul, he again kissed the object of his early affection. The next morning I wanted to go on my journey, in order to make sure of my escape to the Free States. But, as might be expected, my mother, father, brothers, and sisters could ill part with their long lost one; and persuaded me to go into the woods in the day time, and at night come home and sleep there. This I did for about a week; on the next Sunday night, I laid me down to sleep between my two brothers, on a pallet, which my mother had prepared for me; about twelve o'clock I was suddenly awoke, and found my bed surrounded by twelve slave holders with pistols in hand, who took me away (not allowing me to bid farewell to those I loved so dearly) to the Red House, where they confined me in a room the rest of the night, and in the morning lodged me in the gaol of Caswell Court-House.

What was the scene at home, what sorrow possessed their hearts, I am unable to describe, as I never after saw any of them more. I heard, however, that my mother, was soon after I left confined, and was very long before she recovered the effects of this disaster.* I was told afterwards, that some of those men who took me, were professing Christians, but to me, they did not seem

*My mother had seven children living when I last saw her, and the above one was born soon after I left, made the eighth, and they are now all in slavery except myself.

to live up to what they professed; they did not seem, by their practice, at least, to recognize that God as their God, who hath said, "thou shalt not deliver unto his master, the servant which is escaped from his master unto thee, he shall dwell with thee, even among you, in that place which he shall choose, in one of thy gates, where it liketh him best; thou shalt not oppress him."–Deut. xxiii. 15, 16.

I was confined here in a dungeon under ground, the grating of which looked to the door of the gaoler's house. His wife had a great antipathy to me. She was Mr. Roper's wife's cousin. My grandmother used to come to me nearly every day, and bring me something to eat, besides the regular gaol allowance, by which, my sufferings were somewhat decreased. Whenever the gaoler went out, which he often did, his wife used to come to my dungeon, and shut the wooden door over the grating, by which, I was nearly suffocated, the place being very damp and noisome. My master did not hear of my being in gaol for thirty-one days after I had been placed there. He immediately sent his son, and son-in-law, Mr. Anderson, after me. They came in a horse and chaise, took me from the gaol to a blacksmith's shop, and got an iron collar fitted round my neck, with a heavy chain attached, then tied my hands, and fastened the other end of the chain on another horse, and put me on its back. Just before we started, my grandmother came to bid me farewell; I gave her my hand as well as I could, and she having given me two or three presents, we parted. I had felt enough, far too much, for the weak state I was in; but how shall I describe my feelings, upon parting with the *last* relative that I *ever saw*. The reader must judge by what would be his own feelings, under similar circumstances. We then went on for fifty miles; I was very weak, and could hardly sit on the horse. Having been in prison so long, I had lost the southern tan; and as the people could not see my hair, having my hat on, they thought I was a white man–a criminal–and asked what crime I had committed. We arrived late at night, at the house of Mr. Britton. I shall never forget the journey that night. The thunder was one continued roar, and the lightning blazing all around. I expected every minute that my iron collar would attract it, and I should be knocked off the horse, and dragged along the ground. This gentleman, a year or two before had liberated his slaves, and sent them into Ohio, having joined the society of Friends,[13] which society does not allow the holding of slaves. I was, therefore, treated very well there, and they gave me a hearty supper, which did me much good in my weak state.

They secured me in the night, by locking me to the post of the bed on which they slept. The next morning, we went on to Salisbury. At that place we stopped to water the horses; they chained me to a tree in the yard, by the side of their chaise. On my horse they had put the saddle bags which contained the provisions. As I was in the yard, a black man came and asked me what I had been doing; I told him I had run away from my master, after which he told me several tales about the slaves, and among them he mentioned the case of a Quaker, who was then in prison, waiting to be hung, for giving a free passage to a slave. I had been considering all the way, how I could escape from my horse, and once had an idea of cutting his head off, but thought it too cruel; and at last thought of trying to get a rasp and cut the chain by which I was fastened to the horse. As they often let me get on nearly a quarter of a mile before them, I thought I should have a good opportunity of doing this without being seen. The black man procured me a rasp, and I put it into the saddle bags which contained the provisions. We then went on our journey, and one of the sons asked me if I wanted anything to eat; I answered no, though very hungry at the time, as I was afraid of their going to the bags and discovering the rasp. However, they had not had their own meal at the inn as I supposed, and went to the bags to supply themselves, where they discovered the rasp. Upon this, they fastened my horse beside the horse in their chaise, and kept a stricter watch over me. Nothing remarkable occurred till we got within eight miles of Mr. Gooch's, where we stopped a short time; and, taking advantage of their absence, I broke a switch from some boughs above my head, lashed my horse and set off at full speed. I had got about a quarter of a mile before they could get their horse loose from their chaise; one then rode the horse, and the other ran as fast as he could after me. When I caught sight of them, I turned off the main road into the woods, hoping to escape their sight, their horse, however, being much swifter than mine, they soon got within a short distance of me. I then came to a rail fence, which I found it very difficult to get over, but breaking several rails away, I effected my object. They then called upon me to stop more than three times, and I not doing so they fired after me, but the pistol only snapped.

This is according to law; after three calls they may shoot a run-away slave. Soon after the one on the horse came up with me, and catching hold of the bridle of my horse, pushed the pistol to my side, the other soon came up, and breaking off several stout branches from the trees, they gave me about 100 blows. They did this very near to a planter's house, the gentleman was not at home, but his wife came out and begged them not to *kill* me *so near the house*; they took no notice of this, but kept on beating me. They then fastened me to the axle-tree of their chaise, one of them got into the chaise, the other took my horse, and they run me all the eight miles as fast as they could; the one on my horse going behind to guard me.

## CHAPTER IV

### The Author is Flogged and Punished in various ways, but still perseveres in his attempts to Escape, till he was sold to Mr. Wilson.

In this way we came to my old master, Mr. Gooch. The first person I saw was himself; he unchained me from the chaise, and at first seemed to treat me very gently, asking me where I had been, &c. The first thing the sons did was to show the rasp which I had got to cut my chain. My master gave me a hearty dinner, the best he ever did give me, but it was to keep me from dying before he had given me all the flogging he intended. After dinner he took me to a log-house, stripped me quite naked, fastened a rail up very high, tied my hands to the rail, fastened my feet together, put a rail between my feet, and stood on one end of it to hold it down; the two sons then gave me fifty lashes each, the son-in-law another fifty, and Mr. Gooch himself fifty more.

While doing this his wife came out, and begged him not to kill me, the first act of sympathy I ever noticed in her. When I called for water, they brought a pail-full and threw it over my back, ploughed up by the lashes. After this, they took me to the blacksmith's shop, got *two large bars of iron*, which they bent round my feet, each bar *weighing twenty pounds*, and put a heavy log-chain on my neck. This was on Saturday. On the Monday, he chained me to the same female slave as before. As he had to go out that day, he did not give me the punishment which he intended to give me every day, but at night when he came home, he made us walk round his estate, and by all the houses of the slaves, for them to taunt us; when we came home, he told us, we must be up very early in the morning, and go to the fields before the other slaves. We were up at day break, but we could not get on fast, on account of the heavy irons on my feet. It may be necessary to state here, that these irons were first made red hot and bent in a circle, so as just to allow of my feet going through; it having been cooled, and my leg with the iron on lifted up to an anvil, it was made secure round my ankles. When I walked with these irons on, I used to hold them up with my hands by means of cord. We walked *about a mile in two hours*, but knowing the punishment he was going to inflict on us, we made up our minds to escape into the woods, and secrete ourselves. This we did, and he not being able to find us; sent all his slaves, about forty, and his sons, to find us, which they could not do; and about twelve o'clock, when we thought they would give up looking for us at that time, we went on, and came to the banks of the Catarba. Here I got a stone, and opened the ring of the chain on her neck, and got it off; and as the chain round my neck was only passed through a ring, as soon as I had got her's off, I slipped the chain through my ring, and got it off my own neck.*—We then went on by the banks of the river for some distance, and found a little canoe about two feet wide. I managed to get in, although the irons on my feet made it very dangerous, for if I had upset the canoe, I could not swim. The female got in after me, and gave me the paddles, by which we got some distance down the river. The current being very strong, it drove us against a small island; we paddled round the island to the other side, and then made towards the opposite bank. Here again we were stopped by the current, and made up to a large rock in the river, between the island and the opposite shore. As the weather was very rough,

*It may be well to state here, that the ring which fastened the log chain together around the female's neck; was an open ring, similar to those used at the end of watch chains.

we landed on the rock and secured the canoe, as it was not possible to get back to the island. It was a very dark night and rained tremendously; and as the water was rising rapidly towards the top of the rock, we gave all up for lost, and sometimes hoped, and sometimes feared to hope, that we should never see the morning. But Providence[14] was moving in our favour; the rain ceased, the water reached the edge of the rock, then receded, and we were out of danger from this cause. We remained all night upon the rock, and in the morning reached the opposite shore, and then made our way through the woods till we came to a field of Indian corn, where we plucked some of the green ears and eat them, having had nothing for two days and nights. We came to the estate of —, where we met with a coloured man who knew me, and having run away himself from a bad master, he gave us some food, and told us we might sleep in the barn that night. Being very fatigued, we overslept ourselves; the proprietor came to the barn, but as I was in one corner under some Indian corn tops, and she in another, he did not perceive us, and we did not leave the barn before night, (Wednesday.) We then went out, got something to eat, and strayed about the estate till Sunday. On that day, I met with some men, one of whom had had irons on his feet the same as me; he told me that his master was going out to see his friends, and that he would try and get my feet loose; for this purpose I parted with this female, fearing, that if she were caught with me, she would be forced to tell who took my irons off. The man tried some time without effect, he then gave me a file and I tried myself, but was disappointed on account of their thickness.

On the Monday, I went on towards Lancaster, and got within three miles of it that night; and went towards the plantation of Mr. Crockett, as I knew some of his slaves, and hoped to get some food given me. When I got there, however, the dogs smelt me out and barked; upon which, Mr. Crockett came out, followed me with his rifle, and came up with me. He put me on a horse's back, which put me to extreme pain, from the great weight hanging from my feet. We reached Lancaster gaol that night, and he lodged me there. I was placed in the next dungeon to a man who was going to be hung. I shall never forget his cries and groans, as he prayed all night for the mercy of God. Mr. Gooch did not hear of me for several weeks: when he did, he sent his son-in-law, Mr. Anderson, after me. Mr. Gooch himself came within a mile of Lancaster, and waited until Mr. Anderson brought me. At this time I had but one of the irons on my feet, having got so thin round my ankles that I had slipped one off while in gaol. His son-in-law tied my hands, and made me walk along till we came to Mr. Gooch. As soon as we arrived at M'Daniel's Ford, two miles above the Ferry, on the Catarba River, they made me wade across, themselves going on horseback. The water was very deep, and having irons on one foot and round my neck, I could not keep a footing. They dragged me along by my chain, on the top of the water. It was as much as they could do to hold me by the chain, the current being very strong. They then took me home, flogged me, put extra irons on my neck and feet, and put me under the driver, with more work than ever I had before. He did not flog me so severely as before, but continued it every day. Among the instruments of torture employed, I here describe one:–

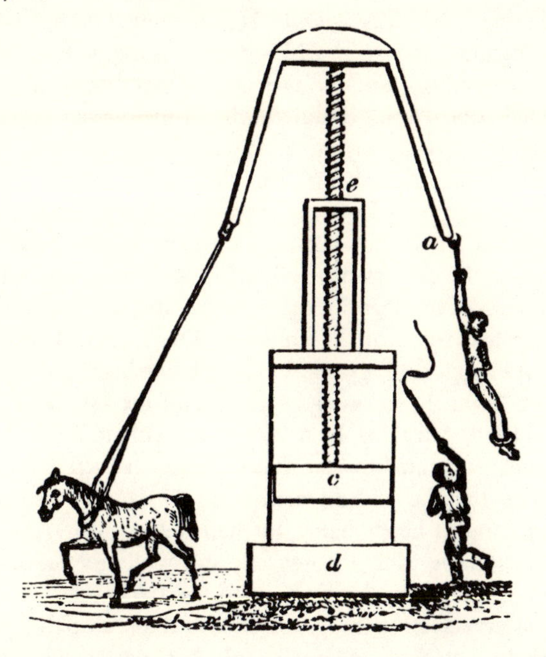


The author hanging by his hands tied to a cotton screw.*

This is a machine used for packing and pressing cotton. By it he hung me up by the hands at letter *a*, a horse, and at times, a man moving round the screw *e*, and carrying it up and down, and pressing the block *c* into the box *d*, into which the cotton is put. At this time he hung me up for a quarter of an hour. I was carried up ten feet from the ground, when Mr. Gooch asked me if I was tired? He then let me rest for five minutes, then carried me round again, after which, he let me down and put me into the box *d*, and shut me down in it for about ten minutes. After this torture, I stayed with him several months, and did my work very well. It was about the beginning of 1832, when he took off my irons, and being in dread of him, he having threatened me with more punishment, I attempted again to escape from him. At this time I got into North Carolina: but a reward having been offered for me, a Mr. Robinson caught me, and chained me to a chair, upon which he sat up with me all night, and next day proceeded home with me. This was Saturday. Mr. Gooch had gone to church, several miles from his house. When he came back, the first thing he did was to pour some tar on my head, then rubbed it all

*This screw is sometimes moved round by hand, when there is a person hanging on it. The screw is made with wood, a large tree cut down, and carved in the shape of a screw.

over my face, took a torch with pitch on, and set it on fire; he put it out before it did me very great injury, but the pain which I endured was most excruciating, nearly all my hair having been burnt off. On Monday, he put irons on me again, weighing nearly fifty pounds. He threatened me again on the Sunday with another flogging; and on the Monday morning, before day-break, I got away again, with my irons on, and was about three hours, going a distance of two miles.* I had gone a good distance, when I met with a coloured man, who got some wedges, and took my irons off. However, I was caught again, and put into prison in Charlotte, where Mr. Gooch came, and took me back to Chester. He asked me how I got my irons off? They having been got off by a slave, I would not answer his question, for fear of getting the man punished. Upon this, he put the fingers of my hands into a vice, and squeezed all my nails off. He then had my feet put on an anvil, and ordered a man to beat my toes, till he smashed some of my nails off. The marks of this treatment still remain upon me, some of my nails never having grown perfect since. He inflicted this punishment, in order to get out of me how I got my irons off, but never succeeded. After this, he hardly knew what to do with me; the whole stock of his cruelties seemed to be exhausted. He chained me down in the log-house. Soon after this, he sent a female slave to see if I was safe. Mr. Gooch had not secured me as he thought; but had only run my chain through the ring, without locking it. This I observed; and while the slave was coming, I was employed in loosening the chain with the hand that was not wounded. As soon as I observed her coming, I drew the chain up tight, and she observing, that I seemed fast, went away and told her master, who was in the field ordering the slaves. When she was gone. I drew the chain through the ring, escaped under the flooring of the log-house, and went on under it, till I came out at the other side, and ran on; but, being sore and weak, I had not got a mile before I was caught, and again carried back. He tied me up to a tree in the woods at night, and made his slaves flog me. I cannot say how many lashes I received; but it was the worst flogging I ever had, and the last which Mr. Gooch ever gave me.

There are several circumstances which occurred on this estate while I was there, relative to other slaves, which it may be interesting to mention. Hardly a day ever passed without some one being flogged. To one of his female slaves he had given a dose of castor oil and salts[15] together, as much as she could take;† he then got a box, about six feet by two and a half, and one and a half feet deep; he put this slave under the box, and made the men fetch as many logs as they could get, and put them on the top of it; under this she was made to stay all night. I believe, that if he had given this slave one, he had given her three thousand lashes. Mr. Gooch was a member of a Baptist Church. His

*It must be recollected, that when a person is two miles from a house, in that part of the country, that he can hide himself in the woods for weeks, and I knew a slave who was hid for six months without discovery, the trees being so thick.

†The female whom Mr. Gooch chained me to.

slaves thinking him a very bad sample of what a professing Christian ought to be, would not join the connexion he belonged to, thinking they must be a very bad set of people: there were many of them members of the Methodist Church.* On Sunday, the slaves can only go to church at the will of their master, when he gives them a pass for the time they are to be out. If they are found by the patrole after the time to which their pass extends, they are severely flogged.

On Sunday nights a slave, named Allen, used to come to Mr. Gooch's estate for the purpose of exhorting and praying with his brother slaves, by whose instrumentality many of them had been converted. One evening, Mr. Gooch caught them all in a room, turned Allen out, and threatened his slaves with one hundred lashes each, if they ever brought him there again. At one time Mr. Gooch was ill and confined to his room; if any of the slaves had done anything which he thought deserving a flogging, he would have them brought into his bed-room and flogged before his eyes.

With respect to food, he used to allow us one peck[16] of Indian meal[17] each per week, which, after being sifted and the bran[18] taken from it, would not be much more than half a peck. Meat we did not get for sometimes several weeks together; however, he was proverbial for giving his slaves more food than any other slave-holder. I stayed with Mr. Gooch a year and a half; during that time the scenes of cruelty I witnessed and experienced, are not at all fitted for these pages. There is much to excite disgust in what has been narrated, but hundreds of other cases might be mentioned.

## CHAPTER V

**I was not long with Mr. Wilson, who was a Negro trader, before he exchanged me to Mr. Rowland, who was also a trader for another slave, and after being with him about one year, was sold to Mr. Goodly, who exchanged me again to Mr. Louis.**

After this, Mr. Gooch seeing that I was determined to get away from him, chained me and set me with another female slave, whom he had treated very cruelly, to Mr. Britton, son of the before-mentioned, a slave-dealer. We were to have gone to Georgia to be sold, but a bargain was struck before we arrived there. Mr. Britton had put chains on me to please Mr. Gooch, but having gone some little distance we came up with a white man, who begged Mr. Britton to unchain me, he then took off my handcuffs. We then went on to Union Court House, where we met a drove of slaves belonging to Mr. Wilson, who

*In fact, in some of the States nearly all the slaves are Methodists; and when in the field at work, they may be often heard singing these words, "I am happy, I am happy, Lord pity poor me.–Me never know what happiness was, until I joined de Methodists.–I am happy, Lord pity poor me."

ultimately bought me and sent me to his drove; the girl was sold to a planter in the neighbourhood as bad as Mr. Gooch.* In court week the negro traders and slaves encamp a little way out of the town. The traders here will often sleep with the best looking female slaves among them, and they will often have many children in the year, which are said to be slave holder's children, by which means, through his villany, he will make an immense profit of this intercourse, by selling the babe with its mother. They often keep an immense stock of slaves on hand; many of them will be with the trader a year or more before they are sold. Mr. Marcus Rowland, the drover[19] who bought me, then returned with his slaves to his brother's house (Mr. John Rowland), where he kept his drove on his way to Virginia. He kept me as a kind of servant. I had to grease the faces of the blacks every morning with sweet oil, to make them shine, before they are put up to sell. After he had been round several weeks and sold many slaves, he left me and some more at his brother's house, while he went on to Washington, about 600 miles, to buy some more slaves, the drove having got very small. We were treated very well while there, having plenty to eat and little work to do, in order to make us fat. I was brought up more as a domestic slave, as they generally prefer slaves of my colour for that purpose. When Mr. Rowland came back, having been absent about five months, he found all the slaves well except one female, who had been grieving very much at being parted from her parents, and at last died of grief. He dressed us very nicely and went on again. I travelled with him for a year, and had to look over the slaves and see that they were dressed well, had plenty of food, and to oil their faces. During this time we stopped once at White House Church, a Baptist Association; a protracted camp meeting was holding there, on the plan of the revival meetings[20] in this country. We got there at the time of the meeting, and sold two female slaves on the Sunday morning, at the time the meeting broke up, to a gentleman who had been attending the meeting the whole of the week. While I was with Mr. Rowland, we were at many such meetings; and the members of the churches are by this means so well influenced towards their fellow-creatures at these meetings for the worship of God, that it becomes a fruitful season for the drover, who carries on an immense traffic with the attendants at these places. This is common to Baptists and Methodists. At the end of the year, he exchanged me to a farmer, Mr. David Goodley, for a female slave in Greenville, about fourteen miles from Greenville Court House. The gentleman was going to Missouri to settle, and on his way had to pass through Ohio, a free State. But having learnt after he bought me, that I had before tried to get away, to the free States, he was afraid to take me with him, and I was again exchanged to a Mr. Louis.

*As I am often asked "What became of the female I was chained to?" The above is the girl, whom I have seen once since she was last sold, and from what I saw of her then, I do not think she can be alive now. Before Mr. R. left, he had it in contemplation, on account of my being too white, and fearing that I would run away, to mark or write on my face with powder, similar to the way in which sailors are marked on the arm.

## CHAPTER VI

**Travels with Mr. Louis to Pendleton Indian Springs, from thence to Columbus, where I was sold at auction to Mr. Beveridge. Travels and history with Mr. Beveridge.**

Mr. Marvel Louis was in the habit of travelling a great deal, and took me as a domestic slave to wait on him. Mr. Louis boarded at the house of Mr. Clevelin, a very rich planter at Greenville, South Carolina. Mr. L. was paying his addresses to the daughter of this gentleman, but was surprised and routed in his approaches, by a Colonel Dorkins, of Union Court House, who ultimately carried her off in triumph. After this, Mr. Louis took to drinking, to drown his recollection of disappointed love. One day he went to Pendleton Races, and I waited on the road for him; returning intoxicated, he was thrown from his horse into a brook, and was picked up by a gentleman, and taken to an inn, and I went there to take care of him. Next day, he went on to Punkintown with Mr. Warren R. Davis, a member of Congress; I went with him. This was at the time of the agitation of the Union and Nullifying party,[21] which was expected to end in a general war. The Nullifying party had a grand dinner on the occasion, after which, they gave their slaves all their refuse, for the purpose of bribing them to fight on the side of their party. The scene on this occasion was humorous, all the slaves scrambling after bare bones and crumbs, as if they had had nothing for weeks. When Mr. Louis had got over this fit of drunkenness, we returned to Greenville, where I had little to do except in the warehouse. There was preaching in the Court-house on the Sunday; but scarcely had the sweet savour of the worship of God passed away, when, on Monday, a public auction was held for the sale of slaves, cattle, sugar, iron, &c. by Z. Davis, the high constable and others.

On these days I was generally very busy in handing out the different articles for inspection, and was employed in this way for several months. After which, Mr. Louis left this place for Pendleton; but his health getting worse, and fast approaching consumption, he determined to travel. I went with him over Georgia to the Indian Springs, and from there to Columbus; here he left me with Lawyer Kemp, a member of the State Assembly, to take care of his horses and carriage till he came back from Cuba, where he went for the benefit of his health. I travelled round with Mr. Kemp, waiting until my master came back. I soon after heard, that Mr. Louis had died at Appalachicola, and had been buried at Tennessee Bluff. I was very much attached to the neighbourhood of Pendleton and Greenville, and feared, from Mr. Louis's death, I should not get back there.

As soon as this information arrived, Mr. Kemp put me, the carriage and horses, a gold watch, and cigars, up to auction, on which I was much frightened, knowing there would be some very cruel masters at the sale; and fearing, I should again be disappointed in my attempt to escape from bondage. Mr.

Beveridge, a Scotchman, from Appalachicola, bought me, the horses, and cigars.* He was not a cruel master; he had been in America eighteen years, and I believe, I was the first slave he ever bought. Mr. Kemp had no right to sell me, which he did, before he had written to Mr. Louis's brother.

Shortly after this, Mr. Kemp, having had some altercation with General Woodfork, it ended in a duel, in which Mr. W. was killed. A few weeks after, as Mr. Kemp was passing down a street, he was suddenly shot dead by Mr. Milton, a rival lawyer. When I heard this, I considered it a visitation of God on Mr. Kemp for having sold me unjustly, as I did not belong to him. This was soon discovered by me, Mr. Louis's brother having called at Mackintosh Hotel, Columbus, to claim me, but which he could not effect. After this, I travelled with Mr. Beveridge, through Georgia, to the warm springs, and then came back to Columbus, going on to Marianna, his summer-house, in Florida.

Here I met with better treatment than I had ever experienced before; we travelled on the whole summer; at the fall, Mr. Beveridge went to Appalachicola on business. Mr. Beveridge was contractor for the mail, from Columbus to Appalachicola, and owner of three steamboats, the Versailles, Andrew Jackson, and Van Buren. He made me steward on board the Versailles, the whole winter. The river then got so low that the boats could not run. At this time, Mr. Beveridge went to Mount Vernon. On our way, we had to pass through the Indian nation. We arrived at Columbus, where I was taken dangerously ill of a fever. After I got well, Mr. Beveridge returned to Marianna, through the Indian nation. Having gone about twelve miles, he was taken very ill. I took him out of the carriage to a brook, and washed his hands and face until he got better, when I got him into the carriage again, and drove off till we came to General Irving's, where he stopped several days on account of his health. While there, I observed on the floor of the kitchen several children, one about three months old, without any body to take care of her; I asked, where her mother was, and was told, that Mrs. Irving had given her a very hard task to do at washing, in a brook, about a quarter of a mile distant. We heard after, that not being able to get it done, she had got some cords, tied them round her neck, climbed up a tree, swung off, and hung herself. Being missed, persons were sent after her, who observed several buzzards flying about a particular spot, to which they directed their steps, and found the poor woman nearly eaten up.

After this, we travelled several months without anything remarkable taking place.

*How Mr. Beveridge ever became a slave-holder, I cannot account for, for I believe him to be the only kind slave-holder in America, and not only that, I have been in England three years, and have never met with a kinder man than Mr. Beveridge, and have often prayed that God would deliver him from that one sin, a sin which he was kept from eighteen years.

## CHAPTER VII

**The Author's last Attempt and final Escape from Marianna to Savannah, from thence to New York; Quarantined at Statten Island.**

In the year 1834, Mr. Beveridge, who was now residing in Appalachicola, a town in West Florida, became a bankrupt, when all his property was sold, and I fell into the hands of a very cruel master, Mr. Register, a planter in the same State; of whom, knowing his savage character, I always had a dread. Previously to his purchasing me, he had frequently taunted me, by saying, "you have been a gentleman long enough, and, whatever may be the consequences, I intend to buy you." To which I remarked, that I would on no account live with him if I could help it. Nevertheless, intent upon his purpose, in the month of July, 1834, he bought me; after which I was so exasperated, that I cared not whether I lived or died; in fact, whilst I was on my passage from Appalachicola, I procured a quart bottle of whiskey, for the purpose of so intoxicating myself, that I might be able either to plunge myself into the river, or so to enrage my master that he should dispatch me forthwith. I was, however, by a kind Providence, prevented from committing this horrid deed by an old slave on board, who, knowing my intention, secretly took the bottle from me; after which my hands were tied, and I was led into the town of Ochesa, to a warehouse, where my master was asked by the proprietor of the place, the reason for his confining my hands, in answer to which, Mr. Register said, that he had purchased me. The proprietor, however, persuaded him to untie me; after which, my master being excessively drunk, asked for a cowhide, intending to flog me, from which the proprietor dissuaded him, saying, that he had known me for some time, and he was sure that I did not require to be flogged. From this place we proceeded about mid-day on our way, he placing me on the bare back of a half-starved old horse which he had purchased, and upon which sharp *surface*, he kindly intended I should ride about eighty miles, the distance we were then from his home. In this unpleasant situation I could not help reflecting upon the prospects before me, not forgetting that I had heard that my new master had been in the habit of stealing cattle and other property, and among other things a slave woman, and that I had said, as it afterwards turned out, in the hearing of some one who communicated the saying to my master, that I had been accustomed to live with a gentleman and not with a rogue; and, finding that he had been informed of this, I had the additional dread of a few hundred lashes for it, on my arrival at my destination.

About two hours after we started it began to rain very heavily, and continued to do so until we arrived at Marianna, about twelve at night, where we were to rest till morning. My master here questioned me as to whether I intended to run away or not; and, I not then knowing the sin of lying, at once told him that I would not. He then gave me his clothes to dry; I took them to the kitchen for that purpose, and he retired to bed, taking a bag of clothes belonging to me with him, as a kind of security, I presume, for my safety. In an hour or two afterwards, I took his clothes to him dried, and found him fast asleep. I placed them by his side, and said that I would then take my own to dry too, taking care to speak loud enough to ascertain whether he was asleep or not, knowing that he had a dirk[22] and a pistol by his side, which he would not have hesitated using against me, if I had attempted secretly to have procured them. I was glad to find that the effects of his drinking the day before had caused his sleeping very soundly, and I immediately resolved on making my escape; and without loss of time started with my few clothes into the woods, which were in the immediate neighbourhood; and, after running many miles, I came to the river Chapoli, which is very deep, and so beset with alligators that I dared not attempt to swim across. I paced up and down this river, with the hope of finding a conveyance across, for a whole day, the succeeding night, and till noon the following day, which was Saturday. About twelve o'clock on that day I discovered an Indian canoe, which had not from all appearance been used for some time; this, of course, I used to convey myself across, and after being obliged to go a little way down the river, by means of a piece of wood I providentially found in the boat, I landed on the opposite side. Here I found myself surrounded by planters looking for me, in consequence of which, I hid myself in the bushes until night, when I again travelled several miles to the farm of a Mr. Robinson, a large sugar and cotton planter, where I rested till morning in a field. Afterwards I set out working my way through the woods, about twenty miles towards the east; this I knew by my knowledge of the position of the sun at its rising. Having reached the Chattahoochee river, which divides Florida from Georgia, I was again puzzled to know how to cross; it was about three o'clock in the day, when a number of persons were fishing; having walked for some hours along the banks, I at last, after dark, procured a ferry-boat, which not being able, from the swiftness of the river, to steer direct across, I was carried many miles down the river, landing on the Georgian side, from whence I proceeded on through the woods two or three miles, and came to a little farm house about twelve at night; at a short distance from the house I found an old slave hut, into which I went, and informed the old man, who appeared seventy or eighty years old, that I had had a very bad master, from whom I had run away; and asked him, if he could give me something to eat, having had no suitable food for three or four days; he told me he had nothing but a piece of dry Indian bread, which he cheerfully gave me; having eaten it, I went on a short distance from the hut, and laid down in the wood to rest for an hour or two. All the following day (Monday) I continued travelling through the woods, was greatly distressed for want of water to quench my thirst, it being a very dry country, till I came to Spring Creek, which is a wide, deep stream, and with some of which I gladly quenched my thirst. I then proceeded to cross the same, by a bridge close by, and continued my way until dusk. I came to a gentleman's house in the woods, where I inquired how far it was to the next house, taking care to watch an opportunity to ask some individual whom I could master, and get away from, if any interruption to my progress was attempted. I went on for some time, it being a very fine moonlight night, and was presently alarmed by the howling of a wolf very near me; which I concluded, was calling other wolves to join him in attacking me, having understood that they always assemble in numbers for such a purpose; the howling increased, and I was still pursued, and the numbers were evidently increasing fast; but I was happily rescued from my dreadful fright, by coming to some cattle, which attracted, as I supposed, the wolves, and saved my life; for I could not get up the trees for safety, they being very tall pines, the lowest branches of which were, at least, forty or fifty feet from the ground, and the trunks very large and smooth.

About two o'clock I came to the house of a Mr. Cherry, on the borders of the Flint River; I went up to the house, and called them up to beg something to eat; but having nothing cooked, they kindly allowed me to lie down in the porch, where they made me a bed. In conversation with this Mr. Cherry, I discovered that I had known him before, having been in a steam-boat, the Versailles, some months previous, which sunk very near his house, but which I did not at first discern to be the same. I then thought that it would not be prudent for me to stop there, and, therefore, told them, I was in a hurry to get on, and must start very early again, he having no idea who I was; and I gave his son six cents to take me across the river, which he did when the sun was about half an hour high, and unfortunately landed me where there was a man building a boat, who knew me very well, and my former master too,— he, calling me by name, asked me where I was going.

I was very much frightened at being discovered, but summoned up courage, and said, that my master had gone on to Tallyhassa[23] by the coach, and that there was not room for me, and I had to walk round to meet him. I then asked the man to put me in the best road to get there, which, however, I knew as well as he did, having travelled there before; he directed me the best way; but I, of course, took the contrary direction, wanting to get on to Savannah. By this hasty and wicked deception, I saved myself from going to Bainbridge prison, which was close by, and to which I should surely have been taken had it been known that I was making my escape.

Leaving Bainbridge, I proceeded about forty miles, travelling all day under a scorching sun, through the woods in which I saw many deer and serpents, until I reached Thomas Town, in the evening. I there inquired the way to Augusta, of a man whom I met, and also asked where I could obtain lodgings, and was told that there was a poor minister about a mile from the place, who would give me lodgings. I accordingly went, and found them in a little log-house, where, having awakened the family, I found them all lying on the bare boards, where I joined them, for the remainder of the night.

In the morning, the old gentleman prayed for me, that I might be preserved on my journey; he had previously asked me where I was going, and I knowing, that if I told him the right place, any that inquired of him for me would be able to find me, asked the way to Augusta, instead of Savannah, my real destination. I also told him, that I was partly Indian and partly white, but I am also partly African, but this I omitted to tell him, knowing if I did I should be apprehended. After I had left this hut, I again inquired for Augusta, for the purpose of misleading my pursuers, but I afterwards took my course through the woods, and came into a road, called the Coffee road, which General Jackson cut down for his troops at the time of the war, between the Americans and Spaniards, in Florida; in which road there are but few houses, and which I preferred for the purpose of avoiding detection.

After several days I left this road, and took a more direct way to Savannah, where I had to wade through two rivers before I came to the Alatamah, which I crossed in a ferry-boat, about a mile below the place where the rivers Oconee and Ocmulgee run together into one river, called the Alatamah. I here met with some cattle drovers, who were collecting cattle to drive to Savannah. On walking on before them, I began to consider in what way I could obtain a passport for Savannah, and determined on the following plan:–

I called at a cottage, and after I had talked sometime with the wife, who began to feel greatly for me, in consequence of my telling her a little of my history, (her husband being out hunting) I pretended to show her my passport,[24] feeling for it everywhere about my coat and hat, and not finding it; I went back a little way, pretending to look for it, but came back, saying, I was very sorry, but I did not know where it was. At last, the man came home, carrying a deer upon his shoulders, which he brought into the yard, and began to dress it.[25] The wife then went out to tell him my situation, and after long persuasion, he said he could not write, but that if I could tell his son what was in my passport, he should write me one; and knowing that I should not be able to pass Savannah without one, and having heard several free coloured men read theirs, I thought, I could tell the lad what to write. The lad sat down and wrote what I told him, nearly filling a large sheet of paper for the passport, and another sheet with recommendations. These being completed, I was invited to partake of some of the fresh venison, which the woman of the house had prepared for dinner, and having done so, and feeling grateful for their kindness, I proceeded on my way. Going along, I took my papers out of my pocket, and looking at them, although I could not read a word, I perceived that the boy's writing was very unlike other writing that I had seen, and was greatly blotted besides; consequently, I was afraid that these documents would not answer my purpose, and began to consider what other plan I could pursue to obtain another pass.

I had now to wade through another river to which I came, and which I had great difficulty in crossing, in consequence of the water overflowing the banks of several rivers to the extent of upwards of twenty miles. In the midst of the water, I passed one night upon a small island, and the next day, I went through the remainder of the water. On many occasions, I was obliged to walk upon my toes, and consequently, found the advantage of being six feet two inches high, (I have grown three inches since,) and at other times was obliged to swim. In the middle of this extremity, I felt it would be imprudent for me to return; for if my master was in pursuit of me, my safest place from him was in the water, if I could keep my head above the surface. I was, however, dreadfully frightened, and most earnestly prayed that I might be kept from a watery grave, and resolved, that if again I landed, I would spend my life in the service of God.

Having, through mercy, again started on my journey, I met with the drovers; and having, whilst in the waters, taken the pass out of my hat, and so dipped it in the water as to spoil it, I showed it to the men, and asked them where I could get another. They told me, that in the neighbourhood, there lived a rich cotton-merchant who would write me one. They took me to him, and gave their word, that they saw the passport before it was wet, (for I had previously showed it to them,) upon which, the cotton-planter wrote a free pass and a recommendation, to which the cow-drovers affixed their marks.

The recommendation was as follows;

"John Roper, a very interesting young lad, whom I have seen and travelled with for eighty or ninety miles on his road from Florida, is a free man, descended from Indian and white. I trust, he will be allowed to pass on without interruption, being convinced from what I have seen, that he is free, and though dark, is not an African. I had seen his papers before they were wetted."

These cow-drovers, who procured me the passport and recommendation from the cotton-planter, could not read; and they were intoxicated when they went with me to him. I am part African, as well as Indian and white, my father, being a white man, Henry Roper, Esq., Caswell County, North Carolina, U.S., a very wealthy slave-holder, who sold me when quite a child, for the strong resemblance I bore to him. My mother is part Indian, part African; but I dared not disclose that, or I should have been taken up. I then had eleven miles to go to Savannah, one of the greatest slave-holding cities in America, and where they are always looking out for run-away slaves. When at this city, I had travelled about five hundred miles.* It required great courage to pass through this place. I went through the main street with apparent confidence, though much alarmed; did not stop at any house in the city, but went down immediately to the Docks, and inquired for a berth,[26] as a steward to a vessel to New York. I had been in this capacity before on the Appalachicola River. The person whom I asked to procure me a berth, was steward of one of the New York Packets; he knew Captain Deckay, of the schooner Fox, and got me a situation on board that vessel, in five minutes, after I had been at the Docks. The schooner Fox was a very old vessel, twenty-seven years old, laden

*The distance between these two places is much less than five hundred miles; but I was obliged to travel round about, in order to avoid being caught.

with lumber and cattle for New York; she was rotten, and could not be insured. The sailors were afraid of her; but I ventured on board, and five minutes after, we dropped from the Docks into the river. My spirits then began to revive and I thought I should get to a free country directly. We cast anchor in the stream, to keep the sailors on, as they were so dissatisfied with the vessel, and lay there four days; during which time, I had to go into the city several times, which exposed me to great danger, as my master was after me, and I dreaded meeting him in the city.

Fearing the Fox would not sail before I should be seized, I deserted her, and went on board a brig sailing to Providence, that was towed out by a steam-boat,* and got thirty miles from Savannah. During this time, I endeavoured to persuade the steward to take me as an assistant, and hoped to have accomplished my purpose; but the captain had observed me attentively, and thought I was a slave, he therefore ordered me, when the steam-boat was sent back, to go on board her to Savannah, as the fine for taking a slave from that city to any of the Free States, is five hundred dollars. I reluctantly went back to Savannah, among slave-holders and slaves. My mind was in a sad state; and I was under strong temptation to throw myself into the river. I had deserted the schooner Fox, and knew that the captain might put me into prison, till the vessel was ready to sail; if this had happened, and my master had come to the jail in search of me, I must have gone back to slavery. But when I reached the Docks at Savannah, the first person I met was the captain of the Fox, looking for another steward in my place. He was a very kind man, belonging to the Free States, and inquired if I would go back to his vessel. This usage was very different to what I expected, and I gladly accepted his offer. This captain did not know that I was a slave. In about two days we sailed from Savannah for New York.

I am (August, 1834) unable to express the joy I now felt. I never was at sea before, and, after I had been out about an hour, was taken with sea-sickness, which continued five days. I was scarcely able to stand up, and one of the sailors was obliged to take my place. The captain was very kind to me all this time; but even after I recovered, I was not sufficiently well to do my duty properly, and could not give satisfaction to the sailors, who swore at me, and asked me why I shipped, as I was not used to the sea? We had a very quick passage; and in six days, after leaving Savannah, we were in the harbour at Statten Island, where the vessel was quarantined for two days, six miles from New York. The captain went to the city, but left me aboard with the sailors, who had most of them been brought up in the slave holding States, and were very cruel men. One of the sailors was particularly angry with me, because he had to perform the duties of my place; and while the captain was in the city, the sailors called me to the fore-hatch, where they said they would treat me.

*An iron boat, the first that was ever built in America, belonging to Mr. Lemayor, and this was also the first time she sailed.

I went, and while I was talking, they threw a rope round my neck, and nearly choked me. The blood streamed from my nose profusely. They also took up ropes with large knots, and knocked me over the head. They said, I was a negro; they despised me; and I expected they would have thrown me into the water. When we arrived at the city, these men, who had so ill treated me, ran away that they might escape the punishment which would otherwise have been inflicted on them.

## CHAPTER VIII

### Arrived in New York, on to Poughkeepsie, Albany, Bogister, Vermont, Boston, and return to New York–Embarked for England, November, 1834.

When I arrived in the city of New York, I thought I was free; but learned I was not, and could be taken there. I went out into the country several miles, and tried to get employment; but failed, as I had no recommendation. I then returned to New York; but finding the same difficulty there to get work, as in the country, I went back to the vessel, which was to sail eighty miles up the Hudson River, to Poughkeepsie. When I arrived, I obtained employment at an inn, and after I had been there about two days, was seized with the cholera,[27] which was at that place. The complaint was, without doubt, brought on by my having subsisted on fruit only, for several days, while I was in the slave States. The landlord of the inn came to me when I was in bed, suffering violently from cholera, and told me, he knew I had that complaint, and as it had never been in his house, I could not stop there any longer. No one would enter my room, except a young lady, who appeared very pious and amiable, and had visited persons with the cholera. She immediately procured me some medicine at her own expense, and administered it herself; and, whilst I was groaning with agony, the landlord came up and ordered me out of the house directly. Most of the persons in Poughkeepsie had retired for the night; and I lay under a shed on some cotton bales. The medicine relieved me, having been given so promptly; and next morning I went from the shed, and laid on the banks of the river below the city. Towards evening, I felt much better, and went on in a steamboat, to the city of Albany, about eighty miles. When I reached there, I went into the country, and tried for three or four days to procure employment, but failed.

At that time I had scarcely any money, and lived upon fruit; so I returned to Albany, where I could get no work, as I could not show the recommendations I possessed, which were only from slave States; and I did not wish any one to know I came from them. After a time, I went up the western canal, as steward, in one of the boats. When I had gone about 350 miles up the canal, I found I was going too much towards the slave States; in consequence of which, I returned to Albany, and went up the northern canal, into one of the New England States–Vermont. The distance I had travelled, including the 350 miles I had to return from the west, and the 100 to Vermont, was 2300 miles. When I reached Vermont, I found the people very hospitable and kind: they seemed opposed to slavery, so I told them I was a run-away slave. I hired myself to a firm in Sudbury.* After I had been in Sudbury some time, the neighbouring farmers told me, that I had hired myself for much less money than I ought. I mentioned it to my employers, who were very angry about it; I was advised to leave by some of the people round, who thought the gentlemen I was with would write to my former master, informing him where I was, and obtain the reward fixed upon me. Fearing I should be taken, I immediately left, and went into the town of Ludlow, where I met with a kind friend, Mr. ——,† who sent me to school for several weeks. At this time, I was advertised in the papers, and was obliged to leave. I went a little way out of Ludlow, to a retired place, and lived two weeks with a Mr. ——, deacon of a Baptist church at Ludlow: at this place I could have obtained education, had it been safe to have remained.‡ From there I went to New Hampshire, where I was not safe, so went to Boston, Massachusetts, with the hope of returning to Ludlow, to which place I was much attached. At Boston, I met with a friend, who kept a shop, and took me to assist him for several weeks. Here I did not consider myself safe, as persons from all parts of the country were continually coming to the shop, and I feared some might come who knew me. I now had my head shaved, and bought a wig, and engaged myself to a Mr. Perkins, of Brookline, three miles from Boston, where I remained about a month. Some of the family discovered that I wore a wig, and said that I was a run-away slave; but the neighbours all round thought I was a white, to prove which, I have a document in my possession to call me to military duty. The law is, that no slave or coloured person performs this, but every other person in America, of the age of twenty-one, is called upon to perform military duty, once or twice in the year, or pay a fine.

*During my stay in this town, I thought of the vow I made in the water, (page [77],) and I became more thoughtful about the salvation of my soul. I attended the Methodist Chapel, where a Mr. Benton preached, and there I began to feel that I was a great sinner. During the latter part of my stay here, I became more anxious about salvation, and I entertained the absurd notion that religion would come to me in some extraordinary way. With this impression, I used to go into the woods two hours before day-light to pray, and expected something would take place, and I should become religious.

†It would not be proper to mention any names, as a person in any of the States in America, found harbouring a slave, would have to pay a heavy fine.

‡Whilst in this neighbourhood, I attended the Baptist Meeting, and trust the preaching of the gospel was much blessed to my soul. As this was the first time I was ever favoured with any education, I was very intent upon learning to read the Bible, and in a few weeks I was able, from my own reading, to repeat by heart the whole of the last chapter of Matthew. I also attended the prayer and inquiry meetings, where the attendants used to relate their experience, and I was requested to do the same. I found these meetings a great blessing, and they were the means, under God, of communicating to my mind a more clear and distinct knowledge of the way of salvation by Jesus Christ.

**COPY OF THE DOCUMENT.**

"Mr. Moses Roper,

"You being duly enrolled as a soldier in the Company, under the command of Captain Benjamin Bradley, are hereby notified and ordered to appear at the Town House, in Brookline, on Friday, 28th instant, at 3 o'clock, P.M., for the purpose of filling the vacancy in said Company, occasioned by the promotion of Lieut. Nathaniel M. Weeks, and of filling any other vacancy which may then and there occur in said Company, and there wait further orders.

"By order of the Captain,

"F. P. Wentworth, Clerk.

"*Brookline, August,* 14*th*, 1835.*

I then returned to the city of Boston, to the shop where I was before.† Several weeks after I had returned to my situation, two coloured men informed me, that a gentleman had been inquiring for a person, whom, from the description, I knew to be myself, and offered them a considerable sum if they would disclose my place of abode; but they being much opposed to slavery, came and told me; upon which information, I secreted myself till I could get off. I went into the Green mountains for several weeks, from thence to the city of New York, and remained in secret several days, till I heard of a ship, the Napoleon, sailing to England, and on the 11th of November, 1835, I sailed, taking with me letters of recommendation, to the Rev. Drs. Morrison, and Raffles, and the Rev. Alex. Fletcher. The time I first started from slavery, was in July, 1834, so that I was nearly sixteen months in making my escape.

## CHAPTER IX

### The Author arrives at Liverpool, November 29th, 1835.–Manchester.–London.

On the 29th of November, 1835, I reached Liverpool; and my feelings when I first touched the shores of Britain were indescribable, and can only be properly understood by those who have escaped from the cruel bondage of slavery.

*Being very tall, I was taken to be twenty-one; but my correct age, as far as I can tell, is stated in page [54].

†During the first part of my abode in this city, I attended at the coloured church in Bellnap Street; and I hope I found both profit and pleasure in attending the means of divine grace. I now saw the wicked part I had taken in using so much deception in making my escape. After a time, I found slave-owners were in the habit of going to this coloured chapel to look for run-away slaves. I became alarmed, and afterwards attended the preaching of the Rev. Dr. Sharp. I waited upon the Doctor to request he would baptize me, and admit me a member of his church; and after hearing my experience, he wished me to call again. This I did, but he was gone into the country, and I saw him no more.

" 'Tis liberty alone, that gives the flower of fleeting life its lustre and perfume;
And we are weeds without it."

"Slaves cannot breathe in England:
If their lungs receive our air, that moment they are free
They touch our country, and their shackles fall."
*Cowper.*

When I reached Liverpool, I proceeded to Dr. Raffles, and handed my letters of recommendation to him. He received me very kindly, and introduced me to a member of his church, with whom I stayed the night. Here I met with the greatest attention and kindness. The next day I went on to Manchester, where I met with many kind friends; among others, Mr. Adshead, of that town, to whom I desire, through this medium, to return my most sincere thanks for the many great services which he rendered me, adding both to my spiritual and temporal comfort. I would not, however, forget to remember here Mr. Leese, Mr. Giles, Mr. Crewdson, and Mr. Clare, the latter of whom, gave me a letter to Mr. Scoble, the secretary of the Anti-slavery Society. I remained here several days, and then proceeded to London, December 12th, 1835, and immediately called on Mr. Scoble, to whom I delivered my letter. This gentleman procured me a lodging. I then lost no time in delivering my letters to Dr. Morison and the Rev. Alexander Fletcher, who received me with the greatest kindness; and shortly after this, Dr. Morison sent my letter from New York, with another from himself, to the *Patriot* Newspaper, in which he kindly implored the sympathy of the public in my behalf. The appeal was read by Mr. Christopherson, a member of Dr. Morison's church, of which gentleman, I express but little of my feelings and gratitude, when I say, that throughout he has been towards me a parent, and for whose tenderness and sympathy I desire ever to feel that attachment which I do not know how to express.

I stayed at his house several weeks, being treated as one of the family. The appeal in the *Patriot*, referred to getting a suitable academy for me, which the Rev. Dr. Cox recommended at Hackney, where I remained half a year, going through the rudiments of an English education. At this time, I attended the ministry of Dr. Cox, which I enjoyed very much, and to which I ascribe the attainment of clearer views of divine grace than I had before. I had attended here several months, when I expressed my wish to Dr. Cox, to become a member of his church, I was proposed; and after stating my experience, was admitted, March 31st, 1836. Here I feel it a duty to present my tribute of thankfulness, however feebly expressed, to the affectionate and devoted attention of the Rev. Doctor, from whom, under God, I received very much indeed of spiritual advice and consolation, as well as a plentiful administration to my temporal necessities. I would not forget also to mention the kindness of his church generally, by whom I was received with Christian love and charity. Never, I trust, will be effaced from my memory, the parental care of the Rev. Dr. Morison, from whom I can strictly say, I received the greatest kindness I ever met with, and to whom, as long as God gives me lips to utter, or mind to reflect, I desire to attribute the comfort to which I have experienced, since I set my foot upon the happy shores of England.

Here it is necessary that I should draw this narrative to a close, not that my materials are exhausted, but that I am unwilling to extend it to a size which might preclude many well-wishers from the possession of it.

But I must remark, that my feelings of happiness at having escaped from cruel bondage, are not unmixed with sorrow of a very touching kind. *"The Land of the Free"* still contains the mother,* the brothers, and the sisters of Moses Roper, not enjoying liberty, not the possessors of like feelings with me, not having even a distant glimpse of advancing towards freedom, but still slaves! This is a weight which hangs heavy on me. As circumstances at present stand, there is not much prospect of ever again seeing those dear ones, from whom on the Sunday night, I was torn away by armed slave-holders, and carried into cruel bondage.† And nothing would contribute so much to my entire happiness, if the kindness of a gracious Providence should ever place me in such favourable circumstances, as to be able to purchase their freedom. But I desire to express my entire resignation to the will of God. Should that Divine Being who made of one flesh all the kindreds of the earth, see fit that I should again clasp them to my breast, and see in them the reality of free men and free women, how shall I, a poor mortal, be enabled to sing a strain of praise sufficiently appropriate to such a boon from heaven.

But if the all-wise disposer of all things should see fit to keep them still in suffering and bondage, it is a mercy to know, that he orders all things well, that he is still the judge of all the earth, and that under such dispensations of his providence, he is working out that which shall be most for the advantage of his creatures.

Whatever I may have experienced in America, at the hands of cruel task-masters, yet I am unwilling to speak in any but respectful terms of the land of my birth. It is far from my wish to attempt to degrade America in the eyes of Britons. I love her institutions in the Free States, her zeal for Christ; I bear no enmity even to the slave-holders, but regret their delusions, many I am aware are deeply sensible of the fault, but some I regret to say are not, and I could wish to open their eyes to their sin; may the period come, when God shall wipe off this deep stain from her constitution, and may America soon be *indeed* the land of the free.

*About five months ago the Author wrote to Dr. Gallon, his mother's master, to know what sum would be sufficient to purchase her freedom, and he has received the following painful answer:–

*Milton, North Carolina,*

*Aug. 28th, 1839.*

"Your mother and her family were transferred from this place, two or three years ago, to Grunsborough, in the State of Alabama, and I regret to inform you that your mother is since dead."

†See page [62].

In conclusion, I thank my dear friends in England for their affectionate attentions, and may God help me to show by my future walk in life, that I am not wanting in my acknowledgments of their kindness. But above all, to the God of all grace, I desire here before his people, to acknowledge that all the way in which he has led me has been the right way, and as in his mercy and wisdom, he has led me to this country, where I am allowed to go free, may all my actions tend to lead me on, through the mercy of God in Christ, in the right way, to a city of habitation.

### Lines,* Written on the Occasion of the Escape to England of Mr. Moses Roper, Late an American Slave—now a Freeman of Great Britain. Heb. xiii. 1, 2, 3.[28]

Who is my Brother?—Ask the waves that come
From Afric's shores to greet our Island home;
Who is my Brother?—Ask the winds that stray
From Indian realms to chase our clouds away;
Who is my Brother?—Ask the suns that shine
On southern seas, then turn to smile on thine;
Who is my Brother?—Ask the stars that roll
Their nightly journey round from pole to pole;
These all shall tell thee that their wand'rings find
But one vast Family in all Mankind;—
Nor colour, clime, nor caste can e'er efface,
The kindred likeness of the wide-spread race—
Nor break the chain that at the first began,
To bind in one the Family of Man.
Come then—awake thy sympathies to feel,
A Brother's interest in a brother's weal,
God's wisdom and his goodness both decreed,
That from one stock all nations should proceed,
That wheresoe'er He cast His creature's lot,
Kindness and love might consecrate the spot.
Behold thy Brother! on his form confess'd
Thy nature's dignity is seen impress!
In every look—in every gesture—Man?
Wipe off the stamp of Manhood, ye who can.
Beats not his breast with warm affection's glow?
Breathes not his mind with thoughts' impassion'd flow?
Is there a joy—a grief—man ever knew
But in his bosom finds a birth-place too?
What though a tyrant's hand might strive to bind
With iron grasp the energies of mind—
As well might chains and stripes control the wave

*These lines were written by Miss Tuckey, of Cork, after I had addressed a meeting in that city.

The soul! the soul! can never be a slave.
  Brother–by that Creative Power whose Word
One common nature on our race conferr'd;
Brother–still closer–by the love that sent
The Son of God to bear sin's punishment;
Brother, by Grace Divine that poured its light
On the dark horrors of our heathen night:
We give the hand of fellowship to thee,
We bid thee welcome, and we hail thee free?
Thou art a slave no longer–on thy brow
The air of freedom breathes in triumph now,
Thine heart rejoices o'er the broken chain,
Whose links are sever'd ne'er to meet again:–
But sweeter still that Liberty to know,
Which Christ the Saviour only can bestow,–
And feel whate'er thy future lot may be,
The truth! the truth! hath made thy spirit free.
Through all thy touching story glad we trace
The ways of Providence, the power of Grace,
And see thy countless trials join to prove
The God of Glory is–the God of Love.
  Go then–still guided by his mighty hand
Where'er His will, His wisdom may command.
His love direct thy steps, as when of old,
He led the shepherd of His chosen fold.
Thy tale like his–whose name is borne by thee–
Marked out for death in helpless infancy;
Like him the child of servitude and shame,
Born of a race that bear the captive name:
Daily indebted to a tyrant's nod
For the free mercies of a bounteous God;
Holding the very life *He* gave,–at will
Of those, who though they cannot save, can kill;
Like him, "when come to years," by Grace Divine–
Led to embrace a Saviour's Cross as thine:
Like him cast from the land that gave thee birth
And driven a wanderer on the face of earth:
Like him in all thy wand'rings may'st thou find,
Some Jethro's kindness soothe and cheer thy mind.
Still be thy tale like his–to thee be given
To bear on earth the messages of Heaven:
To tell the Pharaohs who enslave thy race,
That God will scatter plagues on every place,–
Where proud oppression dares his wrath defy,
And brave his arm, and scorn his searching eye.
Sound out his thunders, 'till the dead in sin
Shall hear the voice of conscience speak within,
Believe,–and tremble at the dread decree,

Break every chain,–bid every slave be Free!
Then when thy Brethren forth from bondage come,
Be thine to lead them to their better home:
That land of Promise–where their feet shall rest,
With Peace and Liberty for ever blest,
And through the wilderness that lies between
Their wearied spirits and the joys unseen,–
Be God to thee and them, a shade by day,
A light by night to mark their onward way:
Till all the Freemen of the Lord shall meet,
To cast their crowns at Jesu's sacred feet
And own the link that shall for ever bind,
Even as one Soul–all nations of Mankind.

*M. B. Tuckey.*
*Cork, Ferney, Oct.* 31, 1838.

## EDITORIAL NOTES TO *A NARRATIVE OF THE ADVENTURES AND ESCAPE OF MOSES ROPER*

1. Starling, *The Slave Narrative*, 106–7.

2. The British slave trade.

3. Andrew Jackson (1767–1845) was the seventh president of the United States (1829–37). He was a founder of the Democratic Party, which advocated the rights of individual states to define and finance domestic improvements. President Jackson was also responsible for a number of other reforms intended to strengthen the legislative decisions of individual states.

4. Jail.

5. Generally, a two-wheeled carriage for one or two people. It is usually drawn by a single horse.

6. Chains, shackles, and/or handcuffs.

7. A mechanized enclosure used in canals to raise and lower boats to different levels.

8. A tool with spikes or teeth used to break-up and smooth soil.

9. A large cask or barrel.

10. Of black ancestry.

11. Subsequent chapters.

12. This area of the Bible tells the story of Joseph, the eleventh of Jacob's twelve sons. At age seventeen, Joseph was given a coat by his father. His older brothers realized that Joseph was a favorite of Jacob's, became jealous, and sold Joseph into Egyptian slavery. Joseph ingratiated himself with the Pharaoh by interpreting his dreams. As thanks, Pharaoh appointed Joseph to the post of supervising his grain. After twenty years, Joseph's brothers arrived in Egypt from Canaan to buy grain during a famine. Joseph, realizing they did not recognize them, tested their character before making himself known to them. After their reunion, he brought the entire family to Egypt. Since Joseph and his brothers were descendants of the Twelve Tribes of Israel, their story connects Genesis with the deliverance from captivity that occurs in Exodus.

13. The name commonly used for members of the Religious Society of Friends, originally founded in England in 1647 by George Fox. Their beliefs encourage humanitarianism, racial equality, prison reform, and quality education.

14. A benign power seen as guiding individuals through danger with care or, when necessary, intervention.

15. A mixture commonly used as a laxative.

16. A dry measure equaling approximately eight quarts.

17. Ground corn.

18. The coarse chaff of ground grain, usually wheat.

19. Usually, one who drives sheep, pigs, and other domestic animals to market.

20. An evangelical meeting, often characterized by emotional excitement.

21. Possibly a reference to the controversial issue of nullification, which was the theory that states (rather than any section of the federal government) should have the power to declare unconstitutional (nullify) laws passed by Congress. This issue of the supremacy of states' rights over federal law was ultimately resolved by the Civil War.

22. A short sword or dagger.

23. Tallahassee, Florida.

24. A note or letter of permission from their owner that all slaves were required to carry during travel.

25. The process of preparing skins for tanning and dyeing without separating the fur from the pelt.

26. An employment situation or position.

27. A bacterial infection of the small intestine.

28. Hebrews 13:1–3, "Let brotherly love continue. Be not forgetful to entertain strangers: for thereby some have entertained angels unawares. Remember them that are in bonds, as bound with them; and them which suffer adversity, as being yourselves also in the body."

# 3

# LUNSFORD LANE (1803–?)

## The Narrative of Lunsford Lane

What is known about Lunsford Lane is primarily contained in the information he presents in his *Narrative*. Lane was born near Raleigh, North Carolina, on May 30, 1803. The *Narrative* is a Franklinesque story illustrating the importance of hard work and economic independence as necessary steps toward freedom and self-determination. Lane's *Narrative* places the potential his entrepreneurial skills provide him in direct relationship to the confining, limiting nature of the slave system. Even his earliest awareness of slavery is juxtaposed against his mindfulness that the slave system, above all things, functions around the buying and selling of human bodies as much as it operates on the concept of subjugation based on race. Lane writes that "To know, also, that I was never to consult my own will, but was, while I lived, to be entirely under the control of another, was another state of mind hard for me to bear. Indeed all things now made me *feel*, what I had before known only in words, that *I was a slave*. Deep was this feeling and it preyed upon my heart like a never-dying worm."

Other narrators tend to balance their feelings of being a slave against their desire to escape. Henry Bibb's *Narrative*, for example, is almost entirely structured by his pattern of escape and recapture. For Lane, however, escape is replaced by his talent for business. Lane discovers his talent for trade soon after he realizes his enslavement: "One day, while I was in this state of mind, my father gave me a small basket of peaches. I sold them for thirty cents, which was the first money I ever had in my life. Afterwards I won some marbles, and sold them for sixty cents, and some weeks after, Mr. Hog, from Fayetteville, came to visit my master, and on leaving gave me one dollar. After that, Mr. Bennahan, from Orange county, gave me a dollar, and a son of my master fifty cents. These sums, and the hope that then entered my mind of purchasing at some future time my freedom, made me long for money: and the plans for money-making took the principal possession of my thoughts. . . . Now I began to think seriously of becoming able to buy myself; and cheered by this hope, I went on from one thing to another, laboring 'at dead of night,' after the long weary day's toil for my master was over, till I found I had collected one hundred dollars." With his father's help, Lane developed a process for preparing smoking tobacco that allowed him "to manufacture a good article out of a very indifferent material."

His financial success allowed him, even as a slave, to marry in 1828, start a family, and begin to save funds in hopes of eventually purchasing their freedom. Lane purchased his own freedom on September 9, 1835. Unlike other narratives, where writers often see their lowest point as being when they are beaten and otherwise fully deprived of any sense of humanity, Lane's lowest moment arrived when the cost of providing for his family caused him to exhaust his savings: "So that by the expense of providing for my wife and children, all the money I had earned, and could earn, by my night labor, was consumed, till I found myself reduced to five dollars, and this I lost one day in going to the plantation. My light of hope now went out." Lane's opportunity for financial independence arrived when his master died and his master's widow agreed to allow him to hire himself out: "This was a privilege which comparatively few slaves at the south enjoy; and in this I felt truly blessed." By 1842, Lane had fulfilled the agreement to purchase his family. He relocated them to New England in the hope of starting a new business.

As he promises to do in his preface to the *Narrative*, Lane resolutely describes the "bright" side of his experiences. He does, however, enigmatically indicate that for the person so inclined, parts of his narrative "might be twisted to convey an idea more than should be expressed." As William L. Andrews observes, this dual narrative role is precisely the role Lane chooses for himself throughout the *Narrative*. While a slave, Lane hid both his prosperity and his intelligence from fellow slaves and slaveholders alike. Similarly, as a narrator, he has obscured the bite of his social critique by claiming in his preface to present "only a simple narration of such facts connected with my own case, as I thought would be most interesting and instructive to readers generally."[1]

The *Narrative* reprinted here is from the third edition of the text, originally published in 1845. The first edition of the *Narrative* was published in 1842.

## FURTHER READING

William L. Andrews, *To Tell a Free Story* (1986); Marion Wilson Starling, *The Slave Narrative* (1988); Gay Wilentz, "Authenticating Experience: North Carolina Slave Narratives and the Politics of Race" (1992).

# THE NARRATIVE OF LUNSFORD LANE, FORMERLY OF RALEIGH, N. C.

EMBRACING AN ACCOUNT OF HIS EARLY LIFE,
THE REDEMPTION BY PURCHASE OF HIMSELF
AND FAMILY FROM SLAVERY,
AND HIS BANISHMENT FROM THE PLACE OF HIS
BIRTH FOR THE CRIME OF WEARING A
COLORED SKIN.

PUBLISHED BY HIMSELF.

THIRD EDITION.

BOSTON:
PRINTED FOR THE PUBLISHER:
HEWES AND WATSON'S PRINT.
No. 60. . . . Congress St.
1845.

## NOTE TO THE THIRD EDITION

The rapidity with which the first and second editions of this work has been sold, renders it necessary to put another edition to press, without any enlargement or material alteration.

Thanks to those friends who have aided me in the sale of the former editions,–to those editors who have so favorably noticed the work,–and to those who have so freely purchased. May I not justly hope for a continuance of the same kind regards?

L. L.
BOSTON, JULY 4, 1845.

## TO THE READER

The following Narrative has been prepared at the solicitation of very many friends. Whatever my own judgment might be, I should yield to theirs. In the hope that these pages may produce an impression favorable to my countrymen in bondage; also that I may realize something from the sale of my work towards the support of a numerous family, I have committed this publication to press. It might have been made two or three, or even six times larger, without diminishing from the interest of any one of its pages–*indeed with an increased interest*–but the want of the pecuniary means, and other considerations, have induced me to present it as here seen.

I have not, in this publication, attempted or desired to argue anything. It is only a simple narration of such facts connected with my own case, as I thought would be most interesting and instructive to readers generally. The facts will, I think, cast some light upon the policy of a slave-holding community, and the effect on the minds of the more enlightened, the more humane, and the *Christian* portion of the southern people, of holding and trading in the bodies and souls of men.

I have said in the following pages, that my condition as a slave was comparatively a happy, indeed a highly favored one; and to this circumstance is it owing that I have been able to come up from bondage and relate the story to the public; and that my wife, my mother, and my seven children, are here with me this day. If for anything this side the invisible world I bless Heaven, it is that I was not born a plantation slave, nor even a house servant under what is termed a hard and cruel master.

It has not been any part of my object to describe slavery generally, and in the narration of my own case I have dwelt as little as possible upon the dark side–have spoken mostly of the bright. In whatever I have been obliged to say unfavorable to others, I have endeavored not to overstate, but have chosen rather to come short of giving the full picture–omitting much which it did not seem important to my object to relate. And yet I would not venture to say that this publication does not contain a single period which might be twisted to convey an idea more than should be expressed.

Those of whom I have had occasion to speak, are regarded, where they are known, as among the most kind men to their slaves. Mr. Smith, some of whose conduct will doubtless seem strange to the reader, is sometimes taunted with being an abolitionist, in consequence of the interest he manifests towards the colored people. If to any his character appear like a riddle, they should remember that men, like other things, have "two sides," and often a top and a bottom in addition.

While in the South, I succeeded, by stealth, in learning to read and write a little, and since I have been in the North I have learned more. But I need not say that I have been obliged to employ the services of a friend, in bringing this Narrative into shape for the public eye. And it should perhaps be said on the part of the writer, that it has been hastily compiled, with little regard to style, only to express the ideas accurately, and in a manner to be understood.

LUNSFORD LANE.
BOSTON, JULY 4, 1845.

## NARRATIVE

The small city of Raleigh, North Carolina, it is known, is the capital of the State, situated in the interior, and containing about thirty-six hundred inhabitants. Here lived Mr. SHERWOOD HAYWOOD, a man of considerable respectability, a planter, and the cashier of a bank. He owned three plantations, at the distances, respectively, of seventy-five, thirty, and three miles from his residence in Raleigh. He owned in all about two hundred and fifty slaves, among the rest my mother, who was a house servant to her master, and of course a resident in the city. My father was a slave to a near neighbor. The apartment where I was born and where I spent my childhood and youth, was called "the kitchen," situated some fifteen or twenty rods[2] from the "great house." Here the house servants lodged and lived, and here the meals were prepared for the people in the mansion. The "field hands," of course, reside upon the plantation.

On the 30th of May, 1803, I was ushered into the world; but I did not begin to see the rising of its dark clouds, nor fancy how they might be broken and dispersed, until some time afterwards. My infancy was spent upon the floor, in a rough cradle, or sometimes in my mother's arms; my early boyhood, in playing with the other boys and girls, colored and white, in the yard, and occasionally doing such little matters of labor as one of so young years could. I knew no difference between myself and the white children: nor did they seem to know any in turn. Sometimes my master would come out and give a biscuit to me, and another to one of his own white boys; but I did not perceive the difference between us. I had no brothers or sisters, but there were other colored families living in the same kitchen, and the children playing in the same yard, with me and my mother.

When I was ten or eleven years old, my master set me regularly to cutting wood, in the yard, in the winter, and working in the garden in the summer. And when I was fifteen years of age, he gave me the care of the pleasure horses, and made me his carriage driver: but this did not exempt me from other labor, especially in the summer. Early in the morning, I used to take his three horses to the plantation, and turn them into the pasture to graze, and myself into the cotton or cornfield, with a hoe in my hand, to work through the day: and after sunset I would take these horses back to the city, a distance of three miles, feed them, and then attend to any other business my master or any of his family had for me to do, until bed time, when, with my blanket in my hand, I would go into the dining room to rest through the night. The next day the same round of labor would be repeated, unless some of the family wished to ride out, in which case I must be on hand with the horses to wait upon them, and in the meantime to work about the yard. On Sunday I had to drive to church twice, which, with other things necessary to be done, took the whole day. So my life went wearily on from day to day, from night to night, and from week to week.

When I began to work, I discovered the difference between myself and my master's white children. They began to order me about, and were told to do so by my master and mistress. I found, too, that they had learned to read, while I was not permitted to have a book in my hand. To be in the possession of anything written or printed, was regarded as an offence. And then there was the fear that I might be sold away from those who were dear to me, and conveyed to the far south. I had learned, that, being a slave, I was subject to this worst (to us) of all calamities; and I knew of others in similar situations to myself, thus sold away. My friends were not numerous; but in proportion as they were few they were dear; and the thought that I might be separated from them forever, was like that of having the heart torn from its socket; while the idea of being conveyed to the far south seemed infinitely worse than the terrors of death. To know, also, that I was never to consult my own will, but was, while I lived, to be entirely under the control of another, was another state of mind hard for me to bear. Indeed all things now made me *feel*, what I had before known only in words, that *I was a slave.* Deep was this feeling, and it preyed upon my heart like a never-dying worm. I saw no prospect that my condition would ever be changed. Yet I used to plan in my mind from day to day, and from night to night, how I might be free.

One day, while I was in this state of mind, my father gave me a small basket of peaches. I sold them for thirty cents, which was the first money I ever had in my life. Afterwards I won some marbles, and sold them for sixty cents, and some weeks after, Mr. Hog, from Fayetteville, came to visit my master, and on leaving gave me one dollar. After that, Mr. Bennahan, from Orange county, gave me a dollar, and a son of my master fifty cents. These sums, and the hope that then entered my mind of purchasing at some future time my freedom, made me long for money: and plans for money-making took the principal possession of my thoughts. At night I would steal away with my axe, get a load of wood to cut for twenty-five cents, and the next morning hardly escape a whipping for the offence. But I persevered until I had obtained twenty dollars. Now I began to think seriously of becoming able to buy myself; and cheered by this hope, I went on from one thing to another, laboring "at dead of night," after the long weary day's toil for my master was over, till I found I had collected one hundred dollars. This sum I kept hid, first in one place and then in another, as I dare not put it out, for fear I should lose it.

After this, I lit upon a plan which proved of great advantage to me. My father suggested a mode of preparing smoking tobacco, different from any then or since employed. It had the double advantage of giving the tobacco a peculiarly pleasant flavor, and of enabling me to manufacture a good article out of a very indifferent material. I improved somewhat upon his suggestion, and commenced the manufacture, doing, as I have before said, all my work in the night. The tobacco I put up in papers of about a quarter of a pound each, and sold them at fifteen cents. But the tobacco could not be smoked without a pipe, and as I had given the former a flavor peculiarly grateful, it occurred to me that I might so construct a pipe as to cool the smoke in passing through it, and thus meet the wishes of those who are more fond of smoke than heat. This I effected by means of a reed, which grows plentifully in that region: I made a passage through the reed with a hot wire, polished it, and attached a clay pipe to the end, so that the smoke should be cooled in flowing through the stem, like whiskey or rum in passing from the boiler through the worm of the still. These pipes I sold at ten cents a-piece. In the early part of the night I would sell my tobacco and pipes, and manufacture them in the latter part. As the Legislature sat in Raleigh every year, I sold these articles considerably to the members, so that I became known not only in the city, but in many parts of the State, as a *tobacconist.*

Perceiving that I was getting along so well, I began, slave as I was, to think about taking a wife. So I fixed my mind upon Miss Lucy Williams, a slave of Thomas Devereaux, Esq., an eminent lawyer in the place; but failed in my undertaking. Then I thought I never would marry; but at the end of two or three years my resolution began to slide away, till finding I could not keep it longer, I set out once more in pursuit of a wife. So I fell in with her to whom I am now united, Miss MARTHA CURTIS, and the bargain between *us* was completed. I next went to her master, Mr. Boylan, and asked him, according to the custom, if I might "marry his woman." His reply was, "Yes, if you will behave yourself." I told him I would. "And make her behave herself?" To this I also assented: and then proceeded to ask the approbation of my master, which was granted. So in May, 1828, I was bound as fast in wedlock as a slave can be. God may at any time sunder that band in a freeman; either master may do the same at pleasure in a slave. The bond is not recognized in law. But in my case it has never been broken; and now it cannot be, except by a higher power.

When we had been married nine months and one day, we were blessed with a son, and two years afterwards with a daughter. My wife also passed from the hands of Mr. Boylan, into those of Mr. BENJAMIN B. SMITH, a merchant, a member and class-leader in the methodist church, and in much repute for his deep piety and devotion to religion. But grace (of course,) had not wrought in the same *manner* upon the heart of Mr. Smith, as nature had done upon that of Mr. Boylan, who made no religious profession. This latter gentleman used to give my wife, who was a favorite slave, (her mother nursed every one of his own children,) sufficient food and clothing to render her comfortable, so that I had to spend for her but little, except to procure such small articles of extra comfort as I was prompted to from time to time. Indeed, Mr. Boylan was regarded as a very kind master to all the slaves about him,—that is, to his house servants; nor did he personally inflict much cruelty, if any, upon his field hands. The overseer on his nearest plantation (I know but little about the rest,) was a very cruel man; in one instance, as it was said among the slaves, he whipped a man *to death*; but of course he denied that the man died in consequence of the whipping. Still it was the choice of my wife to pass into the hands of Mr. Smith, as she had become attached to him in consequence of belonging to the same church, and receiving his religious instruction and counsel as her class-leader, and in consequence of the peculiar devotedness to the cause of religion for which he was noted, and which he always seemed to manifest. But when she became his slave, he withheld both from her and her children, the needful food and clothing, while he exacted from them to the uttermost all the labor they were able to perform. Almost every article of clothing worn either by my wife or children, especially every article of much value, I had to purchase; while the food he furnished the family amounted to less than a meal a day, and that of the coarser kind. I have no remembrance that he ever gave us a blanket, or any other article of bedding, although it is considered a rule at the south that the master shall furnish each of his slaves with one blanket a year. So that, both as to food and clothing, I had in fact to support both my wife and the children, while he claimed them as his property, and received all their labor. She was a house servant to Mr. Smith, sometimes cooked the food for his family, and usually took it from the table; but her mistress was so particular in giving it out to be cooked, or so watched it, that she always knew whether it was all returned; and when the table was cleared away, the stern old lady would sit by and see that every dish (except the very little she would send into the kitchen,) was put away, and then she would turn the key upon it, so as to be sure her slaves should not die of gluttony. This practise is common with some families in that region, but with others it is not. It was not so in that of her less pious master, Mr. Boylan, nor was it precisely so at my master's. We used to have corn bread enough, and some meat. When I was a boy, the pot-liquor, in which the meat was boiled for the "great house," together with some little corn-meal balls that had been thrown in just before the meat was done, was poured into a tray and set in the middle of the yard, and a clam-shell or pewter spoon given to each of us children, who would fall upon the delicious fare as greedily as pigs. It was not generally so much as we wanted, consequently it was customary for some of the white persons who saw us from the piazza of the house where they were sitting, to order the more stout and greedy ones to eat slower, that those more young and feeble might have a chance. But it was not so with Mr. Smith; such luxuries were more than he could afford, kind and Christian man as he was considered to be. So that by the expense of providing for my wife and children, all the money I had earned, and could earn, by my night labor, was consumed, till I found myself reduced to five dollars, and this I lost one day in going to the plantation. My light of hope now went out. My prop seemed to have given way from under me. Sunk in the very night of despair respecting my freedom, I discovered myself, as though I had never known it before, a husband, the father of two children, a family looking up to me for bread, and I a slave, penniless, and well watched by my master, his wife, and his children, lest I should, perchance, catch the friendly light of the stars to make something in order to supply the cravings of nature in those with whom my soul was bound up; or lest some plan of freedom might lead me to trim the light of diligence after the day's labor was over, while the rest of the world were enjoying the hours in pleasure or sleep.

At this time an event occurred, which, while it cast a cloud over the prospects of some of my fellow slaves, was a rainbow over mine. My master died; and his widow, by the will, became sole executrix of his property. To the surprise of all, the bank of which he had been cashier, presented a claim against the estate for forty thousand dollars. By a compromise, this sum was reduced to twenty thousand dollars: and my mistress, to meet the amount, sold some of her slaves, and hired out others. I hired my time of her,* for which I paid her a price varying from one hundred dollars to one hundred and twenty dollars per year. This was a privilege which comparatively few slaves at the south enjoy; and in this I felt truly blessed.

I commenced the manufacture of pipes and tobacco on an enlarged scale. I opened a regular place of business, labelled my tobacco in a conspicuous manner with the names of *"Edward and Lunsford Lane,"* and of some of the persons who sold it for me,–establishing agencies for the sale in various parts of the State, one at Fayetteville, one at Salisbury, one at Chapel Hill, and so on,–sold my articles from my place of business, and about town, also deposited them in stores on commission: and thus, after paying my mistress for my time, and rendering such support as was necessary to my family, I found in the space of some six or eight

*It is contrary to the laws of the State for a slave to have command of his own time in this way, but in Raleigh it is sometimes winked at. I knew one slave-man, who was *doing well for himself*, taken up by the public authorities and hired out for the public good, three times in succession for this offence. The time of hiring in such a case is one year. The master is subject to a fine. But generally, as I have said, if the slave is *orderly*, and appears to be *making nothing*, neither he nor the master is interfered with.

years, that I had collected the sum of one thousand dollars. During this time I had found it politic to go shabbily dressed, and to appear to be very poor, but to pay my mistress for my services promptly. I kept my money hid, never venturing to put out a penny, nor to let any body but my wife know that I was making any. The thousand dollars was what I supposed my mistress would ask for me, and so I determined now what I would do.

I went to my mistress and inquired what was her price for me. She said a thousand dollars. I then told her that I wanted to be free, and asked her if she would sell me to be made free. She said she would; and accordingly I arranged with her, and with the master of my wife, Mr. Smith, already spoken of, for the latter to take my money* and buy of her my freedom, as I could not legally purchase it, and as the laws forbid emancipation, except for "meritorious services." This done, Mr. Smith endeavored to emancipate me formally, and to get my manumission recorded; I tried also; but the court judged that I had done nothing "meritorious," and so I remained, nominally only, the slave of Mr. Smith for a year; when, feeling unsafe in that relation, I accompanied him to New York, whither he was going to purchase goods, and was there regularly and formally made a freeman, and there my manumission was recorded. I returned to my family in Raleigh, and endeavored to do by them as a freeman should. I had known what it was to be a slave, and I knew what it was to be free.

But I am going too rapidly over my story. When the money was paid to my mistress and the conveyance fairly made to Mr. Smith, I felt that I was free. And a queer and a joyous feeling it is to one who has been a slave. I cannot describe it, only it seemed as though I was in heaven. I used to lie awake whole nights thinking of it. And oh, the strange thoughts that passed through my soul, like so many rivers of light; deep and rich were their waves as they rolled;–these were more to me than sleep, more than soft slumber after long months of watching over the decaying, fading frame of a friend, and the loved one laid to rest in the dust. But I cannot describe my feelings to those who have never been slaves: then why should I attempt it? He who has passed from spiritual death to life, and received the witness within his soul that his sins are forgiven, may possibly form some distant idea, like the ray of the setting sun from the far off mountain top, of the emotions of an emancipated slave. That opens heavens. To break the bonds of slavery, opens up at once both earth and heaven. Neither can be truly seen by us while we are slaves.

And now will the reader take with me a brief review of the road I had trodden. I cannot here dwell upon its dark shades, though some of these were black as the pencillings of midnight, but upon the light, that had followed my path from my infancy up, and had at length conducted me quite out of the

*Legally*, my money belonged to my mistress; and she could have taken it and refused to grant me my freedom. But she was a very kind woman for a slave owner; and she would under the circumstances scorn to do such a thing. I have known of slaves, however, served in this way.

deep abyss of bondage. There is a hymn opening with the following stanza, which very much expresses my feelings:

> "When all thy mercies, Oh my God,
> My rising soul surveys,
> Transported with the view, I'm lost
> In wonder, love, and praise."

I had endured what a freeman would indeed call hard fare; but my lot, on the whole, had been a favored one for a slave. It is known that there is a wide difference in the situations of what are termed house servants, and plantation hands. I, though sometimes employed upon the plantation, belonged to the former, which is the favored class. My master, too, was esteemed a kind and humane man; and altogether I fared quite differently from many poor fellows whom it makes my blood run chill to think of, confined to the plantation, with not enough of food and that little of the coarsest kind, to satisfy the gnawings of hunger,–compelled oftentimes, to hie away in the night-time, when worn down with work, and *steal*, (if it be stealing,) and privately devour such things as they can lay their hands upon,–made to feel the rigors of bondage with no cessation,–torn away sometimes from the few friends they love, friends doubly dear because they are few, and transported to a climate where in a few hard years they die,–or at best conducted heavily and sadly to their resting place under the sod, upon their old master's plantation,–sometimes, perhaps, enlivening the air with merriment, but a forced merriment, that comes from a stagnant or a stupefied heart. Such as this is the fate of the plantation slaves generally, but such was not my lot. My way was comparatively light, and what is better, it conducted to freedom. And my wife and children were with me. After my master died, my mistress sold a number of her slaves from their families and friends–but not me. She sold several children from their parents–but my children were with me still. She sold two husbands from their wives–but I was still with mine. She sold one wife from her husband–but mine had not been sold from me. The master of my wife, Mr. Smith, had separated members of families by sale–but not of mine. With me and my house, the tenderer tendrils of the heart still clung to where the vine had entwined; pleasant was its shade and delicious its fruits to our taste, though we knew, and what is more, we *felt* that we were slaves. But all around I could see where the vine had been torn down, and its bleeding branches told of vanished joys, and of new wrought sorrows, such as, slave though I was, had never entered into my practical experience.

I had never been permitted to learn to read; but I used to attend church, and there I received instruction which I trust was of some benefit to me. I trusted, too, that I had experienced the renewing influences of the gospel; and after obtaining from my mistress a written *permit*, (a thing *always* required in such a case,) I had been baptised and received into fellowship with the Baptist denomination. So that in religious matters, I had been indulged in the exercise of my own conscience—a favor not always granted to slaves. Indeed I, with others, was often told by the minister how good God was in bringing us over to this country from dark and benighted Africa, and permitting us to listen to the sound of the gospel. To me, God also granted temporal freedom, which man without God's consent, had stolen away.

I often heard select portions of the scriptures read. And on the Sabbath there was one sermon preached expressly for the colored people which it was generally my privilege to hear. I became quite familiar with the texts, "Servants be obedient to your masters."[3]—"Not with eye service as men pleasers."[4]—"He that knoweth his master's will and doeth it not, shall be beaten with many stripes,"[5] and others of this class: for they formed the basis of most of these public instructions to us. The first commandment impressed upon our minds was to obey our masters, and the second was like unto it, namely, to do as much work when they or the overseers were not watching us as when they were. But connected with these instructions there was more or less that was truly excellent; though mixed up with much that would sound strangely in the ears of freedom. There was one very kind hearted Episcopal minister whom I often used to hear; he was very popular with the colored people. But after he had preached a sermon to us in which he argued from the Bible that it was the will of heaven from all eternity we should be slaves, and our masters be our owners, most of us left him; for like some of the faint hearted disciples in early times we said,—"This is a hard saying, who can bear it?"[6]

My manumission, as I shall call it—that is, the bill of sale conveying me to Mr. Smith, was dated Sept. 9th, 1835. I continued in the tobacco and pipe business as already described, to which I added a small trade in a variety of articles; and some two years before I left Raleigh, I entered also into a considerable business in wood, which I used to purchase by the acre standing, cut it, haul it into the city, deposit it in a yard and sell it out as I advantageously could. Also I was employed about the office of the Governor, as I shall hereafter relate. I used to keep one or two horses, and various vehicles, by which I did a variety of work at hauling about town. Of course I had to hire more or less help, to carry on my business.

In the manufacture of tobacco I met with considerable competition, but none that materially injured me. The method of preparing it having originated with me and my father, we found it necessary, in order to secure the advantage of the invention, to keep it to ourselves, and decline, though often solicited, going into partnership with others. Those who undertook the manufacture could neither give the article a flavor so pleasant as ours, nor manufacture it so cheaply, so they either failed in it, or succeeded but poorly.

Not long after obtaining my own freedom, I began seriously to think about purchasing the freedom of my family. The first proposition was that I should buy my wife, and that we should jointly labor to obtain the freedom of the children afterwards, as we were able. But that idea was abandoned when her master, Mr. Smith, refused to sell her to me for less than one thousand dollars, a sum which then appeared too much for me to raise.

Afterwards, however, I conceived the idea of purchasing at once the entire family. I went to Mr. Smith to learn his price, which he put at *three thousand dollars* for my wife and six children, the number we then had. This seemed a large sum, both because it was a great deal for me to raise, and also because Mr. Smith, when he bought my wife and *two* children, had actually paid but five hundred and sixty dollars for them, and had received, ever since, their labor, while I had almost entirely supported them, both as to food and clothing. Altogether, therefore, the case seemed a hard one, but as I was entirely in his power I must do the best I could. At length he concluded, perhaps partly of his own motion, and partly through the persuasion of a friend, to sell the family for $2,500, as I wished to free them, though he contended still that they were worth three thousand dollars. Perhaps they would at that time have brought this larger sum, if sold for the Southern market. The arrangement with Mr. Smith was made in December, 1838. I gave him five notes of five hundred dollars each, the first due in January, 1840, and one in January each succeeding year; for which he transferred my family into my own possession, with a *bond* to give me a bill of sale when I should pay the notes. With this arrangement, we found ourselves living in our own house,–a house which I had previously purchased,–in January, 1839.

After moving my family, my wife was for a short time sick, in consequence of her labor and the excitement in moving, and her excessive joy. I told her that it reminded me of a poor shoemaker in the neighborhood, who purchased a ticket in a lottery; but not expecting to draw, the fact of his purchasing it had passed out of his mind. But one day as he was at work on his last, he was informed that his ticket had drawn the liberal prize of ten thousand dollars; and the poor man was so overjoyed, that he fell back on his seat, and immediately expired.

In this new and joyful situation we found ourselves getting along very well, until September, 1840, when, to my surprise, as I was passing the street one day, engaged in my business, the following note was handed me. "Read it," said the officer, "or if you cannot read, get some white man to read it to you." Here it is, *verbatim*:

*To Lunsford Lane, a free man of Color*:

Take notice, that whereas complaint has been made to us, two Justices of the Peace for the county of Wake and State of North Carolina, that you are a free negro from another State, who has migrated into this State contrary to the provisions of the act of assembly concerning free negroes and mulattoes, now notice is given you that unless you leave and remove out of this State within twenty days, that you will be proceeded against for the penalty prescribed by said act of assembly, and be otherwise dealt with as the law directs. Given under our hands and seals this the 5th Sept. 1840.

WILLIS SCOTT, JP (Seal)
JORDAN WOMBLE, JP (Seal).

This was a terrible blow to me, for it prostrated at once all my hopes in my cherished object of obtaining the freedom of my family, and led me to expect nothing but a separation from them forever.

In order that the reader may understand the full force of the foregoing notice, I will copy the law of the State under which it was issued:

SEC. 65. It shall not be lawful for any free negro or mulatto to migrate into this State: and if he or she shall do so, contrary to the provisions of this act, and being thereof informed, shall not, within twenty days thereafter, remove out of the State, he or she being thereof convicted in the manner hereafter directed, shall be liable to a penalty of five hundred dollars; and upon failure to pay the same, within the time prescribed in the judgment awarded against such person or persons, he or she shall be liable to be held in servitude and at labor a term of time not exceeding ten years, in such manner and upon such terms as may be provided by the court awarding such sentence, and the proceeds arising therefrom shall be paid over to the county trustee for county purposes: Provided, that in case any free negro or mulatto shall pay the penalty of five hundred dollars, according to the provisions of this act, it shall be the duty of such free negro or mulatto to remove him or herself out of this State within twenty days thereafter, and for every such failure, he or she shall be subject to the like penalty as is prescribed for a failure to remove in the first instance.—*Revised Statutes North Carolina, chap.* 111.

The next section provides that if the free person of color so notified, does not leave within the twenty days after receiving the notice, he may be arrested on a warrant from any Justice, and be held to bail for his appearance at the next county court, when he will be subject to the penalties specified above; or in case of his failure to give bonds, he may be sent to jail.

I made known my situation to my friends, and after taking legal counsel, it was determined to induce, if possible, the complainants to prosecute no farther at present, and then as the Legislature of the State was to sit in about two months, to petition that body for permission to remain in the State until I could complete the purchase of my family; after which I was willing, if necessary, to leave.

From January 1st, 1837, I had been employed, as I have mentioned, in the office of the Governor of the State, principally under the direction of his private Secretary, in keeping the office in order, taking the letters to the Post Office, and doing such other duties of the sort as occurred from time to time. This circumstance, with the fact of the high standing in the city of the family of my former master, and of the former masters of my wife, had given me the friendship of the first people in the place generally, who from that time forward acted towards me the friendly part.

Mr. BATTLE, then private Secretary to Governor Dudley, addressed the following letter to the prosecuting attorney in my behalf:

RALEIGH, Nov. 3, 1840.

DEAR SIR:–Lunsford Lane, a free man of color, has been in the employ of the State under me since my entering on my present situation. I understand that under a law of the State, he has been notified to leave, and that the time is now at hand.

In the discharge of the duties I had from him, I have found him prompt, obedient and faithful. At this particular time, his absence to me would be much regretted, as I am now just fixing up my books and other papers in the new office, and I shall not have time to learn another what he can already do so well. With me the period of the Legislature is a very busy one, and I am compelled to have a servant who understands the business I want done, and one I can trust. I would not wish to be an obstacle in the execution of any law, but the enforcing of the one against him will be doing me a serious inconvenience, and the object of this letter is to ascertain whether I could not procure a suspension of the sentence till after the adjournment of the Legislature, say about 1st January, 1841,

I should feel no hesitation in giving my word that he will conduct himself orderly and obediently.

I am, most respectfully,
Your obedient servant,
C. C. BATTLE.

G. W. HAYWOOD, Esq.,
*Attorney at Law, Raleigh, N. C.*

To the above letter the following reply was made:

RALEIGH, Nov. 3, 1840.

MY DEAR SIR:–I have no objection, so far as I am concerned, that all further proceedings against Lunsford should be postponed until after the adjournment of the Legislature.

The process now out against him is one issued by two magistrates, Messrs. Willis Scott and Jordan Womble, over which I have no control. You had better see them today, and perhaps, at your request, they will delay further action on the subject.

Respectfully yours,
GEO. W. HAYWOOD.

Mr. Battle then enclosed the foregoing correspondence to Messrs. Scott and Womble, requesting their "favorable consideration." They returned the correspondence, but neglected to make any reply.

In consequence, however, of this action on the part of my friends, I was permitted to remain without further interruption, until the day the Legislature commenced its session. On that day a warrant was served upon me, to appear before the county court, to answer for the sin of having remained in the place of my birth for the space of twenty days and more after being warned out. I escaped going to jail through the kindness of Mr. Haywood, a son of my former master, and Mr. Smith, who jointly became security for my appearance at court.

This was on Monday; and on Wednesday I appeared before the court; but as my prosecutors were not ready for the trial, the case was laid over three months, to the next term.

I then proceeded to get up a petition to the Legislature. It required much hard labor and persuasion on my part to start it; but after that, I readily obtained the signatures of the principal men in the place. Then I went round to the members, many of whom were known to me, calling upon them at their rooms, and urging them for my sake, for humanity's sake, for the sake of my wife and little ones, whose hopes had been excited by the idea that they were even now free; I appealed to them as husbands, fathers, brothers, sons, to vote in favor of my petition, and allow me to remain in the State long enough to purchase my family. I was doing well in business, and it would be but a short time before I could accomplish the object. Then, if it was desired, I and my wife and children, redeemed from bondage, would together seek a more friendly home, beyond the dominion of slavery. The following is the petition presented, endorsed as the reader will see:

*To the Hon. General Assembly of the State of North Carolina.*

GENTLEMEN:–The petition of Lunsford Lane humbly shews–That about five years ago, he purchased his freedom from his mistress, Mrs. Sherwood Haywood, and by great economy and industry has paid the purchase money; that he has a wife and seven children whom he has agreed to purchase, and for whom he has paid a part of the purchase money; but not having paid in full, is not yet able to leave the State, without parting with his wife and children.

Your petitioner prays your Honorable Body to pass a law, allowing him to remain a limited time within the State, until he can remove his family also. Your petitioner will give bond and good security for his good behavior while he remains.

Your petitioner will ever pray, &c.
–LUNSFORD LANE.

The undersigned are well acquainted with Lunsford Lane, the petitioner, and join in his petition to the Assembly for relief.

Charles Manly,
R. W. Haywood,
Eleanor Haywood,
William Hill,
R. Smith,
William Peace,
Jos. Peace,
Drury Lacy,
Will. Peck,
W. A. Stith,
A. B. Stith,
J. Brown,
William White,
George Simpson,

| | |
|---|---|
| William M'Pheeters, | Jno. I. Christophers, |
| William Boylan, | John Primrose, |
| Fabius J. Haywood, | Hugh M'Queen, |
| D. W. Stone, | Alex. J. Lawrence, |
| T. Merideth, | C. L. Hinton. |
| A. J. Battle, | |

Lunsford Lane, the petitioner herein, has been servant to the Executive Office since the 1st of January, 1837, and it gives me pleasure to state that, during the whole time, without exception, I have found him faithful and obedient, in keeping every thing committed to his care in good condition. From what I have seen of his conduct and demeanor, I cheerfully join in the petition for his relief.

C. C. BATTLE, *P. Secretary to Gov. Dudley.*
RALEIGH, Nov. 20, 1840.

The foregoing petition was presented to the Senate. It was there referred to a committee. I knew when the committee was to report, and watched about the State House that I might receive the earliest news of the fate of my petition. I should have gone within the senate chamber, but no colored man has that permission. I do not know why, unless for fear he may hear the name of *Liberty*. By and by a member came out, and as he passed me, said, *"Well, Lunsford, they have laid you out; the nigger bill is killed."* I need not tell the reader that my feelings did not enter into the merriment of this honorable senator. To me, the fate of my petition was the last blow to my hopes. I had done all I could do, had said all I could say, laboring night and day, to obtain a favorable reception to my petition; but all in vain. Nothing appeared before me but I must leave the State, and leave my wife and my children, never to see them more. My friends had also done all they could for me.

And why must I be banished? Ever after I entertained the first idea of being free, I had endeavored so to conduct myself as not to become obnoxious to the white inhabitants, knowing as I did their power, and their hostility to the colored people. The two points necessary in such a case I had kept constantly in mind. First, I had made no display of the little property or money I possessed, but in every way I wore as much as possible the aspect of poverty. Second, I had never appeared to be even so intelligent as I really was. This all colored people at the south, free and slaves, find it peculiarly necessary to their own comfort and safety to observe.

I should, perhaps, have mentioned that on the same day I received the notice to leave Raleigh, similar notices were presented to two other free colored people, who had been slaves; were trying to purchase their families; and were otherwise in a like situation to myself. And they took the same course I did to endeavor to remain a limited time. ISAAC HUNTER, who had a family with five children, was one; and WALLER FREEMAN, who had six children, was the other. Mr. Hunter's petition went before mine; and a bill of some sort passed the Senate, which was so cut down in the Commons, as to allow him only *twenty days* to remain in the State. He has since, however, obtained the freedom of his family, who are living with him in Philadelphia.

Mr. Freeman's petition received no better fate than mine. His family were the property of Judge BADGER, who was afterwards made a member of Mr. Harrison's cabinet. When Mr. Badger removed to Washington, he took with him among other slaves this family; and Freeman removed also to that city. After this, when Mr. B. resigned his office, with the other members of the cabinet under President Tyler, he entered into some sort of contract with Freeman, to sell him this family, which he left at Washington, while he took the rest of his slaves back to Raleigh. Freeman is now endeavoring to raise money to make the purchase.

It was now between two and three months to the next session of the court; and I knew that before or at that time I must leave the State. I was bound to appear before the court; but it had been arranged between my lawyer and the prosecuting attorney, that if I would leave the State, and pay the costs of court, the case should be dropped, so that my bondsmen should not be involved. I therefore concluded to stay as long as I possibly could, and then leave. I also determined to appeal to the kindness of the friends of the colored man in the north, for assistance, though I had but little hope of succeeding in this way. Yet it was the only course I could think of, by which I could see any possible hope of accomplishing the object.

I had paid Mr. Smith six hundred and twenty dollars, and had a house and lot worth five hundred dollars, which he had promised to take when I had raised the balance. He gave me also a bill of sale of one of my children, Laura, in consideration of two hundred and fifty dollars of the money already paid; and her I determined to take with me to the north. The costs of court, which I had to meet, amounted to between thirty and forty dollars, besides the fee of my lawyer.

On the 18th of May, 1841, three days after the court commenced its session, I bid adieu to my friends in Raleigh, and set out for the city of New York. I took with me a letter of introduction and recommendation from Mr. John Primrose, a very estimable man, a recommendatory certificate from Mr. Battle, and a letter from the church of which I was a member, together with such papers relating to the affair as I had in my possession. Also I received the following:

RALEIGH, N. C., May, 1841.

The bearer, Lunsford Lane, a free man of color, for some time a resident in this place, being about to leave North Carolina in search of a more favorable location to pursue his trade, has desired us to give him a certificate of his good conduct heretofore.

We take pleasure in saying that his habits are temperate and industrious, that his conduct has been orderly and proper, and that he has for these qualities been distinguished among his caste.

| | |
|---|---|
| William Hall, | R. Smith, |
| Weston R. Gales, | C. Dewey. |
| C. L. Hinton, | |

The above was certified to officially in the usual form, by the clerk of the Court of Common Pleas and Quarter Sessions.

My success in New York was at first small; but at length I fell in with two friends who engaged to raise for me three hundred dollars, provided I should first obtain from other sources the balance of the sum required, which balance would be one thousand and eighty dollars. Thus encouraged, I proceeded to Boston; and in the city and vicinity the needful sum was contributed by about the 1st of April, 1842. My thanks I have endeavored to express in my poor way to the many friends who so kindly and liberally assisted me. I cannot reward them; I hope they will receive their reward in another world. If the limits of this publication would permit, I should like to record the names of many to whom I am very especially indebted for their kindness and aid, not only in contributing, but in introducing me, and opening various ways of access, to others.

On the 5th of February, 1842, finding that I should soon have in my possession the sum necessary to procure my family, and fearing that there might be danger in visiting Raleigh for that purpose, in consequence of the strong opposition of many of the citizens against colored people, their opposition to me, and their previously persecuting me from the city, I wrote to Mr. Smith, requesting him to see the Governor, and obtain, under his hand, a permit to visit the State for a sufficient time to accomplish this business. I requested Mr. Smith to publish the permit in one or two of the city papers, and then to enclose the original to me. This letter he answered, under date of Raleigh, 19th Feb. 1842, as follows:

LUNSFORD:–Your letter of the 5th inst. came duly to hand, and in reply I have to inform you, that owing to the absence of Gov. Morehead, I cannot send you the permit you requested, but this will make no difference, for you can come home, and after your arrival you can obtain one to remain long enough to settle up your affairs. You ought of course to apply to the Governor immediately on your arrival, before any malicious person would have time to inform against you; I don't think by pursuing this course you need apprehend any danger. * * * *

We are all alive at present in Raleigh on the subjects of temperance and religion. We have taken into the temperance societies about five hundred members, and about fifty persons have been happily converted. * * * The work seems still to be spreading, and such a time I have never seen before in my life. Glorious times truly.

Do try to get all the religion in your heart you possibly can, for it is the only thing worth having after all.

Your, &c. B. B. SMITH.

The way now appeared to be in a measure open; also I thought that the religious and temperance interest mentioned in the latter portion of Mr. Smith's letter, augured a state of feeling which would be a protection to me. But fearing still that there might be danger in visiting Raleigh without the permit from the Governor, or at least wishing to take every possible precaution, I addressed another letter to Mr. Smith, and received under date of March 12th, a reply, from which I copy as follows:

"The Governor has just returned, and I called upon him to get the permit, as you requested, but he said he had no authority by law to grant one; and *he told me to say to you that you might in perfect safety come home* in a quiet manner, and remain twenty days without being interrupted. I also consulted Mr. Manly, (a lawyer,) and he *told me the same thing.* * * * *Surely you need not fear any thing under these circumstances. You had therefore better come on just as soon as possible.*"

I need not say, what the reader has already seen, that my life so far had been one of joy succeeding sorrow, and sorrow following joy; of hope, of despair, of bright prospects, of gloom; and of as many hues as ever appear on the varied sky, from the black of midnight, or of the deep brown of a tempest, to the bright warm glow of a clear noon day. On the 11th of April, it was noon with me; I left Boston on my way for Raleigh with high hopes, intending to pay over the money for my family and return with them to Boston, which I designed should be my future home; for there I had found friends, and there I would find a grave. The visit I was making to the south was to be a farewell one; and I did not dream that my old cradle, hard as it once had jostled me, would refuse to rock me a pleasant, or even an affectionate good bye. I thought, too, that the assurances I had received from the Governor, through Mr. Smith, and the assurances of other friends, were a sufficient guaranty that I might visit the home of my boyhood, of my youth, of my manhood, in peace, especially as I was to stay but for a few days and then to return. With these thoughts, and with the thoughts of my family and freedom, I pursued my way to Raleigh, and arrived there on the 23d of the month. It was Saturday, about four o'clock, P.M., when I found myself once more in the midst of my family. With them I remained over the Sabbath, as it was sweet to spend a little time with them after so long an absence, an absence filled with so much of interest to us, and as I could not do any business until the beginning of the week. On Monday morning, between eight and nine o'clock, while I was making ready to leave the house for the first time after my arrival, to go to the store of Mr. Smith, where I was to transact my business with him, two constables, Messrs. Murray and Scott, entered, accompanied by two other men, and summoned me to appear immediately before the police. I accordingly accompanied them to the City Hall, but as it was locked and the officers could not at once find the key, we were told that the court would be held in Mr. Smith's store, a large and commodious room. This was what is termed in common phrase, in Raleigh, a "call court." The Mayor, Mr. Loring, presided, assisted by William Boylan and Jonathan Busbye, Esqs., Justices of the Peace. There were a large number of people together–more than could obtain admission to the room–and a large company of mobocratic spirits crowded around the door. Mr. Loring read the writ, setting forth that I had been guilty of *delivering abolition lectures in the State of Massachusetts.* He asked me whether I was guilty or not guilty. I told him I did not know whether I had given abolition lectures or not, but if it pleased the court, I would relate the course I had pursued during my absence from Raleigh. He then said that I was at liberty to speak.

The circumstances under which I left Raleigh, said I, are perfectly familiar to you. It is known that I had no disposition to remove from this city, but resorted to every lawful means to remain. After I found that I could not be permitted to stay, I went away, leaving behind everything I held dear, with the exception of one child, whom I took with me, after paying two hundred and fifty dollars for her. It is also known to you and to many other persons here present, that I had engaged to purchase my wife and children of their master, Mr. Smith, for the sum of twenty-five hundred dollars, and that I had paid of this sum (including my house and lot,) eleven hundred and twenty dollars, leaving a balance to be made up of thirteen hundred and eighty dollars. I had previously to that lived in Raleigh, a slave, the property of Mr. Sherwood Haywood, and had purchased my freedom by paying the sum of one thousand dollars. But being driven away,–no longer permitted to live in this city to raise the balance of the money due on my family,–my last resort was to call upon the friends of humanity in other places, to assist me.

I went to the city of Boston, and there I related the story of my persecutions here, the same as I have now stated to you. The people gave ear to my statements; and one of them, Rev. Mr. Neale, wrote back, unknown to me, to Mr. Smith, inquiring of him whether the statements made by me were correct. After Mr. Neale received the answer, he sent for me, informed me of his having written, and read to me the reply. The letter fully satisfied Mr. Neale and his friends. He placed it in my hands, remarking that it would, in a great measure, do away the necessity of using the other documents in my possession. I then, with that letter in my hands, went out from house to house, from place of business to place of business, and from church to church, relating, where I could gain an ear, the same heart-rending and soul-trying story which I am now repeating to you. In pursuing that course, the people, first one and then another, contributed, until I had succeeded in raising the amount alluded to, namely, thirteen hundred and eighty dollars. I may have had contributions from abolitionists; but I did not stop to ask those who assisted me whether they were anti-slavery or pro-slavery, for I considered that the money coming from either would accomplish the object I had in view. These are the facts; and now, sir, it remains for you to say, whether I have been giving abolition lectures or not.

In the course of my remarks, I presented the letter of Mr. Smith to Mr. Neale, showing that I had acted the open part while in Massachusetts; also I referred to my having written to Mr. Smith, requesting him to obtain for me the permit of the Governor; and I showed to the court Mr. Smith's letters in reply, in order to satisfy them that I had reason to believe I should be unmolested in my return.

Mr. Loring then whispered to some of the leading men; after which he remarked that he saw nothing in what I had done, according to my statements, implicating me in a manner worthy of notice. He called upon any present who might be in possession of information tending to disprove what I had said, or to show any wrong on my part, to produce it, otherwise I should be set at liberty. No person appeared against me; so I was discharged.

I started to leave the house; but just before I got to the door I met Mr. James Litchford, who touched me on the shoulder, and I followed him back. He observed to me that if I went out of that room I should in less than five minutes be a dead man; for there was a mob outside waiting to drink my life. Mr. Loring then spoke to me again, and said that notwithstanding I had been found guilty of nothing, yet public opinion was law; and he advised me to leave the place the next day, otherwise he was convinced I should have to suffer death. I replied, "not to-morrow, but to-day." He answered that I could not go that day, because I had not done my business. I told him that I would leave my business in his hands and in those of other such gentlemen as himself, who might settle it for me and send my family to meet me at Philadelphia. This was concluded upon, and a guard appointed to conduct me to the depot. I took my seat in the cars, when the mob that had followed us surrounded me, and declared that the cars should not go, if I were permitted to go in them. Mr. Loring inquired what they wanted of me; he told them that there had been an examination, and nothing had been found against me; that they were at the examination invited to speak if they knew aught to condemn me, but they had remained silent, and that now it was but right I should be permitted to leave in peace. They replied that they wanted a more thorough investigation, that they wished to search my trunks (I had but one trunk) and see if I was not in possession of abolition papers. It now became evident that I should be unable to get off in the cars; and my friends advised me to go the shortest way possible to jail, for my safety. They said they were persuaded that what the rabble wanted was to get me into their possession, and then to murder me. The mob looked dreadfully enraged, and seemed to lap for blood. The whole city was in an uproar. But the first men and the more wealthy were my friends; and they did everything in their power to protect me. Mr. Boylan, whose name has repeatedly occurred in this publication, was more than a father to me; and Mr. Smith and Mr. Loring, and so many other gentlemen, whose names it would give me pleasure to mention, were exceedingly kind.

The guard then conducted me through the mob to the prison; and I felt joyful that even a prison could protect me. Looking out from the prison window, I saw my trunk in the hands of Messrs. Johnson, Scott, and others, who were taking it to the City Hall for examination. I understood afterwards that they opened my trunk; and as the lid flew up, Lo! a paper! a paper!! Those about seized it, three or four at once, as hungry dogs would a piece of meat after forty days famine. But the meat quickly turned to a stone; for the paper it happened, was one *printed in Raleigh*, and edited by Weston R. Gales, a nice man to be sure, but no abolitionist. The only other printed or written things in the trunk were some business cards of a firm in Raleigh–not incendiary.

Afterwards I saw from the window Mr. Scott, accompanied by Mr. Johnson, lugging my carpet-bag in the same direction my trunk had gone. It was opened at the City Hall, and found actually to contain a pair of old shoes, and a pair of old boots!–but they did not conclude that these were incendiary.

Mr. Smith now came to the prison and told me that the examination had been completed, and nothing found against me; but that it would not be safe for me to leave the prison immediately. It was agreed that I should remain in prison until after nightfall, and then steal secretly away, being let out by the keeper, and pass unnoticed to the house of my old and tried friend Mr. Boylan. Accordingly I was discharged between nine and ten o'clock. I went by the back way leading to Mr. Boylan's; but soon and suddenly a large company of men sprang upon me, and instantly I found myself in their possession. They conducted me sometimes high above ground and sometimes dragging me along, but as silently as possible, in the direction of the gallows, which is always kept standing upon the Common, or as it is called "the pines," or "piny old field." I now expected to pass speedily into the world of spirits; I thought of that unseen region to which I seemed to be hastening; and then my mind would return to my wife and children, and the labors I had made to redeem them from bondage. Although I had the money to pay for them according to a bargain already made, it seemed to me some white man would get it, and they would die in slavery, without benefit from my exertions and the contributions of my friends. Then the thought of my own death, to occur in a few brief moments, would rush over me, and I seemed to bid adieu in spirit to all earthly things, and to hold communion already with eternity. But at length I observed those who were carrying me away, changed their course a little from the direct line to the gallows, and hope, a faint beaming, sprung up within me; but then as they were taking me to the woods, I thought they intended to murder me there, in a place where they would be less likely to be interrupted than in so public a spot as where the gallows stood. They conducted me to a rising ground among the trees, and set me down. "Now," said they, "tell us the truth about those abolition lectures you have been giving at the north." I replied that I had related the circumstances before the court in the morning; and could only repeat what I had then said. "But that was not the truth–tell us the truth." I again said that any different story would be false, and as I supposed I was in a few minutes to die, I would not, whatever they might think I would say under other circumstances, pass into the other world with a lie upon my lips. Said one, "you were always, Lunsford, when you were here, a clever fellow, and I did not think you would be engaged in such business as giving abolition lectures." To this and similar remarks, I replied, that the people of Raleigh had always said the abolitionists did not believe in buying slaves, but contended that their masters ought to free them without pay. I had been laboring to buy my family; and how then could they suppose me to be in league with the abolitionists?

After other conversation of this kind, and after they seemed to have become tired of questioning me, they held a consultation in a low whisper among themselves. Then a bucket was brought and set down by my side; but what it contained, or for what it was intended, I could not divine. But soon, one of the number came forward with a pillow, and then hope sprung up, a flood of light and joy within me. The heavy weight on my heart rolled off; death had passed by and I unharmed. They commenced stripping me till every rag of clothes was removed; and then the bucket was set near, and I discovered it to contain tar. One man,–I will do him the honor to record his name,–Mr. WILLIAM ANDRES, a journeyman printer, when he is anything except a tar-and-featherer, put his hands the first into the bucket, and was about passing them to my face. "Don't put any in his face or eyes," said one.* So he desisted; but he, with three other "gentlemen," whose names I should be happy to record if I could recall them, gave me as nice a coat of tar all over, face only excepted, as any one would wish to see. Then they took the pillow and ripped it open at one end, and with the open end commenced the operation at the head and so worked downwards, of putting a coat of its contents over that of the contents of the bucket. A fine escape from the hanging this will be, thought I, provided they do not with a match set fire to the feathers. I had some fear they would. But when the work was completed they gave me my clothes, and one of them handed me my watch, which he had carefully kept in his hands; they all expressed great interest in my welfare, advised me how to proceed with my business the next day, told me to stay in the place as long as I wished, and with other such words of consolation they bid me good night.

After I had returned to my family, to their inexpressible joy, as they had become greatly alarmed for my safety, some of the persons who had participated in this outrage, came in, (probably influenced by a curiosity to see how the tar and feathers would be got off,) and expressed great sympathy for me. They said they regretted that the affair had happened,–that they had no objections to my living in Raleigh,–I might feel perfectly safe to go out and transact my business preparatory to leaving,–I should not be molested.

Meanwhile, my friends, understanding that I had been discharged from prison, and perceiving I did not come to them, had commenced a regular

*I think this was Mr. Burns, a blacksmith in the place, but I am not certain. At any rate, this man was my *friend* (if so he may be called,) on this occasion; and it was fortunate for me that the company generally seemed to look up to him for wisdom.

search for me, on foot and on horseback, everywhere; and Mr. Smith called upon the Governor to obtain his official interference; and after my return, a guard came to protect me; but I chose not to risk myself at my own house, and so went to Mr. Smith's, where this guard kept me safely until morning. They seemed friendly indeed, and were regaled with a supper during the night by Mr. Smith. My friend, Mr. Battle, (late Private Secretary to the Governor,) was with them; and he made a speech to them, setting forth the good qualities I had exhibited in my past life, particularly in my connection with the Governor's office.

In the morning, Mr. Boylan, true as ever, and unflinching in his friendship, assisted me in arranging my business,* so that I should start with my family *that day* for the north. He furnished us with provisions more than sufficient to sustain the family to Philadelphia, where we intended to make a halt; and sent his own baggage wagon to convey our baggage to the depot, offering also to send his carriage for my family. But my friend, Mr. Malone, had been before him in this kind offer, which I had agreed to accept.

Brief and sorrowful was the parting from my kind friends; but the worst was the thought of leaving my mother. The cars were to start at ten o'clock in the morning. I called upon my old mistress, Mrs. Haywood, who was affected to weeping by the considerations that naturally came to her mind. She had been kind to me; the day before, she and her daughter, Mrs. Hogg, now present, had jointly transmitted a communication to the court, representing that in consequence of my good conduct from my youth, I could not be supposed to be guilty of any offence. And now, "with tears that ceased not flowing," they gave me their parting blessing. My mother was still Mrs. Haywood's slave, and I her only child. Our old mistress could not witness the sorrow that would attend the parting with my mother. She told her to go with me; and said that if I ever became able to pay two hundred dollars for her, I might; otherwise it should be her loss. She gave her the following paper, which is in the ordinary form of a *pass*:

RALEIGH, N. C., April 26, 1842.

Know all Persons by these Presents, That the bearer of this, Clarissa, a slave, belonging to me, hath my permission to visit the city of New York with her relations, who are in company with her; and it is my desire that she may be protected and permitted to pass without molestation or hindrance, on good behavior. Witness my hand this 26th April, 1842.

ELEANOR HAYWOOD.

Witness–J. A. CAMPBELL.

*Of course I was obliged to sacrifice much on my property, leaving in this hurried manner. And while I was in the north, a kind *friend* had removed from the wood-lot wood that I had cut and corded, for which I expected to receive over one hundred dollars; thus saving me the trouble of making sale of it, or of being burdened with the money it would bring. I suppose I have no redress. I might add other things as bad.

On leaving Mrs. Haywood's, I called upon Mrs. Badger, another daughter, and wife of Judge Badger, previously mentioned. She seemed equally affected; she wept as she gave me her parting counsel. She and Mrs. Hogg, and I, had been children together, playing in the same yard, while yet none of us had learned that they were of a superior and I of a subject[7] race. And in those infant years there were pencillings made upon the heart, which time and opposite fortunes could not all efface. May these friends never be slaves as I have been; nor their bosom companions and their little ones be slaves like mine.

When the cars were about to start, the whole city seemed to be gathered at the depot; and, among the rest, the mobocratic portion, who appeared to be determined still that I should not go peaceably away. Apprehending this, it had been arranged with my friends and the conductor, that my family should be put in the cars and that I should go a distance from the city on foot, and be taken up as they passed. The mob, therefore, supposing that I was left behind, allowed the cars to start.

Mr. Whiting, known as the agent of the rail-road company, was going as far as Petersburg, Va.; and he kindly assisted in purchasing our tickets, and enabling us to pass on unmolested. After he left, Capt. Guyan, of Raleigh, performed the same kind office as far as Alexandria, D. C., and then he placed us in the care of a citizen of Philadelphia, whose name I regret to have forgotten, who protected us quite out of the land of slavery. But for this we should have been liable to be detained at several places on our way, much to our embarrassment, at least, if nothing had occurred of a more serious nature.

One accident only had happened; we lost at Washington a trunk containing most of our valuable clothing. This we have not recovered; but our lives have been spared to bless the day that conferred freedom upon us. I felt when my feet struck the pavements in Philadelphia, as though I had passed into another world. I could draw in a full long breath, with no one to say to the ribs, "why do ye so?"

On reaching Philadelphia we found that our money had all been expended, but kind friends furnished us with the means of proceeding as far as New-York; and thence we were with equal kindness aided on to Boston.

In Boston and in the vicinity, are persons almost without number, who have done me favors more than I can express. The thought that I was now in my loved, though recently acquired home–that my family were with me where the stern, cruel, hated hand of slavery could never reach us more–the greetings of friends–the interchange of feeling and sympathy–the kindness bestowed upon us, more grateful than rain to the thirsty earth–the reflections of the past that would rush into my mind,–these and more almost overwhelmed me with emotion, and I had deep and strange communion with my own soul. Next to God from whom every good gift proceeds, I feel under the greatest obligations to my kind friends in Massachusetts. To be rocked in their cradle of Liberty,–oh, how unlike being stretched on the pillory of slavery! May that cradle rock forever; may many a poor care-worn child of sorrow, many a spirit-bruised (worse than lash-mangled) victim of oppression, there sweetly sleep to the lullaby of Freedom, sung by Massachusetts' sons and daughters.

A number of meetings have been held at which friends have contributed to our temporal wants, and individuals have sent us various articles of provision and furniture and apparel, so that our souls have been truly made glad. There are now ten of us in the family, my wife, my mother, and myself, with seven children, and we expect soon to be joined by my father, who several years ago received his freedom by legacy. The wine fresh from the clustering grapes never filled so sweet a cup as mine. May I and my family be permitted to drink it, remembering whence it came!

I suppose such of my readers as are not accustomed to trade in human beings, may be curious to see the Bills of Sale, by which I have obtained the right to my wife and children. They are both in the hand writing of Mr. Smith. The first–that for Laura–is as follows:

STATE OF NORTH CAROLINA, WAKE COUNTY.

Know all Men by these Presents, That for and in consideration of the sum of two hundred and fifty dollars, to me in hand paid, I have this day bargained and sold, and do hereby bargain, sell and deliver, unto Lunsford Lane, a free man of color, a certain negro girl by the name of Laura, aged about seven years, and hereby warrant and defend the right and title of the said girl to the said Lunsford and his heirs forever, free from the claims of all persons whatsoever.

In Witness whereof, I have hereunto set my hand and seal, at Raleigh, this 17th May, 1841.

B. B. SMITH, [Seal.]

Witness–ROBT. W. HAYWOOD.

Below is the Bill of Sale for my wife and other six children, to which the papers that follow are attached:

STATE OF NORTH CAROLINA, WAKE COUNTY.

Know all Men by these Presents, That for and in consideration of the sum of eighteen hundred and eighty dollars, to me in hand paid, the receipt of which is hereby acknowledged, I have this day bargained, sold and delivered, unto Lunsford Lane, a free man of color, one dark mulatto woman named Patsy, one boy named Edward, one boy also named William, one boy also named Lunsford, one girl named Maria, one boy also named Ellick, and one girl named Lucy, to have and to hold the said negroes free from the claims of all persons whatsoever.

In Witness whereof, I have hereunto affixed my hand and seal, this 25th day of April, 1842.

B. B. SMITH, [Seal.]

Witness–TH. L. WEST.

STATE OF NORTH CAROLINA, WAKE COUNTY.

*Office of Court of Pleas &. Quarter Sessions, Apr.* 26, 1842.

The execution of the within Bill of Sale was this day duly acknowledged before me, by B. B. Smith, the executor of the same.

In Testimony whereof, I have hereunto affixed the seal of said Court, and subscribed my name at Office, in Raleigh, the date above.

JAS. T. MARRIOTT, *Clerk.*

STATE OF NORTH CAROLINA, WAKE COUNTY.

I, William Boylan, presiding magistrate of the Court of Pleas and Quarter Sessions for the County aforesaid, certify that Jas. T. Marriott, who has written and signed the above certificate, is Clerk of the Court aforesaid, that the same is in due form, and full faith and credit are due to such his official acts.

Given under my hand and private seal, (having no seal of office,) this 26th day of April, 1842.

WM. BOYLAN, P. M. [Seal.]

THE STATE OF NORTH CAROLINA.

*To all to whom these Presents shall come—Greeting:*

Be it Known, That William Boylan, whose signature appears in his own proper hand writing to the annexed certificate, was, at the time of signing the same, and now is, a Justice of the Peace and the Presiding Magistrate for the County of Wake, in the State aforesaid, and as such he is duly qualified and empowered to give such certificate, which is here done in the usual and proper manner; and full faith and credit are due to the same, and ought to be given to all the official acts of the said William Boylan, as Presiding Magistrate aforesaid.

In Testimony whereof, I, J. M. Morehead, Governor, Captain General and Commander in Chief, have caused the Great Seal of the State to be hereunto affixed, and signed the same, at the city of Raleigh, on the 26th day of April, in the year of our Lord one thousand eight hundred and forty-two, and in the sixty-sixth year of the Independence of the United States.

J. M. MOREHEAD.

*By the Governor.*

P. REYNOLDS, *Private Secretary.*

## EDITORIAL NOTES TO *THE NARRATIVE OF LUNSFORD LANE*

1. Andrews, *To Tell a Free Story*, 115–18.

2. A measure containing 5½ yards or 16½ feet.

3. Titus 2:9–10, "Exhort servants to be obedient unto their own masters, and to please them well in all things; not answering again; Not purloining, but shewing all good fidelity; that they may adorn the doctrine of God our Saviour in all things"; Ephesians 6:5, "Servants, be obedient to them that are your masters according to the flesh, with fear and trembling, in singleness of your heart, as unto Christ."

4. Ephesians 6:6, "Not with eyeservice, as menpleasers; but as the servants of Christ, doing the will of God from the heart."

5. Luke 12:47, "And that servant, which knew his lord's will, and prepared not himself, neither did according to his will, shall be beaten with many stripes."

6. John 6:60, "Many therefore of his disciples, when they had heard this, said, This is an hard saying; who can hear it?"

7. Subordinate or inferior.

# 4

# LEWIS CLARKE (1815–1897) AND MILTON CLARKE (?–?)

## NARRATIVES OF THE SUFFERINGS OF LEWIS AND MILTON CLARKE

William L. Andrews refers to Frederick Douglass's *Narrative*, which was published in 1845, as "the great enabling text of the first century of Afro-American autobiography."[1] This "enabling" quality is especially true in terms of what its immense popularity meant in the marketplace. Douglass's *Narrative* sold an unprecedented 4,500 copies within its first five months of publication and was subsequently issued in English, Irish, and French editions.[2] The attention given to Douglass's *Narrative* caused a surge in the demand for other narratives that could convey the humanity of the enslaved and the injustice of the slave system. Douglass also "enabled" narratives stylistically. Rather than limiting narrators to unvarnished recitations of individual and collective slave experience, Douglass expanded the form to incorporate personal qualities of the narrator's voice.

Lewis Clarke's narrative was published in 1845, as a result of the attention Douglass's *Narrative* was creating. Lewis Clarke's narrative sold 3,000 copies within its first year of publication. His brother, Milton Clarke, had also produced a narrative and, at the suggestion of Joseph C. Lovejoy, agreed to expand his description of some of the incidents in his life and reissue the narrative combined with the second edition of his brother Lewis's in 1846. The combined edition was also extremely popular.

Like Douglass, Lewis Clarke was an active speaker on behalf of the abolitionist cause. His narrative is characterized by a homespun, folksy, colloquial quality that was undoubtedly the result of speaking engagements that gave him the opportunity to rehearse and refine his presentation of the most compelling aspects of his life. What may also have contributed to the colloquial quality is the fact that Lewis dictated his narrative to the abolitionist minister Joseph C. Lovejoy (1805–1871) rather than writing it himself. Lovejoy, whose brothers Owen and Elijah P. Lovejoy were also involved with the abolitionist movement, served as an amanuensis for both Lewis and Milton and, in the prefaces to their narratives, offers fairly standard comments about the importance and accuracy of their stories and the limits of his editorial involvement.[3] Of Lewis, Lovejoy writes that "I first became acquainted with Lewis Clarke in December, 1842. I well remember the deep impression made upon my mind on hearing his Narrative from his own lips. It gave me a new and more vivid impression of the wrongs of Slavery than I had ever before felt." Lewis's narrative was produced on the basis of the compelling nature of his story and the strength of his character. "Many persons, who have heard him lecture, have expressed a strong desire that his story might be recorded in a connected form. He has, therefore, concluded to have it printed." The boundaries, of course, of Lovejoy's involvement are impossible to clarify fully.

What is clear, however, are the compelling circumstances of Lewis's life. He was born in Madison County, Kentucky, in 1815. His mother, Letitia Campbell (who was known as Letty), was the daughter of Samuel Campbell, the owner of the plantation. He promised her her freedom upon his death. In the meantime, Letty married and eventually gave birth to ten children. At age six, Lewis was claimed as being the rightful property of Betsey Campbell Banton, who was Letty's married half-sister. Her cruelty throughout the narrative illustrates the irresponsible power of the slaveholder. In 1831, Samuel Campbell died. No will freeing his daughter Letty was ever found. In the wake of financial downturn by Betsey Campbell Banton, Lewis was hired out. He eventually escaped to Port Stanley, Ontario. His abolitionist involvement began when he returned to Oberlin, Ohio in search of his brother. Milton's narrative adds his own remembrances of his childhood and eventual escape. Appendixes to the combined edition of their narratives include a sketch of the Clarke family and a list of the most commonly asked questions (along with his responses) that Lewis received on the abolitionist platform.

In addition to his oratorical skills and the popularity of his narrative, Lewis is also well-known as Harriet Beecher Stowe's model for the character George Harris in *Uncle Tom's Cabin* (1852). In her *Key to Uncle Tom's Cabin* (1856) Stowe writes that "Lewis Clarke is an acquaintance of the writer. Soon after his escape from slavery, he was received into the family of a sister-in-law of the author, and there educated. His conduct during this time was such as to win for him uncommon affection and respect, and the author has frequently heard him spoken of in the highest terms by all who knew him." The incisive, homespun style of the narrative combined with the expansion of popular interest in the slave narrative genre and Stowe's glowing appraisal helped catapult the narrative to a prominent place among abolitionist literature.[4]

The *Narratives* reprinted here are taken from the 1846 edition of the text, originally published in Boston, Massachusetts.

## FURTHER READING

William L. Andrews, *To Tell a Free Story* (1986); John W. Blassingame, *Slave Testimony* (1977); Marion Wilson Starling, *The Slave Narrative* (1988).

Lewis Clarke

# NARRATIVES
## OF THE SUFFERINGS OF
# LEWIS AND MILTON CLARKE,
## SONS OF A SOLDIER OF THE REVOLUTION,
## DURING A
# CAPTIVITY OF MORE THAN TWENTY YEARS
## AMONG THE
# SLAVEHOLDERS OF KENTUCKY,
## ONE OF THE
# SO CALLED CHRISTIAN STATES OF NORTH AMERICA.

DICTATED BY THEMSELVES.

BOSTON:
PUBLISHED BY BELA MARSH,
NO. 25 CORNHILL.
1846.

All Orders to be sent to the Publisher.

## PREFACE

I first became acquainted with LEWIS CLARKE in December, 1842. I well remember the deep impression made upon my mind on hearing his Narrative from his own lips. It gave me a new and more vivid impression of the wrongs of Slavery than I had ever before felt. Evidently a person of good native talents and of deep sensibilities, such a mind had been under the dark cloud of slavery for more than twenty-five years. Letters, reading, all the modes of thought awakened by them, had been utterly hid from his eyes; and yet his mind had evidently been active, and trains of thought were flowing through it which he was utterly unable to express. I well remember, too, the wave on wave of deep feeling excited in an audience of more than a thousand persons, at Hallowell, Me., as they listened to his story, and looked upon his energetic and manly countenance, and wondered if the dark cloud of slavery could cover up–hide from the world, and degrade to the condition of brutes–*such* immortal minds. His story, there and wherever since told, has aroused the most utter abhorrence of the Slave System.

For the last two years, I have had the most ample opportunity of becoming acquainted with Mr. Clarke. He has made this place his home, when not engaged in giving to public audiences the story of his sufferings and the sufferings of his fellow-slaves. Soon after he came to Ohio, by the faithful instruction of pious friends, he was led, as he believes, to see himself a sinner before God, and to seek pardon and forgiveness through the precious blood of the Lamb. He has ever manifested an ardent thirst for religious, as well as for other kinds of knowledge. In the opinion of all those best acquainted with him, he has maintained the character of a sincere Christian. That he is what he professes to be,–a slave escaped from the grasp of avarice and power,–there is not the least shadow of doubt. His Narrative bears the most conclusive internal evidence of its truth. Persons of discriminating minds have heard it repeatedly, under a great variety of circumstances, and the story, in all substantial respects, has been always the same. He has been repeatedly recognized in the Free States, by persons who knew him in Kentucky, when a slave. During the summer of 1844, Cassius M. Clay[5] visited Boston, and, on seeing Milton Clarke, recognized him as one of the Clarke family, well known to him in Kentucky. Indeed, nothing can be more surely established than the fact that Lewis and Milton Clarke are no impostors. For three years they have been engaged in telling their story in seven or eight different states, and no one has appeared to make an attempt to contradict them. The capture of Milton in Ohio, by the kidnappers, as a *slave*, makes assurance doubly strong. Wherever they have told their story, large audiences have collected, and every where they have been listened to with great interest and satisfaction.

Cyrus is fully equal to either of the brothers in sprightliness of mind–is withal a great wit, and would make an admirable lecturer, but for an unfortunate impediment in his speech. They all feel deeply the wrongs they have suffered, and are by no means forgetful of their brethren in *bonds*. When Lewis first came to this place, he was frequently noticed in silent and deep meditation. On being asked what he was thinking of, he would reply, "O, of the poor slaves! Here I am free, and they suffering *so much*." Bitter tears are often seen coursing down his manly cheeks, as he recurs to the scenes of his early suffering. Many persons, who have heard him lecture, have expressed a strong desire that his story might be recorded in a connected form. He has, therefore, concluded to have it printed. He was anxious to spread the story of his sufferings as extensively as possible before the community, that he might awaken more hearts to feel for his down-trodden brethren. Nothing seems to grieve him to the heart, like finding a minister of the gospel, or a professed Christian, indifferent to the condition of the slave. As to doing much for the instruction of the minds of the slaves, or for the salvation of their souls, till they are EMANCIPATED, *restored* to the rights of men, in his opinion it is utterly impossible.

When the master, or his representative, the man who justifies slaveholding, comes with the whip in one hand and the Bible in the other, the slave says, at least in his heart, Lay down *one* or the *other*. Either make the tree good and the fruit good, or else both corrupt together. Slaves do not believe that THE RELIGION which is from God, bears *whips and chains*. They ask, emphatically, concerning their FATHER in heaven,

> "Has He bid you buy and sell us;
> Speaking from his throne, the sky?"

For the facts contained in the following Narrative, Mr. Clarke is of course alone responsible. Yet, having had the most ample opportunities for testing his accuracy, I do not hesitate to say, that I have not a shadow of doubt but in all material points every word is true. Much of it is in his own language, and all of it according to his own dictation.

J. C. LOVEJOY.
CAMBRIDGEPORT, April, 1845.

## NARRATIVE OF LEWIS CLARKE

I was born in March, as near as I can ascertain, in the year 1815, in Madison county, Kentucky, about seven miles from Richmond, upon the plantation of my grandfather, Samuel Campbell. He was considered a very respectable man, among his fellow-robbers, the slaveholders. It did not render him less honorable in their eyes, that he took to his bed Mary, his slave, perhaps half white, by whom he had one daughter, LETITIA CAMPBELL. This was before his marriage.

My father was from "beyond the flood"—from Scotland, and by trade a weaver. He had been married in his own country, and lost his wife, who left to him, as I have been told, two sons. He came to this country in time to be in the earliest scenes of the American revolution. He was at the battle of Bunker Hill,[6] and continued in the army to the close of the war. About the year 1800, or before, he came to Kentucky, and married Miss Letitia Campbell, then held as a slave by her *dear* and *affectionate* father. My father died, as near as I can recollect, when I was about ten or twelve years of age. He had received a wound in the war, which made him lame as long as he lived. I have often heard him tell of Scotland, sing the merry songs of his native land, and long to see its hills once more.

Mr. Campbell promised my father that his daughter Letitia should be made free in his will. It was with this promise that he married her. And I have no doubt that Mr. Campbell was as good as his word, and that, by his *will*, my mother and her nine children were made free. But ten persons in one family, each worth three hundred dollars, are not easily set free among those accustomed to live by continued robbery. We did not, therefore, by an instrument from the hand of the dead, escape the avaricious grab of the slaveholder. It is the common belief that the will was destroyed by the heirs of Mr. Campbell.

The night in which I was born, I have been told, was dark and terrible—black as the night for which Job prayed,[7] when he besought the clouds to pitch their tent round about the place of his birth; and my life of slavery was but too exactly prefigured by the stormy elements that hovered over the first hour of my being. It was with great difficulty that any one could be urged out for a necessary attendant for my mother. At length, one of the sons of Mr. Campbell, William, by the promise from his mother of the child that should be born, was induced to make an effort to obtain the necessary assistance. By going five or six miles, he obtained a female professor of the couch.

William Campbell, by virtue of this title, always claimed me as his property. And well would it have been for me if this claim had been regarded. At the age of six or seven years, I fell into the hands of his sister, Mrs. Betsey Banton, whose character will be best known when I have told the horrid wrongs which she heaped upon me for ten years. If there are any *she* spirits that come up from hell, and take possession of one part of mankind, I am sure she is one of that sort. I was consigned to her under the following circumstances: When she was married, there was given her, as part of her dower, as is common among the Algerines of Kentucky, a *girl*, by the name of Ruth, about fourteen or fifteen years old. In a short time, Ruth was dejected and injured, by beating and abuse of different kinds, so that she was sold, for a half-fool, to the more tender mercies of the sugar-planter in Louisiana. The amiable Mrs. Betsey obtained then, on loan from her parents, another slave, named Phillis. In six months she had suffered so severely, under the hand of this monster-woman, that she made an attempt to kill herself, and was taken home by the parents of Mrs. Banton. This produced a regular slaveholding family brawl; a regular war, of *four* years, between the *mild* and peaceable Mrs. B. and her own parents. These wars are very common among the Algerines in Kentucky; indeed, slaveholders have not arrived at that degree of civilization that enables them to live in tolerable peace, though united by the nearest family ties. In them is fulfilled what I have heard read in the Bible—"The father is against the son, and the daughter-in-law against the mother-in-law, and their *foes* are of their own household."[8] Some of the slaveholders may have a *wide* house; but one of the *cat-handed*, snake-eyed, brawling women, which slavery produces, can fill it from cellar to garret. I have heard every place I could get into any way ring with their screech-owl voices. Of all the animals on the face of this earth, I am most afraid of a real mad, passionate, raving, slaveholding woman. Somebody told me, once, that Edmund Burke declared that the natives of India fled to the jungles, among tigers and lions, to escape the more barbarous cruelty of Warren Hastings.[9] I am sure I would sooner lie down to sleep by the side of tigers than near a raging-mad slave woman. But I must go back to *sweet* Mrs. Banton. I have been describing her in the *abstract*. I will give a full-grown portrait of her right away. For four years after the trouble about Phillis she never came near her father's house. At the end of this period, another of the amiable sisters was to be married, and sister Betsey could not repress the tide of curiosity urging her to be present at the nuptial ceremonies. Beside, she had another motive. Either shrewdly suspecting that she might deserve less than any member of the family, or that some ungrounded partiality would be manifested toward her sister, she determined, at all hazards, to be present, and see that the scales which weighed out the children of the plantation should be held with even hand. The wedding-day was appointed; the sons and daughters of this joyful occasion were gathered together, and then came also the fair-faced, but black-hearted, Mrs. B. Satan, among the sons of God, was never less welcome than this fury[10] among her kindred. They all knew what she came for,—to make mischief, if possible. "Well, now, if there ain't Bets!" exclaimed the old lady. The father was moody and silent, knowing that she inherited largely of the disposition of her mother; but he had experienced too many of her retorts of courtesy to say as much, for dear experience had taught him the discretion of silence. The brothers smiled at the prospect of fun and frolic; the sisters trembled for fear, and word flew round among the slaves, "The old she-bear has come home! look out! look out!"

The wedding went forward. Polly, a very good sort of a girl to be raised in that region, was married, and received, as the first instalment of her dower[11] a *girl* and a *boy*. Now was the time for Mrs. Banton, sweet, good Mrs. Banton. "Poll has a girl and a *boy*, and I only had that fool of a girl. I reckon, if I go home without a boy too, this house wont be left standing."

This was said, too, while the sugar of the wedding-cake was yet melting upon her tongue. How the bitter words would flow when the guests had retired, all began to imagine. To arrest this whirlwind of rising passion, her mother promised any boy upon the plantation, to be taken home on her return. Now, my evil star was right in the top of the sky. Every boy was ordered in, to pass before this female sorceress, that she might select a victim for her unprovoked malice, and on whom to pour the vials of her wrath for years. I was that unlucky fellow. Mr. Campbell, my grandfather, objected, because it would divide a family, and offered her Moses, whose father and mother had been sold south. Mrs. Campbell put in for William's claim, dated *ante natum*[12]—before I was born; but objections and claims of every kind were swept away by the wild passion and shrill-toned voice of Mrs. B. Me she would have, and none else. Mr. Campbell went out to hunt, and drive away bad thoughts; the old lady became quiet, for she was sure none of her blood run in my veins, and, if there was any of her husband's there, it was no fault of hers. Slave women are always revengeful toward the children of slaves that have any of the blood of their husbands in them. I was too young, only seven years of age, to understand what was going on. But my poor and affectionate mother understood and appreciated it all. When she left the kitchen of the mansion-house, where she was employed as cook, and came home to her own little cottage, the tear of anguish was in her eye, and the image of sorrow upon every feature of her face. She knew the female Nero,[13] whose rod was now to be over me. That night sleep departed from her eyes. With the youngest child clasped firmly to her bosom, she spent the night in walking the floor, coming ever and anon to lift up the clothes and look at me and my poor brother, who lay sleeping together. *Sleeping*, I said. Brother slept, but not I. I saw my mother when she first came to me, and I could not sleep. The vision of that night—its deep, ineffaceable impression—is now before my mind with all the distinctness of yesterday. In the morning, I was put into the carriage with Mrs. B. and her children, and my weary pilgrimage of suffering was fairly begun. It was her business on the road, for about twenty-five or thirty miles, to initiate her children into the art of tormenting their new victim. I was seated upon the bottom of the carriage, and these little imps were employed in pinching me, pulling my ears and hair; and they were stirred up by their mother, like a litter of young wolves, to torment me in every way possible. In the mean time, I was compelled by the old she-wolf to call them "Master," "Mistress," and bow to them, and obey them at the first call.

During that day, I had, indeed, no very agreeable foreboding of the torments to come; but, sad as were my anticipations, the reality was infinitely beyond them. Infinitely more bitter than death were the cruelties I experienced at the hand of this merciless woman. Save from one or two slaves on the plantation, during my ten years of captivity here, I scarcely heard a kind word, or saw a smile toward me from any living being. And now that I am where people look kind, and act kindly toward me, it seems like a dream. I hardly seem to be in the same world that I was then. When I first got into the free states, and saw every body look like they loved one another, sure enough, I thought, this must be the *"Heaven"* of LOVE I had heard something about. But I must go back to what I suffered from that wicked woman. It is hard work to keep the mind upon it; I hate to think it over—but I must tell it—the world must know what is done in Kentucky. I cannot, however, tell all the ways by which she tormented me. I can only give a few instances of my suffering, as specimens of the whole. A book of a thousand pages would not be large enough to tell of all the tears I shed, and the sufferings endured, in THAT TEN YEARS OF PURGATORY.[14]

A very trivial offence was sufficient to call forth a great burst of indignation from this woman of ungoverned passions. In my simplicity, I put my lips to the same vessel, and drank out of it, from which her children were accustomed to drink. She expressed her utter abhorrence of such an act, by throwing my head violently back, and dashing into my face two dippers of water. The shower of water was followed by a heavier shower of *kicks*; yes, delicate reader, this *lady* did not hesitate to *kick*, as well as cuff in a very plentiful manner; but the words, bitter and cutting, that followed, were like a storm of hail upon my young heart. "She would teach me better manners than that; she would let me know I was to be brought up to her hand; she would have *one* slave that knew his place; if I wanted water, go to the spring, and not drink there in the house." This was new times for me; for some days I was completely benumbed with my sorrow. I could neither eat nor sleep. If there is any human being on earth, who has been so blessed as never to have *tasted* the cup of sorrow, and therefore is unable to conceive of *suffering*; if there be one so lost to all feeling as even to say, that the slaves do not suffer when *families* are separated, let such a one go to the ragged quilt which was my couch and pillow, and stand there night after night, for long, weary hours, and see the bitter tears streaming down the face of that more than orphan boy, while, with half-suppressed sighs and sobs, he calls again and again upon his absent mother.

> "Say, mother, wast thou conscious of the tears I shed?
> Hovered thy spirit o'er thy sorrowing son?
> Wretch even *then*! life's journey just begun."

Let him stand by that couch of bitter sorrow through the terribly lonely night, and then wring out the wet end of those rags, and see how many tears yet remain, after the burning temples had absorbed all they could. He will not doubt, he cannot doubt, but the slave has feeling. But I find myself running away again from Mrs. Banton—and I don't much wonder neither.

There were several children in the family, and my first main business was to wait upon them. Another young slave and myself have often been compelled to sit up by turns all night, to rock the cradle of a little, peevish scion of slavery. If the cradle was stopped, the moment they awoke a dolorous cry was sent forth to mother or father, that Lewis had gone to sleep. The reply to this call would be a direction from the mother for these petty tyrants to get up and take the whip, and give the good-for-nothing scoundrel a smart whipping. This was the midnight pastime of a child ten or twelve years old. What might you expect of the future man?

There were four house-slaves in this family, including myself; and though we had not, in all respects, so hard work as the field hands, yet in many things our condition was much worse. We were constantly exposed to the whims and passions of every member of the family; from the least to the greatest their anger was wreaked upon us. Nor was our life an easy one, in the hours of our toil or in the amount of labor performed. We were always required to sit up until all the family had retired; then we must be up at early dawn in summer, and before day in winter. If we failed, through weariness or for any other reason, to appear at the first morning summons, we were sure to have our hearing quickened by a severe chastisement. Such horror has seized me, lest I might not hear the first shrill call, that I have often in dreams fancied I heard that unwelcome voice, and have leaped from my couch, and walked through the house and out of it before I awoke. I have gone and called the other slaves, in my sleep, and asked them if they did not hear master call. Never, while I live, will the remembrance of those long, bitter nights of fear pass from my mind.

But I want to give you a few specimens of the abuse which I received. During the ten years that I lived with Mrs. Banton, I do not think there were as many days, when she was at home, that I, or some other slave, did not receive some kind of beating or abuse at her hands. It seemed as though she could not live nor sleep unless some poor back was smarting, some head beating with pain, or some eye filled with tears, around her. Her tender mercies were indeed cruel. She brought up her children to imitate her example. Two of them manifested some dislike to the cruelties taught them by their mother, but they never stood high in favor with her; indeed, any thing like humanity or kindness to a slave, was looked upon by her as a great offence.

Her instruments of torture were ordinarily the raw hide, or a bunch of hickory-sprouts seasoned in the fire and tied together. But if these were not at hand, nothing came amiss. She could relish a beating with a chair, the broom, tongs, shovel, shears, knife-handle, the heavy heel of her slipper, or a bunch of keys; her zeal was so active in these barbarous inflictions, that her invention was wonderfully quick, and some way of inflicting the requisite torture was soon found out.

One instrument of torture is worthy of particular description. *This was an oak club, a foot and a half in length and an inch and a half square.* With this delicate weapon she would beat us upon the hands and upon the feet until they were blistered. This instrument was carefully preserved for a period of four years. Every day, for that time, I was compelled to see that hated tool of cruelty lying in the chair by my side. The least degree of delinquency either in not doing all the appointed work, or in look or behavior, was visited with a beating from this oak club. That club will always be a prominent object in the picture of horrors of my life of more than twenty years of bitter bondage.

When about nine years old, I was sent in the evening to catch and kill a turkey. They were securely sleeping in a tree–their accustomed resting-place for the night. I approached as cautiously as possible, and selected the victim I was directed to catch; but, just as I grasped him in my hand, my foot slipped, and he made his escape from the tree, and fled beyond my reach. I returned with a heavy heart to my mistress with the story of my misfortune. She was enraged beyond measure. She determined, at once, that I should have a whipping of the worst kind, and she was bent upon adding all the aggravations possible. Master had gone to bed drunk, and was now as fast asleep as drunkards ever are. At any rate, he was filling the house with the noise of his snoring and with the perfume of his breath. I was ordered to go and call him–wake him up–and ask him to be *kind* enough to give me fifty good smart lashes. To be *whipped* is bad enough–to *ask* for it is worse–to ask a drunken man to whip you is too bad. I would sooner have gone to a nest of rattlesnakes, than to the bed of this drunkard. But go I must. Softly I crept along, and gently shaking his arm, said, with a trembling voice, "Master, master, mistress wants you to wake up." This did not go to the extent of her command, and in a great fury she called out, "What, you wont ask him to whip you, will you?" I then added, "Mistress wants you to give me fifty lashes." A bear at the smell of a lamb was never roused quicker. "Yes, yes, that I will; I'll give you such a whipping as you will never want again." And, sure enough, so he did. He sprang from the bed, seized me by the hair, lashed me with a handful of switches, threw me my whole length upon the floor; beat, kicked, and cuffed me worse than he would a dog, and then threw me, with all his strength, out of the door, more dead than alive. There I lay for a long time, scarcely able and not daring to move, till I could hear no sound of the furies within, and then crept to my couch, longing for death to put an end to my misery. I had no friend in the world to whom I could utter one word of complaint, or to whom I could look for protection.

Mr. Banton owned a blacksmith's shop, in which he spent some of his time, though he was not a very efficient hand at the forge. One day, mistress told me to go over to the shop and let master give me a flogging. I knew the mode of punishing there too well. I would rather die than go. The poor fellow who worked in the shop, a very skilful workman, one day came to the determination that he would work no more, unless he could be paid for his labor. The enraged master put a handful of nail-rods into the fire, and when they were *red-hot,* took them out, and *cooled* one after another of them in the blood and flesh of the poor slave's back. I knew this was the shop mode of punishment. I would not go; and Mr. Banton came home, and his amiable lady told him the story of my refusal. He broke forth in a great rage, and gave me a most unmerciful beating; adding that, if I had come, he would have burned the hot nail-rods into my back.

Mrs. Banton, as is common among slaveholding women, seemed to hate and abuse me all the more, because I had some of the blood of her father in my veins. There are no slaves that are so badly abused, as those that are related to some of the women, or the children of their own husband; it seems as though they never could hate these quite bad enough. My sisters were as white and good-looking as any of the young ladies in Kentucky. It happened once of a time, that a young man called at the house of Mr. Campbell, to see a sister of Mrs. Banton. Seeing one of my sisters in the house, and pretty well dressed, with a strong family look, he thought it was Miss Campbell; and, with that supposition, addressed some conversation to her which he had intended for the private ear of Miss C. The mistake was noised abroad, and occasioned some amusement to young people. Mrs. Banton heard of it, and it made her caldron of wrath sizzling hot; every thing that diverted and amused other people seemed to enrage her. There are hot-springs in Kentucky; she was just like one of them, only brimful of boiling poison.

She must wreak her vengeance, for this innocent mistake of the young man, upon me. "She would fix me, so that nobody should ever think I was white." Accordingly, in a burning hot day, she *made me take off every rag of clothes, go out into the garden*, and pick herbs for hours, in order to *burn* me black. When I went out, she threw cold water on me, so that the sun might take effect upon me; when I came in, she gave me a severe beating on my blistered back.

After I had lived with Mrs. B. three or four years, I was put to spinning hemp, flax, and tow,[15] on an old-fashioned foot-wheel. There were four or five slaves at this business, a good part of the time. We were kept at our work from daylight to dark in summer, from long before day to nine or ten o'clock in the evening in winter. Mrs. Banton, for the most part, was near, or kept continually passing in and out, to see that each of us performed as much work as she thought we ought to do. Being young, and sick at heart all the time, it was very hard work to go through the day and evening and not suffer exceedingly for want of more sleep. Very often, too, I was compelled to work beyond the ordinary hour, to finish the appointed task of the day. Sometimes I found it impossible not to drop asleep at the wheel.

On these occasions, Mrs. B. had her peculiar contrivances for keeping us awake. She would sometimes sit, by the hour, with a dipper of vinegar and salt, and throw it in my eyes to keep them open. My hair was pulled till there was no longer any pain from that source. *And I can now suffer myself to be lifted by the hair of the head, without experiencing the least pain.*

She very often kept me from getting water to satisfy my thirst, and in one instance kept me for two entire days without a particle of food. This she did, in order that I might make up for lost time. But, of course, I lost rather than gained upon my task. Every meal taken from me made me less able to work. It finally ended in a terrible beating.

But all my severe labor, and bitter and cruel punishments, for these ten years of captivity with this worse than Arab family, all these were as nothing to the sufferings I experienced by being separated from my mother, brothers, and sisters; the same things, with them near to sympathize with me, to hear my story of sorrow, would have been comparatively tolerable.

They were distant only about thirty miles; and yet, in ten long, lonely years of childhood, I was only permitted to see them three times.

My mother occasionally found an opportunity to send me some token of remembrance and affection, a sugar-plum or an apple; but I scarcely ever ate them; they were laid up, and handled and wept over till they wasted away in my hand.

My thoughts continually by day, and my dreams by night, were of mother and home; and the horror experienced in the morning, when I awoke and behold it was a dream, is beyond the power of language to describe.

But I am about to leave this den of robbers, where I had been so long imprisoned. I cannot, however, call the reader from his new and pleasant acquaintance with this amiable pair, without giving a few more incidents of their history. When this is done, and I have taken great pains, as I shall do, to put a copy of this portrait in the hands of this Mrs. B., I shall bid her farewell. If she sees something awfully hideous in her picture, as here presented, she will be constrained to acknowledge it is true to nature. I have given it from no malice, no feeling of resentment towards her, but that the world may know what is done by *slavery*, and that slaveholders may know that their crimes will come to light. I hope and pray that Mrs. B. will repent of her many and aggravated sins before it is too late.

The scenes between her and her husband, while I was with them, strongly illustrate the remark of Jefferson[16] that slavery fosters the worst passions of the master. Scarcely a day passed, in which bitter words were not bandied from one to the other. I have seen Mrs. B., with a large knife drawn in her right hand, the other upon the collar of her husband, swearing and threatening to cut him *square in two.* They both drank freely, and swore like highwaymen. He was a gambler and a counterfeiter. I have seen and handled his moulds and his false coin. They finally quarrelled openly, and separated; and the last I knew of them, he was living a sort of poor vagabond life in his native state, and she was engaged in a protracted lawsuit with some of her former friends, about her father's property.

Of course, such habits did not produce great thrift in their worldly condition, and myself and other slaves were mortgaged, from time to time, to make up the deficiency between their income and expenses. I was transferred, at the age of sixteen or seventeen, to a Mr. K., whose name I forbear to mention, lest, if he or any other man should ever claim *property* where they never had any, this, my own testimony, might be brought in to aid their wicked purposes.

In the exchange of masters, my condition was, in many respects, greatly improved. I was free, at any rate, from that kind of suffering experienced at the hand of Mrs. B., as though she delighted in cruelty for its own sake. My situation, however, with Mr. K. was far from enviable. Taken from the work in and around the house, and put at once, at that early age, to the constant work of a full-grown man, I found it not an easy task always to escape the lash of the overseer. In the four or five years that I was with this man, the overseers were often changed. Sometimes we had a man that seemed to have some consideration, some mercy; but generally their eye seemed to be fixed upon one object, and that was, to get the greatest possible amount of work out of every slave upon the plantation. When stooping to clear the tobacco-plants from the worms which infest them,–a work which draws most cruelly upon the back,–some of these men would not allow us a moment to rest at the end of the row; but, at the crack of the whip, we were compelled to jump to our places, from row to row, for hours, while the poor back was crying out with torture. Any complaint or remonstrance under such circumstances is sure to be answered in no other way than by the lash. As a sheep before her shearers is dumb, so a slave is not permitted to open his mouth.

There were about one hundred and fifteen slaves upon this plantation. Generally, we had enough, in quantity, of food. We had, however, but two meals a day, of corn-meal bread and soup, or meat of the poorest kind. Very often, so little care had been taken to cure and preserve the bacon, that, when it came to us, though it had been fairly killed once, it was more alive than dead. Occasionally, we had some refreshment over and above the two meals, but this was extra, beyond the rules of the plantation. And, to balance this gratuity, we were also frequently deprived of our food, as a punishment. We suffered greatly, too, for want of water. The slave-drivers have the notion that slaves are more healthy, if allowed to drink but little, than they are if freely allowed nature's beverage. The slaves quite as confidently cherish the opinion that, if the master would drink less peach brandy and whisky, and give the slave more water, it would be better all round. As it is, the more the master and overseer drink, the less they seem to think the slave needs.

In the winter, we took our meals before day in the morning, and after work at night; in the summer, at about nine o'clock in the morning, and at two in the afternoon. When we were cheated out of our two meals a day, either by the cruelty or caprice of the overseer, we always felt it a kind of special duty and privilege to make up, in some way, the deficiency. To accomplish this, we had many devices; and we sometimes resorted to our peculiar methods, when incited only by a desire to taste greater variety than our ordinary bill of fare afforded.

This sometimes led to very disastrous results. The poor slave who was caught with a chicken or a pig, killed from the plantation, had his back scored most unmercifully. Nevertheless, the pigs would die without being sick or squealing once; and the hens, chickens, and turkeys sometimes disappeared, and never stuck up a feather to tell where they were buried. The old goose would sometimes exchange her whole nest of eggs for round pebbles; and, patient as that animal is, this quality was exhausted, and she was obliged to leave her nest with no train of offspring behind her.

One old slave woman upon this plantation was altogether too keen and shrewd for the best of them. She would go out to the corn-crib with her basket, watch her opportunity, with one effective blow pop over a little pig, slip him into her basket, and put the cobs on top, trudge off to her cabin, and look just as innocent as though she had a right to eat of the work of her own hands. It was a kind of first principle, too, in her code of morals, that they that *worked* had a right to eat. The moral of all questions in relation to taking food was easily settled by aunt Peggy. The only question with her was, *how* and *when* to do it.

It could not be done openly, that was plain. It must be done secretly; if not in the daytime, by all means in the night. With a dead pig in the cabin, and the water all hot for scalding, she was at one time warned by her son that the Philistines were upon her. Her resources were fully equal to the sudden emergency. Quick as thought, the pig was thrown into the boiling kettle, a door was put over it, her daughter seated upon it, and, with a good, thick quilt around her, the overseer found little Clara taking a steam-bath for a terrible cold. The daughter, acting well her part, groaned sadly; the mother was very busy in tucking in the quilt, and the overseer was blinded, and went away without seeing a bristle of the pig.

Aunt P. cooked for herself, for another slave named George, and for me. George was very successful in bringing home his share of the plunder. He could capture a pig or a turkey without exciting the least suspicion. The old lady often rallied me for want of courage for such enterprises. At length, I summoned resolution, one rainy night, and determined there should be one from the herd of swine brought home by my hands. I went to the crib of corn, got my ear to shell, and my cart-stake to despatch a little roaster. I raised my arm to strike, summoned courage again and again, but to no purpose. The scattered kernels were all picked up, and no blow struck. Again I visited the crib, selected my victim, and *struck*! The blow glanced upon the side of the head, and, instead of falling, he ran off, squealing louder than ever I heard a pig squeal before. I ran as fast, in an opposite direction, made a large circuit, and reached the cabin, emptied the hot water, and made for my couch as soon as possible. I escaped detection, and only suffered from the ridicule of old Peggy and young George.

Poor Jess, upon the same plantation, did not so easily escape. More successful in his effort, he killed his pig; but he was found out. He was hung up by the hands, with a rail between his feet, and full three hundred lashes scored in upon his naked back. For a long time his life hung in doubt; and his poor wife, for becoming a partaker after the fact, was most severely beaten.

Another slave, employed as a driver upon the plantation, was compelled to whip his own wife, for a similar offence, so severely that she never recovered from the cruelty. She was literally *whipped to death by her own husband.*

A slave, called Hall, the hostler[17] on the plantation, made a successful sally, one night, upon the animals forbidden to the Jews.[18] The next day, he went into the barn-loft, and fell asleep. While sleeping over his abundant supper, and dreaming, perhaps, of his feast, he heard the shrill voice of his master, crying out, "The hogs are at the horse-trough; where is Hall?" The "hogs" and "Hall," coupled together, were enough for the poor fellow. He sprung from the hay, and made the best of his way off the plantation. He was gone six months; and, at the end of this period, he procured the intercession of the son-in-law of his master, and returned, escaping the ordinary punishment. But the transgression was laid up. Slaveholders seldom *forgive*; they only *postpone* the time of revenge. When about to be severely flogged, for some pretended offence, he took two of his grandsons, and escaped as far towards Canada as Indiana. He was followed, captured, brought back, and whipped most horribly. All the old score had been treasured up against him, and his poor back atoned for the whole at once.

On this plantation was a slave, named Sam, whose wife lived a few miles distant; and Sam was very seldom permitted to go and see his family. He worked in the blacksmith's shop. For a small offence, he was hung up by the hands, a rail between his feet, and whipped in turn by the master, overseer, and one of the waiters, till his back was torn all to pieces; and, in less than two months, Sam was in his grave. His last words were, "Mother, tell master he has killed me at last, for nothing; but tell him if God will forgive him I will."

A very poor white woman lived within about a mile of the plantation house. A female slave, named Flora, knowing she was in a very suffering condition, shelled out a peck of corn, and carried it to her in the night. Next day, the old man found it out, and this deed of charity was atoned for by one hundred and fifty lashes upon the bare back of poor Flora.

The master with whom I now lived was a very passionate man. At one time he thought the work on the plantation did not go on as it ought. One morning, when he and the overseer waked up from a drunken frolic, they swore the hands should not eat a morsel of any thing, till a field of wheat of some sixty acres was all cradled. There were from thirty to forty hands to do the work. We were driven on to the extent of our strength, and, although a brook ran through the field, not one of us was permitted to stop and taste a drop of water. Some of the men were so exhausted that they reeled for very weakness; two of the women fainted, and one of them was severely whipped, to revive her. They were at last carried helpless from the field and thrown down under the shade of a tree. At about five o'clock in the afternoon the wheat was all cut, and we were permitted to eat. Our suffering for want of water was excruciating. I trembled all over from the inward gnawing of hunger and from burning thirst.

In view of the sufferings of this day, we felt fully justified in making a foraging expedition upon the milk-room that night. And when master, and overseer, and all hands were locked up in sleep, ten or twelve of us went down to the spring house; a house built over a spring, to keep the milk and other things cool. We pressed altogether against the door, and open it came. We found half of a good baked pig, plenty of cream, milk, and other delicacies; and, as we felt in some measure delegated to represent all that had been cheated of their meals the day before, we ate plentifully. But after a successful plundering expedition within the gates of the enemy's camp, it is not easy always to cover the retreat. We had a *reserve* in the pasture for this purpose. We went up to the herd of swine, and, with a milk-pail in hand, it was easy to persuade them there was more where that came from, and the whole tribe followed readily into the spring house, and we left them there to wash the dishes and wipe up the floor, while we retired to rest. This was not malice in us; we did not love the waste which the hogs made; but we must have something to eat, to pay for the cruel and reluctant fast; and when we had obtained this, we must of course cover up our track. They watch us narrowly; and to take an egg, a pound of meat, or any thing else, however hungry we may be, is considered a great crime; we are compelled, therefore, to waste a good deal sometimes, to get a little.

I lived with this Mr. K. about four or five years; I then fell into the hands of his son. He was a drinking, ignorant man, but not so cruel as his father. Of him I hired my time at $12 a month; boarded and clothed myself. To meet my payments, I split rails, burned coal, peddled grass seed, and took hold of whatever I could find to do. This last master, or owner, as he would call himself, died about one year before I left Kentucky. By the administrators I was hired out for a time, and at last put up upon the auction block, for sale. No *bid* could be obtained for me. There were two reasons in the way. One was, there were two or three old mortgages which were not settled, and the second reason given by the bidders was, I had had too many privileges; had been permitted to trade for myself and go over the state; in short, to use their phrase, I was a "spoilt nigger." And sure enough I was, for all their purposes. I had long thought and dreamed of LIBERTY; I was now determined to make an effort, to gain it. No tongue can tell the doubt, the perplexities, the anxiety which a slave feels, when making up his mind upon this subject. If he makes an effort, and is not successful, he must be laughed at by his fellows; he will be beaten unmercifully by the master, and then watched and used the harder for it all his life.

And then, if he gets away, *who, what* will he find? He is ignorant of the world. All the white part of mankind, that he has ever seen, are enemies to him and all his kindred. How can he venture where none but white faces shall greet him? The master tells him, that abolitionists *decoy* slaves off into the free states, to catch them and sell them to Louisiana or Mississippi; and if he goes to Canada, the British will put him in a *mine under ground, with both eyes put out, for life.* How does he know what, or whom, to believe? A horror of great darkness comes upon him, as he thinks over what may befall him. Long, very long time did I think of escaping before I made the effort.

At length, the report was started that I was to be sold for Louisiana. Then I thought it was time to act. My mind was made up. This was about two weeks before I started. The first plan was formed between a slave named Isaac and myself. Isaac proposed to take one of the horses of his mistress, and I was to take my pony, and we were to ride off together; I as master, and he as slave. We started together, and went on five miles. My want of confidence in the plan induced me to turn back. Poor Isaac plead like a good fellow to go forward. I am satisfied from experience and observation that both of us must have been captured and carried back. I did not know enough at that time to travel and manage a waiter. Every thing would have been done in such an awkward manner that a keen eye would have seen through our plot at once. I did not know the roads, and could not have read the guide-boards; and ignorant as many people are in Kentucky, they would have thought it strange to see a man with a waiter, who could not read a guide-board. I was sorry to leave Isaac, but I am satisfied I could have done him no good in the way proposed.

After this failure, I staid about two weeks; and after having arranged every thing to the best of my knowledge, I saddled my pony, went into the cellar where I kept my grass-seed apparatus, put my clothes into a pair of saddle-bags, and them into my seed-bag, and, thus equipped, set sail for the north star. O what a day was that to me! This was on Saturday, in August, 1841. I wore my common clothes, and was very careful to avoid special suspicion, as I already imagined the administrator was very watchful of me. The place from which I started was about fifty miles from Lexington. The reason why I do not give the *name* of the place, and a more accurate location, must be obvious to any one who remembers that, in the eye of the law, I am yet accounted a slave, and no spot in the United States affords an asylum for the wanderer. True, I feel protected in the hearts of the many warm friends of the slave by whom I am surrounded; but this protection does not come from the LAWS of any one of the United States.

But to return. After riding about fifteen miles, a Baptist minister overtook me on the road, saying, "How do you do, boy? are you free? I always thought you were free, till I saw them try to sell you the other day." I then wished him a thousand miles off, preaching, if he would, to the whole plantation, "Servants, obey your masters;"[19] but I wanted neither sermons, questions, nor advice from him. At length I mustered resolution to make some kind of a reply. "What made you think I was free?" He replied, that he had noticed I had great privileges, that I did much as I liked, and that I was almost white. "O yes," I said, "but there are a great many slaves as white as I am." "Yes," he said, and then went on to name several; among others, one who had lately, as he said, run away. This was touching altogether too near upon what I was thinking of. Now, said I, he must know, or at least reckons, what I am at—*running away*.

However, I blushed as little as possible, and made strange of the fellow who had lately run away, as though I knew nothing of it. The old fellow looked at me, as it seemed to me, as though he would read my thoughts. I wondered what in the world *slaves could* run away for, especially if they had such a chance as I had had for the last few years. He said, "I suppose you would not run away on any account, you are so well treated." "O," said I, "I do very well, very well, sir. If you should ever hear that I had run away, be certain it must be because there is some great change in my treatment."

He then began to talk with me about the seed in my *bag*, and said that he should want to buy some. Then, I thought, he means to get at the truth by looking in my *seed bag*, where, sure enough, he would not find *grass* seed, but the seeds of Liberty. However, he dodged off soon, and left me alone. And although I have heard say, poor company is better than none, I felt much better without him than with him.

When I had gone on about twenty-five miles, I went down into a deep valley by the side of the road, and changed my clothes. I reached Lexington about seven o'clock that evening, and put up with brother Cyrus. As I had often been to Lexington before, and stopped with him, it excited no attention from the slaveholding gentry. Moreover, I had a pass from the administrator, of whom I had hired my time. I remained over the Sabbath with Cyrus, and we talked over a great many plans for future operations, if my efforts to escape should be successful. Indeed, we talked over all sorts of ways for me to proceed. But both of us were very ignorant of the roads, and of the best way to escape suspicion. And I sometimes wonder that a slave, so ignorant, so timid, as he is, *ever* makes the attempt to get his freedom. *"Without* are *foes, within* are *fears."*[20]

Monday morning, bright and early, I set my face in good earnest toward the Ohio River, determined to see and tread the north bank of it, or *die* in the attempt. I said to myself, One of two things,—FREEDOM OR DEATH![21] The first night I reached Mayslick, fifty odd miles from Lexington. Just before reaching this village, I stopped to think over my situation, and determine how I would pass that night. On that night hung all my hopes. I was within twenty miles of Ohio. My horse was unable to reach the river that night. And besides, to travel and attempt to cross the river in the night, would excite suspicion. I must spend the night *there*. But *how*? At one time, I thought, I will take my pony out into the field and give him some corn, and sleep myself on the grass. But then the *dogs* will be out in the evening, and, if caught under such circumstances, they will take me for a *thief* if not for a runaway. That will not do. So, after weighing the matter all over, I made a plunge right into the heart of the village, and put up at the tavern.

After seeing my pony disposed of, I looked into the bar-room, and saw some persons that I thought were from my part of the country, and would know me. I shrunk back with horror. What to do I did not know. I looked across the street, and saw the shop of a silversmith. A thought of a pair of spectacles, to hide my face, struck me. I went across the way, and began to barter for a pair of double-eyed green spectacles. When I got them on, they blind-folded *me*, if they did not others. Every thing seemed right up in my eyes. Some people buy spectacles to see out of; I bought mine to keep from being seen. I hobbled back to the tavern, and called for supper. This I did to avoid notice, for I felt like any thing but eating. At tea, I had not learned to measure distances with my new eyes, and the first pass I made with my knife and fork at my plate went right into my lap. This confused me still more, and, after drinking one cup of tea, I left the table, and got off to bed as soon as possible. But not a wink of sleep that night. All was confusion, dreams, anxiety, and trembling.

As soon as day dawned, I called for my horse, paid my reckoning, and was on my way, rejoicing that *that* night was gone, any how. I made all diligence on my way, and was across the Ohio, and in Aberdeen by noon, that day!

What my feelings were, when I reached the free shore, can be better imagined than described. I trembled all over with deep emotion, and I could feel my hair rise up on my head. I was on what was called a *free* soil, among a people who had no slaves. I saw white men at work, and no slave smarting beneath the lash. Every thing was indeed *new* and wonderful. Not knowing where to find a friend, and being ignorant of the country–unwilling to inquire, lest I should betray my ignorance, it was a whole week before I reached Cincinnati. At one place, where I put up, I had a great many more questions put to me than I wished to answer. At another place, I was very much annoyed by the officiousness of the landlord, who made it a point to supply every guest with newspapers. I took the copy handed me, and turned it over, in a somewhat awkward manner, I suppose. He came to me to point out a veto, or some other very important news. I thought it best to decline his assistance, and gave up the paper, saying my eyes were not in a fit condition to read much.

At another place, the neighbors, on learning that a Kentuckian was at the tavern, came, in great earnestness, to find out what my business was. Kentuckians sometimes came there to kidnap their citizens. They were in the habit of watching them close. I at length satisfied them, by assuring them that I was not, nor my father before me, any slaveholder at all; but, lest their suspicions should be excited in another direction, I added, my grandfather was a slaveholder.

At Cincinnati, I found some old acquaintances, and spent several days. In passing through some of the streets, I several times saw a great slave-dealer from Kentucky, who knew me, and, when I approached him, I was very careful to give him a wide berth. The only advice that I here received was from a man who had once been a slave. He urged me to sell my pony, go up the river, to Portsmouth, then take the canal for Cleveland, and cross over to Canada. I acted upon this suggestion, sold my horse for a small sum, as he was pretty well used up, took passage for Portsmouth, and soon found myself on the canal-boat, headed for Cleveland. On the boat, I became acquainted with a Mr. Conoly, from New York. He was very sick with fever and ague,[22] and, as he was a stranger, and alone, I took the best possible care of him, for a time. One day, in conversation with him, he spoke of the slaves, in the most harsh and bitter language, and was especially severe on those who *attempted to run away*. Thinks I, you are not the man for me to have much to do with. I found the *spirit* of slaveholding was not all south of the Ohio River.

No sooner had I reached Cleveland, than a trouble came upon me from a very unexpected quarter. A rough, swearing, reckless creature, in the shape of a man, came up to me, and declared I had passed a bad five dollar bill upon his wife, in the boat, and he demanded the silver for it. I had never seen him, nor his wife, before. He pursued me into the tavern, swearing and threatening all the way. The travellers, that had just arrived at the tavern, were asked to give their names to the clerk, that he might enter them upon the book. He called on me for my name, just as this ruffian was in the midst of his assault upon me. On leaving Kentucky, I thought it best, for my own security, to take a new name, and I had been entered on the boat as Archibald Campbell. I knew, with such a charge as this man was making against me, it would not do to change my name from the boat to the hotel. At the moment, I could not recollect what I had called myself, and, for a few minutes, I was in a complete puzzle. The clerk kept calling, and I made believe deaf, till, at length, the name popped back again, and I was duly enrolled a guest at the tavern, in Cleveland. I had heard, before, of persons being frightened out of their *Christian* names, but I was fairly scared out of both mine for a while. The landlord soon protected me from the violence of the bad-meaning man, and drove him away from the house.

I was detained at Cleveland several days, not knowing how to get across the lake, into Canada. I went out to the shore of the lake again and again, to try and see the other side, but I could see no hill, mountain, nor city of the asylum I sought. I was afraid to inquire *where* it was, lest it would betray such a degree of ignorance as to excite suspicion at once. One day, I heard a man ask another, employed on board a vessel, "and where does this vessel trade?" Well, I thought, if that is a proper question for you, it is for me. So I passed along, and asked of every vessel, "Where does this vessel trade?" At last, the answer came, "over here in Kettle Creek, near Port Stanley." And where is that? said I. "O, right over here, in *Canada*." That was the sound for me; "over here in Canada." The captain asked me if I wanted a passage to Canada. I thought it would not do to be too earnest about it, lest it would betray me. I told him I some thought of going, if I could get a passage cheap. We soon came to terms on this point, and that evening we set sail. After proceeding only nine miles, the wind changed, and the captain returned to port again. This, I thought, was a very bad omen. However, I stuck by, and the next evening, at nine o'clock, we set sail once more, and at daylight we were in Canada.

When I stepped ashore here, I said sure enough, I AM FREE. Good heaven! what a sensation, when it first visits the bosom of a full-grown man; one *born* to bondage—one who had been taught, from early infancy, that this was his inevitable lot for life. Not till *then* did I dare to cherish, for a moment, the feeling that *one* of the limbs of my body was my own. The slaves often say, when cut in the hand or foot, "Plague on the old foot" or "the old hand; it is master's—let him take care of it. Nigger don't care, if he never get well." My hands, my feet, were now my own. But what to do with them, was the next question. A strange sky was over me, a new earth under me, strange voices all around; even the animals were such as I had never seen. A flock of prairie-hens and some black geese were altogether new to me. I was entirely alone; no human being, that I had ever seen before, where I could speak to him or he to me.

And could I make that country ever seem like *home?* Some people are very much afraid all the slaves will run up north, if they are ever free. But I can assure them that they will run *back* again, if they do. If I could have been assured of my freedom in Kentucky, then, I would have given any thing in the world for the prospect of spending my life among my old acquaintances, where I first saw the sky, and the sun rise and go down. It was a long time before I could make the sun work right at all. It would rise in the wrong place, and go down wrong; and, finally, it behaved so bad, I thought it could not be the same sun.

There was a little something added to this feeling of strangeness. I could not forget all the horrid stories slaveholders tell about Canada. They assure the slave that, when they get hold of slaves in Canada, they make various uses of them. Sometimes they *skin* the *head*, and wear the wool on their coat collars—put them into the lead-mines, with both eyes out—the young slaves they eat; and as for the red coats, they are sure death to the slave. However ridiculous to a well-informed person such stories may appear, they work powerfully upon the excited imagination of an ignorant slave. With these stories all fresh in mind, when I arrived at St. Thomas, I kept a bright look-out for the red coats.[23] As I was turning the corner of one of the streets, sure enough, there stood before me a *red coat*, in full uniform, with his tall bear-skin cap, a foot and a half high, his gun shouldered, and he standing as erect as a guide-post. Sure enough, that is the fellow that they tell about catching the slave. I turned on my heel, and sought another street. On turning another corner, the *same* soldier, as I thought, faced me, with his black cap and stern look. Sure enough, my time has come now. I was as near scared to death, then, as a man can be and breathe. I could not have felt any worse if he had shot me right through the heart. I made off again, as soon as I dared to move. I inquired for a tavern. When I came up to it, there was a great brazen lion sleeping over the door, and, although I knew it was not alive, I had been so well frightened that I was almost afraid to go in. Hunger drove me to it at last, and I asked for something to eat.

On my way to St. Thomas I was also badly frightened. A man asked me who I was. I was afraid to tell him a runaway slave, lest he should have me to the mines. I was afraid to say, "I am an American," lest he should shoot me, for I knew there had been trouble between the British and Americans. I inquired, at length, for the place where the greatest number of colored soldiers were. I was told there were a great many at New London; so for New London I started. I got a ride, with some country people, to the latter place. They asked me who I was, and I told them from Kentucky; and they, in a familiar way, called me "Old Kentuck." I saw some soldiers, on the way, and asked the men what they had soldiers for. They said they were kept "to get *drunk* and be *whipped*;" that was the chief use they made of them. At last, I reached New London, and here I found soldiers in great numbers. I attended at their parade, and saw the guard driving the people back; but it required no guard to keep me off. I thought, "If you will let me alone, I will not trouble you." I was as much afraid of a red coat as I would have been of a bear. Here I asked again for the colored soldiers. The answer was, "Out at Chatham, about seventy miles distant." I started for Chatham. The first night, I stopped at a place called the Indian Settlement. The door was barred, at the house where I was, which I did not like so well, as I was yet somewhat afraid of their Canadian tricks. Just before I got to Chatham, I met two colored soldiers, with a white man, bound, and driving him along before them. This was something quite new. I thought, then, sure enough, this is the land for me. I had seen a great many colored people bound, and in the hands of the whites, but this was changing things right about. This removed all my suspicions, and, ever after, I felt quite easy in Canada. I made diligent inquiry for several slaves, that I had known in Kentucky, and at length found one, named Henry. He told me of several others, with whom I had been acquainted, and from him, also, I received the first correct information about brother Milton. I knew that he had left Kentucky about a year before I did, and I supposed, until now, that he was in Canada. Henry told me he was at Oberlin, Ohio.

At Chatham, I hired myself for a while, to recruit my purse a little, as it had become pretty well drained by this time. I had only about sixty-four dollars, when I left Kentucky, and I had been living upon it now for about six weeks. Mr. Everett, with whom I worked, treated me kindly, and urged me to stay in Canada, offering me business on his farm. He declared "there was no 'free state' in America; all were *slave* states, bound to slavery, and the slave could have no asylum in any of them." There is certainly a great deal of truth in this remark. I have *felt*, wherever I may be in the United States, the kidnappers may be upon me at any moment. If I should creep up to the top of the monument on Bunker's Hill, beneath which my father fought, I should not be safe, even there. The slave-mongers have a right, by the laws of the United States, to seek me, even upon the top of the monument, whose base rests upon the bones of those who fought for freedom.

I soon after made my way to Sandwich, and crossed over to Detroit, on my way to Ohio, to see Milton. While in Canada, I swapped away my pistol, as I thought I should not need it, for an old watch. When I arrived at Detroit, I found my watch was gone. I put my baggage, with nearly every cent of money I had, on board the boat for Cleveland, and went back to Sandwich to search for the old watch. The ferry here was about three-fourths of a mile, and, in my zeal for the old watch, I wandered so far that I did not get back in season for the boat, and had the satisfaction of hearing her *last* bell just as I was about to leave the Canada shore. When I got back to Detroit I was in a fine fix; my money and my clothes gone, and I left to wander about in the streets of Detroit. A man may be a man for all clothes or money, but he don't feel quite so well, any how. What to do now I could hardly tell. It was about the first of November. I wandered about and picked up something very cheap for supper, and paid nine-pence for lodging. All the next day no boat for Cleveland. Long days and nights to me. At length another boat was up for Cleveland. I went to the Captain, to tell him my story; he was very cross and savage; said a man had no business from home without money; that so many told stories about losing money that he did not know what to believe. He finally asked me how much money I had. I told him sixty-two and a half cents. Well, he said, give me that, and pay the balance when you get there. I gave him every cent I had. We were a day and a night on the passage, and I had nothing to eat except some cold potatoes, which I picked from a barrel of fragments, and cold victuals. I went to the steward, or cook, and asked for something to eat, but he told me his orders were strict to give away nothing, and, if he should do it, he would lose his place at once.

When the boat came to Cleveland it was in the night, and I thought I would spend the balance of the night in the boat. The steward soon came along, and asked if I did not know that the boat had landed, and the passengers had gone ashore. I told him I knew it, but I had paid the captain all the money I had, and could get no shelter for the night unless I remained in the boat. He was very harsh and unfeeling, and drove me ashore, although it was very cold, and snow on the ground. I walked around a while, till I saw a light in a small house of entertainment. I called for lodging. In the morning, the Frenchman, who kept it, wanted to know if I would have breakfast. I told him, no. He said then I might pay for my lodging. I told him I would do so before I left, and that my outside coat might hang there till I paid him.

I was obliged at once to start on an expedition for raising *some cash.* My resources were not very numerous. I took a *hair* brush, that I had paid three York shillings for a short time before, and sallied out to make a sale. But the wants of every person I met seemed to be in the same direction with my own; they wanted *money* more than hair brushes. At last, I found a customer who paid me ninepence *cash,* and a small balance in the shape of something to eat for breakfast. I was started square for that day, and delivered out of my present distress. But hunger will return, and all the quicker when a man don't know how to satisfy it when it does come. I went to a plain boarding-house, and told the man just my situation; that I was waiting for the boat to return from Buffalo, hoping to get my baggage and money. He said he would board me two or three days and risk it. I tried to get work, but no one seemed inclined to employ me. At last, I gave up in despair, about my luggage, and concluded to start as soon as possible for Oberlin. I sold my great-coat for two dollars, paid one for my board, and with the other I was going to pay my fare to Oberlin. That night, after I had made all my arrangements to leave in the morning, the boat came. On hearing the bell of a steam-boat, in the night, I jumped up and went to the wharf, and found my baggage; paid a quarter of a dollar for the long journey it had been carried, and glad enough to get it again at that.

The next morning, I took the stage for Oberlin; found several abolitionists from that place in the coach. They mentioned a slave named Milton Clarke, who was living there, that he had a brother in Canada, and that he expected him there soon. They spoke in a very friendly manner of Milton, and of the slaves; so, after we had a long conversation, and I perceived they were all friendly, I made myself known to them. To be thus surrounded at once with friends, in a land of strangers, was something quite new to me. The impression made by the kindness of these strangers upon my heart, will never be effaced. I thought, there must be some new principle at work here, such as I had not seen much of in Kentucky. That evening I arrived at Oberlin, and found Milton boarding at a Mrs. Cole's. Finding here so many friends, my first impression was that all the abolitionists in the country must live right there together. When Milton spoke of going to Massachusetts, "No," said I, "we better stay here where the *abolitionists* live." And when they assured me that the friends of the slave were more numerous in Massachusetts than in Ohio, I was greatly surprised.

Milton and I had not seen each other for a year; during that time we had passed through the greatest change in outward condition, that can befall a man in this world. How glad we were to greet each other in what we then *thought* a *free* State may be easily imagined. We little dreamed of the dangers sleeping around us. Brother Milton had not encountered so much danger in getting away as I had. But his time for suffering was soon to come. For several years before his escape, Milton had hired his time of his master, and had been employed as a steward in different steamboats upon the river. He had paid as high as two hundred dollars a year for his time. From his master he had a written pass, permitting him to go up and down the Mississippi and Ohio rivers when he pleased. He found it easy, therefore, to land on the north side of the Ohio river, and concluded to take his own time for returning. He had caused a letter to be written to Mr. L., his pretended owner, telling him to give himself no anxiety on his account; that he had found by experience he had wit enough to take care of himself, and he thought the care of his master was not worth the two hundred dollars a year which he had been paying for it, for four years; that, on the whole, if his master would be quiet and contented, he thought he should do very well. This letter, the escape of two persons belonging to the same family, and from the same region, in one year, waked up the fears and the *spite* of the slaveholders. However, they let us have a little respite, and, through the following winter and spring, we were employed in various kinds of work at Oberlin and in the neighborhood.

All this time I was deliberating upon a plan by which to go down and rescue Cyrus, our youngest brother, from bondage. In July, 1842, I gathered what little money I had saved, which was not a large sum, and started for Kentucky again. As near as I remember, I had about twenty dollars. I did not tell my plan to but one or two at Oberlin, because there were many slaves there, and I did not know but that it might get to Kentucky in some way through them sooner than I should. On my way down through Ohio, I advised with several well known friends of the slave. Most of them pointed out the dangers I should encounter, and urged me not to go. One young man told me to go, and the God of heaven would prosper me. I knew it was dangerous, but I did not then dream of all that I must suffer in body and mind before I was through with it. It is not a very comfortable feeling, to be creeping round day and night, for nearly two weeks together, in a den of lions, where, if one of them happens to put his paw on you, it is certain death, or something much worse.

At Ripley, I met a man who had lived in Kentucky; he encouraged me to go forward, and directed me about the roads. He told me to keep on a back route not much travelled, and I should not be likely to be molested. I crossed the river at Ripley, and when I reached the other side, and was again upon the soil on which I had suffered so much, I *trembled, shuddered*, at the thoughts of what might happen to me. My fears, my feelings, overcame for the moment all my resolution, and I was for a time completely overcome with emotion. Tears flowed like a brook of water. I had just left kind friends; I was now where every man I met would be my enemy. It was a long time before I could summon courage sufficient to proceed. I had with me a rude map, made by the Kentuckian whom I saw at Ripley. After examining this as well as I could, I proceeded. In the afternoon of the first day, as I was sitting in a stream to bathe and cool my feet, a man rode up on horseback, and entered into a long conversation with me. He asked me some questions about my travelling, but none but what I could easily answer. He pointed out to me a house where a white woman lived, who, he said, had recently suffered terribly from a fright. Eight slaves, that were running away, called for something to eat, and the poor woman was sorely scared by them. For his part, the man said, he hoped they never would find the slaves again. Slavery was the curse of Kentucky. He had been brought up to work, and he liked to work, but slavery made it disgraceful for any white man to work. From this conversation I was almost a good mind to trust this man, and tell him my story; but, on second thought, I concluded it might be just as *safe* not to do it. A hundred or two dollars for returning a slave, for a poor man, is a heavy temptation. At night, I stopped at the house of a widow woman, not a tavern, exactly; but they often entertained people there. The next day, when I got as far as Cynthiana, within about twenty miles of Lexington, I was sore all over, and lame, from having walked so far. I tried to hire a horse and carriage, to help me a few miles. At last, I agreed with a man to send me forward to a certain place, which he said was twelve miles, and for which I paid him, in advance, three dollars. It proved to be only seven miles. This was now Sabbath day, as I had selected that as the most suitable day for making my entrance into Lexington. There is much more passing in and out on that day, and I thought I should be much less observed than on any other day.

When I approached the city, and met troops of idlers, on foot and on horseback, sauntering out of the city, I was very careful to keep my umbrella before my face, as people passed, and kept my eyes right before me. There were many persons in the place who had known me, and I did not care to be recognized by any of them. Just before entering the city, I turned off to the field, and lay down under a tree and waited for night. When its curtains were fairly over me, I started up, took two pocket handkerchiefs, tied one over my forehead, the other under my chin, and marched forward for the city. It was not then so dark as I wished it was. I met a young slave, driving cows. He was quite disposed to condole with me, and said, in a very sympathetic manner, "Massa sick?" "Yes, boy," I said, "Massa sick; drive along your cows." The next colored man I met, I knew him in a moment, but he did not recognize me. I made for the wash-house of the man with whom Cyrus lived. I reached it without attracting any notice, and found there an old slave, as true as steel. I inquired for Cyrus; he said he was at home. He very soon recollected me; and, while the boy was gone to call Cyrus, he uttered a great many exclamations of wonder, to think I should return.

"Good Heaven, boy! what you back here for? What on arth you here for, my son? O, I scared for you! They kill you, just as sure as I alive, if they catch you! Why, in the name of liberty, didn't you stay away, when you gone so slick? Sartin, I never did 'spect to see you again!" I said, "Don't be scared." But he kept repeating, "I scared for you! I scared for you!" When I told him my errand, his wonder was somewhat abated; but still his exclamations were repeated all the evening, "What brought you back here?" In a few minutes, Cyrus made his appearance, filled with little less of wonder than the old man had manifested. I had intended, when I left him, about a year before, that I would return for him, if I was successful in my effort for freedom. He was very glad to see me, and entered, with great animation, upon the plan for his own escape. He had a wife, who was a free woman, and consequently he had a home. He soon went out, and left me in the wash-room with the old man. He went home to apprize his wife, and to prepare a room for my concealment. His wife is a very active, industrious woman, and they were enabled to rent a very comfortable house, and, at this time, had a spare room in the attic, where I could be thoroughly concealed.

He soon returned, and said every thing was ready. I went home with him, and, before ten o'clock at night, I was stowed away in a little room, that was to be my prison-house for about a week. It was a comfortable room; still the confinement was close, and I was unable to take exercise, lest the people in the other part of the house should hear. I got out, and walked around a little, in the evening, but suffered a good deal, for want of more room to live and move in. During the day, Cyrus was busy making arrangements for his departure. He had several little sums of money, in the hands of the foreman of the tan-yard, and in other hands. Now, it would not do to go right boldly up and demand his pay of every one that owed him; this would lead to suspicion at once. So he contrived various ways to get in his little debts. He had seen the foreman, one day, counting out some singular coin of some foreign nation. He pretended to take a great liking to that foreign money, and told the man, if he would pay him what was due him in *that* money, he would give him two or three dollars. From another person he took an order on a store; and so, in various ways, he got in his little debts as well as he could. At night, we contrived to plan the ways and means of escaping. Cyrus had never been much accustomed to walking, and he dreaded, very much, to undertake such a journey. He proposed to take a couple of horses, as he thought he had richly earned them, over and above all he had received. I objected to this, because, if we were caught, either in Kentucky or out of it, they would bring against us the charge of stealing, and this would be far worse than the charge of running away.

I firmly insisted, therefore, that we must go on foot. In the course of a week, Cyrus had gathered something like twenty dollars, and we were ready for our journey. A family lived in the same house with Cyrus, in a room below. How to get out, in the early part of the evening, and not be discovered, was not an easy question. Finally, we agreed that Cyrus should go down and get into conversation with them, while I slipped out with his bundle of clothes, and repaired to a certain street, where he was to meet me.

As I passed silently out at the door, Cyrus was cracking his best jokes, and raising a general laugh, which completely covered my retreat. Cyrus soon took quiet and unexpected leave of his friends in that family, and leave, also, of his wife above, for a short time only. At a little past eight of the clock we were beyond the bounds of the city. His wife did all she could to assist him in his effort to gain his inalienable rights. She did not dare, however, to let the slaveholders know that she knew any thing of his attempt to run away. He had told the slaves that he was going to see his sister, about twelve miles off. It was Saturday night, when we left Lexington. On entering the town, when I went in, I was so intent upon covering up my face, that I took but little notice of the roads. We were very soon exceedingly perplexed to know what road to take. The moon favored us, for it was a clear, beautiful night. On we came, but, at the cross of the roads, what to do we did not know. At length, I climbed one of the guide-posts, and *spelled* out the names as well as I could. We were on the road to freedom's boundary, and, with a strong step, we measured off the path: but again the cross roads perplexed us. This time, we took hold of the sign-post and lifted it out of the ground, and turned it upon one of its horns, and spelled out the way again. As we started from this goal, I told Cyrus we had not put up the sign-post. He pulled forward, and said he guessed we would do that when we came back. Whether the sign-board is up or down, we have never been there to see.

Soon after leaving the city, we met a great many of the patrols; but they did not arrest us, and we had no disposition to trouble them.

While we were pressing on, by moonlight, and sometimes in great doubt about the road, Cyrus was a good deal discouraged. He thought, if we got upon the wrong road, it would be almost certain death for us, or something worse. In the morning, we found that, on account of our embarrassment in regard to the roads, we had only made a progress of some twenty or twenty-five miles. But we were greatly cheered to find they were so many miles in the right direction. Then we put the best foot forward, and urged our way as fast as possible. In the afternoon it rained very hard; the roads were muddy and slippery. We had slept none the night before, and had been, of course, very much excited. In this state of mind and of body, just before dark, we stopped in a little patch of bushes, to discuss the expediency of going to a house, which we saw at a distance, to spend the night.

As we sat there, Cyrus became very much excited, and, pointing across the road, exclaimed, "Don't you see that animal there?" I looked, but saw nothing; still he affirmed that he saw a dreadful ugly animal looking at us, and ready to make a spring. He began to feel for his pistols, but I told him not to fire there; but he persisted in pointing to the animal, although I am persuaded he saw nothing, only by the force of his imagination. I had some doubts about telling this story, lest people would not believe me; but a friend has suggested to me that such things are not uncommon, when the imagination is strongly excited.

In travelling through the rain and mud, this afternoon, we suffered beyond all power of description. Sometimes we found ourselves just ready to stand, fast asleep, in the middle of the road. Our feet were blistered all over. When Cyrus would get almost discouraged, I urged him on, saying we were walking for *freedom now.* "Yes," he would say, "freedom is good, Lewis, but this is a *hard, h-a-r-d* way to get it." This he would say, half asleep. We were so weak, before night, that we several times fell upon our knees in the road. We had crackers with us, but we had no appetite to eat. *Fears* were behind us; *hope* before; and we were driven and drawn as hard as ever men were. Our limbs and joints were so stiff that, if we took a step to the right hand or left, it seemed as though it would shake us to pieces. It was a dark, weary day to us both.

At length, I succeeded in getting the consent of Cyrus to go to a house for the night. We found a plain farmer's family. The good man was all taken up in talking about the camp-meeting held that day, about three miles from his house. He only asked us where we were from, and we told him our home was in Ohio. He said the young men had behaved unaccountably bad at the camp-meeting, and they had but little comfort of it. They mocked the preachers, and disturbed the meeting badly.

We escaped suspicion more readily, as I have no doubt, from the supposition, on the part of many, that we were going to the camp-meeting. Next morning, we called at the meeting, as it was on our way, bought up a little extra gingerbread against the time of need, and marched forward for the Ohio. When any one inquired why we left the meeting so soon, we had an answer ready: "The young men behave so bad, we can get no good of the meeting."

By this time we limped badly, and we were sore all over. A young lady whom we met, noticing that we walked lame, cried out, mocking us, "O my feet, my feet, how sore!" At about eleven o'clock, we reached the river, two miles below Ripley. The boatman was on the other side. We called for him. He asked us a few questions. This was a last point with us. We tried our best to appear unconcerned. I asked questions about the boats, as though I had been there before; went to Cyrus, and said, "Sir, I have no change; will you lend me enough to pay my toll? I will pay you before we part." When we were fairly landed upon the northern bank, and had gone a few steps, Cyrus stopped suddenly, on seeing the water gush out at the side of the hill. Said he, "Lewis, give me that tin cup." "What in the world do you want of a tin cup now? We have not time to stop." The cup he would have. Then he went up to the spring, dipped and drank, and dipped and drank; then he would look round, and drink again. "What in the world," said I, "are you fooling there for?" "O," said he, "this is the first time I ever had a chance to drink water that ran out of the *free* dirt." Then we went a little further, and he sat down on a log. I urged him forward. "O," said he, "I must sit on this free timber a little while."

A short distance further on, we saw a man, who seemed to watch us very closely. I asked him which was the best way to go, *over* the hill before us, or *around* it. I did this, to appear to know something about the location. He went off, without offering any obstacles to our journey. In going up the hill, Cyrus would stop, and lay down and roll over. "What in the world are you about, Cyrus? Don't you see Kentucky is over there?" He still continued to roll and kiss the ground; said it was a game horse that could roll clear over. Then he would put face to the ground, and roll over and over. "First time," he said, "he ever rolled on *free* grass."

After he had recovered a little from his sportive mood, we went up to the house of a good friend of the slave at Ripley. We were weary and worn enough; though ever since we left the river, it seemed as though Cyrus was young and spry as a colt; but when we got where we could *rest*, we found ourselves *tired*. The good lady showed us into a good bedroom. Cyrus was skittish. He would not go in and lie down. "I am afraid," said he, "of old mistress. She is too good–too good–can't be so–they want to catch us both." So, to pacify him, I had to go out into the orchard and rest there. When the young men came home, he soon got acquainted, and felt sure they were his friends. From this place we were sent on by the friends, from place to place, till we reached Oberlin, Ohio, in about five weeks after I left there to go for Cyrus. I had encountered a good deal of peril; had suffered much from anxiety of feeling; but felt richly repaid in seeing another brother free.

We stopped at Oberlin a few days, and then Cyrus started for Canada. He did not feel exactly safe. When he reached the lake, he met a man from Lexington who knew him perfectly; indeed, the very man of whom his wife hired her house. This man asked him if he was free. He told him yes, he was free, and he was hunting for brother Milton, to get him to go back and settle with the old man for his freedom. Putnam told him that was all right. He asked Cyrus if he should still want that house his wife lived in. "O, yes," said Cyrus, "we will notify you when we don't want it any more. You tell them, I shall be down there in a few days. I have heard of Milton, and expect to have him soon to carry back with me." Putnam went home, and, when he found what a fool Cyrus had made of him, he was vexed enough. "A rascal," he said, "I could have caught him as well as not."

Cyrus hastened over to Canada. He did not like that country so well as the states, and in a few weeks returned. He had already sent a letter to his wife, giving her an account of his successful escape, and urging her to join him as soon as possible. He had the pleasure of meeting his wife, and her three children by a former husband, and they have found a quiet resting-place, where, if the rumor of oppression reaches them, they do not feel its scourge, nor its chains. And there is no doubt entertained by any of his friends but he can take care of himself.

He begins already to appreciate his rights, and to maintain them as a freeman. The following paragraph concerning him was published in the Liberty Press about one year since:–

**"PROGRESS OF FREEDOM**

"*Scene at Hamilton Village, N.Y.*

"Mr. Cyrus Clarke, a brother of the well-known Milton and Lewis Clarke, (all of whom, till within a short time since, for some twenty-five years, were slaves in Kentucky,) mildly, but firmly, presented his ballot at the town meeting board. Be it known that said Cyrus, as well as his brothers, are *white*, with only a sprinkling of the African; just enough to make them bright, quick, and intelligent, and scarcely observable in the color except by the keen and scenting slaveholder. Mr. Clarke had all the necessary qualifications of white men to vote.

"*Slave.* Gentlemen, here is my ballot; I wish to vote. (Board and by-standers well knowing him, all were aghast–the waters were troubled–the slave legions were 'up in their might.')

"*Judge E.* You can't vote! Are you not, and have you not been a slave?

"*Slave.* I shall not *lie* to vote. I am and have been a slave, so called; but I wish to vote, and I believe it my right and duty.

"*Judge E.* Slaves can't vote.

"*Slave.* Will you just show me in your books, constitution, or whatever you call them, where it says a slave can't vote?

"*Judge E.* (Pretending to look over the law, &c., well knowing he was 'used up.') Well, well, you are a colored man, and can't vote without you are worth $250.

"*Slave.* I am as white as *you*; and don't *you vote?*

"(Mr. E. is well known to be very dark; indeed, as dark or darker than Clarke. The current began to set against Mr. E. by murmurs, sneers, laughs, and many other demonstrations of dislike.)

"*Judge E.* Are you not a *colored* man? and is not your hair curly?

"*Slave.* We are both colored men; and all we differ is, that you have not the handsome wavy curl; you raise *Goat's wool*, and I come, as you see, a little nearer *Saxony.*

"At this time the fire and fun was at its height, and was fast consuming the judge with public opprobrium.

"*Judge E.* I challenge this man's vote, he being a colored man, and not worth $250.

"Friends and foes warmly contested what constituted a colored man by the New York statute. The board finally came to the honorable conclusion that, to be a *colored* man, he must be at least one half blood African. Mr. Clarke, the SLAVE, then voted, he being nearly full white. I have the history of this transaction from Mr. Clarke, in person. In substance it is as told me, but varying more or less from his language used.

J. THOMPSON.

"PARIS, *March*, 12, 1844."

Martha, the wife of Cyrus, had a long story of the wrath of the slaveholders, because he ran away. Monday morning she went down, in great distress, to the overseer to inquire for her husband. She, of course, was in great anxiety about him. Mr. Logan threatened her severely, but she, having a little mixture of the Indian, Saxon, and African blood, was quite too keen for them. She succeeded in so far lulling their suspicions as to make her escape, and was very fortunate in her journey to her husband.

We remained but a short time after this in Ohio. I spent a few days in New York; found there a great many warm friends; and, in the autumn of 1843, I came to old Massachusetts. Since that time, I have been engaged a large part of the time in telling the story of what I have felt and seen of slavery.

I have generally found large audiences, and a great desire to hear about slavery. I have been in all the New England States except Connecticut; have held, I suppose, more than five hundred meetings in different places, sometimes two or three in a place. These meetings have been kindly noticed by many of the papers, of all parties and sects. Others have been very bitter and unjust in their remarks, and tried to throw every possible obstacle in my way. A large majority of ministers have been willing to give notice of my meetings, and many of them have attended them. I find that most ministers say they are abolitionists, but truth compels me to add, that, in talking with them, I find many are more zealous to apologize for the slaveholders, than they are to take any active measures to do away slavery.

Since coming to the free states, I have been struck with great surprise at the quiet and peaceable manner in which families live. I had no conception that *women* could live without quarrelling, till I came into the free states.

After I had been in Ohio a short time, and had not seen nor heard any scolding or quarrelling in the families where I was, I did not know how to account for it. I told Milton, one day, "What a faculty these women have of keeping all their bad feelings to themselves! I have not seen them quarrel with their husbands, nor with the girls, or children, since I have been here." "O," said Milton, "these women are not like our women in Kentucky; they don't fight at all." I told him I doubted that; "I guess they do it somewhere; in the kitchen, or down cellar. It can't be," said I, "that a woman can live, and not scold or quarrel." Milton laughed, and told me to watch them, and see if I could catch them at it. I have kept my eyes and ears open from that day to this, and I have not found the place where the women get mad and rave like they do in Kentucky yet. If they do it here, they are uncommon sly; but I have about concluded that they are altogether different here from what they are in the slave states. I reckon slavery must work upon their minds and dispositions, and make them ugly.

It has been a matter of great wonder to me, also, to see all the children, rich and poor, going to school. Every few miles I see a school-house, here; I did not know what it meant when I saw these houses, when I first came to Ohio. In Kentucky, if you should feed your horse only when you come to a school-house, he would starve to death.

I never had heard a church bell only at Lexington, in my life. When I saw steeples and meeting-houses so thick, it seemed like I had got into another world. Nothing seems more wonderful to me now, than the different way they keep the Sabbath there, and here. In the country, in summer, there the people gather in groups around the meeting-house, *built of logs*, or around in the groves where they often meet; one company, and perhaps the minister with them, are talking about the price of niggers, pork, and corn; another group are playing cards; others are swapping horses, or horse-racing; all in sight of the meeting-house or place of worship. After a while the minister tells them it is time to begin. They stop playing and talking for a while. If they call him right smart, they hear him out; if he is "no account," they turn to their cards and horses, and finish their devotion in this manner.

The slaveholders are continually telling how poor the white people are in the free states, and how much they suffer from poverty; no masters to look out for them. When, therefore, I came into Ohio, and found nearly every family living in more real comfort than almost any slaveholder, you may easily see I did not know what to make of it. I see how it is now; every man in the free states *works*; and as they work for themselves, they do twice as much as they would do for another.

In fact, my wonder at the contrast between the slave and the free states has not ceased yet. The more I see here, the more I *know* slavery curses the master as well as the slave. It curses the soil, the houses, the churches, the schools, the burying-grounds, the flocks, and the herds; it curses man and beast, male and female, old and young. It curses the child in the cradle, and heaps curses upon the old man as he lies in his grave. Let all the people, then, of the civilized world get up upon Mount Ebal,[24] and curse it with a long and bitter curse, and with a loud voice, till it withers and dies; till the year of jubilee dawns upon the south, till the sun of a FREE DAY sends a beam of light and joy into every cabin.

I wish here sincerely to recognize the hand of a kind Providence in leading me from that terrible house of bondage, for raising me up friends in a land of strangers, and for leading me, as I hope, to a saving knowledge of the truth as it is in Christ. A slave cannot be sure that he will always enjoy his religion in peace. Some of them are beaten for acts of devotion. I can never express to God all the gratitude which I owe him for the many favors I now enjoy. I try to live in love with all men. Nothing would delight me more than to take the worst slaveholder by the hand, even Mrs. Banton, and freely forgive her, if I thought she had repented of her sins. While she, or any other man or woman, is trampling down the image of God, and *abusing* the life out of the poor slave, I cannot believe they are Christians, or that they ought to be allowed the Christian name for one moment. I testify against them now, as having none of the spirit of Christ. There will be a cloud of swift witnesses against them at the day of judgment. The testimony of the slave will be heard then. He has no voice at the tribunals of earthly justice, but he will one day be heard; and then such revelations will be made, as will fully justify the opinion which I have been compelled to form of slaveholders. They are a SEED of *evil-doers–corrupt* are they–they have done abominable works.

## PREFACE

The Narrative of LEWIS CLARKE was published a year since; and a large edition–three thousand copies–was exhausted in less than a year. There is a call for more; and MILTON CLARKE has concluded to add a few of the incidents of his life, and a more particular account of the attempt to kidnap him in Ohio. I have no doubt, that, with the slight mistakes in regard to circumstances incident to things so long kept only in memory, the following Narrative, as well as that which precedes, may be relied on as true. It is not among the least interesting of the marks of progress in the cause of Freedom, that now, from Ohio, the assistant kidnappers of Jerry Phinney are calling loudly upon their principals in Kentucky to help them out of prison, where they suffer justly. This shows that neither Ohio, nor any other free state, can much longer be made the hunting-ground of the slaveholders.

J. C. L.
*May,* 1846.

## NARRATIVE OF MILTON CLARKE

When I was about six years of age, the estate of Samuel Campbell, my grandfather, was sold at auction. His sons and daughters were all present at the sale, except Mrs. Banton. Among the articles and animals put upon the

catalogue, and placed in the hands of the auctioneer, were a large number of slaves. When every thing else had been disposed of, the question arose among the heirs, "What shall be done with Letty (my mother) and her children?" John and William Campbell came to mother, and told her they would divide her family among the heirs, but none of them should go out of the family. One of the daughters–to her everlasting honor be it spoken–remonstrated against any such proceeding. Judith, the wife of Joseph Logan, told her brothers and sisters, "Letty is our own half sister, and you know it; father never intended they should be sold." Her protest was disregarded, and the auctioneer was ordered to proceed. My mother, and her infant son Cyrus, about one year old, were put up together and sold for $500!! Sisters and brothers selling their own sister and her children!! My venerable old father, who was now in extreme old age, and debilitated from the *wounds* received in the war of the Revolution, was, nevertheless, roused by this outrage upon his rights and upon those of his children.

"He had never expected," he said, "when fighting for the liberties of this country, to see his own wife and children sold in it to the highest bidder." But what were the entreaties of a quivering old man, in the sight of eight or ten hungry heirs? The bidding went on; and the whole family, consisting of mother and eight children, were sold at prices varying from $300 to $800. Lewis, the reader will recollect, had been previously given to that paragon of excellence, Mrs. Banton. It was my fortune, with my mother, brother Cyrus, and sister Delia, to fall into the hands of aunt Judith; and had she lived many years, or had her husband shared with her the virtues of humanity, I should probably have had far less to complain of, for myself and some of the family. She was the only one of all the family that I was ever willing to own, or call my aunt.

The third day after the sale, father, mother, Delia, Cyrus, and myself, started for our home at Lexington, with Mr. Joseph Logan, a tanner. He was a tall, lank, gray-eyed, hard-hearted, cruel wretch; coarse, vulgar, debauched, corrupt and corrupting; but in good and regular standing in the Episcopalian church. We were always protected, however, from any very great hardships during the life of his first wife.

At her death, which happened in about two years, we were sincere mourners; although her husband was probably indulging far other emotions than those of sorrow. He had already entered, to a considerable extent, into arrangements for marrying a younger sister of his wife, Miss Minerva Campbell. She was a half fool, besides being underwitted. If any body falls into such hands, they will know what Solomon meant, when he said, "Let a bear robbed of her whelps meet a man, rather than a *fool* in his folly."[25] There are a great many bears in Kentucky, but none of them quite equal to a slaveholding woman.

I had a regular battle with this young mistress, when I was about eleven years old. She had lived in the family while her sister was alive, and from the clemency of Judith, in protecting the slaves, the authority of Miss Minerva was in a very doubtful state when she came to be installed mistress of the house. Of course, every occasion was sought to show her authority. She attempted to give me a regular breaking-in, at the age above stated. I used the weapons of defence "God and nature gave me;" I bit and scratched, and well nigh won the battle; but she sent for Logan, whose shadow was more than six feet, and I had to join the *non-resistance* society right off. It was all day with me then. He dashed me down upon my head, took the raw hide and ploughed up my young back, and that grinning fool, his wife, was looking on; this was a great aggravation of the flogging, that she should see it and rejoice over it.

When I was about twelve years old, I was put to grinding bark in the tannery. Not understanding the business, I did not make such progress as Logan thought I ought to make. Many a severe beating was the consequence. At one time, the shoulder of the horse was very sore, and Logan complained that I did not take good care of him. I tried to defend myself as well as I could, but his final argument was thumping my head against the post. Kings have their *last* argument, and so have slaveholders. I took the old horse into the stable, and, as I had no one else to talk with, I held quite a dialogue with old Dobbin. Unluckily for me, Logan was hid in another stall, to hear his servant curse him. I told the horse, "Master complains that I don't grind bark enough; complains that I work you too hard; don't feed you enough; now, you old rascal, you know it is a lie, the whole of it; I have given you fifteen ears of corn three times a day, and that is enough for any horse; Cæsar says that is enough, and Moses says that is enough; now eat your corn, and grow fat." At the end of this apostrophe, I gave the old horse three good cuts on the face, and told him to walk up and eat the corn. I then stepped out into the floor and threw in fifteen ears more, and said, "See if the old man will think that is enough."

Scarcely had the words passed my lips, when I heard a rustling in the next stall, and Joe Logan was before me, taller than ever I saw him before, and savage as a cannibal. I made for the door, but he shut it upon me, and caught me by one leg. He began kicking and cuffing, till, in my despair, I seized him, like a young bear, by the leg, with my teeth, and, with all his tearing and wrenching, he could not get me off. He called one of the white hands from the tanyard, and just as he came in, Logan had his knife out, and was about to cut my throat. The man spoke, and told him not to do that. They tied me and gave me *three hundred lashes*; my back was peeled from my shoulders to my heels.

Mother was in the house, and heard my screams, but did not dare to come near me. Logan left me weltering in my blood; mother then came and took me up, and carried me into her own room. About 8 o'clock that evening, Logan came out and asked mother if I was alive or dead. She told him I was alive. I laid there four weeks, before I went out of the door. Let fathers and mothers think what it would be to see a child whipped to the very gate of death, and not be permitted to say a word in their behalf. Words can never tell what I suffered, nor what mother suffered. I shuddered at the countenance of Joseph Logan for many months after. The recollection now makes me shudder, as I go back to that bitter day.

Such a cruel wretch could not, of course, manage with much discretion a silly, but high-tempered wife. Their social intercourse was like the meeting of the sirocco and the earthquake. She would scorch terribly with her provoking tongue; he would *shake* her terribly in his anger. Finally, he held her out at arms length and gave her the horsewhip to the tune of about thirty stripes. She hopped and danced at this, to the infinite amusement of the slaves when we were alone; of course, in their presence we were very serious. We had good reason for rejoicing in this flogging, for she was never known to prescribe raw hide for a slave after that. She soon, however, left her husband and went to live with Mrs. Anderson, where, by her cruelty, she showed her reform was only temporary.

Then began that series of bitter cruelties by which Logan attempted to subdue sister Delia to his diabolical wishes. She was, at this time, some sixteen or eighteen years of age. At first, persuasion was employed. This was soon exchanged for stripes.

One morning, I was a witness of the torture which he inflicted. Sister asked me to speak to mother; I ran and called her; she hesitated a good deal, but the shrieks of her child at length overcame every fear, and she rushed into the presence of, and began to remonstrate with, this brute. He was only the more enraged. He turned around with all the vengeance of a fury, and knocked poor mother down, and injured her severely; when I saw the blood streaming from the shoulders of my sister, and my mother knocked down, I became completely frantic, and ran and caught an axe, and intended to cut him down at a blow. My mother had recovered her feet just in time to meet me at the door. She persuaded me not to go into the spinning-room, where this whipping took place. Sister soon came out, covered with blood. Mother washed her wounds as well as she could. In six days after this, sister was chained to a gang of a hundred and sixty slaves, and sent down to New Orleans. Mother begged for her daughter; said she would get some one to buy her; a gentleman offered to do this, after she was sold to the slave-driver; but the inhuman monster was inexorable; this was the punishment threatened, if he was refused the sacrifice of her innocence.

Sister was therefore carried down the river to New Orleans, kept three or four weeks, and then put up for sale. The day before the sale, she was taken to the barber's, her hair dressed, and she was furnished with a new silk gown, and gold watch, and every thing done to set off her personal attractions, previous to the time of the bidding. The first bid was $500; then $800. The auctioneer began to extol her virtues. Then $1000 was bid. The auctioneer says, "If you only knew the *reason* why she is sold, you would give any sum for her. She is a *pious*, good girl, member of the Baptist church, *warranted* to be a virtuous girl." The bidding grew brisk. *"Twelve!"* "thirteen," "fourteen," "fifteen," "sixteen hundred," was at length bid, and she was knocked off to a Frenchman, named Coval. He wanted her to live with him as his housekeeper and mistress. This she utterly refused, unless she were emancipated and made his wife. In about one month, he took her to Mexico, emancipated, and married her. She visited France with her husband, spent a year or more there and in the West Indies. In four or five years after her marriage, her husband died, leaving her a fortune of twenty or thirty thousand dollars. A more just and remarkable reward of sterling virtue in an unprotected girl, cannot be found in all the books of romance.

But I must return to my own story. Soon after the sale of my sister, the father of Joseph Logan, Deacon Archibald Logan, purchased his estate in Lexington, and all his slaves; mother, Cyrus, and myself, among the number. I was then valued at one thousand dollars. Mother, I should rather say, was given away in her old age to old Mrs. Logan, the wife of the deacon. In three or four years after this, Joseph Logan came to the house of his father, sick with the consumption, and died. He professed to be penitent upon his deathbed, and asked forgiveness of mother and myself for all the wrong done to our family.

I was then taken by the deacon for his body servant; travelled with him, and was often supposed to be his son.

I have little complaint to make of the old man, except that he kept me a *slave.* Cyrus was put into the tanyard, and fared very differently. For some reason, the old deacon treated him with great cruelty.

In 1833, my poor mother ended her sorrows, cut off very suddenly by the cholera. Our condition was then desolate indeed. Father had died several years before. The prospect before us was interminable, lonely bondage. The thought of it sometimes drove us almost to despair. I soon began to hire my time, by the day, or week, as I could make a bargain. I was a very good bass drummer, and had learned to play on the bugle. The deacon would hire me out to play for volunteers, that were then and soon after *training* for a campaign in Texas. He received three dollars for half a day for my services. When I found this out, I sold my bugle and drum. He was very sorry I had sold them; would have bought them himself, if he had known I wanted to sell. I told him, I was tired of playing. We soon compromised the matter, however; I bought my instruments, and was to have half I earned with them. I then began to lay up money, and had a shrewd notion that I could take care of myself. I frequently heard the Declaration of Independence read; and listened with great wonder to the Texas orators, as they talked about liberty. I thought it might be as good for me as for others. I could never reason myself into the belief, that the old deacon had any right to the annual rent which I paid for my own body. I then was paying to this old miser two hundred dollars a year for my time, boarding and clothing myself. I joined a company of musicians, and we made money fast and easy by attending balls and parties.

But before leaving the deacon, I wish to give a few recollections of his family matters, to illustrate the workings of good society among slaveholders. The deacon lost his wife about the time of the death of my mother. He was an elder of the Presbyterian church, and afterwards became a deacon of a Congregational church; and there was a widow named Robb, of the same communion; a good name for the whole clan of slaveholding tyrants, male and female; they are all *robbers* of the worst kind. The good women of the deacon's acquaintance visited him, and pitied his lonely condition, and hinted, that Mrs. Robb would be a great comfort to him in his affliction.

The negotiation was commenced, and soon terminated, to the *present* satisfaction of both parties. But two old people, with habits firmly fixed, do not often, like kindred drops, mingle into one. Each one wanted to keep their household fixings for their own children.

She was younger than the deacon, more artful, and could easily outwit him. The daughters of Mr. Logan had come to the house, before the marriage, and carefully marked the bedding. The deacon gave me the keys of his rooms, and attempted to limit the freedom of his new spouse in the house of which she was installed mistress. This produced confusion and abundance of sparring. She treated *her* slaves better than she did *his*, and this set all the old servants against her. She got to the old man's closet, drank his wine, and then charged it to the slaves. We were not long in pointing out to the deacon the true channel in which his wine flowed. Her servants were frequently despatched, with buckets of sugar and coffee, to the daughters of Mrs. Logan. It was nuts for us to find this out and tell the deacon. Here was new fuel for the fires of dispute that crackled every day in this habitation of the *Patriarchs*. They quarrelled openly; it was a public scandal; till, one day, his old withered hand seized the horsewhip and crowned their bliss with a dozen or two good smart lashes. The flame was all abroad, then. Many waters could not quench the *fires* of this loving pair. She left him, and her son-in-law threatened the old man's back with the cowskin.

The church interposed and called him to account. He owned up, as to the whipping; but justified, under the plea, that he afflicted the *body* for the good of the *soul*. It would not do. He bought off from his wife, and she left him. The church excommunicated the deacon. He made application, very soon, for admission to a Congregational church. They would not receive him, till he made some sort of a confession. He acknowledged the fact, but plead a good motive–the benefit of her soul. He was at length received, and presently began to garner the sanctuary of oppression–a southern church. The house was soon carpeted; the pulpit was renovated, dressed in velvet; a new bell hung, and new life infused into the waning church, which had just received such an ornament to its virtues and holiness. The unlucky minister had a little bit of decency, if not of conscience left. He had opposed the whole proceeding. Educated at the north, he one day dropped some word of condemnation of the sin of oppression. This was too much for the deacon. The minister was forthwith dismissed, and a more supple tool employed. The old man could hardly be trained to the exemplary habits becoming an office-bearer of the standards of Zion.[26] Frequent attempts were made to discipline him; but the deacon, with his great wealth, had such ascendency over the minds of his brethren, that a vote of censure or suspension could never be obtained. He lived and died in "good and regular standing," so far as came to my knowledge or belief.

The only beating that I had, after I came into the hands of Deacon Logan, was at the instigation of his son Joseph. Only about thirty lashes were put on by the public whipper, in the watch-house. I was tied, hands and feet, and whipped by the servile wretch, who does this business at a dollar a head for men–the *same* for women.

I did not witness as many scenes of cruelty among the slaves as many have; I was usually employed about the house, and was not in a situation to see what others have. One or two instances I can mention of what I personally knew of the cruelty of slaveholders. Joseph Logan had a slave, named Priscilla. She did the work in the kitchen. One morning, the biscuit came upon the table badly scorched. Mistress Minerva threw them in her face, struck her with the shovel, then heated the tongs, and took her by the nose. She raised her hand, to resist this act of wanton cruelty. Logan was called for, came out, and knocked her down with a large club; called in his men, and had her tied and beaten most unmercifully. He then put a log chain on her, and compelled her to drag it for days. She never recovered; her mind was destroyed, and she was soon after sold, for little or nothing, as an idiot.

Joseph Logan had another slave, named Peter. The wife of Peter was the slave of Thomas Kennedy, who lived forty-five miles from Lexington. Kennedy consented to sell Milly only on condition that, if she was ever resold, he should have the refusal of her. She lived with her husband till she had two children, and then her mistress, Minerva, resolved she should be sold. The tears and entreaties of her husband, the despair upon the countenance of the victim herself, were all in vain. She, with her two children, was sold to Warren Orford, one of the *soul* drivers, for twelve or thirteen hundred dollars. The husband became melancholy, sank down under his burden, turned to the intoxicating cup, and became a drunkard.

In the year 1838, I hired my time of Deacon Logan, for the purpose of going in a steamboat up and down the Ohio and Mississippi Rivers. I was at New Orleans three or four times, before I could find any thing of sister Delia. At last, through the assistance of an old acquaintance, I found where she lived. I went to the house, but I was so changed, by the growth of seven or eight years, that she did not know me. When I told her who I was, she was very incredulous; and, to test my identity, brought forward a small article of clothing, and asked me if ever I had seen it. I told her it once belonged to mother. "Ah! then," she said, "you must be my brother." She was very glad to see me, and hear from her brothers and sisters.

The next summer, she visited Kentucky with me, and spent two or three months. Deacon Logan treated her with great politeness; said his son did very wrong to sell her as he did; that, if he had then owned the family, it should not have been done. While in Kentucky, she advanced the money, in part, to pay for the freedom of Dennis, and, as soon as she returned to New Orleans, she sent up the balance.

She also made arrangements with Deacon Logan, to purchase brother Cyrus and myself for sixteen hundred dollars.

In the autumn of 1840, I started to go to New Orleans, to get the money to pay for Cyrus and myself. When I arrived at Louisville, I met the sorrowful tidings that sister was dead! This was a sudden, withering blast of all my well-founded hopes of deliverance from slavery. The same letter that brought the tidings of her death also informed me that she had left her property, by will, to me, for the purpose of buying myself, and all the family, from bondage. I was now told that, if I went down and took the property, my master could claim and take the whole of it. I went directly back to Lexington, and asked Mr. Logan to make me free, and I would pay him a thousand dollars, the first money that I received from the estate of my sister. This he said he would not do; but he gave me a free paper, to pass up and down the river as I pleased, and to transact any business as though I was free. With this paper, I started for New Orleans, but could get no more than sixty dollars and a suit of clothes. The person with whom it was left, said it was in real estate, and he had no authority to sell it. I then began to think that the day of my freedom was a great way off. I concluded, with a great many other persons in desperate circumstances, to go to Texas. I took boat for Galveston. Here it looked worse than slavery, if any thing can be worse. I soon returned, and came up to Louisville. Here I met three slaves of Doctor Graham, of Harrodsburg, Kentucky. Their names were Henry, Reuben, and George; all smart, fine fellows, good musicians, and yielding the doctor a handsome income. In the same company were three others, all of the same craft.

"Now," said I, "boys, is the time to strike for liberty. I go for Ohio tomorrow. What say you?" They pondered the question, and we all determined to start, as a company of musicians, to attend a great *ball* in Cincinnati–and, sure enough, it was the grandest ball we ever played for. We came to Cincinnati, and the friends there advised us to go farther north. Doctor Graham's boys struck for Canada, while I stopped at Oberlin, Ohio. It was well they did, for the doctor was close upon them, offering a large reward. He reached Detroit within a few hours after they had crossed the ice to Malden. He attempted to hire some one to go over, and capture them; no one would attempt this. He hired a man, at last, to go over and hire them to get on a boat, and go to Toledo, to play for a ball. Doctor Graham was to be in the boat, when it touched at Malden. For some reason, the boys were quite cautious, and very reluctant to go. When the wolf in sheep's clothing offered them five hundred dollars to go and play for one ball, they were more suspicious than ever. When the boat touched at the wharf, the boys were on the wharf, playing a gypsy waltz, a great favorite of Doctor Graham's. When the doctor found his plan did not work, sure enough, he came out to hear his favorite singers. He landed, and spent several days in fruitless endeavors to persuade them to return to Kentucky. They still persist in preferring a monarchy to the *patriarchal* form of government.

While at Oberlin, there was an attempt to capture a Mr. Johnson and his wife, residents in that place. They had once, to be sure, had a more southern home; but they believed the world was free for them to choose a home in, as well as for others. Johnson worked in a blacksmith's shop, with another man. To this individual he confided the name and place of the robber who had claimed him in Ohio. This wretch went to another, blacker-hearted one, named *Benedict*, of Illyria. Let no mother ever use that name again for her new-born son. It was disgraced enough by Benedict Arnold[27]–it should, with him, be covered in oblivion. But this lawyer, Benedict of Illyria, has made the infamy around that name thicker and blacker than it was before. He wrote to the pretended owner of Johnson where he could be found. In hot haste he came;

but, thanks to an honest justice, his evidence was not sufficient. He returned for better testimony; as he came back, he was suddenly grasped by the hand of death, and died within ten miles of Oberlin, with an oath upon his lips. Johnson and his wife broke jail, and were carried forward to Canada. There were a great many forwarding houses in Ohio at that time; they have greatly increased since, and nearly all of them are doing a first-rate business.

During the summer of 1841, the emigration to Canada, through Oberlin, was very large. I had the pleasure of giving the "right hand of fellowship" to a goodly number of my former acquaintances and fellow-sufferers. The masters accused me of *stealing* several of them. This is a great lie. I never stole one in my life. I have assisted several to get into possession of the true owner, but I never assisted any man to steal another away from himself. God has given every man the true title-deed to himself, written upon his face. It cannot be blotted entirely out. The slaveholders try hard to do it, but it can yet be read; all other titles are shams and forgeries. Among others, I assisted a Mrs. Swift, and her two children, to get over to Canada, where they can read titles more clearly than they do in some of the states. This was brought up as a heavy charge against me by Mr. Postlewaite, the illustrious catchpole of the slaveholders.

In the autumn of this year, I was delighted to meet brother Lewis at Oberlin. The happiness which we both experienced at meeting each other, as we supposed, securely free, in a free state, may be well imagined.

In 1842, there were nine slaves reached Oberlin by one arrival, all from one plantation. A Mr. Benningale, of Kentucky, was close upon them, impiously claiming that he had property in these images of God; ay, that they were *property*, and entirely his, to all intents and purposes. This is not the doctrine taught by a great many good men in Ohio. These men came to Oberlin. The next day, Benningale arrived. He lined the lake with watchmen. **Benedict** (do, printers, put that name in *black* type, if you can) of Illyria was on the alert; thirty pieces of silver were always the full price of innocent blood with him. Benningale, finding they were hid in the village, threatened to burn the town. The colored people were on guard all night. They met two persons, whom they suspected as spies of the kidnappers. They told them, if they caught them out again, they should be hung right up, as spies against liberty. The fugitives were at length put into a wagon, carried to the lake, and shipped for Canada. The pursuers offered a thousand dollars for their arrest. No one was found sufficiently enterprising to claim the reward. They landed safe upon the other side. Soon after this, there were seven more slaves arrived at Oberlin. The miserable Benedict, assisted by the Chapmans, set their traps around the village. Seven hundred dollars reward was offered for their arrest. Power of attorney had been sent on to the traitor Benedict. The slaves were kept concealed, till, as in the case of Moses, it was no longer safe for them. There were six men and one woman in the company. A plan was contrived to put the kidnappers upon a false scent. Six colored men were selected to personate the men, and I was dressed in female attire, to be passed off for the woman. A telltale[28] was informed that the slaves would start for the lake at such a time, and go in a certain direction. He was solemnly enjoined not to tell a word of it. Those who knew him understood what he would do. The secret was too precious for him to keep. He ran right to Benedict with it. We left Oberlin in one direction, and the real objects of pursuit started, soon after, upon another road. The *ruse* took; Benedict and Company were in full pursuit, with sheriff, writ, and all the implements of kidnapping. We selected one of our number, George Perry, to act as spokesman for the gang. Just as we arrived at the village of Illyria, eight miles from Oberlin, Benedict and Company surrounded our carriage, and ordered the driver to stop. Platt, the driver, challenged his authority. Benedict pulled out his advertisement, six men and one woman, with the description of their persons. Platt told him he thought they were not the persons he was after. The traitor affirmed he knew they were. The driver turned to his passengers, and said he could do no more for them. George then began to play his part: "Well, 'den, 'dis nigger must get out." We accordingly left the carriage, and were conducted into the tavern. In the tavern were two travellers, who were very inquisitive. "Where are you from?" George answered, "Don't care where I from." Benedict, when he began to suspect that all was not exactly right, came up to me for a more minute examination of my person. I had kept my head and face under my hood and cloak. He ordered me to hold up my head. George says, "Let 'dat gal alone, Mr. white man; de nigger gal plague enough in slave state–you just let her alone, here, if you please." One of the travellers called for cider; George stepped up and drank it for him. The table was furnished for some of the guests, and George, without any ceremony, declared " 'Dis nigger hungry," and swept the table for himself and comrades. The landlord threatened to flog him. The colored men all spoke up together, "You strike 'dat nigger if you dare." At last, they got a justice of the peace; but he had been let into the whole secret. Benedict began his plea; produced his evidence; said that ungrateful girl (pointing to me) had left a kind mistress, right in the midst of a large ironing!!! The justice finally said, he did not see but he must give us up to Mr. Benedict as slaves, fugitives from service. Our friends then gave the signal, and I threw off my bonnet and cloak, and stood up a man. Such a shout as the spectators raised would do the heart of freedom good. "Why, your woman has turned into a man, Mr. Benedict." "It may be these others, that appear to be men, are all women." Benedict saw through the plot, and took his saddle without any rejoinder to his plea. The tavern-keeper ordered us out of the house, and we took carriage for Oberlin. Meanwhile the real objects of pursuit were sailing on the waters of the blue lake.

Benedict was terribly angry at me. He swore he would have me captured. He wrote immediately to Deacon Logan, that no slaves could be captured there while Milton Clarke was at large.

The slaveholders of Lexington had a meeting, and determined to send a

Mr. Postlewaite, a crack slavebreaker, and a Mr. M'Gowan, after me. They came and lingered about Oberlin, watching their opportunity. They engaged two wretches named Chapman, of Illyria, to assist in the capture. Brother Lewis and I went up to Madison, Lake county, to spend a few days. We had a meeting on Sabbath evening, at which we addressed the people. There was a traitor there named Warner, from Lexington, who told Postlewaite where we were. Monday morning, my brother and myself rode up to Dr. Merriam's, accompanied by two or three of Mr. Winchester's family, with whom we had spent the Sabbath. I sat a few minutes in the carriage; and a little girl out of health, the niece of Dr. Merriam, and his own daughter, came out and wanted to ride. I took them in, and had not driven a mile when a close carriage overtook and passed me, wheeled right across the road, and four men leaped out of it and seized my horse. I had no conjecture who they were. I asked them what they wanted–"if money, I have only fifty cents in the world; you are welcome to that." "We want not *money*, but *you!*" The truth then flashed upon my mind in a moment–"They are kidnappers."

I jumped from the carriage for the purpose of running for life. My foot slipped, and I fell. In a moment, four men were upon me. They thrust my head down upon the ground, bound me hand and foot, put me into the carriage, and started for Judge Page's; a judge prepared beforehand for their purposes. Soon after we started, we met a man in the road. I spoke to him, and asked him to take care of the girls in the buggy, and to tell Lewis the kidnappers from Kentucky had got me. Postlewaite and M'Gowan took off my hat, and gave me a beating upon the head. One of the Chapmans spoke and said, "Now we have got you, my good fellow; you are the chap that has enticed away so many slaves; we will take care of you; we will have Lewis soon." They then took me to Mr. Judge Page. The sheriff of the county was there. He asked me what I had done, that they had tied me up so close. "Have you murdered any body?" I said, "No." "Have you been stealing?" "No, sir." "What have you done?" "Nothing, sir." "What have they tied you for, then?" Postlewaite told him it was none of his business. The sheriff said it was his business, and, "if he has committed no crime, you must untie him." He then came up to take off the cords from me. Postlewaite drew his pistols, and threatened to shoot him. Judge Page told the sheriff he had better not touch the gentleman's *property*. The sheriff said he would see whose property he was. By this time the alarm was spread, and a large company had gathered around the tavern. The sheriff told the people to see that that man was not removed till he came back. He went out, and summoned the posse of farmers in every direction. They left their ploughs, and jumped upon their horses, with the collars yet on their necks, and rode with all speed for the scene of action. "The kidnappers had got the white nigger," was the watchword.

Postlewaite began to be alarmed. He asked Mr. Page which was the best way for him to go. Could he go safely to the lake, and take a steamboat for Cleveland? "Why, no, the abolitionists watch all the landing-places." Could he go to Painesville? "Why, no, General Paine, a red-hot abolitionist, is there." Postlewaite asked for a place to take me, where I should be secure. They carried me to the counting-room of the judge. They then began to coax. The judge said, "You better go back, Clarke, willingly; it will be better for you, when you get there." "Did not your master treat you well?" asked the very gracious Mr. Postlewaite. "Yes," I said, "he treated me well; no fault to find with him on that score." "What did you run away for, then?" "I came, sir, to get my freedom. I offered him eight hundred dollars for my liberty, and he would not take it. I had paid him about that much for my time, and I thought I might as well have what I earned, as to pay it to him." "Well, sir, if you had come off alone, the deacon would not have cared so much about it; but you led others off; and now we are going to carry you back, and whip you, on the public square in Lexington."

The judge had appointed three o'clock in the afternoon for my trial, as my friends said they wished to procure evidence that I came away with the consent of Deacon Logan. In the mean time, Postlewaite & Co. were full of joy at their success, and despatched a letter to Lexington, announcing the capture of Milton Clarke, and assuring their friends there, that they should have Lewis before sundown. "We shall be in Lexington with them about Thursday or Friday." This was great news to the deacon and his friends; but, alas for them, the result was not exactly to answer to the expectation. They assembled in great numbers on both days, as I have been told, and watched, with eager interest, the arrival of the stage; but no Clarke, and no Postlewaite, were in it. Many a triumph has been enjoyed only in anticipation.

Dinner came on, at length, and I was moved back into the tavern. Postlewaite had a rope around me, which he kept in his hand all the time. They called for dinner for six—the driver and myself among the number. When they sat down, I was placed at a short distance from the table. The landlady asked if I was not to sit down. Postlewaite said, no nigger should sit at table with him. She belabored him in good womanly style; told him he was a thief, and a scoundrel, and that, if she was a *man*, he should never carry me away. The people were gathered, all this time, around the windows, and in the road, discussing the matter, and getting up the steam, to meet the Kentucky bowie knives and pistols. Postlewaite sent out, and got a man to come in and watch me, while he eat his dinner. The people at the windows were preparing to take me out. He watched the movement, and had me brought up nearer to the table.

At three o'clock, my trial came on. My friends claimed, that I should have a trial as a *white* man. Robert Harper plead for the oppressors, assisted by another, whose name is unknown to me. For me, lawyer Chase, and another, appeared. To these gentlemen, and all others, who were friendly to me on this occasion, I feel an obligation which I can never express. It was to me, indeed, a dark hour, and they were friends in time of need. General Paine arrived about the commencement of the trial, and presented a firm front to the tyrants.

My lawyer asked by what law they claimed me. They said, under the black law of Ohio. The reply was, that I was not a black man. Postlewaite said he arrested me, as the property of Archibald Logan, under the article of the constitution, that persons *"owing service,"* and fleeing from one state to another, shall be given up to the person to whom such service is due. He then read the power of attorney, from Deacon Logan to him, authorizing him to seize one Milton Clarke–describing me as a person five feet two and a half inches tall, probably trying to pass myself off as white. "His hair is straight, but curls a little at the lower end." After reading this, he read his other papers, showing that I was the slave of Logan. He produced a bill of sale, from Joseph to Deacon Logan. He then asked me if I had not lived, for several years, with Deacon Logan. General Paine said, if I spoke at all, I might tell the whole story–that I had a free pass to go where I chose, (and this was the fact.) The suggestion of General Paine frightened Postlewaite; he told me to shut up my jaws, or he would smash my face in for me. The people cried out, "Touch him if you dare; we will string you up, short metre." He then said to me, "D–n you; we will pay you for all this, when we get home." The anxiety on my part, by this time, was beyond any thing I ever felt in my life. I sometimes hoped the people would rescue me, and then feared they would not. Many of them showed sympathy in their countenances, and I could see that the savageism of Postlewaite greatly increased it. My lawyer then asked, for what I *owed* service to Deacon Logan; told Harper & Co., if Mr. Clarke owed the deacon, present his bill, and, if it is a reasonable one, his friends will pay it. He then asked me if I owed Deacon Logan, of Kentucky. I told him no–the deacon owed me about eight hundred dollars; I owed him nothing. Postlewaite said, then, he arrested me as the *goods* and *chattels* of Logan. Mr. Chase said, "Mr. Clarke had permission to come into the free states." "Yes," said Postlewaite, "but not to *stay* so long." Finally, Mr. Chase asked, "Where did Joseph Logan get *his* right to Clarke?" On this point, he had no specific evidence. He then resorted to the general testimony of several letters, which he took from his pocket. One was from General Coombs, another from McCauly, one from John Crittenden, one from Morehead, Governor Lecher, John Speed Smith, and, last of all, from HENRY CLAY.[29] These gentlemen all represented Mr. Postlewaite as a most *pious* and excellent man, whose word was to be taken in every thing; stating, also, that they knew Milton Clarke, and that he was the property of Deacon A. Logan. This array of names closed the testimony. Bob Harper then made his infamous plea; said, finally, the judge could possibly do no otherwise than give me up, on the testimony of so many great names. Judge Page had received his fee, as I verily believe, before he gave judgment; and he very soon came to the conclusion, that Deacon Logan had proved his claim. I was delivered over to the tender mercies of Postlewaite & Co. Just as we were going out at the door, the sheriff met us, and arrested Postlewaite, McGowan, and the Chapmans, for assault and battery on the person of Milton Clarke. They were told, their trial would come on the next day, at ten o'clock, before Justice Cunningham. Postlewaite swore terribly at this; said it was an abolition concern. Some one asked the sheriff what should be done with me. He said he did not want me–it was the others that he had arrested. I was then tied to Postlewaite. Some one said, "Cut him loose." Postlewaite replied, "The first that attempts to touch him, I will blow him through." I asked the people if I should be carried back, as I had committed no crime. They said, "No, no; never." General Paine said he would call out the militia, before I should be carried back.

Postlewaite ordered out his carriage, to accompany the sheriff. He drove me into it, came in with his partners, McGowan and the Chapmans, and Judge Page. We then started for Unionville, distant about two miles from Centreville. A very great crowd followed us, on every side. My friends had not been idle; they had been over to Jeffersonville, in Ashtabula county, and obtained a writ of Habeas Corpus[30] for me. Unionville was upon the border of *two* counties. The road through it divided them. The people had fixed their carriages so that ours must pass upon the Ashtabula side. Soon as the wheels passed the border of this county, the carriage was stopped, and the sheriff of Ashtabula demanded the body of Milton Clarke. The people shouted, came up and unhitched the horses, and turned them face to the carriage. Postlewaite cried out, "Drive on." Driver replied, "The horses are faced about." P. began to be very angry. The people asked the driver what he was there for, assisting in such business as this. The poor fellow begged they would not harm his horses; he did not know what they wanted him for, or he never would have come. He begged for his horses, and himself. Postlewaite said, if they meddled with the horses, he would shoot a hundred of them. The people told him, if he put his head out of that carriage, he would never shoot again. At this stage of the business, Robert Harper, Esq., came up, to read the riot act. The people were acting under a charter broader and older than any statutes passed on earth. Harper was glad to escape himself, or justice would have speedily been meted out to him. The friends came up to the carriage, and told me not to be alarmed; they would have me, at any rate. Among others in the crowd, was a huge Buckeye blacksmith, six feet tall. At first, he took sides with the thieves; said he wanted no niggers there. My friends told him to come up to the carriage, and pick out the nigger, if there was any there. He came, and looked into the carriage some time, and at last, pointing to Postlewaite, said, "That is the nigger." The chivalric Mr. P. told him no man called him nigger with impunity. The Buckeye insisted upon it he was the nigger. P. told him he lied, three times. The northern lion was waked up, and he slapped the armed knight in the face. Postlewaite drew his bowie knife, and threatened to cut him. The Ohioan asked him what it was. He said, a bowie knife. "What are you going to do with it?" "Put it into you, if you put your head in here again." "Ay, ay, you are going to booy me, are you? Then I'll booy you." He ran to the fence, and seized a sharp rail, and said he was going to booy, too. The sheriff, that had the writ to take me, let down the steps; and the people called out, "Let us kill them." The man armed with the rail, began to beat the door, and told them to let me out. General Paine spoke, and urged the multitude not to proceed to violence. Judge Page began to feel quite uneasy, in his new position. He exhorted me to keep still, or they would kill us all. The sheriff then gave Postlewaite and Company five minutes' time to release me, or take the consequences; said the carriage would be demolished in two minutes, when he spoke the word to the people. The pistols and bowie knives were quietly put away, and the tone of the stationary passengers, inside the carriage, very suddenly changed. Judge Page said, "Better let Clarke get out; they will kill us, if you don't." The cowardly Chapmans began to plead for mercy: "You can't say that we touched you, Clarke." "Yes you did," I told them; "you all jumped on me at once." The people became more and more clamorous outside the carriage—those inside more and more uneasy. They at length were more eager to get rid of me than they ever had been to catch me. "Get out; get out, Clarke," rung round on every side of me.

Soon as my feet touched the ground, the rope was cut, and once more I felt free. I was hurried into a wagon, and, under the care of the sheriff, driven off toward Austinburg, while the other sheriff took the kidnappers in another direction into Lake county. They soon stopped to give me something to eat; but I had no appetite for food, either then or for a week afterwards.

Postlewaite hired a man to follow and watch me. But my friends soon contrived to put him on a false scent. It was now dark, and I exchanged seats with a Mr. Winchester, and the watch-dog soon found he was on the wrong trail. The sheriff that had me in keeping was not very careful of his charge, and he soon lost all knowledge of my whereabouts. I was concealed for two or three days at Austinburg, as lonely as mortal man could well be. One night I went out and slept upon the haystack in the field, fearing they might search the house. The man who owned it came next day to Mr. Austin's, where I stopped, to know if it was so; said, if he had known that a nigger slept there, he would have burned the hay and him all up together. "Let him go back, where he belongs."

He then turned to me, and asked me if I had seen that nigger. I told him I had; I knew him very well. Mr. Austin asked him what he would say, if they should come and attempt to take me into slavery; why, said he, "I would shoot them." His philanthropy was graduated, like many others, upon nothing more substantial than color.

In a few days I had the pleasure to learn that Postlewaite and Company, after a trial before Mr. Cunningham, had returned to Kentucky. I have since been told they crept into the city of Lexington as silently as possible; that they left the stage before it entered the city, and went in under the shade of night. When they were visible, the inquiries were thick and fast, "Where are the Clarkes? What have you done with the Clarkes?"

Both the little girls in the carriage when I left it were thrown out, and one so injured that she never recovered. She died in a few days.

The citizens called a meeting at Austinburg, and Lewis and I began to lecture on the subject of slavery. From that time to the present, we have had more calls for meetings than we could attend. We have been in eight different states, and hundreds of thousands have listened with interest to the story of our wrongs, and the wrongs of our countrymen in bonds. If God spares our lives, we hope to see the day when the trump of jubilee shall sound,[31] and liberty shall be proclaimed throughout the land to all the inhabitants thereof.

## APPENDIX

### A Sketch of the Clarke Family by Lewis Clarke

My mother was called a very handsome woman. She was very much esteemed by all who knew her; the slaves looked up to her for advice. She died, much lamented, of the cholera, in the year 1833. I was not at home, and had not even the melancholy pleasure of following her to her grave.

1. The name of the oldest member of the family was Archy. He never enjoyed very good health, but was a man of great ingenuity, and very much beloved by all his associates, colored and white. Through his own exertions, and the kindness of C. M. Clay, and one or two other friends, he procured his freedom. He lived to repay Mr. Clay and others the money advanced for him, but not long enough to enjoy for many years the freedom for which he had struggled so hard. He paid six hundred dollars for himself. He died about seven years since, leaving a wife and four or five children in bondage; the inheritance of the widow and poor orphans is, LABOR WITHOUT WAGES; WRONGS WITH NO REDRESS; SEPARATION FROM EACH OTHER FOR LIFE, and no being to hear their complaint, but that God who is the *widow's God and Judge.* "Shall I not be avenged on such a nation as this?"

2. Sister Christiana was next to Archy in age. She was first married to a free colored man. By him she had several children. Her master did not like this connection, and her husband was driven away, and told never to be seen there again. The name of her master is Oliver Anderson; he is a leading man in the Presbyterian church, and is considered one of the best among slaveholders. Mr. Anderson married Polly Campbell, at the time I was given to Mrs. Betsey Banton. I believe she and Mrs. Banton have not spoken together since they divided the slaves at the death of their father. They are the only two sisters now living of the Campbell family.

3. Dennis is the third member of our family. He is a free man in Kentucky, and is doing a very good business there. He was assisted by a Mr. William L. Stevenson, and also by his sister, in getting his freedom. He never had any knowledge of our intention of running away, nor did he assist us in any manner whatever.

4. Alexander is the fourth child of my mother. He is the slave of a Dr. Richardson; has with him a very easy time; lives as well as a man can and be

a slave; has no intention of running away. He lives very much like a second-hand gentleman, and I do not know as he would leave Kentucky on any condition.

5. My mother lost her fifth child soon after it was born.

6. Delia came next. Hers was a most bitter and tragical history. She was so unfortunate as to be uncommonly handsome, and, when arrived at woman's estate, was considered a great prize for the guilty passions of the slaveholders.

7. To No. 7 I, Lewis Clarke, respond, and of me you have heard enough already.

8. Milton comes next, and he is speaking for himself. He is almost constantly engaged in giving lectures upon the subject of slavery; has more calls usually than he can attend to.

9. Manda, the ninth child, died when she was about fifteen or sixteen years of age. She suffered a good deal from Joseph Logan's second wife.

10. Cyrus is the youngest of the family, and lives at Hamilton, New York.

## Questions and Answers by Lewis Clarke

The following questions are often asked me, when I meet the people in public, and I have thought it would be well to put down the answers here.

*How many holidays in a year do the slaves in Kentucky have?*–They usually have six days at Christmas, and two or three others in the course of the year. Public opinion generally seems to require this much of slaveholders; a few give more, some less; some *none*, not a day nor an hour.

*How do slaves spend the Sabbath?*–Every way the master pleases. There are certain kinds of work which are respectable for Sabbath day. Slaves are often sent out to salt the cattle, collect and count the pigs and sheep, mend fences, drive the stock from one pasture to another. Breaking young horses and mules, to send them to market, yoking young oxen, and training them, is proper Sabbath work; piling and burning brush, on the back part of the lot, grubbing brier patches that are out of the way, and where they will not be seen. Sometimes corn must be shelled in the corn-crib; hemp is baled in the hemp-house. The still-house[32] must be attended on the Sabbath. In these, and various other such like employments, the more avaricious slaveholders keep their slaves busy a good part of every Sabbath. It is a great day for visiting and eating, and the house servants often have more to do on that than on any other day.

*What if strangers come along, and see you at work?*–We must quit shelling corn, and go to play with the cobs; or else we must be clearing land, on our own account. We must cover up master's sins as much as possible, and take it all to ourselves. It is hardly fair; for he ought rather to account for our sins, than we for his.

*Why did you not learn to read?*–I did not *dare* to learn. I attempted to spell some words when a child. One of the children of Mrs. Banton went in, and told her that she heard Lewis spelling. Mrs. B. jumped up as though she had been shot. "Let me ever know you to spell another word, I'll take your *heart* right out of you." I had a strong desire to learn. But it would not do to have slaves learn to read and write. They could read the guide-boards. They could write passes for each other. They cannot leave the plantation on the Sabbath without a written pass.

*What proportion of slaves attend church on the Sabbath?*–In the country, not *more* than *one in ten on an average.*

*How many slaves have you ever known that could read?*–I never saw more than three or four that could properly read at all. I never saw but one that could write.

*What do slaves know about the Bible?*–They generally believe there is somewhere a real Bible, that came from God; but they frequently say the Bible now used is master's Bible; most that they hear from it being, "Servants, obey your masters."[33]

*Are families often separated? How many such cases have you personally known?–I never knew a whole family to live together till all were grown up, in my life.* There is almost always, in every family, some one or more keen and bright, or else sullen and stubborn slave, whose influence they are afraid of on the rest of the family, and such a one must take a walking ticket to the south.

There are other causes of separation. The death of a large owner is the occasion usually of many families being broken up. Bankruptcy is another cause of separation, and the hard-heartedness of a majority of slaveholders another and a more fruitful cause than either or all the rest. *Generally* there is but little more scruple about separating families than there is with a man who keeps sheep in selling off the lambs in the fall. On one plantation where I lived, there was an old slave named Paris. He was from fifty to sixty years old, and a very honest and apparently pious slave. A slave-trader came along one day, gathering hands for the south. The old master ordered the waiter or coachman to take Paris into the back room, *pluck out* all his gray hairs, rub his face with a greasy towel, and then had him brought forward and sold for a *young* man. His wife consented to go with him, upon a promise from the trader that they should be sold together, with their youngest child, which she carried in her arms. They left two behind them, who were only from four to six or eight years of age. The speculator collected his drove, started for the market, and, before he left the state, he *sold that infant child* to pay one of his tavern bills, and took the balance in cash. This was the news which came back to us, and was never disputed.

I saw one slave mother, named Lucy, with seven children, put up by an administrator for sale. At first the mother and three small children were put up together. The purchasers objected: one says, "I want the woman and the babe, but not the other children;" another says, "I want that little girl;" and another, "I want the boy." "Well," says the administrator, "I must let you have them to the best advantage." So the children were taken away; the mother and infant were first sold, then child after child–the mother looking on in perfect agony; and as one child after another came down from the auction block, they would run and cling, weeping, to her clothes. The poor mother stood, till nature gave way; she fainted and fell, with her child in her arms. The only sympathy she received from most of the hard-hearted monsters, who had riven her heart-strings asunder, was, "She is a d–d deceitful bitch; I wish she was mine; I would teach her better than to cut up such shines as that here." When she came to, she moaned wofully, and prayed that she might die, to be relieved from her sufferings.

I knew another slave, named Nathan, who had a slave woman for a wife. She was killed by hard usage. Nathan then declared he would never have another slave wife. He selected a free woman for a companion. His master opposed it violently. But Nathan persevered in his choice, and in consequence was sold to go down south. He returned once to see his wife, and she soon after died of grief and disappointment. On his return south, he leaped from the boat, and attempted to swim ashore; his master, on board the boat, took a gun and deliberately shot him, and he drifted down the current of the river.

On this subject of separation of families, I must plant one more rose in the garland that I have already tied upon the brow of the sweet Mrs. Banton. The reader cannot have forgotten her; and in the delectable business of tearing families asunder, she, of course, would have a hand. A slave by the name of Susan was taken by Mrs. Banton on mortgage. She had been well treated where she was brought up, had a husband, and they were very happy together. Susan mourned in bitterness over her separation, and pined away under the cruel hand of Mrs. Banton. At length she ran away, and hid herself in the neighborhood of her husband. When this came to the knowledge of Mrs. B., she charged her husband to go for "Suke," and never let her see his face unless she was with him. "No," said she, "if you are offered a double price, don't you take it. I want my satisfaction out of her, and then you may sell her as soon as you please." Susan was brought back in fetters, and Mr. and Mrs. B. both took their *satisfaction*; they beat and tortured poor Susan till her premature offspring perished, and she almost sank beneath their merciless hands, and then they sold her to be carried a hundred miles farther away from her husband. Ah! slavery is like running the dissecting knife around the heart, among all the tender fibres of our being.

A man by the name of Bill Myers, in Kentucky, went to a large number of auctions, and purchased women about forty years old, with their youngest children in their arms. As they are about to cease bearing at that age, they are sold cheap. The children he took and shut up in a log pen, and set some old worn-out slave women to make broth and feed them. The mothers he gathered in a large drove, and carried them south and sold them. He was detained there for months longer than he expected; and, winter coming on, and no proper provision having been made for the children, many of them perished with cold and hunger, some were frostbitten, and all were emaciated to skeletons. This was the only attempt that I ever knew for gathering young children together, like a litter of pigs, to be raised for the market. The success was not such as to warrant a repetition on the part of Myers.

Jockey Billy Barnett had a slave-prison, where he gathered his droves of husbands, fathers, and wives, separated from their friends; and he tried to keep up their spirits by employing one or two fiddlers to play for them, while they danced over and upon the torn-off fibres of their hearts. Several women were known to have died in that worse than Calcutta Black Hole of grief. They mourned for their children, and would not be comforted, because they were not.

*How are the slave cabins usually built?*–They are made of small logs, about from ten to twenty feet square. The roof is covered with splits, and *dirt* is thrown in to raise the bottom, and then it is beat down hard for a floor. The chimneys are made of cut sticks and clay. In the corners, or at the sides, there are pens made, filled with straw, for sleeping. Very commonly, two or three families are huddled together in one cabin, and in cold weather they sleep together promiscuously, old and young. Some few families are indulged in the privilege of having a few hens or ducks around them; but this is not very common.

*What amount of food do slaves have in Kentucky?*–They are not put on allowance; they generally have enough of corn bread; and meat and soup are dealt to them occasionally.

*What is the clothing of a slave for a year?*–For summer, he has usually a pair of tow and linen pants, and two shirts of the same material. He has a pair of shoes, a pair of woolsey pants, and a round jacket for winter.

The account current of a slave with his master stands about thus:–

**ICHABOD LIVE-WITHOUT-WORK, *IN ACCOUNT WITH* JOHN WORK-WITHOUT-PAY.**

*Dr.*[34]

To one man's work, one year, .................................................. $100 00

*Contra, Cr.*[35]

By 13 bushels of corn meal, at 10 cents, .......................... $1 30
" 100 lbs. mean bacon and pork, at 1½ cents, ....................... 1 50
" Chickens, pigs, &c., taken without leave, say, ....................... 1 50
" 9 yds. of tow and linen, for shirts and pants, at 12½ cents, ......... 1 12½
" 1 pair of shoes, ................................................ 1 50
" Cloth for jacket and winter pants, 5½ yds., at 2 shillings, ........... 1 84
" Making clothes, ................................................ 1 00
" 1 Blanket, ................................................ 1 00
" 2 Hats or caps, ................................................ 75
$11 51½
" Balance due the slave every year, ............................................ $88 48½

The account stands unbalanced thus till the great day of reckoning comes.

Now, allow that one half of the slaves are capable of labor; that they can earn, on an average, one half the sum above named; that would give us $50 a year for 1,500,000 slaves, which would be *seventy-five millions* as *the sum robbed* from the slaves every year!! "Woe unto him that useth his neighbor's service without wages!"[36] Woe unto him that buildeth his house by iniquity, "for the stone shall cry out of the wall, and the beam out of the timber shall answer it!"[37] "Behold, the hire of the laborers, who have reaped down your fields, which is of you kept back by fraud, crieth; and the cries of them which have reaped are entered into the ears of the Lord of Sabaoth. Ye have lived in pleasure on the earth, and been wanton; ye have *nourished your hearts, as in a day of slaughter*."[38]

*Have you ever known a slave mother to kill her own children?*–There was a slave mother near where I lived, who took her child into the cellar and killed it. She did it to prevent being separated from her child. Another slave mother took her three children and threw them into a well, and then jumped in with them, and they were all drowned. Other instances I have frequently heard of. At the death of many and many a slave child, I have seen the two feelings struggling in the bosom of a mother–joy, that it was beyond the reach of the slave monsters, and the natural grief of a mother over her child. In the presence of the master, grief seems to predominate; when away from them, they rejoice that there is one whom the slave-driver will never torment.

*How is it that masters* KILL *their slaves, when they are worth so much money?*–They do it to gratify passion; this must be done, cost what it may. Some say a man will not kill a horse worth a hundred dollars, much less a slave worth several hundred dollars. A horse has no such *will* of his own, as the slave has; he does not provoke the man, as a slave does. The master knows there is *contrivance* with the slave to outwit him; the horse has no such contrivance. This conflict of the *two* WILLS is what makes the master so much more passionate with his slave than with a horse. A slaveholder must be master on the plantation, or he knows the *example* would destroy all authority.

*What do they do with old slaves, who are past labor?*–Contrive all ways to keep them at work till the last hour of life. Make them shell corn and pack tobacco. They hunt and drive them as long as there is any life in them. Sometimes they turn them out to do the best they can, or die. One man, on moving to Missouri, sold an old slave for one dollar, to a man not worth a cent. The old slave was turned out to do the best he could; he fought with age and starvation a while, but was soon found, one morning, *starved* to death, out of doors, and half eaten up by animals. I have known several cases where slaves were left to starve to death in old age. Generally, they sell them south, and let them die there; send them, I mean, before they get very old.

*What makes them wash slaves in salt and water after they whip them?*–For two reasons; one is to make them smart, and another to prevent mortification in the lacerated flesh. I have seen men and women both washed after they had been cruelly beaten. *I have done it with my own hands.* It was the hardest work I ever did. The flesh would crawl, and creep, and quiver, under my hands. This slave's name was Tom. He had not started his team Sunday morning early enough. The neighbors *saw* that Mr. Banton had work done on the Sabbath. Dalton, the overseer, attempted to whip him. Tom knocked him down and trod on him, and then ran away. The patrols caught him, and he was whipped—*three hundred* lashes. Such a back I never saw; such work I pray that I may never do again.

*Do not slaves often say that they love their masters very much?*—Say so? yes, certainly. And this loving master and mistress is the hardest work that slaves have to do. When any stranger is present, we have to love them very much. When master is sick, we are in great trouble. Every night the slaves gather around the house, and send up one or two to see how master does. They creep up to the bed, and with a very soft voice, inquire, "How is dear massa? O massa, how we want to hear your voice out in the field again!" Well, this is what they say up in the sick room. They come down to their *anxious* companions. "How is the old man?" "Will he die?" "Yes, yes; he sure to go, this time; he never whip the slave no more." "Are you sure? Will he die?" "O yes! surely gone for it, now." Then they all look glad, and go to the cabin with a merry heart.

Two slaves were sent out to dig a grave for old master. They dug it very deep. As I passed by, I asked Jess and Bob what in the world they dug it so deep for. It was down six or seven feet. I told them there would be a fuss about it, and they had better fill it up some. Jess said it suited him exactly. Bob said he would not fill it up; he wanted to get the old man as near *home* as possible. When we got a stone to put on his grave, we hauled the largest we could find, so as to fasten him down as strong as possible.

Another story illustrates the feeling of the slaves on taking leave of their masters. I will not vouch for the truth of it; but it is a story slaves delight to tell each other. The master called the slave to his sick bed. "Good-by, Jack; I have a long journey to go; farewell." "Farewell, massa! pleasant journey: you soon be dere, massa—*all de way down hill!*"

*Who are the patrols?*—They are men appointed by the county courts to look after all slaves without a pass. They have almost unlimited power over the slaves. They are the sons of run-down families. The greatest scoundrel is always captain of the band of patrols. They are the offscouring of all things; the refuse, the fag end, the ears and tails of slavery; the scales and fins of fish; the tooth and tongues of serpents. They are the very fool's cap of baboons, the echo of parrots, the wallet and satchel of polecats, the scum of stagnant pools, the exuvial, the worn-out skins of slaveholders; they dress in their old clothes. They are, emphatically, the servants of servants, and slaves of the devil; they are the meanest, and lowest, and worst of all creation. Like starved wharf rats, they are out nights, creeping into slave cabins, to see if they have an old bone there; drive out husbands from their own beds, and then take their places. They get up all sorts of pretences, false as their lying tongues can make them, and then whip the slaves and carry a gory lash to the master, for a piece of bread.

The rascals run me with their dogs six miles, one night, and I was never nearer dead than when I reached home that night. I only escaped being half torn to pieces by the dogs, by turning their attention to some calves that were in the road. The dogs are so trained that they will seize a man as quick as any thing else. The dogs come very near being as mean as their masters.

Cyrus often suffered very much from these wretches. He was hired with a man named Baird. This man was reputed to be very good to his slaves. The patrols, therefore, had a special spite toward his slaves. They would seek for an opportunity to abuse them. Mr. Baird would generally give his slaves a pass to go to the neighbors, once or twice a week, if requested. He had been very good to Cyrus in this respect, and therefore Cyrus was unwilling to ask too often. Once he went out without his pass. The patrols found him and some other slaves on another plantation without any passes. The other slaves belonged to a plantation where they were often whipped; so they gave them a moderate punishment and sent them home. Cyrus, they said, they would take to the woods, and have a regular whipping spree. It was a cold winter night, the moon shining brightly. When they had got into the woods, they ordered him to take off his outside coat, then his jacket; then he said he had a new vest on; he did not want that whipped all to pieces. There were seven men standing in a ring around him. He looked for an opening, and started at full speed. They took after him, but he was too spry for them. He came to the cabin where I slept, and I lent him a hat and a pair of shoes. He was very much excited; said they were all around him, but couldn't whip him. He went over to Mr. Baird, and the patrols had got there before him, and had brought his clothes and told their story. It was now eight or nine o'clock in the evening. Mr. Baird, when a young man, had lived on the plantation of Mr. Logan, and had been treated very kindly by mother. He remembered this kindness to her children. When Cyrus came in, Mr. Baird took his clothes and handed them to him, and told him, "Well, boy, they came pretty near catching you." Cyrus put on his clothes, went into the room where the patrols were, and said, "Good evening, gentlemen. Why, I did not think the patrols would be out to-night. I was thinking of going over to Mr. Reed's; if I had, I should have gone without a pass. They would have caught me, sure enough. Mr. Baird, I wish you would be good enough to give me a pass, and then I won't be afraid of these fellows." Mr. Baird enjoyed the fun right well, and sat down and wrote him a pass; and the patrols started, and had to find the money for their peach brandy somewhere else.

There were several other times when he had but a hair-breadth escape for his skin. He was generally a little too shrewd for them. After he had outwitted them several times, they offered a premium to any one who would whip him.

*How do slaves get information of what is doing in the free states?*—In different ways. They get something from the waiters, that come out into the free states and then return with their masters. Persons from the free states tell them many things; the free blacks get something; and slaves learn most of all from hearing their masters talk.

*Don't slaves that run away return sometimes?*—Yes; there was one returned from Canada, very sorry he had run away. His master was delighted with him; thought he had him sure for life, and made much of him. He was sent round to tell how bad Canada was. He had a sermon for the public,—the ear of the masters,—and another for the slaves. How many he enlightened about the best way to get there, I don't know. His master, at last, was so sure of him, that he let him take his wife and children and go over to Ohio, to a camp-meeting, all fitted out in good style, with horse and wagon. They never stopped to hear any preaching, till they heard the waves of the lakes lift up their cheerful voices between them and the oppressor. George then wrote an affectionate note to his master, inviting him to take tea with him in Canada, beyond the waters, the barrier of freedom. Whether the old people ever went up to Canada, to see their affectionate children, I have not learned. I have heard of several instances very much like the above.

*If the slaves were set free, would they cut the throats of their masters?*—They are far more likely to kill them, if they don't set them free. Nothing but the hope of emancipation, and the fear they might not succeed, keeps them from rising to assert their rights. They are restrained, also, from affection for the children of those who so cruelly oppress them. If none would suffer but the masters themselves, the slaves would make many more efforts for freedom. And, sooner or later, unless the slaves are *given free*, they will take freedom, at all hazards. There are multitudes that chafe under the yoke, sorely enough. They could run away themselves, but they would hate to leave their families.

*Did the slaves in Kentucky hear of the emancipation in the West Indies?*—They did, in a very short time after it took place. It was the occasion of great joy. They expected they would be free next. This event has done much to keep up the hopes of the slave to the present hour.

*What do slaves think of the* PIETY *of their masters?*—They have very little confidence in them about any thing. As a specimen of their feelings on this subject, I will tell an anecdote of a slave.

A slave, named George, was the property of a man of high standing in the church. The old gentleman was taken sick, and the doctor told him he would die. He called George, and told him if he would wait upon him attentively, and do every thing for him possible, he would remember him in his will: he would do something handsome for him.

George was very much excited to know what it might be; hoped it might be in the heart of his master to give him his freedom. At last, the will was made. George was still more excited. The master noticed it, and asked what the matter was. "Massa, you promise do something for me in your will. Poor nigger! what massa done for George?" "O George, don't be concerned; I have done a very handsome thing for you—such as any slave would be proud to have done for him." This did not satisfy George. He was still very eager to know what it was. At length the master saw it necessary to tell George, to keep him quiet, and make him attend to his duty. "Well, George, I have made provision that, when you die, you shall have a good coffin, and be put into the same vault with me. Will not that satisfy you, George?" "Well, massa, one way I am satisfied, and one way I am not." "What, what," said the old master, "what is the matter with that?" "Why," says George, "I like to have good coffin when I die." "Well, don't you like to be in the same vault with me and other rich masters?" "Why, yes, massa, one way I like it, and one way I don't." "Well, what don't you like?" "Why, I fraid, massa, when de debbil come take you body, he make mistake, and get mine."

The slaves uniformly prefer to be buried at the greatest possible distance away from master. They are superstitious, and fear that the slave-driver, having whipped so much when alive, will, somehow, be beating them when dead. I was actually as much afraid of my old master when dead, as I was when he was alive. I often dreamed of him, too, after he was dead, and thought he had actually come back again, to torment me more.

*Do slaves have conscientious scruples about taking things from their masters?*—They think it wrong to take from a neighbor, but not from their masters. The only question with them is, "Can we keep it from master?" If they can keep their backs safe, conscience is quiet enough on this point. But a slave that will steal from a slave, is called *mean* as *master.* This is the lowest comparison slaves know how to use: "just as mean as white folks." "No right for to complain of white folks, who steal us all de days of our life; nigger dat what steal from nigger, he meaner nor all."

There is no standard of morality in the slave states. The master stands before the slave a robber and oppressor. His words count nothing with the slaves. The slaves are disrobed of the attributes of men, so that they cannot hold up the right standard, and there is none. The slaves frequently have discussions upon moral questions. Sol and Tom went, one night, to steal the chickens of a neighbor. Tom went up, to hand them down to Sol. While engaged in this operation, he paused a minute. "Sol, you tink dis right, to steal dese chicken from here?" "What dat you say, Tom?" "I say, you tink him right to steal dese chicken, Sol?" "What you come talk dat way, now, for? Dat quession you ought settle 'fore you come here." "Me did tink about it, but want to hear what you say, Sol. Don't you tink it kind of wrong to take dese here chicken?" "I tell you, Sol, no time for 'scuss dat now. Dat is *de* great moral question. Make haste; hand me down anudder one; let us git away from here 'fore de daylight come."

*Do you think it was right for you to run away, and not pay any thing for yourself?*—I would be willing to pay, if I knew who to pay it to. But when I think it over, I can't find any body that has any better right to me than myself. I can't pay father and mother, for they are dead. I don't owe Mrs. Banton any thing for bringing me up the way she did. I worked five or six years, and earned more than one hundred dollars a year, for Mr. K. and family, and received about a dozen dollars a year in clothing. Who do I owe, then, in Kentucky? If I catch one of the administrators on here, I intend to sue him for wages, and interest, for six years' hard work. There will be a small bill of damages for abuse; old Kentucky is not rich enough to pay me for that.

*Soon after you came into Ohio, did you let yourself to work?*–I did.–*Was there any difference in your feelings while laboring there, and as a slave in Kentucky?*–I made a bargain to work for a man in Ohio. I took a job of digging a cellar. Before I began, the people told me he was bad pay; they would not do it for him. I told them I had agreed to do it. So at it I went, worked hard, and got it off as soon as possible, although I did not expect to get a cent for it; and yet I worked more readily, and with a better mind, than I ever did in Kentucky. If I worked for nothing then, I knew I had made my own bargain; and working with that thought made it easier than any day's work I ever did for a master in Kentucky. That *thought* was worth more than any pay I ever got in slavery. However, I was more fortunate than many thought I should be; through the exertions of a good friend, I got my pay soon after the work was done.

*Why do slaves dread so bad to go to the south–to Mississippi or Louisiana?*–Because they know that slaves are driven very hard there, and worked to death in a few years.

*Are those who have* GOOD *masters afraid of being sold south?*–They all suffer very much for fear master's circumstances will change, and that he may be compelled to sell them to the "SOUL-DRIVERS," a name given to the dealers by the slaves.

*What is the highest price you ever knew a slave to sell for?*–I have known a man sold for $1465. He was a waiter-man, very intelligent, very humble, and a good house servant. A good blacksmith, as I was told, was once sold in Kentucky for $3000. I have heard of handsome girls being sold in New Orleans for from $2000 to $3000. The common price of females is about from $500 to $700, when sold for plantation hands, for house hands, or for *breeders.*

*Why is a black slave-driver worse than a white one?*–He must be very strict and severe, or else he will be turned out. The master selects the hardest-hearted and most unprincipled slave upon the plantation. The overseers are usually a part of the patrols. Which is the worst of the two characters, or *officers,* is hard to tell.

*Are the masters afraid of insurrection?*–They live in constant and great fear upon this subject. The least unusual noise at night alarms them greatly. They cry out, "What is that?" "Are the boys all in?"

*What is the worst thing you ever saw in Kentucky?*–The worst thing I ever saw was a woman, stripped all naked, hung up by her hands, and then whipped till the blood ran down her back. Sometimes this is done by a young master, or mistress, to an aged mother, or even a grandmother. Nothing the slaves abhor as they do this.

*Which is the worst, a master or a mistress?*–A mistress is far worse. She is forever and ever tormenting. When the master whips it is done with; but a mistress will blackguard, scold, and tease, and whip the life out of a slave.

*How soon do the children begin to exercise their authority?*–From the very breast of the mother. I have seen a child, before he could talk a word, have a stick put into his hand, and he was permitted to whip a slave, in order to quiet him. And from the time they are born till they die, they live by whipping and abusing the slave.

*Do you suffer from cold in Kentucky?*–Many people think it so warm there that we are safe on this score. They are much mistaken. The weather is far too cold for our thin clothing; and in winter, from rain, sleet, and snow, to which we are exposed, we suffer very severely. Such a thing as a great-coat the slave very seldom has.

*What do they raise in Kentucky?*–Corn and hemp, tobacco, oats, some wheat and rye; SLAVES, mules, hogs, and horses, for the southern market.

*Do the masters drink a great deal?*–They are nearly all *hard* drinkers–many of them drunkards; and you must not exclude mistress from the honor of drinking, as she is often *drunk*, too.

*Are you not afraid they will send up and catch you, and carry you back to Kentucky?*–They may make the *attempt*; but I made up my mind, when I left slavery, never to go back there and continue alive. I fancy I should be a load for one or two of them to carry back, any how. Besides, they well know that they could not take me out of any state this side of Pennsylvania. There are very few in New England that would sell themselves to help a slaveholder; and if they should, they would have to run their country. They would be hooted at as they walked the streets.

Now, in conclusion, I just want to say, that all the abuses which I have here related are *necessary*, if slavery must continue to exist. It is impossible to cut off these abuses and keep slavery alive. Now, if you do not approve of these horrid sufferings, I entreat you to lift up your voice and your hand against the whole system, and, with one united effort, overturn the abominations of centuries, and restore scattered families to each other; pour light upon millions of dark minds, and make a thousand, yea, ten times ten thousand, abodes of wretchedness and woe to hail and bless you as angels of mercy sent for their deliverance.

## Facts from the Personal Knowledge of Milton Clarke

General Leslie Coombs, of Lexington, owned a man named Ennis, a house carpenter. He had bargained with a slave-trader to take him and carry him down the river. Ennis was determined not to go. He took a broadaxe and cut one hand off; then contrived to lift the axe, with his arm pressing it to his body, and let it fall upon the other, cutting off the ends of his fingers. His master sold him for a nominal price, and down he went to Louisiana.

A slave named Jess, belonging to Deacon Logan, went out one Sabbath evening for the same purpose that many young men have for making calls on that evening. Jack White, a captain of the patrols, followed Jess, and took him out and whipped him, in the presence of the family where Jess was making his call. The indignation of poor Jess was roused. He sought his way by stealthy steps, at night, to the barn of Jack White, and touched it with the match. Jess was suspected, and his master told him, if guilty, he had better own it, and he would send him down the river to save him from being hung. Jess was put in jail on suspicion. Deacon Logan sent his slaves by night; they got Jess out of jail; he was concealed by his master for a few days, and then sold for $700, and sent down the river.

**Hired Slaves–Bagging Factories**

In and around Lexington are numerous factories for spinning and weaving hemp bagging. Young slaves, from ten to fifteen years old, are employed in spinning. They are hired for $20 to $30 a year, and their condition is a very hard and cruel one. They have a weekly task. So much hemp is weighed out; so much filling must be returned, all of the right size, and at the proper time. Want of skill, mistakes of various kinds, subject them to frequent and unmerited stripes.

An overseer of one of these factories, Tom Monks, would tie up his poor boys, and give them from forty to fifty lashes. He kept them sometimes yoked with iron collars, with prongs sticking out, and the name of the owner written on them. Working in these factories takes all the life and spirit out of a young slave, and he soon becomes little better than an idiot. This is the worst kind of slavery in Kentucky. When the life is thus taken out of these poor lads, at the age of eighteen or twenty, they are sold for Louisiana. Here a short but bitter doom awaits them.

They are first carried to New Orleans, and put in pens. When a purchaser comes and inquires of the slave what he can do, he must make pretensions, of course, to great skill and ability, or the seller will abuse him. But what will be his condition with the purchaser, who finds that he cannot do half the things he promised? The sugar-planter blames the slave. He came from the bag factory, but said he was a good field hand; could hold plough, hoe corn, or any other kind of farming work in Kentucky. He has lied to his *present* master, for the benefit of his *former* one. He atones for it by many a cruel flogging. When they find one that is very awkward and ignorant, the master tells the overseer to "put him through for what he is worth;" "use him up as soon as you can;" "get what you can out of him in a short time, and let him die." In a few years, the poor fellow ends his labors and his sorrows.

The bell rings at four o'clock in the morning, and they have half an hour to get ready. Men and women start together, and the women must work as steadily as the men, and perform the same tasks as the men. If the plantation is far from the house, the sucking children are taken out and kept in the field all day. If the cabins are near, the women are permitted to go in two or three times a day to their infant children. The mother is driven out when the child is three to four weeks old. The dews of the morning are very heavy, and wet the slaves all through. Many, from the upper slave states, die from change of climate and diet. At the time of making sugar and molasses, the slaves are kept up half the night; and the worst-looking creatures I ever saw were the slaves that make the sugar for those sensitive ladies and gentlemen, who cannot bear the sight of a colored person, but who are compelled to use the sugar made by the filthiest class of slaves.

O, how would LIBERTY wash away the filth and the misery of millions! Then the slaves would be washed, and clothed, and fed, and instructed, and made happy!

There is another and very different class of slaves sent south. When a body servant refuses to be whipped, or his master breaks with him for any other reason, he is sold south. The purchaser questions him, and he tells the truth. "Can you farm?" "No, sir." "What can you do?" "Work in garden, drive horses, and work around the house." "Ay; gentleman nigger, are you? Well, you are gentleman nigger no longer." He is ordered upon the plantation, and soon acquires skill to perform his task. Always sure to perform all that is required, he does not intend to be beaten by any human being. The overseer soon discovers this spirit, and seeks occasion for a quarrel. The slave will not be whipped. A half a dozen overseers are called together, and the poor fellow is chained, and whipped to the border of his grave. In a week or two, the overseer tries his spirit again; comes into the field and strikes him, by way of insult, and the slave knocks him down, and perhaps kills him with his hoe, and flies for the woods. Then horses, dogs, overseers, planters, lawyers, doctors, ministers, are all summoned out on a grand nigger hunt, and poor Bill Turner is shot dead at the foot of a tree, and the trumpet sounds at once a triumph and a retreat.

I expect nothing but there may be an attempt made to carry me back to slavery; but I give fair warning to all concerned, that now, knowing the value of *liberty*, I prize it far above *life*; and no year of suns will ever shine upon my chains as a slave. I *can* die, but I *cannot* be made a slave again. Lewis says, "Amen! Brother Milton, give me your hand! You speak my mind exactly."

### Calling on Their Masters for Help

The Frankfort (Ky.) "Commonwealth" publishes a rich letter from the Ohio justice of the peace, who assisted the kidnappers of Jerry Phinney. It is addressed to the person who now has possession of Jerry, and calls lustily on him to save the wretched justice from the penitentiary. He, and the man who taught him that "that is property which the law declares to be property," ought both to go to the penitentiary till they can unlearn that diabolical sophism. The fellow really talks as though it made a vast difference in his crime, whether the victim had been entangled in a similar manner before. He writes,–

"I wish you, as a friend, to ascertain if the power of attorney, presented to me by said Forbes, is a lawful and true one, and if the said Jerry Phinney is a slave or not; for if he is not, it will go very hard with us, and is a perjury on the said Forbes, in consequence of the affidavit he filed with me.

"And to you, Kentuckians, I appeal for redress for the severe treatment we have received, in consequence of the seizure and conveying off of a slave, as I verily and solemnly believe Jerry; for I cannot for one moment believe that said power of attorney is a forgery, and that Forbes committed perjury.

"And we earnestly solicit your aid; for, without, the state prison is our doom; although I acted in good faith.

"The abolitionists are determined that we shall be convicted of kidnapping.

"We are very poor, but defy the world to bring a dishonorable act against us, except the one now against us, which they deem a great one; but I deny being guilty of any such charge.

"Unless you aid and assist us, you may rely on it that you never need expect an officer, in this section of the country, ever again to touch any thing of the kind, for fear of the penitentiary; for prejudice and abolitionism are bent to imprison any justice of the peace, who dare make an attempt to examine a fugitive from labor, and more particularly if he is poor, and has not money to carry him through a course of law.

"Prejudice is so great, that I am credibly informed the governor has issued his proclamation, offering a reward of one thousand dollars for the apprehension of said Forbes, and Jacob Armatage, the young man that went with Forbes; the citizens are to pay half of said reward.

"Please favor me with an immediate answer; and inform me what proof can be had that Jerry is a slave, and what relief can be rendered us in our distressing case. You may also look for a letter from our attorneys, F. J. Mathews and Colonel N. H. Swayne, as they will address all those whose signatures are in said power of attorney, which is in their hands at this time; and that is the reason I have not given their Christian names.

"WM. HENDERSON, J. P.
"H. D. HENDERSON.
"D. A. POTTER."

**President Edwards–A Testimony**

On the 15th of September, 1791, the younger Edwards, then pastor of a church in New Haven, preached a sermon before the Connecticut Society for the Promotion of Freedom, &c., in which he has the following remarks:–

"The arguments which have been urged against the slave-trade, are, with little variation, applicable to the holding of slaves. He who holds a slave, continues to deprive him of that liberty which was taken from him on the coast of Africa. And if it were wrong to deprive him of it in the first instance, why not in the second? If this be true, no man has a better right to retain his negro in slavery, than he had to take him from his native African shores. And every man who cannot show that his negro hath, by his voluntary conduct, forfeited his liberty, is obliged *immediately to manumit him.*

"I presume it will not be denied that to commit theft or robbery every day of a man's life, is as great a sin as to commit fornication in one instance. But to steal a MAN, or to rob him of his liberty, is a greater sin than to steal his property, or to take it by violence. And to hold a man in a state of slavery, who has a right to his liberty, is to be every day guilty of robbing him of his liberty, or of *man-stealing.* The consequence is inevitable, that, other things being the same, to hold a negro slave, unless he has forfeited his liberty, *is a greater sin than concubinage and fornication.*

"To convince yourselves that, your information being the same, to hold a negro slave is a greater sin than fornication, theft, or robbery, you need only bring the matter home to yourselves. I am willing to appeal to your own consciousness, whether you would not judge it to be a greater sin for a man to hold you or your children, during life, in such slavery as that of the negroes, than for him to indulge in one instance of licentious conduct, or in one instance to steal or rob. Let conscience speak, and I will submit to its decision."

If the above remarks were correct in 1791, can they be wrong in 1846? If our good divines were correct in calling slaveholders man-stealers, and slaveholding a greater sin in the sight of God than concubinage and fornication, what must we think of the moral state or the heart of those modern D. D.'s, who are willing to receive slaveholders into the church of God, and are ready to weave out of their own hearts a *theological fiction* to palliate the enormous evil? Alas! C. M. Clay[39] is right, when he says, "The *disease is of the heart, and not of the head.* We tell you, brothers, that the American people know well enough that the bloody stain is upon them—but they love its *taint!* If we can't arouse the conscience, and ennoble the heart, our labor is lost. A *seared conscience* and a *heart hardened by sin*—these are the grand supporters of slavery in and out of the church. How can these giants be subdued?—*From the Charter Oak.*

## Order of Exercises for a Slaveholders' Meeting

### *I. Prayer. By Cassius M. Clay.*

#### PRAYER AND SLAVERY.

There are many men, professing the Christian religion, who also profess to believe slavery a divine institution! Now, we have lived thus long, and never yet have heard a prayer offered up to God in its behalf! *If it is of God, Christians, pray for it!* Try it; it will strengthen your faith and purify your souls.

O THOU omnipotent and benevolent God, who hast made all men of one flesh, thou Father of all nations, we do most devoutly beseech thee to defend and strengthen thy institution, American slavery! Do thou, O Lord, tighten the chains of our black brethren, and cause slavery to increase and multiply throughout the world! And whereas many nations of the earth have loved their neighbors as themselves, and have done unto others as they would that others should do unto them, and have broken every bond, and have let the oppressed go free, do thou, O God, turn their hearts from their evil ways, and let them seize once more upon the weak and defenceless, and subject them to eternal servitude!

And, O God, as thou hast commanded us not to muzzle even the poor ox that treadeth out the corn, let them labor unceasingly without reward, and let their own husbands, and wives, and children, be sold into distant lands without crime, that thy name may be glorified, and that unbelievers may be confounded, and forced to confess that indeed thou art a God of justice and mercy! Stop, stop, O God, the escape from the prison-house, by which thousands of these *"accursed"* men flee into foreign countries, where nothing but tyranny reigns; and compel them to enjoy the unequalled blessings of our own *free* land!

Whereas our rulers in the Alabama legislature have emancipated a black man, because of some eminent public service, thus bringing the holy name into shame, do thou, O God, change their hearts, melt them into mercy, and into obedience to thy will, and cause them speedily to restore the chain to that unfortunate soul! And, O God, thou Searcher of all hearts, seeing that many of thine own professed followers, when they come to lie down on the bed of death, and enter upon that bourn whence no traveller returns,–where every one shall be called to account for the deeds done in the body, whether they be good or whether they be evil,–emancipate their fellow-men, failing in faith, and given over to hardness of heart and blindness of perception of the truth, do thou, O God, be merciful to them and the poor recipients of their deceitful philanthropy, *and let the chain enter into the flesh and the iron into the soul forever!*

***II. Hymn.***

**PARODY.**

Come, saints and sinners, hear me tell
How pious priests whip Jack and Nell,[40]
And women buy, and children sell,
And preach all sinners down to hell,
And *sing* of heavenly union.

They'll bleat and baa, dona like goats,
Gorge down black sheep, and strain at motes,
Array their backs in fine black coats,
And seize their negroes by their throats,
And *choke*, for heavenly union.

They'll church you if you sip a dram,[41]
And damn you if you steal a lamb;
Yet rob old Tony, Doll, and Sam,
Of human rights, and bread and ham–
*Kidnapper's* heavenly union.

They'll talk of heaven and Christ's reward,
And bind his image with a cord,
And scold and swing the lash abhorred,
And sell their brother in the Lord
To *handcuffed* heavenly union.

They'll read and sing a sacred song,
And make a prayer both loud and long,
And teach the right and do the wrong;
Hailing the brother, sister throng,
With *words* of heavenly union.

We wonder how such saints can sing,
Or praise the Lord upon the wing,
Who roar and scold, and whip and sting,
And to their slaves and mammon[42] cling,
In guilty conscience union.

They'll raise tobacco, corn, and rye,
And drive and thieve, and cheat and lie,
And lay up treasures in the sky,
By making switch and cowskin fly,
In *hope* of heavenly union.

They'll crack old Tony on the skull,
And preach and roar like Bashan[43] bull,
Or braying ass of mischief full;
Then seize old Jacob by the wool,
And *pull* for heavenly union.

A roaring, ranting, sleek man-thief,
Who lived on mutton, veal, and beef,
And never would afford relief
To needy sable sons of grief,
Was *big* with heavenly union.

Love not the world, the preacher said,
And winked his eye and shook his head;–
He seized on Tom, and Dick, and Ned,
Cut short their meat, and clothes, and bread,
Yet still *loved* heavenly union.

Another preacher, whining, spoke
Of one whose heart for sinners broke;–
He tied old Nanny to an oak,

And drew the blood at every stroke,
  And *prayed* for heavenly union.

Two others oped their iron jaws,
And waved their children-stealing paws;
There sat their children in gewgaws;
By stinting negroes' backs and maws,
  They *keep up* heavenly union.

All good from Jack another takes,
And entertains their flirts and rakes,
Who dress as sleek as glossy snakes,
And cram their mouths with sweetened cakes;
  And *this* goes down for union.

### *III. Sermon. By Old Lorenzo.*

Lord, what is wealth? It will not stay,
But ever flies away, away,
  As restless waters roll;
No sort of goods, beyond the grave,
Will ever meet its owner, save
  A faithful negro's soul.

Brethren, did you ever think of the importance of laying up treasures in heaven?[44] What is gold, or houses, or land, or earthly honors? Will they purchase happiness here? Will they secure heaven hereafter? When you "shuffle off this mortal coil," all these things will become as dross, worthless as the sediments of a blacksmith's forge. You tell me, you are going to buy up a store of good works. But what will that avail you. Can you plead your good works at the bar of heaven? Will good works save you? Be not deceived with such a fatal delusion. How are you going to get your good works performed here on earth, to heaven? I tell you, you must have available funds there. They have got a bank up here in the moon. Suppose you could get one of their bills–what would it be worth here? It might be worth something as a curiosity, but as a medium of commerce, it would be worthless as a rag. So of good works; you can't get them to heaven. They are a sort of bank stock, valuable on earth, to be sure, and "nowhere else but there." A draft in heaven, on the Bank of Good Works, located here on earth, would not sell for its cost in white paper. This laying up good works, to purchase an inheritance in heaven, is like bottling jack-o'-lanterns to light up pandemonium.

My hearers, I see you look discouraged. Despair sits brooding on your hearts. "If good works will not save us," I seem to hear you ask, "what will?" Well, I'll tell you:–you must take something that you can get to heaven; that's plain. You must buy niggers. Niggers have souls, and when they die, if they are Orthodox niggers, they go right off to heaven. But, mind you, they must be Orthodox; if they are not, your fat will be in the fire. First, get them converted to the gospel of submission. Preach to them often, from the text "Servants, obey your masters."[45] You will lose nothing by it. If you want to sell them, you can recommend them then, as Christians, and get your money back again; or, if you prefer, you can flog the souls out of them, and lay up a treasure in heaven. Just think of it, Deacon Ashley. Suppose yourself knocking at heaven's gate, and the old turnkey, St. Peter,[46] demanding, "Who comes there?" "Deacon Ashley," you will reply. "What claim do you present to an entrance here?" inquires Peter. Well, now, you see, if you have no claim, you can't get in; so you up and say, "I have property here." "Property here?" asks Peter, in apparent surprise, though I warrant you he knows all about it; "what property?" You will say, "There was my man Caesar, a member of our church, whom I shot ten years ago, when he attempted to run away. I paid eight hundred dollars for him. I suppose he is here." "Yes," Peter says, "Caesar is here. Walk in, deacon; where a man's treasure is, there must he be also."

So you see the immense importance of owning slaves. Our hopes of everlasting salvation hang on the institution of slavery; and as McDuffie said, (I think 'twas Mac,) it is the chief corner-stone of our republican edifice. When I look at it in this light, and think of the mad efforts that are now made to abolish this heaven-ordained institution, and thus secure the destruction of the only free government on earth, and the endless misery of all its inhabitants, my very blood boils with horror at sight of an abolitionist. To rob a man of his purse on earth, is inhuman enough; but to rob him of his treasure in heaven is absolutely diabolical. How many millions on millions of dollars have been paid for slaves, who have gone to heaven! So many millions of dollars, of course, laid up as a treasure there. And these fanatics would not only cheat us out of our just rights here, but would plunder us of our treasures in heaven. I am utterly alarmed at the supineness of our church. A few years ago, if an abolitionist attempted to inculcate his abominable doctrines, you stoned him, hissed at him, pelted him with bad eggs, poured water on him with fire engines, and even shot him dead. You then maintained your character as God's church militant. You have now settled down as God's church capitulated. May you buckle on your armor afresh, and, with brick-bats and unmerchantable eggs, go forth to defend your treasures in heaven. Amen.

### Our Countrymen in Chains

Our fellow-countrymen in chains,
  Slaves in a land of light and law!
Slaves crouching on the very plains
  Where rolled the storm of Freedom's war!
A groan from Eutaw's haunted wood–
  A wail where Camden's martyrs fell–
By every shrine of patriot blood,
  From Moultrie's wall and Jasper's well.

By storied hill and hallowed grot,
  By mossy wood and marshy glen,
Whence rang of old the rifle-shot,
  And hurrying shout of Marion's men!
The groan of breaking hearts is there—
  The falling lash—the fetter's clank!
Slaves—SLAVES are breathing in that air
  Which old De Kalb and Sumter drank!

What, ho!—our countrymen in chains!
  The whip on WOMAN'S shrinking flesh!
Our soil yet reddening with the stains
  Caught from her scourging, warm and fresh!
What! mothers from their children riven!
  What! God's own image bought and sold!
AMERICANS to market driven,
  And bartered, as the brute, for gold!

Speak! shall their agony of prayer
  Come thrilling to our hearts in vain?
To us, whose fathers scorned to bear
  The paltry menace of a chain?
To us, whose boast is loud and long
  Of holy Liberty and Light—
Say, shall these writhing slaves of wrong
  Plead vainly for their plundered Right?

Shall every flap of England's flag
  Proclaim that all around are free,
From "farthest Ind" to each blue crag
  That beetles o'er the Western Sea?
And shall we scoff at Europe's kings,
  When Freedom's fire is dim with us,
And round our country's altar clings
  The damning shade of Slavery's curse?

Just God! and shall we calmly rest,
  The Christian's scorn—the Heathen's mirth—
Content to live the lingering jest
  And by-word of a mocking Earth?
Shall our own glorious land retain
  That curse which Europe scorns to bear?
Shall our own brethren drag the chain
  Which not e'en Russia's menials wear?

Down let the shrine of Moloch sink,
  And leave no traces where it stood;
No longer let its idol drink
  His daily cup of human blood:

But rear another altar there,
  To Truth, and Love, and Mercy given;
And Freedom's gift, and Freedom's prayer,
  Shall call an answer down from Heaven!

J. G. WHITTIER.[47]

## EDITORIAL NOTES TO *NARRATIVES OF THE SUFFERINGS OF LEWIS AND MILTON CLARKE*

1. Andrews, *To Tell a Free Story*, 138.

2. Quarles, *Frederick Douglass*, 55–56; also cited in Andrews, *To Tell a Free Story*, 138.

3. Elijah Parish Lovejoy (1802–1837) was a clergyman and antislavery activist. Lovejoy edited a religious newspaper, the *St. Louis Observer*, which was very critical of slavery, until he relocated across the Mississippi River in 1837. From his new location, Lovejoy published the *Alton Observer* and helped organize the Illinois Anti-Slavery Society. He was killed in November 1837 by rioters intending to destroy his press. See Simon, *Freedom's Champion*, 77–135, and Simon, *Lovejoy*, 66–117; Dillon, *Elijah P. Lovejoy, Abolitionist Editor*, 159–70; Padgett, "Comeouterism and Antislavery Violence in Ohio's Western Reserve," 193–214.

4. Starling, *The Slave Narrative*, 129–32, 233–35; Logan and Winston, eds., *Dictionary of American Negro Biography*, 116–17.

5. Cassius Marcellus Clay (1810–1903) was a Kentucky politician and abolitionist. He served in the Kentucky Legislature in 1835, 1837, and 1840, worked for Lincoln's election in 1860, and was a minister to Russia in 1861, 1862 and 1863–1869. He was the founder of *The American*, an antislavery newspaper in Lexington, Kentucky. See Richardson, *Cassius Marcellus Clay*.

6. The bloodiest battle of the American Revolution (June 1775). Over 1,000 British troops and 400 Americans were killed.

7. Job 3:3–5, "Let the day perish wherein I was born, and the night in which it was said, There is a man child conceived. Let that day be darkness; let not God regard it from above, neither let the light shine upon it. Let darkness and the shadow of death stain it; let a cloud dwell upon it; let the blackness of the day terrify it."

8. Matthew 10:35–36, "For I am come to set a man at variance against his father, and the daughter against her mother, and the daughter in law against her mother in law. And a man's foes shall be they of his own household."

9. Edmund Burke (1727–1797) agitated the British Parliament for the impeachment of Warren Hasting (1732–1818) as the first British governor-general of India.

10. One of the avenging spirits who brings retribution to those who have violated natural laws.

11. Property a woman brings to a husband in marriage.

12. Before birth.

13. Nero (A.D. 37–68) was emperor of Rome from A.D. 54 until his death. He is most well-known for a fire that destroyed a large portion of Rome in A.D. 64. Nero was rumored to have started the fire, though he blamed Christians for the destruction and began a process of Christian persecution.

14. An intermediate state after death for cleansing venal or mortal sin.

15. Fibers used in making cloth.

16. Thomas Jefferson (1743–1826) served as the third president of the United States (1801–1809). He authored the Declaration of Independence, was elected governor of Virginia in 1779, appointed minister to France in 1785, became secretary of state in 1789, and founded the University of Virginia in 1819.

17. An innkeeper.

18. Deuteronomy 14:8, "And the swine, because it divideth the hoof, yet cheweth not the cud, it is unclean unto you: ye shall not eat of their flesh, nor touch their dead carcase."

19. Titus 2:9, "Exhort servants to be obedient unto their own masters, and to please them well in all things; not answering again"; Ephesians 6:5, "Servants, be obedient to them that are your masters according to the flesh, with fear and trembling, in singleness of your heart, as unto Christ."

20. 2 Corinthians 7:5, "For, when we were come into Macedonia, our flesh had no rest, but we were troubled on every side; without were fightings, within were fears."

21. Patrick Henry (1736–1799) was a Virginia statesman, lawyer, and orator who is best known for the words "Give me liberty or give me death," which he used in a speech given before the Virginia Provincial Convention in 1775. On that occasion, he spoke in favor of calling the Virginia militia to defend the colony against the British.

22. An acute fever.

23. A British soldier.

24. Deuteronomy 27:4, "Therefore it shall be when ye be gone over Jordan, that ye shall set up these stones, which I command you this day, in mount Ebal, and thou shalt plaister them with plaister"; Joshua 8:30, "Then Joshua built an alter unto the Lord God of Israel in mount Ebal."

25. Solomon (?–928? B.C.) was the third king of ancient Israel. He ruled from circa 965 B.C. until his death and has a reputation for diplomacy and wisdom. The passage quoted is from Proverbs 17:12, "Let a bear robbed of her whelps meet a man, rather than a fool in his folly."

26. The place on a hill in Jerusalem where King David built his royal palace. It was originally named the City of David. It was also the site where King Solomon later built the Temple. It came to refer to the homeland of the Israelites. Among Christians, Zion often refers to a heavenly city or heavenly home.

27. Benedict Arnold (1741–1801) was a wealthy businessman in New Haven, Connecticut. During the American Revolution, he became a captain in the Connecticut militia and rose to the rank of colonel. His forces helped capture Fort Ticonderoga in 1775. Arnold is best known for conspiring to surrender West Point to the British in 1780.

28. An informer.

29. Henry Clay (1777–1852) was a Kentucky statesman who served as speaker of the House of Representatives, United States senator, and secretary of state. He is best known for proposing the Missouri Compromise of 1820 and the Compromise of 1850.

30. A common law intended to bring a party before a court or before a judge.

31. Leviticus 25:9, "Then shalt thou cause the trumpet of the jubile to sound on the tenth day of the seventh month, in the day of atonement shall ye make the trumpet sound throughout all your land."

32. A distillery.

33. Titus 2:9; Ephesians 6:5. See note 19 above.

34. Debtor.

35. Creditor.

36. Jeremiah 22:13, "Woe unto him that buildeth his house by unrighteousness, and his chambers by wrong; that useth his neighbour's service without wages, and giveth him not for his work."

37. Habakkuk 2:11, "For the stone shall cry out of the wall, and the beam out of the timber shall answer it."

38. James 5:4–5, "Behold, the hire of the labourers who have reaped down your fields, which is of you kept back by fraud, crieth: and the cries of them which have reaped are entered into the ears of the Lord of Sabaoth. Ye have lived in pleasure on the earth, and been wanton; ye have nourished your hearts, as in a day of slaughter.

39. Cassius Marcellus Clay. See note 5 above.

40. The names throughout the poem are fictitious names representing slaves.

41. A small drink of liquor.

42. Riches.

43. Deuteronomy 3:13, "And the rest of Gilead, and all Bashan, being the kingdom of Og, gave I unto the half tribe of Manasseh; all the region of Argob, with all Bashan, which was called the land of giants."

44. Matthew 6:19–21, "Lay not up for yourselves treasures upon earth, where moth and rust doth corrupt, and where thieves break through and steal: But lay up for yourselves treasures in heaven, where neither moth nor rust doth corrupt, and where thieves do not break through nor steal: For where your treasure is, there will your heart be also."

45. Titus 2:9; Ephesians 6:5. See note 19 above.

46. St. Peter (?–A.D. 64?) was a leading apostle of Jesus. Originally named Simon, Jesus renamed him Peter (Matthew 16:18–19), meaning "rock" in Greek. Peter was a leader of the early Christian church. For Catholics, Peter's role in the church is the basis of the establishment of the position of Pope. Protestants interpret Jesus as establishing the church on Peter's faith. Peter may have been martyred during Emperor Nero's persecution of the Christians in A.D. 64–68.

47. John Greenleaf Whittier (1807–1892) was an American poet and committed abolitionist.

# 5

# WILLIAM HAYDEN (1785–?)

## NARRATIVE OF WILLIAM HAYDEN

*The Narrative of William Hayden* is a bit of an anomaly within the genre of slave narrative writing. Because of its digressive qualities and unwillingness to dwell on the cruelties Hayden experienced, the *Narrative* structurally and thematically differs from the kinds of narratives that had their origins as oral recitations at abolitionist rallies. Hayden's narrative contains few of the stock scenes and little, if any, of the moralizing tone that characterize those writings. Most strikingly, the *Narrative* is not structured around the narrator's eventual escape from slavery. In fact, William Hayden adamantly insists that his liberation will be spiritual rather than physical.

At one point, Hayden's owner, Mr. Phillips, became burdened with debt. Phillips's business partner, Mr. Castleman, became consumed with the prospect of bringing Phillips to financial ruin and purchasing Hayden for himself. "At length he [Mr. Phillips] came to me, and after some preliminary remarks, informed me that on our arrival home, I would have to leave the State, as he was greatly . . . determined to have me sold, in case of his inability to pay him [Mr. Castleman] the debt he owed him." Hayden received a pass from Mr. Phillips and traveled to Ohio, which was a free state: "I was thus soon landed unquestioned and unmolested on the free shores of Ohio–beyond hearing of the overseer's lash–and beyond the oppression of the human panderer, who makes a filthy living of luxury, by bartering his own flesh and blood in a public mart." Yet, out of a dual sense of obligation to Mr. Phillips, and the moment of his impending spiritual liberation, Hayden chooses to return to slavery: "I could not consistently sacrifice the confidence which Phillips had placed in me–and I felt fully assured that the hour of my deliverance had not yet come when I was to shake off my yoke of bondage, and proclaim my Emancipation to the world. I had delved for years–long and tedious years in slavery–and now, that I had touched upon a free soil, armed with a pass and signed by my master, authorizing my freedom to travel where I listed, I might have felt myself secure from the Shylocks of the Law, and laughed defiance at the administrators of Southern justice. But I craved not the aid of the laws of man. My liberation was to be *supernatural*–and effected through my own exertions. Hence, I cared not for the bright prospects which were then held out to me." Instead of the usual pattern of conversion from enslavement to freedom or individual bondsman to outspoken abolitionist working as part of a larger political and social cause, the climactic moment of Hayden's *Narrative* occurs when he is able to free his mother from slavery. Hayden never allows the desperation of his enslavement to place him in a position where he compromises what he sees as his spiritual duty.

Little is known about Hayden's life beyond what he presents in his *Narrative.* He was born in Bell-plains, Virginia in 1785. Hayden was taken from his mother when he was five years old, sold to the first in a long series of owners, and taken to Kentucky. Though he received a great deal of informal instruction, his formal education did not begin until around 1807 when he was sent to a school for African American children. Hayden also learned a number of trades, including rope making, barbering, and confectioner.

Like the majority of slave narratives, the desire for freedom is the controlling motif. But the narrative subverts the traditional outline of the form by locating Hayden's ultimate quest for freedom with his mother. After he achieves his own freedom, Hayden goes in search of his mother, from whom he was separated almost forty years earlier. Without the inclusion of abolitionist doctrine and political invective, Hayden's *Narrative* succeeds as a narrative of continuous spiritual fortitude against the vicissitudes and harsh realities of slavery. The *Narrative* does not achieve (nor does it attempt to achieve) the goal of portraying William Hayden as one of slavery's representative victims. Rather, the *Narrative* chronicles the experiences of an individual who, through spiritual fortitude and strength of will, was able to escape the effects of the system.

The events contained in the *Narrative* conclude in 1828. Hayden relocated to Cincinnati, Ohio in 1835. It was here that Hayden composed the *Narrative* and evidently published it at his own expense.

The *Narrative* reprinted here is from the first edition. This edition was initially published for the author in Cincinnati, Ohio, in 1846.

# NARRATIVE
## OF
# WILLIAM HAYDEN.
## CONTAINING
# A FAITHFUL ACCOUNT OF HIS TRAVELS FOR A NUMBER OF YEARS, WHILST A SLAVE, IN THE SOUTH.

WRITTEN BY HIMSELF.

"Party intolerance is despicable; the true spirit of FREEDOM acknowledges only the supremacy of GOD, and the RIGHTS OF MAN."

Cincinnati, Ohio
1846.



PUBLISHED FOR THE AUTHOR.

**Dedication.**

To the friends of my youth,
who, when a poor Slave Boy, taught me the first rudiments
of an English Education, and to
the friends of the slave,
throughout the Universe, together with all
mothers and daughters,
who, through the wisdom of God may be set apart to raise
and Educate families,
this narrative
is respectfully Dedicated.
By their humble servant,
The Author.
Cincinnati, O.
June 1st, 1846.

## PREFACE

In appearing before the public with this brief Narrative, it becomes me, as a duty, to place before that public, some of the principal reasons, which induced me to the writing of it. It is a custom, now-a-days, on assuming the station of an author, to make an obeisance to those, whom the individual looks upon as private and personal friends; and acting under this impulse, I respectfully doff the cap to *all*, and salute them with a few stray leaves from the Diary of my travels through the Southern States, with the Slave Traders.

When first induced to pen this short narrative, I was but a mere boy—a slave—untutored, and alone in the world, save some few friends, who stood by me through "thick and thin." But from my infancy, I have been led on by degrees from step to step, by a supernatural Power—its voice has ever been with me—and each and every promise which has been made by it, has invariably been fulfilled. Many may smile in incredulity at this assertion, and consider it as a hallucination of the brain; or as an evidence of supercilious superstition. Well, let them—but I feel fully convinced and encouraged in that belief, from the blessings and knowledge which I daily see spread before me. Nor am I without precedence. We read in times gone by of the Spirit appearing to many of the believers in God. In the case of Mary the spirit of the Lord made manifest the birth of her son, Jesus—to the shepherds, too, were the same tidings delivered, through the voice of a spirit—the spirit also encouraged and converted Saul of Tarsus, as he wended his way on a crusade against the Christians—and even John was blest with a knowledge of the upper Heavens, through a supernatural spirit. Nor can I believe that those days have forever gone. A supernatural something has always forewarned me of approaching events, and endowed me with a knowledge, which has enabled me to weather the storms of forty years servitude and servile slavery, and to come forth from the trials with honor to myself, and honor to my nation. Nor has that spirit yet forsaken me—although an old man—some sixty years of age—it holds daily communion with me, and urges me on to deeds of sympathy and good will towards all men, whilst its sweet consolations repay me an hundred fold, for all the trials I am doomed to undergo. God's name be praised.

I have said that I was forty years a slave. Yes, forty of the best years of my life, were passed in servile bondage to my fellow men. Yet, during that time, the body alone was prostrated in that degraded situation—the mind—the image and the best gift of God to man, was always elevated—it spurned the shackles, and soared to Heaven, where it revelled in Elysium; in blissful concert with its Creator.

Hard as was my fate, in being cast into a state of bondage, in witnessing the insult, the degradation—the licenstiousness, and the abuse, which the slave-traders heaped upon the unprotected slaves—yet, I stood firm—unshrinking to the commands of mortal—and centred my every thought upon a higher and a holier power. The body may be debased to purposes, at which the brute creation would shudder—it may be made an instrument in the hands of man to prosecute the most damning crimes—but the soul—the immaterial man—the thought—the mind, can never be chained. It belongs to a higher sphere, and ruled by a higher Being, in whose hands are held the whirlwind and the storm,—the existence and non-existence of all the human family. What cause had I then to fear? My heart laved in the waters of Salvation, and my Guardian Spirits stood forth as beacon lights, pointing the road to freedom and to happiness. I felt that this was the case with me, and I determined that "sink or swim," I would persevere in obedience until the goal was won—and the joyful shout of deliverance and bliss, echoed through the valley.

Mankind should ever bow to the power which rules and sustains him. But that power is not vested in mortal hands—it is coeval with Deity itself, and will ever be exercised with rigid justice by an almighty God. Nor will he permit his creatures to suffer—for he has promised that those who put their trust in Him, shall pass the fiery ordeal of the world, unscathed, and unharmed. To Him, then, must I offer up my prayers for my safe deliverance from all the ills which beseige me during my pilgrimage on Earth.

To some, this may seem as a wild and unfeasable theory—void of common sense in a practical point of view, but it is as true, and unchangeable, as that God exists in His might and power, and will one day come to judge the world in righteousness and justice. Why should I not put my trust in God? I am now sixty years of age; and by His power alone, I have been sustained and upheld, and by His power alone, I have passed through trials and temptations at which the stoutest heart would quail. He has borne me through them all—He has raised me up friends in every part of the world in which I have sojourned, and He has brought me out purified and sanctified of the sins of the world—and all connexion with the evil one. How, then, can I turn a deaf ear to his commandments—and turn aside from the path which He has pointed out to me, wherein to go? Were an earthly friend to do this—were he to extend over me the arm of his protection, during the reign of trial and vexation—were he to shield and protect me in health and in sickness, what would be thought of me by the world, if I should turn aside, and denounce and condemn him as a vain, inconsistent, and ambitious personage? Would they award to me the feelings of common humanity and respect? or, would they place any confidence in the sincerity of any profession I might thereafter make or endeavor to place before a discriminating public? No—most assuredly they would not. I would be looked upon as an ingrate—a wretch, whose feelings were seared in the heated cauldrons of base inhumanity, and corruption.

If the world would then look upon me thus—would treat me as a desperado of the deepest dye; what should I expect from an almighty parent who had sustained and protected me in every vicissitude of an ill-spent life? who has thrown the shadow of his protecting wings over me in health—and upheld me with His might and goodness when death overshadowed my couch, and laid the cold impress of his rigid seal almost upon my brow? What, I say, should be the feelings of a Righteous God, who had endowed me with talent—with understanding, and with a knowledge of good and evil, were I thus knowingly to transcend His commands—to turn ingrate upon His hands, and to say to Him by my actions,—"I am aware that you have been a kind and indulgent benefactor to me through life—but I feel that I am now beyond the influence of sickness, disease, or want, and I ask not your further aid?" Could I reasonably suppose that he would pass by such actions, and not stretch forth his "red, right arm" of vengeance; and smite His ungrateful and blasphemous creature to the earth? No! His vengeance most assuredly would fall upon me, and with such an effect that language would fail to draw the faintest picture of its direful consequences.

Why then, should I cast Him aside, after all the blessings which He has bestowed upon me? No, I will not—I cannot let go my hold upon the Saviour, though the Earth should sink, and bury me in its deep and awful chasms of destruction. He has been a friend, when all others have passed me by in silence and in scorn—He has smiled upon me, when every lip has railed out against me in loud and vehement denunciations—and blessed be His name, he has supported me when all would have gloried in my downfall.

Yes, gentle reader, God has sustained me in every vicissitude in which I have been placed, and I feel well assured that He will continue to sustain me, until He gathers me home, to rest with Him in endless happiness. What, but His mighty arm could have shielded me from the many dangers through which I was compelled to pass, when in the possession of wealthy, influential and relentless slave-traders and slave-holders? What but His power could have snatched me from destruction, when angered men raved at me, and stood with fire-arms pointed at my bared bosom? and who but He could have given me power to brave my oppressors, and declare my rights, when the thong and the scourge were about to be applied to me at Natchez? None,—no, I feel that it was He alone, that thwarted them in their proposed cruelty, and saved His weak and dependant creature from their savage and infamous designs. His holy name be praised–for, He has said that throughout all time, He will protect and encourage all his children, if they will but put their trust in Him.

Nor has He alone shielded me from danger and harm. He has, I have reason to believe, endowed me, as I have before stated, with the power and faculty of foreseeing events, which were to take place in my eventful career–and instructed me as to the path in which I should travel, by which to avoid their evil tendencies. This, I have studiously endeavored to do; and if I have, in any instance transcended my instructions, I can confidently assert, that it has been an "error of the head, and not of the heart." My liberation from bondage was promised me by my spiritual guide in the days of my youth, when the chains of slavery were first rivetted upon me–and the means and influences by which this happy event was to be consummated. Yes–even the year in which I was to become a free man, was made manifest to me, whilst toiling in servitude, and abject misery for the malignant gratification of my fellow man–and it was this knowledge which supported me throughout nearly forty years of unjustifiable bondage. My heart was cheered with the blest conviction, that I was, at that period, to become my own master, and acknowledge the right of none to command or drive me in the commission of earthly acts, save the almighty Father of the human family. And my freedom was brought around in the exact manner which the Spirit had set apart for it. The stern, rigid and independent, yet, at the same time, obedient course which as a slave, I pursued towards my masters, was also, persevered in, for the express purpose of fulfilling to the letter, the commands of my Guardian. Never have I knowingly thwarted its wishes, but once–and heavy, indeed was my punishment, in the loss of a portion of my thumb, and uneasiness of mind for a long time thereafter. All its promises to me, have been rigidly fulfilled–and though the clouds of disaffection, and affliction have lowered heavily o'er my domestic concerns–yet, all, I feel assured will again be set aright in obedience with its stern commands. Man–frail, impotent man has no control over them.–he can neither advance, nor retard them in their nature or their march–and until the hour arrives, in which the spirit is to set matters in their proper light before the world, things must still exist in the uncomfortable way in which they now are.

Reader–this little narrative, which will in its pages show you more conclusively the power which this Spirit has exerted over me during life, and the implicit obedience which I have ever yielded to its dictates–is another object brought forth at its commands. For this purpose I was endowed with an education suitable for the object allotted me–and for this purpose, I have now placed myself before the public as an author of a strange race. You may laugh in incredulity, if you please–you may hoot at the idea of man possessing the power of foretelling events, and you may term me fool, idiot, or what you choose–yet, as I have shown you before that this power was given man in former days—you may rest equally assured, that such power has been endowed me by an allwise God. The work is now before you, and though it springs from a dark and benighted source; yet your humble servant prays you will appreciate its merits in a spirit of kindness and leniency. May God bless you.

### To Mrs. Mary S. Smith, Who for Many Years Was to me a Kind Mistress

Lady,—in childhood, we were wont
To greet each others smile;
Were wont to romp in innocence—
In peace our hours to while,
But since age lower'd on our brow,
He wields his sceptre o'er us now.

The sainted mother blest us then,
And taught us of our God—
She taught our infant minds to bow
To his most righteous rod—
She taught our tongues to lisp his name,
And know He ever is the same.

She loved us both—her kindness seem'd
The love the angels bear—
She guided all our young desires,
Of sin, she said, beware—
And when in after years we stood
Before the world, we nam'd her—good!

Sweet were those hours to you and I,
When kneeling o'er our forms
She raised her hands to heaven, and cried,
Shield them from the storms,
Which rage through life—Great Father, save
Them from sin's dark, polluted grave.

The tears then bathed our youthful cheeks,
We knew not why we wept—
But He was o'er us night and day,
And watched us while we slept;
And led us with a parent's hand,
To study well His each command.

Storms since have lower'd o'er our heads—
Life's ills have sought to lure
Our wayward spirits from His charge,
And all His laws abjure.
But like the leaden weights of sin,
Have failed to touch the soul within.

Lady, I love thee, though I claim
  No kindred with thy race,
But as the playmate of my youth,
  I still can see thy face,
And bless the child of her whom then
I loved to hear–not to condemn.

Thy kindness, too, in after years,
  Was shown to me throughout–
Thy love for me through health and strife,
  Cast evil spirits out–
And I have blest thy name, and wept,
To think of thee, whilst others slept.

O, may thy life be one of joy;
  May care ne'er reach thy mind;
And may the God of Heaven bless
  The friend of human kind–
And grant that His sweet counsel may
Enrich thy soul through endless day.

Calm be thy pillow when in death,
  Thy body shall recline–
When friends shall mourn thy swift decay,
  Then tears of grief be mine.
The lowly sod which hides thy face
Shall water'd be by my poor race.

And now farewell! We ne'er may meet,
  To join again the hand–
But yet in Heaven we shall join.
  In God's ne'er dying band;
And in Love's concert voices swell,
To sing His praise–till then, FAREWELL.

RECOMMENDATION:

We, the undersigned, have for many years known Wm. HAYDEN, the author of this work, and believe him to be an honest, upright man,–and withal, a Christian.

Isaac G. Burne,

Jacob Burnet,

E. A. Sehon,

T. Baker,

John Davison,

J. C. Miller,

Jesse O'Neill,

F. Bodman,

C. Cottman,

C. Woodward,

John E. Williams,

John Griffith,

Mr. Kilbreath.

## NARRATIVE OF WILLIAM HAYDEN

The subject of this narrative was born in the year 1785, at Bell-plains, Stafford county, Virginia. The life of a SLAVE, may be considered by many, as a matter of no curiosity—not even the smallest quota of importance in the great drama of human existence. But when the Divine interposition of Christ interferes with the earthly career of mankind, it is the duty of ALL, to treasure each token, small as it may be, which he, in his gracious providence, may vouchsafe to us, as particles in the great chain of human events, which is to guide us through this "vale of tears," and render us fit to anchor our frail barques on the ever blessed shores of the New Jerusalem.

Hence, it is the object of the writer to relate, and to endeavor in the briefest manner possible, to point out certain matters connected with his history as a man—and as a member of community, to show to his fellow mortals the wonderful means, and the various ways through which God exhibits to us, his wonderful nature. To some, he gives wisdom—to some, wealth—and to others, he yields a complication of gifts, such as, wisdom, a foresight of coming events, &c. Hence, the motto, "coming events cast their shadows before."

The latter was the means which Jehovah[1] has employed with the subject of these few but serious reflections, and historical crumbs; and though they may appear as irrelevant, and non apropos, yet, ere they are finished, and perused by the kind reader to whose indulgence they are given, I feel fully confident that by a critical view of the same, he or she may be led to a full knowledge of God's means; of his supernatural agency in leading all to him, and which is considered by the world, or worldly portion of Creation, as superstition, and unworthy of aught save the contumely heaped upon the ignorant of the present day, and a comparison with the dark ages which have long since elapsed and passed from earth.

But this is all wrong. God works his wonders, not in one man—nor in any particular set of men—but in ALL, unobservant of clime and color. He has, in his wisdom, apportioned us as the beneficiaries of his Divine precepts and gifts. None escape—the high and low—the rich and poor—all alike feel His wisdom, and acknowledge his goodness. It would be unjust, therefore, in man to contend with Deity upon the principle of worldly elevation. The mighty in thought, are generally the very poorest in this world's gear. "All is not gold that glitters"[2]—nor, yet is all unholy, which wears the semblance of the world, or pertains to the machinations of selfish and corrupt man. As an evidence of this, I have but to offer to the reader the case of the Apostle Paul.[3] When worn down with disease; when racked with afflictions in both mind and body; famished and languid; dragged from a prison cell; emaciated, and almost disgusting to the sight of humanity–so cursed was he with vermin and the filth of a prison house, he presented a poor, and I might say, a pitiful contrast, when confronted with the royal Agrippa;[4] the tyrant Felix; the vain-glorious, and coquettish Felicia, who had met to pass judgment upon him. Yet the spirit of the Lord was there–his powerful hand upheld his servant through his trials, and supported him through his afflictions,–it pointed out to him the road he was to travel, and the means he was to employ, in order to overcome the temptation and snares of the wicked, and reach the haven he desired. Rags could not disguise the MAN–the prison habits could not cover him from the admiration of all. Even regal authority, surrounded by its slaves, its worshippers, and its proselytes, was not able to withstand the power, in the hands of God's most humble, abject, and comparatively inefficient agent. The glance and glare of royalty vanished–a kingdom became paralyzed; and the highest power in Christendom, robed with the authority of the land; entrusted with the treasure of the kingdom, surrounded with wealth, wisdom and greatness, quailed before the eyes of Paul; quaked at his words, as they fell trembling from his lips, and the poor, royal trio, quivering in agony, made known their effect through Agrippa, by the fearful assertion: "Thou almost persuadest me to be a Christian." Such was the effect of God's words upon the world's great men, when delivered even by his abject and imprisoned servant; and at this more enlightened age, what may be the result of these few stray leaves, Time, and God's ways alone will determine.

Until I was about five years old, I was permitted to live with my mother, who was the property of Mr. Ware, of Bell-plains, and who resided on the banks of the Potomac creek. When quite an infant, not more than two or three years of age, I was known to crawl to the door of the cabin, and watch the rising of the sun. The Day God as he peered from the chambers of the east, and cast his reflection from the clear bosom of the Potomac, appeared to my infantile mind like two suns–the one in the heavens, and the other in the body of the waters; and every morning, it was my desire, and indeed, my first employment, to repair to the door and witness the rising of the two suns. How anxiously my mother, (fond and endearing as she was,) gazed upon me, as I was engaged in witnessing with joy, the beauties of Heaven, and Heaven's goodness.

This act was considered as remarkable in one so young as me, and many were the predictions, from men of influence and extensive learning, that in me, the slave would find a determined and consistent friend, whilst my race and my color would find a representative of their rights through the means of Christ, of which they should not be ashamed. At this age, too, the Spirit of the Lord was at work in my heart–my path of duty was pointed out–my many vicisitudes were before me–the acknowledged divinity of God was building up in my heart a throne, upon which to receive the offerings of many to a new knowledge of his grace—and through me, his humble agent, to lay down to my fellow creatures a new path—a new belief—a belief, unlike the Egyptian idols, but founded upon the uncontrovertable and inscrutable ways with which man is brought by a supernatural agency, to yield himself to Divine decrees, and throw off the yoke which Satan and the world has placed upon him;

> "To be a man—a meek and lowly worm,
> A firm despiser of all worldly scorn."

Nor was this infantile practice—this pleasure of gazing upon the beauties of Heaven's goodness without its benign effects. One morning, on rising from my straw pallet, to seek the door of the cabin, the bed was discovered to be on fire. A sense of danger was even then apparent to my young mind, and through exertions and persuasions, I was enabled to be the instrument of God's holy wisdom, to save the lives of my sister and brother who slept in the same room. That sister now resides in Cincinnati, and can be seen at my house; having removed with my mother and me from Virginia, when our parent was freed. God's beauties were before my mind; his hand was over me, and leading me on; he made my soul, even at that early age acquainted with the fact, that I was to become an instrument in his hand, to work out in my feeble capacity, a portion of his divine work.

But to my Narrative:

At the age of five years, I was taken from my mother, who, for the preceding four years, had a presentiment, that she was not the one designed by Providence to rear me. The man to whom I was sold in the capacity of a slave, was named John Ware, and resided at Swan's Point, on the Potomac, and from that time until I was seven years old, I was engaged in travelling through various parts of the State, as a nurse. And I must be permitted to say for myself, that those children, who are yet permitted to exist, and whom I had the privilege of nursing, can still bear testimony of the affection I bore them, and which I had every reason to believe was reciprocal upon their parts.

But a change soon came over my master's affairs. He was a gambler and a horse-racer, and becoming involved in debt, he was necessitated to sell me. To some, this change might have appeared as an affliction of the deepest caste. But to me, although satisfied with my situation, is was a change for the better. My heart yearned for my mother, whose cabin I had left, and I hoped through God's goodness, to be enabled to procure a purchaser who resided somewhere in her neighborhood.

But a trial ensued. The nature of a master whose deception causes him to fawn upon, and flatter a slave, worked upon my youthful imagination, as it generally works upon the imaginations of all such, and was attended by a like result. A short period previous to my being sent off for sale, my master and mistress left home without taking me with them as a waiter. This, they had never before done, and I was at a loss to account for the change which had been wrought in their conduct. Previously, I had been a favorite, and having excited thereby the jealousy of my fellow slaves, I soon found that the absence of my master and mistress was attended with any thing but good results. The colored people of the household proved ungrateful, and by them, I was used with extreme harshness; hence, my strong affection for my mother, and the strong desire to be near her proved too much, and in my unguarded moments I caught one of my master's horses, and started on my journey. Herein, then, the reader will see the baneful influence of deception and ill usage towards a growing child. But being young, and unaccustomed to the treatment of a horse, I soon rendered him unfit for service, and was necessarily necessitated to perform the balance of the journey on foot. Hence, turning the horse loose, and tying the bridle around me, I made the best of my way towards my mother's cabin. And now, permit me to relate the consequences of deception. Being conversant with it in my master's family, it was an easy matter for me to coin a palpable lie–so, whenever I was asked where I was going, and what my business was, (as was often the case) my invariable answer was, that I was looking for a stray horse which had broken from my master's fields. My youth, and the fact of my having the bridle with me, proved a sufficient shield, and I was permitted to pass unmolested; and having often travelled the road near where my mother resided, I soon found the place, where I arrived in safety, after having travelled for upwards of a whole day.

When I arrived at my mother's, I was in such a state of nudity, and so apparently altered that she did not recognize me. I remained with her about a week, when the master whom I had formerly served, sent me home, writing at the same time to my then master, requesting him not to punish me, and as I was a great favorite, his request was complied with; but shortly after, I was sent to my mistress's brother, who resided and kept a store near Port Royal. This was in consequence of my master being in debt to him for goods, &c., and though gentle reader, you may think it strange, yet it is nevertheless true, that human flesh and blood–the living image of Jehovah himself, was pledged as an old Jack-knife is now-a-days, to the Shylock money-lenders[5] in payment, until my master could attain the means wherewith to redeem me. To this event I looked forward with hope, but the time passed, and, not being able to obtain the money for my redemption, I was sent to Ashton's Gap, a place on the mountain, where an auction for the sale of slaves was generally held; and in company with five other lads, was doomed to undergo the ordeal of the flesh-barterer's hammer. And what think ye was the sum to be raised from the sale of six human beings? The mean and pitiful sum of $50. Here I remained three or four weeks, but time, which brings about all things, finally brought around the fatal day on which the traffic of flesh and blood was to take place. I have before remarked that from my infancy I was admired for my sprightliness, and whether this was the cause or not, I was the first one brought under the hammer, and strange to say brought the full amount of my master's delinquency. A further sale was deemed unnecessary, and the remainder of the boys were prepared to be returned home. During the day we had feats of wrestling, leaping, &c., at all of which exercises, I came off victorious. My young heart was elated with joy at my success, but when the moment came in which I was to be severed from my young companions, and when running to the carriage which was to convey them to their homes, their mothers, and all they held dear on earth, I was informed that I was doomed to remain, and seek a home with a strange master, my heart swelled within me and a flood of tears was the only balm left the benighted and sorely aggrieved slave. No mother's smiles were decreed to welcome me–no maternal words to soothe my pains, no kind and long known home to yield me sustenance and repose–naught but the clanking chains of slavery–the roof of a stranger, and my own sad reflections were meted out to me. Is it a wonder then, that tears gushed forth, or that the mind bent as a reed shaken by tempestuous blasts. Those who know the endearments of home, can duly appreciate my situation.

The master, whose property I became by this sale, lived in Lincoln county, Kentucky, and although he was deputized by his brother to purchase a slave for him, he having advanced him the money for that purpose, he saw fit to send me to his brother, as being small, and purchased a larger, though a sickly looking youth, whom he kept for himself.

On leaving with my master, we went to Farquar county, and there staid until fall, near Smith's Mills; and here permit me to relate an anecdote of our travels. In returning to the house of my new master, I was compelled to travel on foot, except when going down hill on the mountain. In those days, locks were almost unknown, as used for locking the wheels of the wagons which travelled the roads, and small trees were fastened to them to act as holds back. On these trees would I climb, and for the purpose of displaying my agility, seek the very highest limb; and many a severe fall have I received in being thrown from them to the distance of many yards in front of my high seat of honor, so many, that in fact I began truly to conclude that "they that stand high, have many blasts to shake them, and if they fall, they dash themselves to pieces," insomuch that I concluded to abandon my sport, and take the more modest and unassuming mode of travelling, to wit: "Shank's mare."

Some time after I was sent to my master's brother, whose slave I then became, my purchaser came to pay a visit to my master. He was accompanied with several gentlemen, who were aware of his trick in foisting me upon his brother, and when they saw me, so surprised were they, in comparing me with the one which he had kept, that in their teasing and jeering him on his "profitable trade," they let the "cat out of the bag," telling him that appearances were generally deceitful, if not totally opposite to the world's generally received opinions.

My master's name was Frederick Burdet, who resided near Georgetown, Ky. He was married to a Miss Cave, of whom I shall speak hereafter, as she proved to the friendless slave a mother and a guardian, when no relative was near to cheer his servile hours. Mr. Burdet was poor, owning naught of this world's gear, save me; but his wife was seised of three other slaves, and a small tract of land. But soon misfortune and disease visited the abode of my master. The fell Destroyer[6] laid his chilly hand upon the latch, and bore hence to an unknown world the head of that much loved family. After his death, the Court decreed me to his unborn child.

As my master had raised me in a pious manner, and had intended setting me free, after he should have set before me the evils of the world, it became, as a matter of course, the duty of his wife to carry out his pious intentions. Being young, I generally repaired to a spring close to the house, and watching the sun as he rose, and cast his reflections upon the bosom of the spring, would often weep bitterly. In this I was indulged by my master, but after his death, following the same course, my mistress one day spoke to me, thus: William, if you be a good boy, and cry no more, I will be to you a mother; and placing one hand upon my head, and wiping the tears from her eyes, she raised them to Heaven, and supplicated God that he would enable her to fulfil her promise, and thanked him that he had placed some object in her way, to fill the vacuum occasioned by the death of her husband. To this I consented, but felt loath to abandon the spring, although she strictly fulfilled her promise. But from the spring I sought the chimney corner, where I first held communion with the Spirit, which seems to be my guardian angel to the present day.

When, however, it was known that I had only commanded $50, the neighborhood was greatly surprised, and many a dealer in human flesh, would have been anxious to have purchased me; but my good mistress loved me for her dear husband's sake, and not all the wealth of Mexico could have then induced her to part with me.

Shortly after my master's death, I was received into the house as the servant of my mistress, and when my young mistress was born, was initiated as her nurse, with the assurance, that if I took good care of her, I should be free as soon as Miss Polly arrived at marriageable age. This raised my spirits to a high degree, and I became still more attentive to my duties, determining to deserve, if it were really in my power, my freedom from bondage. It was, too, a matter of surprise and astonishment to witness the difference in my actions. Naught but the thought of being a FREE MAN filled my mind from morning until night, and I felt as if I loved my mistress with a ten-fold ardor, whilst it seemed to me that the Lord was watching over the destinies of the poor, friendless colored boy, who was far beyond the reach of parents and relatives. These thoughts inspired me to good actions; but sorry was I, when my young mistress was about two years of age, to witness the lowering of my first cloud of sorrow. It loomed dark and heavy upon me, and has continued to grow darker and darker around me until the present day. At that time my mistress, needing no doubt the proceeds of my labor, as I was large enough to plough with a shovel-plough, hired me out to a man named Henry Barlow. To him I proved useful, and as I was always brisk in running errands, and doing chores, I was universally liked and admired by both black and white.

I remained, however, but one year with Mr. Barlow, when my mistress's brother, Mr. Henry Cave, without her consent, hired me out for six years to a Mr. Elijah Craig, a rope-maker in Georgetown, and it was in this place that the Almighty, in his wisdom saw fit to reveal to His humble creature, the future destiny of his days–to open to him the various paths in which he was to tread, and to point out to him the straight and surest way by which to arrive at the goal of happiness for which his stricken soul panted. Blessed be his holy name. He has upheld me through good and through evil report, and placing all confidence in his supreme power, I feel that he will continue to watch over and bless his sorrowing creature.

Soon after I came to reside with Mr. Craig, I was placed by him in the rope-walk, for the purpose of learning the rope-making business, and being very attentive, and quick of apprehension, I became a favorite with my employer, and set to work at spinning much sooner than is customary with the generality of boys; but being naturally good humored and quick on foot, I was frequently called from my work to run errands, and it appeared to me as if the fates were arrayed against me, for as soon as one "chore" was done–another stood ready waiting for my attendance. But this state of things was soon brought to an end, for it was soon discovered that I lacked but strength to be a first rate workman, and was accordingly sent with some others to Frankfort, Kentucky, to work in a "walk" of Mr. Craig's, under the management of a Mr. James Davis, with whom I had been but a short time, before I became a general favorite with my employer. And here I must digress for a brief time to return to my mistress.

When I parted with her at Georgetown, it was with tears, in which, kind woman, she, as well as myself, indulged freely. At parting she made, I well remember this remark:

"William, if you are ever whipped by any to whom you are hired, remember, I charge you, to return home immediately, for I can permit no one to correct you but myself."

When, then, I had been some time with Mr. Davis, for some trivial offence I was whipped, and remembering my mistress's words, I returned to her. But what was my surprise on hearing her exclaim, when I had narrated the circumstance to her:

"Go back, my boy, and stay till I send for you."

I was shocked, and although I was several times flogged thereafter, I never returned to her again. But my ruling star was uppermost, and I became a favorite with Mr. Davis's children, who taught me to spell, and for this act of kindness, I was always ready to accommodate them in any way I could. Unlike a majority of slave-holder's children, they were not above teaching the poor colored boy to spell and read, but seemed to pride in my rapid progress, which has endeared them to me through this cold and inhospitable world.

But as youths generally like a little spending money with which to enjoy themselves, I soon cast about me for a means of obtaining it. An opportunity soon presented itself, and as we lived near the Kentucky river, I applied myself during my leisure moments to fishing, at which I was generally successful. These fish I conveyed to market, and obtained a considerable sum of spending money, without, in the least, encroaching on my master's time, as I had in a short time became acquainted with all the inn-keepers, who did not hesitate to purchase my "FINNY TRIBE."[7]

This success was followed immediately by another. Having become intimate in my fish speculation with the principal inn-keeper in Frankfort, I made arrangements with him to work for him on holidays and Sundays, cleaning boots, washing dishes, &c.; and in this capacity was my leisure moments employed, during my whole sojourn at Frankfort.

About six months, however, before my time expired with Mr. Craig, my mistress had me a new suit of clothes made and sent, with directions to Mr. Craig to purchase me shoes, stockings, and other necessary "FIXINS," and charge the same to her: so, that for the first time in my life, I had a suit of Sunday clothes.

I here, about this time too, met with a still greater success, by becoming acquainted with Miss Martha Johnson, who lived near Mr. Toleman's, and to whom, through the interposition of Divine Providence, I am indebted for the completion of my limited education. And now, with the permission of the reader, I will commence giving data of my future events. Previous to this, my memory has failed me, and as it was the events of, I might almost say, my infancy, they have passed to the bourne of things forgotten.

About the year 1802, all the hands hired by the year in the rope-walk at Frankfort, were sent home again; but as my contract was for six years, I was compelled to stay six months longer. In the spring of this year I again went to Georgetown. On arriving there, my mistress did not recognize me, so greatly had I grown, and in fact since I had left Georgetown so great had been the improvement both in growth and mental endowments with my YOUNG mistress, that I was at a loss to recognize her. During my absence, however, my mistress, had taken unto herself a second husband, which so much grieved me, on account of the love I bore her dear departed help-mate, that I felt very loath to return home. But as I had not seen any of them for many years, and as they were all anxious for me to return, I was soon compelled to forego my objections, and seek a home again, under the roof of my mistress.

Whilst I was in Georgetown, a new building, which had been reared during my absence, attracted my attention. On a flag stone in front, I discovered some marks which appeared to me as unintelligible as the hyeroglyphics of the Chinese. But I was determined to ascertain their purport, and accordingly asked a gentleman who was passing, the meaning thereof. He informed me that it was the year in which the building was erected; and from this I was aware that the succeeding year would be 1803. This inspired me with a love of figures, and so intently did I set myself about it, that I was soon a tolerable hand at calculation.

At the end of the year I again left Georgetown, and was hired to a man by the name of Peter January, sr., in Lexington, Ky., who owned a rope-walk there. Here I first saw Mr. Clay, who was then engaged in ornamenting his present residence at Ashland. With this gentleman, I became acquainted through the recommendations given him of me by his children, whose acquaintance, I had made previously, and with him I afterwards became a great favorite.

This gentleman and his lady were set apart by my guardian Spirit as my benefactors in time to come. Mrs. Clay has already proved such to me, having used me with the tenderness and sympathy of an indulgent parent.

Before the year was out, too, it was discovered that I was so good a hand in the rope-walk, and so attentive to all the duties assigned me, that all the factors in the place were anxious to obtain me, so that a choice of homes was thus unexpectedly held out to me, of which I was exceedingly glad.

Casting among these people, then, it was my good fortune to accept the proposals of Mr. J. Ware, who had formed a friendship for me, and with whom I resided eight years.

In 1804, I went to board with a wagon maker, by the name of Edward Howe, who generally employed a great many workmen. For these, I performed all the little offices they asked of me, insomuch that they were so well pleased with me, that they all agreed to teach me my lessons in reading, in order that I might become more perfect. To induce me, however, to devote some portion of my time to pleasure and amusement, for so studious had I become that they feared for my health, they would persuade me to play marbles with them, agreeing to learn me so many lessons, for so many games, so that in a short time, I began to like the amusement, and even progressed farther in my studies.

Soon after I went to board with Mr. Howe, it was my good fortune to meet with Miss Johnson, my former instructress. She was at this time teaching school, which was composed of the first families of the place, and having no one to cut wood, or run errands for her, I made an arrangement with her to do her "chores," provided she would teach me at nights, and on the Sabbaths. This she accordingly did, and she often unconsciously filled me with joy, by remarking, that in the little time I had, I made more rapid progress in learning than many of the white boys with all their boasted privileges, and assiduity.

In the same fall, (1804) I became acquainted with Mr. Postlewate, a tavern-keeper, and went with him to clean boots, &c., as I had previously done in Frankfort.–During this time, I did not charge Miss Johnson any thing for the services which I rendered her, as I considered that the learning which she gave me, more than cancelled the obligation. But as I had now become, as I thought too large for a servile occupation, I began to be ashamed of cleaning boots, and consequently, obtaining an old axe, and putting it through the grinding operation, I concluded to make a good living by chopping wood. Through the influence of Miss Johnson, I obtained the work of all the parents of her scholars, so that I had now as much as I could possibly do.

Shortly after this, some of Miss Johnson's relatives came to Lexington. They were players, and engaged in the theatre in that place, and as they went to house-keeping immediately on their arrival, I soon became their "man of all work," so that I felt myself at home, either at their house or that of Miss Johnson. But in 1805, I again went to rope-spinning, and was soon acknowledged to be the best spinner in the country, so that again a choice of homes was again held out to me. This good fortune induced me to tell Mr. Ware, that I would not stay any longer with him, unless he would advance my wages. This, at first, he refused to do, but at last consented to raise them to $6 per year. At that period, twine was worth more at the South, than it ever has been since, bringing from 75 cents to $1 per pound. My task at spinning was forty-eight pounds–and this was considered a good day's work for two men. This task I generally accomplished–gaining two days in every week, exclusive of the Sabbath. The proceeds of these two days amounted to three dollars, which it was optional with me to make, or devote my time to pleasure, if I saw fit so to do.

And now comes a question which many of my readers may smile at, as deriving its existence from Superstition. Meeting one day with Miss Johnston, I inquired of her, if she had ever known any one who could foretell what was to happen in after days. She replied that she had heard of people who had foretold things, and wished to know why I had proposed the question to her. My eyes brightened–my heart beat with a nervous anxiety, and I informed her that I could foresee the day when I was to become a FREE MAN; and that although I had been torn from my parents in my infancy, the day was in prospective, on which I should again meet with them.

The reason of my making this inquiry, was simply this–I had been for several weeks engaged in burying the chips which fell from the logs which I was chopping, on the lot where the house stood. This act I had been commanded, by the Spirit to do; and that, if I strictly fulfilled its mandates, the house should be removed, and no one should occupy the lot, until I had written a Narrative of my Life. Many years have since elapsed–and yet, the lot is vacant, and none seem disposed to occupy it. When, however, I told Miss Johnson this, she smiled, and doubted the virtue of the Spirit–to which I replied that, in four years from that time, we should meet for the last time upon earth, and part, with many tears. This, in the year 1807, was literally fulfilled–and my prediction, so strangely verified, seemed to remove all doubts of my future destiny from her mind. God bless her–for she was to me, a friend indeed.

And here, gentle reader, permit me to give you a brief outline of my progress, and the means by which my limited education was acquired. The only book which I could command, was composed of the leaves of an old Spelling Book, which I had picked up and sewed together, and from this I gleaned such instruction, that I was soon enabled to read the Testament with ease. From that–I attempted writing; which at first, was a difficult task for my friends to persuade me to undertake, as I was then under the impression that it was without the pale of a colored man's nature, to ever be able to write. The substance of this I remarked, to a friend who worked with me in the rope walk, and who after calling me a fool, informed me that he would guaranty to teach me how to write in a short time. He then got a small stick and pointing it, stooped down and wrote "W. HAYDEN," in the sand. After a long time, I was persuaded to make the attempt of copying it. The trial proved successful, and so great was my joy, that tears of pleasure trickled down my face. After this, I would go round the Court House, and picking up all the fragments of paper, I could find, would bring them home. I was afraid however, to attempt reading them, as my playmates informed me that if the white people, caught me reading or writing they would hang me. Whether this assertion was made in ignorance, or through envy, I never ascertained, but certain it is, that it had the desired effect; and consequently I was compelled to get some of the "walk hands" to read them for me, and when I got by myself, I would, with a stump of a pen which I had picked up, endeavor to copy them. My ink, I made by boiling walnut bark and coperas, and having obtained some paper, abandoned my copies in the sand, and took to pen, ink and paper. In this manner, I succeeded in writing a tolerably legible hand, of which I was extremely proud, and would often reason with myself in this wise: "Yonder is a WHITE man–he has seen the frosts of sixty winters, and during that long period, has never been able to learn to read the word of God, or transmit by writing one solitary thought to his distant relatives and friends; whilst I, a poor, friendless colored boy,–a slave–can read the consolations held forth in the Scriptures, and inform my distant friends of my progress through life. O, the difference! I would not part with my little knowledge, for all the wealth of your illiterate dealer in flesh and blood!"

In the year 1807, there was a school started for some colored children, whose fate it had been to be bound out; and as their masters did not want them taught by a white man, they engaged a colored one, belonging to Dr. Downey, to instruct them in spelling and reading. This man was known among us as "Ned,"–what his surname was, I never ascertained. As there were not enough FREE children to make up the school, notice was given, that any one wishing their servants taught, (if they were willing to entrust them with Ned,) should be permitted to send them to school. On hearing this, I applied to Mr. Ware, and having obtained his consent, started, with three others, from the same factory.

The school was composed of about thirty scholars, and considering myself and my companions, as naught but rope hands, we were for a time reckoned as fit butts for all jeering and jesting. This, however, we heeded not, but attended to our books, and by close attention, I was soon at the head of the first spelling class in the school, They were not aware that I had been to school before, and remembering their former conduct, I cared not to inform them of the fact. Ned, too, raised upon my shoulders, for it was generally considered that it was by his exertions that I made such rapid progress; and as a reward for my diligence he made me sub-teacher, and gave to me the charge of the younger children. Previous to this, however, Ned, rather offended not only myself, but all who were connected with the affairs of the school. Being "Principal," and striving to gain favor with some, he paid strict attention to the free children, and would sometimes neglect hearing us our lessons, for upwards of a day, in order to facilitate them. To this I objected, backed by Mr. Duke, and others. At last broaching the subject, (and merely because I spoke my mind freely,) I was deserted by my backing, and was finally expelled from the school. Sore as this occurrence was to me, the Spirit upheld me, and I was finally rewarded for my obedience to its dictates.

> "____ He stood,
> The proud monument of flesh! Yet still,
> The softest whisper of the Word Unchangeable,
> The Spirit, and the Lord,–bade all return;
> And mortal schemes were lost!"

The Trustees of this School, allowed the citizens to have a Night session, if they could procure a teacher. After looking around, they procured not only a teacher, but a room from Mr. Benj. Duke, or, as many called him Mr. Benjamin Almond; an individual of high standing, having a house of his own, in which he, every Sabbath, and often during the week, held Divine service. At a meeting of the Trustees, he and his brother, who were, great friends of mine, recommended me, and agreed to vouch for my abilities and good conduct. This act of kindness they performed, without my knowledge. When, therefore, in a few days, I was called on by Mr. Duke and his lady, and informed of my nomination and election as teacher, I was greatly surprised, and not knowing what answer to return, I informed them of my total incapacity to teach, and of my want of means to rent a room. But Mrs. Duke overruled these objections, informing me that Mr. Duke had prepared his basement story for me, and that she would see I had no difficulty with the children as she would make them behave. Still diffident, to take charge of a school, I told her that I had no place to sleep. This she also overruled, telling me she had a cot at home, and that I might sleep there; so that I was compelled to reward their kindness by an acceptance of their offer. My closet at this time in which I kept my wardrobe was an old flour barrel, and this I conveyed one dark night to my school room.

Mr. W. W. Watson, and Mr. Henry Blue, who were then youths with myself, will no doubt recollect these occurrences, and testify to their truth. They are both, now, worthy and respectable citizens of Cincinnati.

The news of a school being about to commence, spread like wild fire, and when the children came to the house, inquiring for the master, so abashed was I that for a time I hesitated to say I am he. But this bashfulness soon passed away, and I commenced operations by drawing up and laying down a code of rules, by which my school was to be regulated.

The principal rule was, That there was to be no talking or whispering in school during school hours, which were from seven to ten o'clock, P.M. That this rule applied to both old and young, regardless of merit or standing, and that any disobeying, or knowingly violating the rules laid down should be punished, by being turned out, regardless of the weather–if this appeared too hard, they had better withdraw, as their names should not be enrolled. I informed them, too, that I had been elected their teacher by a board of Trustees, that I knew but little, but what I did know, I was determined to teach to the best of my abilities, and that it was as much to their advantage as it was gain to me, to comply with the rules of the school. This brief code offended many, and the consequence was, that they left the school; but on informing their masters of the cause, so pleased were they, that they induced many gentlemen to send, who would not otherwise have done so, not knowing who or what I was. At length my duties commenced, and I soon gained the respect of my scholars to such a degree, that upon their representations, their masters authorized them to invite me to their houses on the Sabbaths, in order that they might see me. They did so–and when their masters became acquainted with me, they appeared surprised that a slave negro, should be so superior in learning to the free negroes, and declared that a person of my information should be immediately set free.

This was in the latter part of the year 1807, the same in which I had commenced my career as wood-chopper. But now, that I was installed as a schoolmaster, my vanity was touched, and I began to consider myself above my old playmates; (O, the follies of youth!) and having the confidence of both my colored and white friends, among the latter of whom was a lady, whom I called "mother," from the kind treatment which I experienced at her hands; things went on right smoothly.

Whilst I was teaching, however, there came to me a young girl, who was a great favorite with her master, to learn to read. Her master would not permit her to keep company with colored folks, as he considered her much superior in grace and mental endowments, to the generality of her race, which, in fact, she really was. For me she soon formed an attachment, and from her representations of me to her master, he requested her to invite me to come and dine with her on the following Sabbath. I accordingly went, and so pleased were they with me, that Mr. Yaiser, (the master alluded to) took the trouble to inquire of my friends, if I was honest, as he felt disposed to become my friend.

About this time, my term ended, and as I had quit the wood-chopping business, I was at a loss what to engage in as a means of living. The inquires of Mr. Yaizer, however, relative to my character, were answered satisfactorily, and he, being a tanner, and wishing to employ a person in whom he could trust, to attend markets and purchase hides, I was engaged. This business was generally performed before day, and delivered at his yard, he paying me a per centage on every hide delivered. My success at this was various; sometimes making as high as $2.50 per day. Here then, I felt again my indebtedness to the Almighty, for his merciful guardianship over me—for as soon as one business afforded me no longer the means of support; another was provided for me. In this way things progressed until 1809.

During all that time I had not lost the hope of again seeing my parents; and so anxious was I to hear from them, that I inquired of every traveller with whom I met, if they were from the vicinity of Falmouth, Virginia. At last I met with a wagoner, and whilst inquiring from whence he hailed, an old woman who was with him replied that she was from Falmouth. Here my mother had acted in the capacity of midwife; and I concluded that she must know something about her. Whilst revolving in my mind whether to ask her or not, the old lady inquired my name. I told her it was William, and that of my mother was Alcy—and that she belonged to Mr. George Ware, who lived at Bell-plains, Stafford county, Virginia. The old lady eyed me sharply for a few moments, and burst into tears, saying, that I was so much like my poor mother, that she would have known me any where, and informed me that she had just come from where my mother resided, and that she had charged her if she found her son any place in Kentucky, to give him her blessing, and write to her immediately. The old lady could not write,—consequently she got the overseer to write to my mother, the joyful news that the lost was found. I then applied to a friend to indict a letter for me, which I immediately endorsed and dispatched to my poor, dear mother; to which, in a few months I received an answer, which filled my heart with unspeakable joy.

In the fall of 1809, I again went to Georgetown, where my old mistress still continued to reside. The young miss who was but two years of age, when I first left Georgetown, had now budded into womanhood, and was upon the eve of marriage. The reader will remember, that after the death of my master, the court consigned me to her as her property, hence, as she was about taking to herself a husband, it was thought best that I should remain in Georgetown until the event took place; consequently I remained, living mostly at home. But here my pride was aroused—I had travelled considerably, and had resided in large places, and I was illy contented to remain in so small a place as Georgetown; so after a short time, I again went into a rope-walk to work, and notwithstanding there was an experienced white man superintending the business, he could show me nothing that I did not already know; hence I soon became the foreman of the factory. From this time I was treated more as a white man than any thing else, as all were acquainted with my deportment whilst in Lexington; and should this Narrative ever meet the eye of any slaves who can read it, let them take my conduct towards my masters as an example. I can assure them that they will be treated with kindness, and rendered still more happy in the bondage in which Providence has seen fit to cast their lots. Nor did I confine myself exclusively to the rope-spinning business. Whilst I was in Lexington, I had learned to make a good article of blacking, and also a polish for morocco shoes of every color, so that I soon got more work of this kind, than my leisure hours would allow me to perform, from the good citizens of Georgetown.

But the day of my mistress's wedding at length came around, and I was sent for to attend. Previous to this, my old mistress had assured me, that it was her intention, as soon as her daughter became of age, to purchase me for herself, and give me a chance of buying my freedom. Now, that Miss Polly was of age, and about to be married, I considered her promise as about to take effect, and looked forward with pleasure to the brief space of time which was to intervene, and to the day, when I could stand forth as a man, and say to the world, "I AM FREE," "free as the air which scales our hills–or as the streams which leap our rocks." But disappointment is the lot of frail humanity; and on the day of the wedding, all my high hopes of freedom were blasted. Whilst the wedding party were at the table, I unconsciously called the Preacher, who had performed the marriage ceremony, "Old Massa." He demanded of me why I did so; and I informed him, that it was because I had lived in the town with his son-in-law, Mr. Hawkins. He said that he had never seen me there to his recollection, but that he had seen me somewhere else. He then asked my mistress if she had raised me; to which she answered that she had, from the time I was seven years of age. He next inquired of me if I knew where my parents lived, and when I told him, he observed that he had been in search of me for ten years, having known my old master, at whose house he had frequently met with my mother; and that he had at her request sought for me in every gang of boys that he had seen in Kentucky–for when he was in Virginia, he saw my mother, who was well but much distressed on my account, thinking that when I was taken away, I was too young to be raised, and feared that she would never again have the pleasure of beholding her long lost son. He told her that if he ever found me, he would purchase me, and when I grew up, he would send me to see her. He appeared to be surprised, that he had not before recognized me, as the resemblance to my mother was very striking–so much so, that he assured me he would have known me if he had met me in any State in the Union. In a short time, too, he inquired of my mistress if she would sell me, who informed him that I was the property of her daughter–that I would have to be appraised, and that she intended purchasing me herself if she could, for the purpose of setting me FREE, and asked me how I would like to be a free man, to which I replied, with tears in my eyes—"very much, mistress, God bless you!"

The gentleman then remarked that Mr. Smith, the individual who had married Miss Polly, lived upon his place, and that he had expressed a desire to own it—and that if he was still of the same notion, he would endeavor to give him a trade. Mr. Smith, however, observed that I was spoiled, and that he would be under the necessity of bringing my high notions down a few "button holes," which remark grieved me so much, that I told my old mistress that I would not live with him any length of time. This news seemed to distress her to such a degree that I said no more.

In a short time the day came for the giving up of the estate, and Mr. Smith, knowing my determination of not living with him, set me up for sale to the highest bidder. There were present six gentlemen who were anxious to purchase me, and I bid fair to command a high price—a price as infamous to the dealer in human flesh, as the thirty pieces of silver, which bought the Son of God, and yielded him up to an ignominious death. Like an ox brought to the shambles for the scrutiny of butchers, I stood before that flesh-buying crowd, awaiting the last stroke of the hammer—the last tone of the crier's voice, which was to consign me to a strange master, and perhaps a stranger land. Can such deeds prosper? Can the Shylock who deals in human flesh, the flesh and blood of his brethren and his sisters, expect to atone for the dark crimes which he is daily committing? Can Salvation reach his guilty soul with the shriek of the murdered slave ringing in his ears, and the phantoms of departed innocence, hovering about his guilty head? The Lord's will be done.

Among the individuals anxious to purchase me, were Major Carneal, who is now residing in the city of Cincinnati, a worthy and respected citizen; Mr. Robert Wickliffe; Thomas W. Hawkins; Mr. Turner Haden; and Governor Garrard, the gentleman whom I met with at my young mistress's wedding, and who became my purchaser. He, however, still kept me at work for Mr. Hawkins, to whom he afterwards transferred me, with this understanding:—that at the expiration of five years I was to be set free, and furnished as a freedom gift with a horse, saddle and bridle, and a suit of clothes, worth at least $100, to carry me home to Virginia. Here, then was another prospect of freedom, and my mind was filled with naught else than making money to bear my expenses home. But all earthly calculations, unless predicated upon the word of God, are but vanity and vexation of spirit. I was doomed again to be disappoinned; for, in 1811, Mr. H. became bankrupt, and was compelled to part with his property and me, in order to extricate himself from his difficulties. The purchaser was his brother James, who did not act so kindly toward me as was my desire, and my general usage theretofore.

As some of my readers may doubt the events above mentioned, I would refer them to Mr. Carneal, who gave way to Governor Garrard, through motives of delicacy, at the same time stating, that if I chose HIM, he would take me immediately to Cincinnati, where I would be free as soon as I touched the shores of Ohio. But the Spirit commanded me to make no choice—that it would bring me out of my trials unscathed, and I became the property of Governor Garrard. For Mr. Carneal, however, I have ever entertained the greatest kindness and gratitude, for his sympathy to me on that occasion. May God bless and protect him through life.

Here, then, another crisis was before me. The foreman of the factory, and I, having served our time in the same place, were upon such intimate terms, that he refused to punish me for any of my youthful misdemeanors, hence it was thought advisable to remove me from his supervision. Previous to this, however, I had a long spell of sickness, during which, many thought that I was poisoned; but through God's Divine mercy, at the expiration of six months, I was restored to health. My physician was Dr. W. H. Richardson, of Lexington.—From the rope-walk I was sent immediately to Frankfort, to act in the capacity of house-waiter. But—I have inadvertently got ahead of my Narrative, and with your permission, kind reader, will return, and travel back with you again.

Mr. James Hawkins, was, at the time of purchasing me, engaged to be married to a young lady by the name of Miss Chew, who resided in Jefferson county, near Louisville, and as he desired to visit his intended bride, in a style consistent with that of wealth and aristocracy; and as I had now become the possessor of a horse, saddle and bridle, his conclusion was, that I would be an indispensable appendage, in the capacity of waiter to him on his journey. This was what I desired, as I wished again to be travelling; therefore, I embraced the opportunity, and having arrived at the top of my trade, I bade farewell for a season, to the rope-walk. Shortly after I accompanied my master, and staying about a month, we returned. On our return, it was found that they could get along without me in the rope-making department, although at first they had conceived it to be a matter of impossibility; consequently I accompanied my master on a journey to Frankfort, at which place he left me. I was now somewhat at the a loss to know what to do, to earn some money, for strange as it may seem, after so many disappointments, I had not lost the hope of becoming at some period, a FREE man. But Providence again pointed out the path in which I was to tread. I performed so miserably in the house that there was much fault found with me, which induced them to desire me to work out of doors; but as I had never worked in the sun, I could not stand it. This was, however, nothing more than contrariness, as I had my mind so fixed on Freedom, that I was not willing to do ANY THING. I was willing, nevertheless, to do one thing, i.e. to hire my own time, and to pay for it at the rate of $10 per month; but this was refused, and I was sent back to the factory to work. Here I did so badly, that they at last agreed to receive the $10, and permit me to have the use of my time. I had at this time $60 in money, deposited in the store of Mr. McGowan, and a horse worth $60. After I left the rope factory, I commenced cleaning clothes, boots, shoes, &c., for such gentlemen as gave me employment; and at nights I was employed at all the parties to play the tamborine—running errands—carrying messages, &c. My friends now advised me to learn to shave, and I concluded that I had better undertake it.

In the Spring of 1811, I packed up, and went back to Frankfort. I left my horse with a friend of mine with directions to sell him, and after paying himself out of the proceeds for his trouble, to remit me the balance wherewith to pay my hire. I then went to the Barber shop of Mr. John S. Gowans, who had formed a friendship for me during my boyhood, when acting in the capacity of a fish-monger, and who felt disposed to aid me all in his power. Hearing that I had come again to Frankfort, he held out the hand of fellowship to me, and that friendship has left its indelible mark upon my heart which can never be erased, until I meet him again in the Land of Spirits, whither he has long since departed.

After telling my friend my circumstances, and my desires, I asked if he would undertake to learn me the trade. After a long parley, during which he gave me little encouragement, he requested me to call again after breakfast, and he would give me a final answer. I did so, and he told me to watch him, whilst he was shaving some of his customers. This request I rigidly obeyed, as also his manœuvres in cutting hair. After he had finished, he sat down by my side, and conversing long and candidly with me, he gave me a pair of razors to dress.[8] I retired, and in a short time returned, showing him the one on which I had been working. He examined it carefully, and saying that it was as well done as he could do it himself, requested me to undertake the other. I did so, and and having finished it, I again met with a similar praise. The apprentices were rather taken a-back, for at first, they had considered it a capital joke, that a factory boy should presume to learn the Tonsorial art;[9] but who, now, no doubt concluded, with Sam Patch, that "some things can be done as well as others." He then advised me to get a cup and box, and having given me a pair of razors and a hone, he told me to take them, with a clean towel, and go the rounds of the town every morning, shaving as many as I could for half price, and that in the coarse of a few weeks, I would be able to set up shop for myself. Before parting with him, to enter upon the duties of my new occupation, I asked him what he charged for the kindness he had shown me, and the advice and instruction which he had given me? His reply was, "the only recompense I ask, is, that if you ever see any of my children, or grand-children in need, you will aid them as well as you can." To this I gratefully assented.

It was now nearly night; but elated with the prospects before me, I determined to go to Georgetown, and commence business, consequently I started, and reached that place about midnight.

The next morning I visited the inn, then kept by Mr. Leonard George, armed with the implements of my new vocation, and as good luck would have it, there happened to be a stranger present, who had but a few minutes before, been inquiring for a barber, which, previous to my debut, was an article the Georgetownians did not possess. As soon as he saw me enter, he took his seat, and called for a "shave." Now, the idea of "Billy Hayden" turning barber, was a fruitful theme of amusement for many of my friends, who stood around, laughing in their sleeves, and thinking, no doubt, that the whole affair would end as an amusing hoax, at the stranger's expense.

Nothing daunted however, I put my razors in order; and placing my napkin under the stranger's chin, I proceeded to the task of "mowing" off his beard, as confidently as if I was an old and experienced hand at the business. All were surprised,–and the gentleman, when I had finished, acknowledged that he had never received a more "comfortable shave" in his life. But when he was informed that his face was the first that I had ever touched, he appeared utterly astonished, and predicted for me a high standing in my vocation.

For some time I continued to follow the occupation of "street barber" for the Georgetownians,–and at the end of the first month, was much gratified to find that I had made $8, clear of my expenses. At the end of two months, my friends proposed to build me a shop, if I could, by any means, procure a lot. I immediately spoke to Mr. Hawkins, (my master) who consented to lease me a lot, and receive his pay therefor, as fast as I made it at my occupation. Not wishing to tax my friends, too, Mr. Hawkins subsequently agreed to build me a shop, which he did.

I had at this time, a female friend, whom I proposed to hire from her owners, in order that we might live together, and make money much faster than I could alone. This I accomplished–and an opportunity for speculation soon presented itself. There was a room underneath the Court House, which the jailor agreed to let us have, if we would clean it out. We accordingly did so, and stocking it with cakes, candies, mellons, nuts, &c., we embarked in another business, connected with my Tonsorial practice, and the consequence was, that we were soon enabled to lay by a considerable sum of money.

But my good fortune stopped not here. Shortly after we embarked in the cake-selling line, Mr. Job Stephenson had a lottery, at which a lot of saddlery was to be disposed of. After much persuasion, I was induced to take a ticket, and the result was, that I drew a saddle, worth $30. I now began to think myself a really fortunate man. My next chance of speculation, was a new assortment of confectionaries, and as I had a great many acquaintances in Lexington, and bearing a good character for honesty and industry, I was enabled, through their influence, to draw to any amount that I saw fit. Again I met with tolerable success.

Whilst trading in Lexington, however, I became acquainted with an old man of color, known by the name of "Daniel," who belonged to Mr. Wickliffe. For this person I formed a strong attachment, for which I could never account; save, that I had a presentiment that at some future time, he would prove of incalculable service to me. I was, therefore, from this presentiment, induced to give the old man many small sums of money–sometimes a half, and sometimes a dollar. At this act of generosity, as he called it, he was greatly surprised, and often asked me the meaning thereof–in reply to which, I invariably told him that I foresaw, that at some not far distant time, he was destined to assist me to a very great extent.

Thus things went on swimmingly until 1812–when a gentleman, living near Cynthiana, brought upon the tapis another lottery. At this period, a friend of mine, who always felt disposed to assist me in my exertions to prosper in the world, advised me to take a ticket–agreeing to pay for it himself, in case Fortune favored me not. With this inducement before me, I was, after some considerable qualms of conscience, prevailed on again to try my luck. This time I drew a horse and gig, which were valued at $500. Now, thought I, the very acme of happiness is mine–as I have now the means of making a grand display, in returning to my home again in Virginia.

After having been purchased by Governor Garrard, in 1810, and transferred by him to Thomas W. Hawkins, with the proviso of being set free in 1815, and who, by a sham sale, when he became bankrupt, made me over to his brother James, I almost began to despair of ever being set free. But the same supernatural Spirit, kept me still in mind of the Divine mercy of God, and promised me that the day of my liberation was not far distant. The idea of my still remaining in bondage, however, I could not shake off, and as I had no writing to the effect that I was to obtain my freedom in 1815, I concluded to speak of the matter to Mr. Hawkins, which I accordingly did, but who gave me no definite answer: hence, I could not arrive at any conclusion as to his intentions with me, but being headstrong in my opinion, I entertained the notion that they still had the idea of keeping me in bondage. Whether I was right or wrong let the sequel tell. However, permit me to assure you I felt within me, a certain something which seemed to intimate to me that Governor Garrard's promise would one day, if not that specified, be brought about. Various were the advises given me by my friends, when the eventful year of freedom arrived, relative to the course I had better pursue. Many advised me to go to my master, and demand my papers, but this I positively refused, knowing Governor G. as a man of integrity and honor, and determined to await the result, and see if his promise would pass by unheeded. I was aware too, if it did, the fault would not rest with him, but with the fickleness which all earthly things are subjected to. Under this impression, I waited until Christmas, but no one came to hold out the papers, which were to announce me to the world, as a free man, although I previously expected that Captain William Garrard, a son of the Governor's, would be the individual, who would bear to me the happy tidings of Freedom's air fanning my youthful cheek, Captain G. too, was one of the signers of the Bill of Sale to Mr. Hawkins, from his father, who had exacted not only the word, but the written obligation of Mr. Hawkins to free me in 1815. I soon discovered that all was not right, as when I had met Capt. G. he generally contrived to pass me with downcast eyes. I knew him to be an honorable man; what then could be the reason? I could divine nothing else, than that Mr. Hawkins was so embarrassed, that he could not consistently with his own interest fulfil the intent of his written obligation.

Acting under this impression, I visited Governor G. and inquired of him, if Mr. H. designed fulfilling the promises towards me which he had made. The old man appeared grieved, and after a few moments, with his eyes suffused with tears, he broke the sad intelligence of disappointment to me, telling me that Mr. Hawkins was sorely in debt, and that unless I was able to purchase myself, he feared that I must still remain in the same bondage which had ground me down for many years previous—he told me his sorrow at the turn affairs had taken was almost too heavy to be borne—that he always designed to make me a free man, and now that his benevolent purposes had been nipped in the bud, he could say no more, than the Almighty Ruler's will be done! "But, William," he continued, "I will be a friend to you, and aid you as far as I possibly can." So great, however was Mr. Hawkin's embarrassments, that it became necessary for me to be again sold, and Mr. Edward Chew, the brother-in-law of Mr. James Hawkins, being on a visit to him at the time, they insisted on him purchasing me, and conveying me to Bayou Sara, the place where he resided. But this scheme was all blown through, as when the proposals were made to me by Mr. Chew, I informed him I would not go, as I was a free man, nor would I consent any longer to pay the $10 per month for the use of my time, as it was just as consistent to exact $10 per month from any FREE negro in the country, for the use of HIS time, as to exact it from ME. I was now FREE, and as a free man had no hesitation in speaking my mind freely. The cause of my thus speaking so confidently, was the fact of having appointed with the consent and advice of Capt. Garrard, Mr. Timberlake as my guardian, consequently when Mr. Chew called for me, and Mr. Mitchell was directed to get me and sell me for the debt of Mr. Hawkins, I immediately referred them to Mr. Timberlake, who referred them to Captain William Garrard, who informed them that they dare not touch me, as I was within a short space of being free, by the deed of transfer from his father to Mr. Hawkins, to which he was one of the signers. This was too much for them, and they concluded to tack about, and take a new track, which was that of persuasion. But this with me was equally unsuccessful, so that they abandoned all further efforts, and I was left to dream on of the prospects of my freedom.

And now, gentle reader, permit me to indulge in a few moral reflections ere I proceed with my Narrative. The Almighty still had his guardian eye over me—he still held me within the hollow of his hand—blessing and leading unscathed—through the world's wickedness and trials the poor, friendless slave. He poured the oil of compassion into the benevolent heart of my old friend Governor G.—His Divine wisdom and goodness prompted the actions of Captain G. to be those of honor and integrity—he raised up a friend for me in Mr. Timberlake—and passing on through the various graduations of time, he brought me forth, and stood me before the world, a man, free as the first Adam, when enjoying the sweets of Paradise. Can it be wondered then, that his humble and sorrowing creature blesses his ever adorable name for all the goodness that he has shown him—that he looks back to his days of bondage with disgust—that he blesses the names of his many friends, friends who stood by him in his hours of need, and lent a helping hand when the dark clouds of adversity loomed heavy and darkly in the horizon of his after life? O, no! He foresaw the storms which were to arise—he knew the troubles, the trials, and the vexations he was to encounter, and averting all, wrestling with the demon spirit of the slave-dealer, he braved the worst and came forth, singing hyms of deliverance to himself, and praise and thanksgiving to God, and his benefactors. But a boundless futurity is yet spread before him—the last act in the drama of life will soon be enacted,—the trump of the Archangel[10] will soon summon all before the tribunal of God, where each deed must be atoned for—where the righteous will find rest, and the weary cease from sorrowing. There we shall all meet—there, face to face we will be confronted before a holy and a just Judge, and as I hope for happiness, I will deal justly with all whose destiny has been linked with mine on earth. May the friends of whom I have spoken above, be blessed; may they enjoy rest on earth, and eternal happiness hereafter, is the humble prayer of the poor being, who once endured with honesty and meekness their servile bondage. God grant his prayer may be answered.

Thus things went on until the year 1817, when Mr. Hawkins, seeing that he was unable to sell me, was prompted to connive with Mr. Thomas Phillips, a slave-dealer, with the understanding that if he could induce me to sell myself to him, he would let him have me for $650. Mr. H. was aware, that if this arrangement could be made, that I would be removed to a strange place, where none knew me, and that probably I would soon forget the promises made of setting me free. But the Spirit of the Lord was working within me, and although for the purpose of extricating Mr. Hawkins from his embarrassments, I agreed to go with Phillips, yet I felt assured that when I chose to claim my freedom, I was privileged to go where I pleased. I accordingly agreed to go, and Philips despatched me to Mr. Hawkins with a note, which proved to be the Bill of Sale, containing a check for the required sum. When I reached Frankfort, I met Mr. Hawkins, walking arm-in-arm with Mr. John Marshall, in the market place. I called him to one side, and gave him the note—he opened it and read it, and stepping into Mr. Taylor's with me, without asking me a question, save who he was to sign the Bill in favor of, drew up the article which was to sever us forever. I told him to Mr. Philips, with whom I had concluded to go South. After taking farewell of him, I returned to Philips, downcast for the tears which many of my friends indulged in on my departure.

With this man I remained until the year 1824, when I purchased myself. Of my travels with Mr. Philips and my various adventures I will speak hereafter. In 1824 I became my own master, however, and as it was Court week in Paris, I made immediate application for a record of the same upon the archives of the Court. A gentlemen proposed the matter to the Court, when the two associate Judges cried out "no! no! we cannot be bothered with such records." But James Garrard, the presiding Judge, after a few moments, commanded the constable to make room, and bring the poor, friendless slave before them. This was accordingly done, and I was ushered into the presence of the Judges before a large concourse of my fellow citizens. After eyeing me for a few moments, Judge G. asked me who I was?

"Why, Massa James," said I, "do you not know me–Billy Haden."

"Why, Billy Haden," replied he, "and is this you? Poor boy, you are at last free; well I am really glad," and bursting into a flood of tears, he ordered the Clerk to record my freedom.

Here the two associates again demurred, asking who would be security that I would not come on the town for support. "I will!" responded Judge G.; "not only security that he becomes not a pauper, but security, in the face of the whole County and State for all he does or says." The audience were astonished–the associates shrunk back into their insignificance, and I was permitted to leave the Court room filled to overflowing with the thoughts of my freedom, and my eyes wet with tears at the recollection of the scene through which I had just passed.

"———

The King and Peasant are to Him the same;
His forming hand made in His image, all,
Nor placed distinction in an empty name.
Why then should man spurn on his fellow man,
When Heaven's pure light is given unto all?
Why should he wield a power o'er the mind,
And worse than slave, command his fellow fall?
All's free! By Heaven's pure laws we live,
Bound to obey no man in slavery;
The mind unshackled, lives for God alone,
Brothers in flesh–heirs of Eternity!
Bow then the knee to Him who rules the world,
Thy God, thy maker, and thy friend in death–
Place all thy thoughts on His atoning power,
And sing His praises with thy latest breath.

Now, reader, what but the goodness and the justice of God could have induced that high-minded Judge, clad in the ermine of his office, to burst into tears at the sight of a poor, friendless negro. Yes, it was this alone; he was a singer of the deed of transfer to Mr. Hawkins, and feeling almost as much as myself the wrongs which I had suffered, the Lord smote his heart, and caused his benevolence and uprightness to see that justice was done me, although at the eleventh hour. God's name be praised.

And now to return to the intervening epochs of my Narrative, from which I have digressed, in order to show you, that although a slave, I had a great many friends, and a greater than earthly friend, the Lord God of hosts to aid and uphold me.

After I had departed to meet Mr. Hawkins, Philips seemed to be somewhat alarmed with the fear that I would not again return; and he knew full well that the safety of his money depended solely upon my honesty. But I returned to him at the specified time, and giving up my business to my partner, Carter Lightfoot, prepared myself to become the waiting man of Mr. Philips. The only duties he required of me, however, was to call upon him, and shave him daily until we started. This I performed faithfully and much to his satisfaction. In October of 1812, we commenced our voyage, and I was made to steer the boat, and in a short time was considered a good steersman. Our passage went on smoothly until we arrived at Natchez, when Stone desired to take the management of the boat from me. In this, however, he was thwarted by Philips, to whom I considered that I justly and legally belonged. This opposition so irritated Stone, that he determined to be avenged on me. To accomplish this, he proceeded up in the town, and sold me to an individual, named Whitehead. Of this proceeding, Philips knew nothing, until Mr. Whitehead came to the boat to demand the property purchased from Mr. Stone. My master was surprised, and assured Mr. Whitehead that Stone had no authority over me, and as his property, he would never permit of my leaving the boat, without his explicit and entire consent. The consequence of this assertion, was a "flare up" between my master and Stone–the latter insisting that I belonged to the firm, the money of the firm having been used in purchasing me. Philips, however, contended that I was exclusively his own–that I had never been entered upon the books of the firm–and that the firm could never recognize the individual property of any member belonging to it. I was a hearer of all that passed–having retired to the back part of the boat, where lying down on the floor, I feigned to be asleep. The dispute ran so high, that for some time I remained undiscovered; but at length Stone spying me, and thinking that I was only "playing possum," (as he termed it) approached me, and putting his foot upon my head, in no very tender manner, shook me considerably. The only answer elicited, however, was a few confused murmurs, as if disturbed in my slumbers; and a few inward chuckles at the success of my ruse. He finally turned from me, with an oath,–and after some further altercation with Philips, they affected a reconciliation–I remaining, as I had previously, in the possession of Philips.

In a few days, having purchased a new boat, we left Natchez, and embarked for Bayou Sara, where we remained for two months. At this place, they continued to dispose of a number of their cargo of slaves, and hastening thence to Palaquemine, the balance were easily sold. On the road, however, we staid some time at St. Martinsville, where Philips was daily receiving letters from his partners in business. These he would generally leave open, unconscious of my ability to read English manuscript,–hence I was duly advised of all his proceedings by this covert means.

In the traffic of human flesh, their luck appeared to be good–so good, that they determined to return to Virginia, in order to purchase a new cargo.

The first verbal knowledge of this that I received from Philips, was revealed to me whilst in his room. He then asked me, how I would like to go with him to Virginia. Although I was aware that he had a notion of selling me, yet the proposition struck upon the long agitated chord of my heart, and vibrated with ecstacy throughout my whole system. Fancy portrayed to me in her most vivid colors, my long lost mother—the joyful greeting of maternal and filial affection—the checquered scenes of my infancy—the salutations of my playmates, and the blissful recollections of my long deserted home. It was a consummation devoutly to be wished for—and telling Mr. Philips that his will was my pleasure, I set about preparing for our journey. The reason, however, of my ready acquiescence to his proposal, independent of my own anxious wishes of beholding again my mother, was, a determination to ascertain all their intentions with regard to me, and this I expected to accomplish by a care-devil disposition as to what they did with me or mine—and strictly following this line of conduct, I proved successful. Philips now thought that he could dispose of me at any moment he deemed it convenient, and consequently concluded to take me with him for another trip, at least. But this priviledge on my part, was purchased rather than received as a bonus, from him; as I was compelled to furnish my own clothes. But even to this extortion I consented; the more easily to further my designs, as the idea of my remaining in bondage all my days, never entered my mind.

Whilst we were in Bayou Sara, I made considerable progress in learning to speak the French language. This however, I kept a secret, as I knew if the fact was known that no Frenchman would purchase me, thinking that their secrets would be endangered by my knowledge. During the winter that I had been with Mr. Philips, I had managed to save upwards of $75. This amount I gave to him, and took his receipt for the same, at six per cent interest. Thence we embarked for home, where we arrived on the first of June.

We had not been long at home, however, ere another snare was set to entrap me. I have before stated that Castleman was anxious to secure me; and for this purpose, he came down to Philips. He appeared very glad to see me; but the man was known to me, and I was aware that the joy which he exhibited, was more like the joy the wolf feels when pouncing upon a lamb, than any emotions of the better qualities of the heart. He knew, too, that I would not live with him, from my oft repeated assertions to that effect. How, then, to bring about this object, he knew not, until Avarice, Selfishness and Villany, pointed out the road—and if ever fiend had the heart to perform a diabolical action, Castleman was that one. For the purpose of accomplishing his object, Philips, over whom he seemed to exercise a strange authority, for reasons best known I presume to themselves was to take me to Georgia, and after showing me the cruel treatment of the overseers to the field negroes, he supposed by threatening to sell me to one of these, that I would be willing to abide the worst, and become the property of Mr. Castleman. But this was ineffectual. My Spiritual guide protected me; and even in the face of these galling tortures,

I remained obstinate in my refusal–and informed him I did not wish to return. This was to him a matter of extreme surprise, so much so, that he gazed confusedly on me for some time, and silence seemed to have sealed his tongue. Castleman, too, seemed vexed, and with an oath informed Philips that he might keep me, and take me back and sell me.

As soon, then, as we were recruited, we started for Virginia. But previous to this, I wrote to my mother, that I expected to see her in June, and as I would have but a short time to stay, to endeavor by all means to be at home. On our journey we passed through Chillicothe, Ohio. Here, there was a strict watch kept over my actions, lest I should run away, knowing that I was in a free State; but I appeared to be ignorant of the fact, and much relieved of their suspense, I was permitted to wander where I pleased, unmolested. On leaving, we took what is generally known as "THE OLD TRACE," which had not been travelled for some time. This was thickly covered with timber, the principal part of which was young hickories. In passing through this, I had inadvertently fallen into a moody state, and was holding sweet communion with my Spiritual agent. My master, on discovering this, asked me what I was thinking about. Unwilling that he should know the train of my thoughts, I replied, pointing to the young hickories:

"What a folly, if this land were occupied by slave-holders, for a manufacturer of COW-HIDES, to engage in business. Nature seems to have supplied whips for the slave's backs from the thickness of an ox-goad, to the delicate riding-switch of a boarding-school miss."

This reply brought forth, as I anticipated, a general round of laughter, and became the theme of merriment and conversation for many a day afterward. In fact, in passing a copse of small timber ever afterwards, they would recur to the subject, and ask me if that was in my opinion, another of Nature's cow-hide manufactories.

But our course soon brought us to Winchester, Virginia, where we put up at the house of Mr. Van Horn. It was at this house that all the Georgian slave-dealers put up, and here were informed that it was worse than useless for us to go to Falmouth, (where my mother resided) as there were then more traders in that place than could find employment. Hence, it was concluded that we should go to Baltimore, via Harper's Ferry, per stage. On arriving at this conclusion, I was despatched onward with the horses, to await their arrival at the Ferry. I was dressed in the top of fashion, and having a spanking pair of horses in my possession, I concluded to go to Bunker Hill, a place I had often heard of, and longed to see. On the road I was an object of universal remark: The whites seemed surprised, and at a loss to know what I was; and those of my own color, paid due deference to their superior, whenever I passed them. At Bunker Hill, I staid but a short time–long enough only to bate my horses and eat my noon-day meal; when I proceeded on to Baltimore. Previous to this however, I had met my master at the Ferry, and as it was his intention to stay a few days in Fredericktown, I was despatched on to Baltimore alone.

Whilst pursuing this journey, however, I was instructed not to let any one know either who or what I was, nor yet the business of my master. These instructions I faithfully fulfilled, and when interrogated by any, curious to know Mr. Philips' business, I replied to them invariably in French, hence the attempt to ascertain, was generally abandoned as fruitless. This astonished many. The richness of my clothes; the span of horses in my possession, and the fact of a colored man speaking the French language, seemed to them as a new era of things under the sun; and I was treated with a civility, seldom extended to the colored race in the slave-holding states. My course pleased Philips very much; and induced him to extend to me many little privileges which heretofore he had withheld from me. But Jealousy was one great ingredient in the composition of his nature and although, my knowledge of the French, was pleasing to him in our travels through the NORTH, yet it was not agreeable, but filled him with alarm when I indulged in it in the SOUTH–especially among the French population. It ever seemed to him, as if I was recounting his many misdemeanors, and was projecting a scheme to his disadvantage. Of this, however, he need not have feared. I had been informed by my Spiritual counsellor that my freedom was as certain as that the heavens were above me; but that the time must be in accordance with its wishes. All attempts, therefore, to thwart the Spirit, would have had a tendency to my detriment–and well satisfied, I awaited patiently the dawning morn of my deliverance.

When I arrived at Baltimore–which I did some few days before my master, I wrote to my mother to come on to that place, and I would pay her expenses. And here permit me, gentle reader to digress from the regular train of my Narrative to indulge in a few brief emotions of filial affection.

There is perhaps no feeling in the bosom of a child, which is more strong and binding, even unto death, than the feeling of love for his mother. 'Tis the love which Heaven first implanted in the bosom of man, save that which exists with the husband and wife. But the love of a son seems, even then, to have been in the eyes of God, of a more binding nature, as it was through *His only Son* that he exhibited its strength to the world, in the person of Jesus Christ, our Lord. Is it any wonder, then, that I, a poor colored creature, could fail to feel the influence of love for a parent, which was even made an example upon Earth by His master Christ. O, how I longed for the arrival of my poor mother–her whom the galling chains of bondage still bound to a master's servile will–her, whom I almost adored and worshipped–who had given me life,–and nourished me through infancy, clad and upheld me, and taught me to place confidence in the Supreme power of God; and whom I felt–aye, know, must one day be liberated by this hand, and clasped as a mother–a slave, freed from bondage, to the bosom of a long lost son. Every hour seemed an age–every day an eternity, until I should be acquainted with the news of her arrival. My mind was racked with intense anguish–my heart throbbed violently, and I very often found my cheeks bathed with tears, emanating from the vast solicitude which I felt; yea, deeply felt, on account of her whom, by the laws of nature and God, I was called upon to term—*mother*. The feelings of a child can be but poorly appreciated towards parents, until he is torn rudely from their protecting arms, and consigned to waste his youth and manhood in exile from their presence. Such was my case, and my mother I had not seen since the days of my infancy. O, how I yearned once more to behold her—to hold her to my bosom and bathe her sorrows in the tears of filial affection. Yearned to gaze into the tenderness of her eyes, and to exclaim with the poet:

> "A mother's tenderness I see,—
> It binds me ever unto, thee—
> We meet again—my truant heart,
> Proclaims we ne'er again will part."—

But the time was fast approaching, and I felt happy in the mere thought of the anticipated joy held out to me.

At length the appointed day came, and with it the object of my dearest solicitude. But still I was doomed not immediately to be permitted to clasp her to my bosom. From infancy we had never met,—and there was little possibility of our knowing each other when confronted. However, the anxiety was soon satisfied, as one day I was walking near the house where my master had put up, and my attention was attracted by the sounds of an elderly colored lady, in conversation with the landlord. She said, "my dear son has written to me to meet him at this place. I have travelled a long way to enjoy this extreme pleasure, but the Fates have doomed me to disappointment." Her grief seemed, too, as almost insupportable; as she asserted, that in case of her not finding her son, she knew not what to do—as she had expended the small trifle she could command, to bear her expences to the place, and would be without the means of getting again to her home. The kind hearted landlord, however, in order to cheer her spirits bade her take courage, and not to give way to her feelings in such an unmatronly manner; assuring her at the same time, that if her son could not be found, he would advance her the means of returning to the home of her master, in Falmouth. Little did I think that the voice of distress which I had heard, emanated from the fond being I was by the laws of nature compelled to call,—*my mother!* Little, indeed, did the son expect to hear the wailings of a parent; after having braved the dangers of her journey, to meet with him—or to see the tears of parental solicitude poured forth in the anticipated joy of his meeting. O, how fondly would I have soothed her sorrows,—how eagerly would I have wiped away the damp, dewey tears which trickled down her wrinkled cheeks, and fell in profusion on the floor at her feet. But—a doubt seemed to have taken possession of my mind—*Was it my mother?* My heart seemed to tell me it *was*—yet, my eyes seemed to tell me, *nay*. Under this weight of uncertainty, I determined to await the result, and ascertain, if possible, the truth of my surmises, ere I made a definite approach. Of this I was soon informed. One of the maids belonging to the house, and to whom I had spoken previously, in a friendly manner, repeated to me, that an old colored lady had arrived there in search of her son, whom she had not seen since his infancy, and, as she had heard me say, that I expected my mother to be in Baltimore, in a few days, it was more than probable that this lady was the mother I spoke of. She then asked me my name, which I immediately gave her, and hearing which she replied, that she believed it to be the same mentioned by the woman. Upon this information, I determined to gain an interview with the old lady, and convince myself, if she were indeed my long lost mother. This I soon accomplished, as the landlord hesitated not to introduce me to her presence. She was a neat and tidy personage, dressed in the garb of a female overseer of the culinary and domestic duties of her mistress's household. She was past the prime of life, and bore traces upon her once fine features, of much sorrow and tribulation. The crowd which had gathered around her, gave way as I approached, and in a few moments I stood face to face with her who had given me birth, and whose heart now yearned to clasp a wayward son once more in her arms. My salutation was social and friendly; and was returned with a grace and warmness which rather astonished me. I entreated pardon for the apparently rude manner in which I had sought the conference; and begged that she would answer a stranger, the few questions he might ask her. She bowed her acquiescence.

I then asked her if she expected to find a son in this place?

She replied, she did; that he had written to her to meet him in Baltimore, and that he would bear her expenses back to her home–adding, that he had been taken from her at Bell-plains, when he was but an infant, and carried to the South, from which she had never looked for his return. That she had long mourned him as dead, but that she felt assured, he still lived, from his letter to her, and that God had answered her prayers of again seeing him. That her heart throbbed to behold him again, and bathe his cheeks with a mother's tears of joy.

My soul filled with feelings which I could not master, as I listened to the poor woman's tale of woe,–which was so nearly my own,–and the tears trickled down my cheeks in copious floods. As soon as I could command myself, I asked her what name she bore at her master's house. She said–"ALCY SHELTON." The name fell upon my ears like a thunder-bolt. It was indeed my mother; and before her stood the son whom she so ardently sought to fold in a mother's embrace. O Heaven! how bounteous are all thy ways–how glorious are all their achievements, and how grateful should we, poor mortals, be, who have from thee, all our wants and wishes supplied, with tender and parental care. My heart filled with joy unspeakable–my tongue seemed to cleave to the roof of my mouth,–and I felt as if I stood in the presence of one, whom the grave had disgorged to fill my cup of joy to the brim. I gazed anxiously and fondly upon her! I longed to announce to her the end of her sufferings, and to tell her, that I, *her son*, would soon be instrumental in soothing her former anxieties and troubles, and exchanging her path for one of pleasantness and peace through the remaining years of her life. But I felt the task more easy to conceive than to execute; and I remained mute and thankful before the crowd, enjoying the sweet thoughts of a re-union with my mother. How long I remained in this delicious trance I know not; but I can remember that the sweet feelings which I then treasured, passed away, and I again assumed the character of an interrogator.

"My good woman," said I, "will you be so good as to answer me the few more queries, which I may propound to you?"

"With pleasure," returned she.

"And what name, madam, does your son bear?"

"William Hayden," replied she, "the name given him by his first master."

"Are you sure he lives in the South?"

"Yes–it was there they bore him from me, and what would I not give–save the salvation of my soul,–to again gaze upon his features!"

"Then, madam, dry your tears–let your bosom no longer be racked with vague suspicions of his death–*he lives, and now stands before you! I* am William Hayden, your son! Mother again embrace your long lost boy!"

For some time the old lady remained with her eyes rivetted upon me, as if in the last stare of expiring nature, and wildly exclaiming, "IT IS! IT IS!" she flew to my arms, and bathed my cheeks with the tears of heart-felt joy. On releasing her from my embrace, she fell heavily to the floor, in a syncope–the excess of her emotions conquering the strength of nature, which had been severely tried during the whole course of my questioning. The inmates gathered her up, and conveyed her to my room, where they left her in my charge. All eyes were bathed in tears, and many of the boarders, who had now gathered in the house,–it being noon-day,–and witnessed the scene just mentioned, deeply sympathized with me, and offered me, congratulations upon my good fortune in again meeting with my parent. But there was none present, who felt the deep emotions which throbbed in *my* bosom. They were the feelings of the *son* for the *parent*–the strong ties which bind in consanguinity, the various members of the human family.–Before me lay the insensible form of her, who had given me life–hung over my cradle in infancy–consummated my every want–and soothed my every childish fear. She, it was, who taught my feeble steps to walk–and whose smiles partook of Heaven's goodness, as I lay in childish play upon her lap. She it was, who taught my infant tongue to lisp the word, *mother*, and taught me the praise of an all Righteous God. Yes, it was her, who to my heart was dearer than all the wealth of Croesus, or Golconda;[11] for whom I would have laid down my life willingly, and whose happiness it became me now to secure, by every possible means in my power. O, God, how I wished to see her revive, and bless her long lost son; but the long pent up feelings of her bosom was too great, and her syncope, arising from their discharge, proved to be of a long duration. But a son stood over her; and every restorative, his simple mind could call up, was resorted to, but of no avail. At that moment he would not have relinquished his charge, for the most towering height, ambition and human grandeur could invest him with.

O, how strong is the love which prompts the heart of the child, for the mother, to whom he owes all his hopes and fears! What strange and yet heart-felt emotions stir his every thought, when by the hand of cruelty he has been torn away, to waste many years of his glowing manhood in a distant clime, under the eye of a servile master, who recognizes him, not as his fellow man, but merely as goods and chattels. All the feelings of humanity are lost upon the slave-holder, when he contrasts his worldly importance–his increasing wealth and standing in society, with the poor slave–he, whose toils and privations are the very means of acquiring that wealth and standing–whose sinews and thews, are made to work as the beast of burthen, to amass that which is held as a sufficient basis, to found a distinction between his master and his fellow man. The former is looked upon as a man of rank–deified as a God–hosannaha[12] sung at his every approach, and praises lavished upon him by the countless mass,–whilst the other is denied even the common necessaries of a life of poverty, and the title of a *fellow man.* And upon what authority, either human or divine, is this false basis established? Surely upon none. The same God who upholds the mighty, extends his parental protection over the humble–the same power that shields the kings of earth, wards off oppression from the subject–and the same Ruling Being, who secures the life of the millionaire, protects the humble privileges and rights of the beggar. Hence, upon the doctrine of universal protection, the slave-holder, in forming such distinctions, perverts the will of God, and sets at defiance his most sacred mandates.

Again,–Upon the Protection and Equality of Human Ethics.

Nature, in her first principles, designed ALL TO BE EQUAL; she made no relative difference in any of her children, either white or black, and established no basis of distinction between them, save that which virtue, morality, integrity and uprightness of action, of themselves draw, as a natural line of demarkation. And he who, in the self wisdom of his heart, which bears the taint of vice at best, bases a distinction upon aught else, perverts her laws, and stamps infamy upon himself as a tyrant and a self willed wretch. Such are the feelings entertained by the slave-holder, towards his fellow beings, whose unfortunate lot it is to be placed within his power. How sweet, then, was the reflection that I had met with a mother; one who could sympathise with my misery, and whose sympathies were appreciated with filial affection by one she could hold to her bosom, and call by the endearing appellation of–*son.* God grant that those feelings may never leave this bosom, as I feel well assured, they will not;–they even at this moment burn with ten-fold fervor. The will, and wisdom of God, I feel, will uphold me, and carry me safely through the trials and vexations of life, as He has hitherto done. His name be praised.

The syncope,[13] into which my parent fell, lasted until the next morning; and yet, during all the previous night. I watched over her, and cheered myself with the consolation that reviving nature, would bring me back to a full enjoyment of the bliss which I had but merely tasted; and which I longed to drain to the very dregs. During the night, her syncope was disturbed by various visions, and her incoherent murmurings, though often indulged in, gave me but little hope of her mental faculties, on recovery. But the power of God was over her,–and when she finally arose from my bed, she indulged in all the extravagant joy which a mother, re-united to her son, who to her, had been so long considered as dead, could well be conceived to indulge in. My heart was too full for utterance–and I verily believe, that if poor mortal was ever permitted to enjoy a foretaste of Heaven, God had so willed it that I should, in re-uniting with her whom I knew to be an affectionate mother.

My prayers were answered,–and how solemnly did I lift my hands to Heaven, and thank God, that I was yet to become his instrument in relieving the distresses of my parent–and elevating a human being, from the slough of *bondage*, to the blessings of *freedom*–that she might exclaim, with pride,

> "Again, I assume the god-like attributes
> Of man; and stand erect, in triumph;
> Freed from the galling yoke of shame!
> The child of Liberty and Heaven–
> And he, my deliverer, is indeed–MY SON.

Shortly after the recovery of my mother, Mr. Philips, my master, entered the room in which we sat. I immediately introduced her to my master. The deep hypocrisy of this man was well known to me, and I was somewhat startled at his propositions to my mother. His features were wreathed in smiles;

> "Yea, he could smile, and be a villain still."

and for the purpose, as he said, of accommodating the wishes of William, whom he professed to love for his honesty and integrity, he would take her with him to *his* home, and invest her with a house of her own, treating her well as long as life remained. But in this, he was doomed to be disappointed.–Whatever purposes he had conjured up, with regard to my mother, I knew not, but whatever they may have been, the interposition of Divine Providence placed itself between him and his object. To fulfil my promise with my mother, I found I had not sufficient change about my person; and as she was very anxious to return again to Falmouth, in accordance with her promise to her mistress, I felt bound to raise the required sum. To pay her expenses home, was my agreement, and for this purpose I was compelled to apply to Phillips, who held $75 of my money, at an interest of 6 per cent. I was anxious too, to get part of this money from him, on account of other things than merely paying the expenses of my parent; and consequently I visited him in his room. I was surprised, however, on making known my intentions to him, to see that he seemed to have objections in giving it to me; and, in order to accomplish his purpose more thoroughly, he endeavored, by all possible insinuations and persuasions, to induce me to believe that Alcy Shelton was *not my mother*; but that I had been imposed on, by a story trumped up to rob me of my money. This course partially grew out of his desire to keep my money still longer, and partially from the umbrage which he had taken that my mother, who was an excellent midwife, would not fall in with the terms which he had held out to her. Nothing was further from the wishes of my mother, or myself, than that she should go with him; yet, to mollify his feelings, she gave as a reason, that she would first have to return to Falmouth, before she could arrange it so as to take a journey to Kentucky. To back this I informed him that I must have $30 to bear her expenses. At first he hesitated, and finally refused to comply with my demand; telling me he had not the change, but would hand it to me in a few days. This, I felt fully convinced, was a mere "*come off*;" yet what was to be done. My mother remained with me for the time specified, when I again asked him for the amount. He did not much like the idea; but fearing, if he refused, that I might leave him, he at length reluctantly gave it to me. I then asked privilege of him, to see my mother a few miles on her way, which privilege he granted, with strict injunctions not to travel far with her; to which I, as a matter of course, consented. We then started, both in good spirits, I at the thoughts of having once more seen *her*, whom I had never again expected to see; and she, feeling that she could now die happy, as God had permitted her again to behold her son, and being happy in a knowledge of his filial affection. We had not left town far, however, when on looking back, I discovered my master following our steps. His suspicions, I suppose, were aroused, and as a valuable body servant, he felt illy at ease, lest I should escape. Of this, I had not the least intention. The hour of my deliverance had not yet come; and my spiritual adviser warned me to await patiently its approach; consequently, having gone with her some few miles, I parted with her—and sorrowful indeed was that parting. Those alone who have parted from some loved object, can appreciate the misery which a heart feels, when about to sever from some dear one, whom you may never more see. The tears which bathed the cheeks of both, told too plainly the feelings which racked the bosom, as the farewell words still lingered on the tongue.

> There is a deep, dread silence racks the heart
> Of him who from a new-born joy must part;
> There is a feeling none can plainly tell,
> That springs from that sad word, farewell

With this feeling I again turned towards Baltimore, praying Heaven that the hour of my deliverance would quickly come, that I might extend the wishes of a son's heart towards a parent, who was still a bond woman. With these reflections I reached town, where I met my master, who was much pleased at my returning so promptly.

In a few days after the above occurrence, we had made our preparations for departure for the south. During the time we were stationed at Baltimore, the clerk of Mr. Phillips' had remained at Winchester. He had in his possession upwards of two thousand dollars, and with this money he was creating quite a bustle among the youth of Winchester; thereby squandering his master's property, and neglecting his master's business. In order to secure this, my master despatched me to Winchester, to claim and bring the money safely to him. Accordingly, saddling Phillips' horse, I departed on my errand. The horse which I rode was a fine spirited animal, and my own rigging being that which would now-a-days, set off to much advantage the most tenacious dandy, or fop,[14] we became quite an object of observation and surprise. The clerk I met with as expected, and having made known to him the object of my errand, he gave me the funds, though with much apparent chagrin. At first he stated he was on his way to Mr. Phillips, and would be the bearer of the money unto him. To this I objected, stating, that however much I felt for him, yet my instructions from my master were definite, and it was my duty to see them carried into effect—even to the very letter. The clerk was well acquainted with the disposition of Phillips, and therefore, however bitter might have been the morsel, he gulped it down, and consigned to my charge the balance of my master's money. The object of my errand here ceased; yet as Mr. Cunningham had often, during his career as a slave-trader's clerk, exhibited a domineering disposition, and conducted himself with rudeness, to the colored portion of his fellow beings, I was determined to show him, that even a beggar, or the veriest creature of pity that crawls upon the face of the globe, is not void of the power of stinging to the quick, the would-be tyrant. I have before stated, that during his stay in Winchester, he figured pretty largely upon the borrowed plumes and means of his master; hence the only scourge I sought for his merited punishment, was to reduce to the blush of shame, one, who had he been possessed with the power, would have crushed those he even then seemed to think were beneath him. Consequently, having divested him of his authority, as Clerk over the funds of my master, and having secured them in a belt which I wore around my waist, I prepared to start on my journey back. The clerk was soon in readiness, and knowing the subserviency of the slaves, he thought he would yet, for a short time, proclaim his *"consequence,"* and retain his high standing with the youth of Winchester. But he was doomed to disappointment. As soon as he had mounted, instead of riding behind, and bringing up the rear, as slaves are in the general habit of doing, I put spurs to my horse, and was soon carricoling by his side—his equal—and in point of confidence, his *superior.* I pitied the poor wretch, as he cast a rueful glance upon me, and seemed to speak with his eyes, what his tongue refused to give utterance to—but I was determined whilst the opportunity lasted, of teaching him one lesson of humanity which should not for a while escape his memory; and that was, that Nature, having placed us *all* upon a scale of *equality*, I felt no disposition to lessen myself in the eyes of my fellow men, by appearing as the servant of a slave-dealer's clerk. The lesson, during our journey had a good effect, for being treated on the road as his equal, he felt wounded in spirits, and became morose and sullen. This, to me was triumph sufficient; and as an act of punishment to him, I still upheld my character of "consequence," until we arrived at the place I had appointed to meet my master, which was Cumberland; and had delivered to him, a strict account of my stewardship. I then very cordially bid the clerk "good day," and assumed the servility of a slave,–not to an *earthly* master–but to a *spiritual* one. How a reconciliation took place between Mr. Cunningham the clerk, and Mr. Phillips, I know not; but he still remained as our clerk on our downward voyage to the South. It might have been, that the disgrace attached to a slave-dealer's clerk, was of such a revolting nature, that no young man of talent and correct principle, would have accepted the situation, or it might have been, that his services in the south, he being a perfect tyrant in heart, were such, as a set of such reckless panderers in human flesh would most need. Whatever it might have been, he was re-instated in his office, which he maintained during the whole journey.

In a day or so, we started for the south. My conduct and fidelity in the transaction with the clerk, gained me the entire confidence of Phillips. He feared shortly after my departure, that I might make my escape. For this I was, as many of the Swartwouters[15] of the present day might think, well provided; having a splendid horse–upwards of two thousand dollars in cash, and the privilege of Philips to travel where I listed.–But I dare not move save by the warning voice of my guardian spirit. I dare not acknowledge to myself the supremacy of aught, save in obedience to its commands. The hour had not arrived–many clouds were yet to intervene, and lower upon my path, ere I could feel myself justifiable in availing myself of any of the many means held out for my freedom. And with the voice of the spirit I was contented; I knew a supernatural hand guided me onward, and I knew also, that when the moment of my deliverance had really come, I would be enabled to throw off the yoke, and proclaim myself to the world as a *free man*–free as the wind that scales the mountain heights–free as the streams which leap our rocks, or, as the zephyrs, that float through Heaven's space–a MAN–a *Christian*, and responsible to heaven for all my acts! Its approach I felt assured was close upon me, and with a surcharged heart, I waited the dawning of its morn.

The confidence of my master in me, was indeed strong; yet, where the golden god, Mammon,[16] interferes with the heart of a slaveholder, all confidence,–all the ties of consanguinity, are sacrificed; and wealth stands forth before the world in all its accursed force, and immolates upon the altar of vice, the thousand tender feelings of friendship, which man should feel for his fellow man. This confidence seemed, instead of decreasing, to grow,–until we arrived at Washington, Pa.–Here my master knew me to be in a free state, and as I before had shown some signs of such a knowledge myself, when placed in similar circumstances, he was much frightened, lest I should avail myself of the opportunity, and proclaim myself *free.* But his fears were all of his own imagining–he need not for a moment have harbored such an idea. I knew too well, my deliverance, and the means of acquiring it, to play false to my own conscience, and my master's interests. I was aware no human power could much longer hold me in bondage; and I anxiously awaited the warning of the spirit's voice.

From Washington we bent our course for Wheeling, Va., where we arrived in good health, with but little or nothing to vary the monotony of servitude on the part of one, nor the case and authority on the part of the other. After spending a short time at Wheeling, we concluded to wend our way towards the south. Preparations to this effect were made,–and at a favorable time, tide and wind allowing, we were upon the broad bosom of the Ohio, on our downward passage to the southern states. Mr. Stone, I knew to be the partner of Phillips, yet nothing could induce me to call him *master*,–I recognized none but Phillips, and his authority alone I would obey. Stone was a proud, overbearing and haughty tyrant,–one to whom white and black, who bear not the golden talisman, must bow in meek humility. He had outraged humanity, and trampled on the finer feelings of the heart so long, that becoming a dread to the *poor*, he commanded through fear, an implicit obedience. He was a fiend incarnate,–whose only joy was in the torture of feelings more noble and tender than his own; and whose greatest happiness was in witnessing the tears and supplications of the poor oppressed slave,–especially the female portion. What then was his surprise, when he saw that I was determined to stand firmly upon the rights of my manhood–to obey the orders of none, save he, whom I *knew* had paid the price for me, and claimed me as his body servant.–He foamed and sweat–threatened his deep revenge–but naught swayed me. I was as firm as the deep rooted Himmelehs;[17] and unless Phillips ordered, I stirred not to obey. By acts of kindness, too, I had become a general favorite with the poor slaves, who, like myself were considered as negotiable property, and bound for that mart, in which a higher price could be attained for us, than in any other. Among these acts was the furnishing of them with such delicacies they dreamed not of. These, I was enabled to supply them, from the fact that I was Phillips' body servant, and had free access to the shore whenever I chose to claim it, whilst the labor of my own hands, in shaving for the boats, provided me with the needful to supply their wants. Nor were these little acts of kindness without their good result. The slaves, thinking to serve me, and knowing my abhorrence of Stone, would convey to me, his threats of flogging me as soon as we arrived in Natchez. To these threats I merely made a laughing reply–and generally concluded by stating that as that was a two handed game, I very strongly imagined that they would be under the necessity of calling the city guards, to aid them in their *laudable efforts*–that I had strictly obeyed *him*, whom I was confident was my master, so far, at least, as money purchased human flesh–nor had any complaint escaped *him* as to my duty; and that unless *he* was the castigator, they would find me able and willing to defend myself. During our passage down, however, Phillips, who was the partner of Stone, was placed in the capacity of steering the boat. Of this, he soon tired; and I, having in the course of time, become somewhat of an adept in steerage, I was stationed at the oar;—at which, I gave general satisfaction. But the deep damning feeling of revenge burned within the bosom of Stone. "The feelings of that nigger," said he, to his comrades, "must be brought down; and I am determined on his arrival at Natchez, to punish his bravado."

When word of this threat was carried to me, I merely smiled, and replied, "I will see to that," and continued at my duty. Stone soon became aware of my apathy and hatred towards him, and my determination not to obey him. Hence, under some pretext, he contrived to take the oar from me; and placed the steering in charge of a relation of his, called Davis. This passed off well enough for a while,—but one day it was found that from the ignorance of this man, he had changed the course of the craft, and pulled nine miles backward. This mistake was first discovered by the people on the shore, who called to us, and told us that we had passed there the evening before, and that we must undoubtedly be upon the wrong track.

This circumstance was the means of reinstating me in my former birth; and from that time until we reached Natchez, nothing of importance took place. Previous to this, however, Phillips had taken sick, and when we arrived in port he was confined to his bed. We had been in this place but a short time, when Stone and the Clerk came to me, for the purpose of chastising me for my arrogance. I demanded the reason,—and in reply, was only commanded to retire to another part of boat, and strip for a castigation. With this I immediately complied, throwing off my coat, rolling up my sleeves, and arming myself with weapons of defence. When they again confronted me, Stone in a voice of authority wished to know what I intended to do with the weapon which I held in my hand. To this, I simply replied, "if wronged by either look or act, rest assured, sir, I intend to defend myself!" "You do, do you," returned he, we shall see to that, men seize the nigger." "We had rather, Mr. Stone, you would perform that part of the ceremony yourself—we have no idea of losing life for you so easily," replied the clerk, who had until now exhibited himself foremost in the assault; no doubt as a recompense for the past liberty I had assumed, in riding by his side from Winchester to Cumberland. "D—n the cowards," retorted Stone in a passion. "Ho, niggers, come forth, and seize on Billy Hayden!" "Stand back!" cried I, as you value your lives stand back! The first man that dares to seize upon me, lies first a corpse upon the deck. And you, [turning to Stone,] what power have you over Billy Hayden? He is your *equal* in the sight of God—your *superior* in the scale of worth! *Who are you?* Let those who know you tell. Despised by all, both black and white, who have ever heard the accents of your more than contemptible name. *You* talk of punishing Billy Hayden. What has he done? In what consists his crime? *In nothing.* Nay, sir, I have done nothing—and think you, I am a fool to work and rack my sinews throughout life for *nothing*,–and be flogged for the same? If you do, let me tell you, the City Guards will have to be called in to help you. You wretch, you call yourself a gentleman. I challenge any one, I care not who he may be, who has ever known you, to dub you with the title, and *you* talk of venting your revenge upon Billy Hayden,–backed & supported by your myrmidons.[18] Let them come–they will find that Virtue, supported by strong thewes, can keep at bay a thousand tyrants of oppression. Advance, and you know the consequences."

Stone stood some time, expecting a break to be made by his creatures, both black and white,–but no such movement was *offered*, and he retired to his room, muttering curses upon me, and threatening to sell me to the worst master he could possibly find in Natchez. These threats I did not care for–as I was well aware my spiritual guide, who had protected me throughout life, would still protect me until death. But the fracas was not designed to end here: –Phillips, whom I have before said was sick, had heard the noise, and the language I addressed to Stone. Quick as thought, he sprang to the deck, and commanded them to desist any attempts at punishing Billy. 'Tis strange gentlemen, said he "that I cannot have a favorite slave, but he must be imposed upon." "Touch that one," said he, pointing to me, "and you'll meet your reward here," patting the handle of a large bowie knife, which he invariably carried. Those words put a grand quietus to the controversy for that time, and I retired to my room in the boat, greatly elated with my own and my master's success.

On the road from Maysville, too, another occurrence took place, which I have some reason to believe, gained for me the increased confidence and respect of my master. Sleeping in a room adjacent to the slaves, who were ironed,[19] I discerned enough from their conversation to enable me to know that a mutiny was abroad, and that it was the intention of the slaves, in order to effect their freedom, to put to death all the whites on board,–and that I, too, was included,–owing to the attention that was paid me,–with the doomed. By jests and cheerfulness with them, however, I gathered from their detached hints, their every movement. That they had even then provided themselves with a file from the lot of Blacksmith tools on board, and that many were at that moment, free from their chains. This information I immediately carried to my master; and after ascertaining the truth of my statement, he had them again bound more firmly than ever. He then asked me if I knew who was the ringleader of the revolters. I knew enough of the slave-holders' disposition to be aware that it would be to him certain death, on the spot, if discovered–hence I concealed his name; but informed him in place thereof, of the name of him who was possessed of the file. This was immediately taken away, and our passage secured to one of peace and safety. For this information Mr. Phillips was thankful to me; and treated me, as far I could discover, with as much courtesy as a master can well find heart to exercise towards his slave. The name of the ringleader of the revolt was never made known to him, until the individual had been sold; which took place near St. Martinsville, and we were on our way home. Had a breath of suspicion alighted upon him, I feel well convinced he would have been sent to serve his master DEATH, instead of a living overseer.—Hence I felt grateful that I had been instrumental in saving the lives of a boat's crew, and thwarting the punishment of death, which the miscreant who, could in cold blood conceive so damning a plot, richly merited. And for all this, the scene at Natchez was my reward, merited in the estimation of slave-dealers. Such is their gratitude and justice—and such is a faithful character of the *slave-holder's* gratitude *in most instances*, where the slave is the recipient thereof.

From Maysville our course lay to Paris, where we remained until October, when we again embarked and came to Cincinnati. Here we staid for a few hours, and then sailed for Natchez. At Cincinnati I had freedom to go and come when and where I listed, as long as the boat remained, but I soon found that this was not palatable to Phillips, who still entertained the idea, that I might escape, knowing myself to be in a free state. But even of this knowledge I feigned extreme ignorance, as any other course might have been detrimental to my purposes, and abridged me of many little freedoms which were otherwise extended to me. When the hour spoken of by the *Spirit, had come*, I was ready for my freedom; but until *then*, I was in mind and body, a slave. But O how anxiously did I await the arrival of that hour,—how ardently did I pray for its arrival, and thank my God that it was, for me, in store. To be a *free man*, was the height of my ambition; and to administer the same *freedom to an aged parent*, was the only hopes of my future happiness.

After the fracas above recorded, which happened at Natchez, things went on in their usual smooth style, until the slaves were divided between Stone and Philips, and destined for different marts. At Natchez, however, when application was made for the purchase of a slave, which was frequent every day; I behaved myself with such utter indifference and apparent independence, that many of the would-be purchasers were at a loss to know if, in reality, I were a slave, and subject to the hammer.[20] I promenaded the deck, whistling some snatches of an old song, and looking, in regard to *consequence*, more like a master than a slave; so that when I was asked how I would like to serve, I invariably replied, "I don't know how I would like to *serve any man*, until I am tried."

"Well," continued they, "how do you like our looks?"

*"I don't like them at all!"* responded I. This answer generally called for an explanation between Philips and the anxious purchaser.

"Philips," said the latter, "is it possible that fellow is a slave?"

"Yes," replied Philips, "he is my body servant—why do you ask?"

"Because he appears too independent to serve—you must put another brow upon him, before you will be able to sell him in this market. He's entirely too free with the tongue." This was the state of things which I desired; and the power of God soon brought me to a knowledge of the kind care which was bestowed upon me.

When a division of the slaves took place, I still remained with Phillips; and having provided our boat, we proceeded to Bayou Sara, whilst Stone remained at Natchez; at this place I commenced the study of the French language, in which I made such rapid progress that in a short time I was enabled to speak and write it pretty fluently. This was a material advantage to me, although my master was in ignorance of my knowledge of it. By it, I was enabled to understand, more effectually, the various dealings of my master, and also inform myself of the transactions which daily took place between him and his correspondents. I, soon, too, became a general favorite with all the whites at Bayou Sara; one lady, in particular, came on board the boat to me, and wished that I would permit her to pick out a master for me. I replied, that I intended at some day, purchasing myself; but if I failed in this I would then call upon her to aid me in the selection of a kind and benevolent master. By some means or other my master became acquainted with my daily study of the French, and reproached me for studying a language which would be of no use to myself, but might probably be an injury to *him*. To this I replied, that I had merely taken it up to keep myself out of mischief. This was, as he said very well, but begged that I would not bother myself with such an outlandish gibberish. I understood him better probably than he expected, but said nothing, as it would have been of no avail.

From Bayou Sara, we embarked in a few days for Atakapas, where we remained all winter. While stationed at this place, my master often received letters from home, in which my knowledge of French constantly kept me advised of his intentions and plans. Castleman, who was also a partner of Stone's and Phillips; and who had long wanted me for himself, but whom I scorned to serve, had now openly proclaimed to Phillips his determination of securing me. I was well aware that Phillips had purchased me for himself; and aware too that my disposal rested solely with Castleman–hence, Phillips being somehow within the power of Castleman, who had threatened a prosecution in case of a refusal, I knew not what course he might be led to pursue. I watched attentively the face of Phillips whilst he perused the letter containing the threat, in order to read, if possible, his determination, and was ready for any proposition he might make me. For some days he said nothing. At length he came to me, and after some preliminary remarks, informed me that on our arrival home, I would have to leave the State, as he was greatly embarrassed with debt, and that one of his partners was determined to have me sold, in case of his inability to pay him the debt he owed him. "And why not let him have me?" asked I, in order to ascertain better the motives which actuated him. "Because," returned he "you have been to me, a faithful servant, and I cannot spare you at this time." Knowing that it was my interest, as well as his own, that I should comply with his wishes, I unhesitatingly replied that wherever he chose I should go, on our arrival at home, his wishes should be strictly obeyed; and whatever he should desire, to state freely and it should be performed.

In Atakapas I was well known, and by my conduct, had acquired many friends. Near this place too, resided a young lady, who was very anxious to purchase me, in order, as she said, that I might teach her the English language. Her importunities were frequent and strong,–and in order to get rid of her, I promised that when I next visited the country, I would be sold to her. Poor thing, she little dreamed I would never become hers,–that the spirit would work my deliverance from bondage, before the day on which she expected to call me her own, should arrive.

My master in this place, met with an unlooked for sale, and even anticipated, and gleaned a rich profit in a short stay–consequently, having made our preparations, we turned our course towards home. My savings, during this trip was about $100, which with the $100 my master was indebted to me, made the respectable sum of $200. A short time after, Phillips concluded to go to New Orleans, and I was induced to go with him; and as we expected to return to St. Martinsville, where there was no confectionary, I determined on investing my money in the purchase of candy, &c., and as soon as I arrived at St. Martinsville, to engage in the business of a Confectioner. With this determination, on reaching New Orleans, I was introduced to a lady, who kept a Confectionary shop, and who, after she had been apprized of my intentions, assured me that she would give me a bargain of her stock in trade; and further assured me, that if I would consent she would purchase me of my master, and live with me as my wife. Now, this was too much of a good thing for me; so purchasing her candies, which were weighed out, and leaving the *living sweet*, to seek some more suitable husband at her leisure, I left for St. Martinsville. I found no difficulty in selling my confectionaries, and when my sales were concluded, I discovered that a profit was made of 100 per cent, thereon; swelling the sum of one hundred dollars, which I had invested in the purchase, to two hundred dollars, which when added to the $100 already saved, secured me in one half the sum which was asked for my freedom.–Heaven! with what delight did I look upon that money, and long for the remaining $300 that I might lay it in the hands of Phillips, and say, "according to our agreement, sir, I am a free man." But how was I to secure this money? Phillips, in leading his present life, might be snatched off, and what would then become of my savings, or the proof that he held at the time of his death, one half the purchase money for my freedom. This I determined to remedy; and approaching him, I intimated to him the uncertainty of life, and my anxiety of leaving some written evidence for the $100 which he already owed me, and the 200 dollars which I was then ready to pay him. He then asked me if I knew of any friend of mine who would draw up the writings? I told him I would call on Mr. Brent, a gentleman who seemed to think a good deal of me, and see if I could get him to do it; accordingly, I waited on Mr. Brent, and making known my errand, he informed me that as he was acquainted with Mr. Phillips, he could not, unless he was present, and gave his consent, comply with my request: as it might be the cause of ill feelings between them afterwards. I had mentioned to him also, in the presence of Mr. McElvain, that I was to have my freedom for $650, and that the $300 for which I wished the writings drawn were the first payments thereon; but that I feared Phillips had some sinister motives in view, and designed to cheat me out of my money and my freedom. Mr. Brent requested that *I* would go and bring Mr. Phillips to the store, which *I* accordingly did, after cautioning Mr. McElvain to watch the countenance of Phillips, and see if he could not plainly discover guilt of thought and action.–This, he promised to do. When Mr. Phillips came into the store, *I* placed myself in front of him and riveted my eyes upon him. He seemed embarrassed, and his face flashed like a living coal. Mr. Brent then told him what *I* had requested him to do–stating, at the same time he considered it nothing more than right that *I* should have security for my money, in case of his death; and after some hesitation my master concurred. The writings were then drawn up, and signed by Phillips, and attested by the gentlemen present; Mr. Brent counting out the money to Phillips. After he had signed the note, he told me *I* had better leave it at the store, in the keeping of Mr. Brent. To this *I* replied, that *I* intended to do so, and turning to Mr. B., *I* said, presenting him a letter from my mother, "here sir, is a letter from my mother. *I*n case of my death, *I* wish you to send that and the money to her, as the present of an affectionate son. *I*t is my will, and *I* hope you will not consider it as an insult to request you to act as the Executor of a poor slave!" Mr. Brent promised faithfully to see my wishes carried out, and with tears in my eyes, *I* left the store, grateful to Heaven for the kind protection which *I* had received through the goodness of God.

My master was at this time very much embarrassed, and Castleman, one of his partners in business was determined to leave nothing unresorted to, to secure me, and ruin Phillips.–Consequently my master was obliged to take up his boarding with the Sheriff of Bourbon Co., Mr. John Reins. He told me to answer no questions relative to him, and that, if Castleman came to ask for him to tell him, *I* knew nothing of him.–*I*t was but a short time before this rank hypocrite–bent upon the persecution of his victim,–in every manner, he could possibly do it, came. He appeared to be very glad to see me, but *I* discovered and knew that it was the same joy he felt, as that evinced by the hungry wolf, when the unwary lamb approaches its hideous jaws. His first question, after shaking hands very cordially with me, was for Phillips. *I* told him *I* knew nothing about him. This answer seemed to surprise him, as he gazed at me for some considerable length of time, in silence, when turning on his heel, and casting one malignant glance around him, which *I* shall never forget, he departed. *I* immediately went to Phillips, and communicated to him what had passed. He told me that *I* must instantly leave the State; and giving me $15 in money, and a pass to carry me to Cincinnati, *I* forthwith proceeded on my journey. Fortunately there was a wagon passing on the Georgetown road, at this time for Cincinnati.–*I* had, however, some friends whom *I* wished to visit ere *I* left the State, and having shown the wagoner my pass, which he recognized as genuine, he permitted me to take a birth in his wagon as far as

Williamsport. As *I* left Paris, the Court House Bell was ringing. The first case before the Court was the case of Castleman vs. Phillips. On the appearance of Castleman in Court, *I* afterwards understood, the first query was for me.–Castleman stated that he had seen me but a few moments since, and that for the purpose of securing my evidence, he did not deem it necessary to put me in close custody; but that he had no doubt I could be brought before the court, after a very little delay. The court, however, having but little time to lose, owing to cases of importance being upon the tapis, it adjourned the case of my master with Castleman–without a hearing. Thus the scheme of my master was accomplished, by my absence, and by an act of treachery and vice he was enabled to elude the swift arm of justice. But, his day was soon to come, and the spirit spoke of my triumph over his viliany, as a matter beyond the reach of cavil. Upon the road we passed on smoothly, until we came to Williamsport, where some of the friends of the wagoner began to rally him on the quick sale of his marketing, and appearing not to believe him, they approached the wagon, and removing the hay under which I was safely ensconsed, they charged him with harboring a runaway slave. To this the wagoner stoutly replied that he scorned the idea of harboring a runaway slave, that the man he had there, *was as free as either of them*; and that he was responsible for the safe passage of me, to the end of his journey–and this authority he took upon himself, upon the pass which he now held in his possession. If any man dared to doubt him, and lay a finger upon me, with a design to capture me, they would first have to trample over his dead body. In this he was warmly seconded by his father-in-law, and after a few words of altercation, the melee ended, and the crowd dispersed, apparently well satisfied, and I was taken by my benefactor to his house. Here I had to tell my story over and over again to his wife, and many of their friends, who visited them, and all seemed to sympathize deeply with me, and pray me God speed in all my undertakings. After remaining under his roof for several days, aiding and assisting my kind friend in many things about his place; and being treated by him and his amiable lady, more like a member of the family, than as a stranger, I departed on the morning of the fourth day, in the stage, for Cincinnati, with their blessings and well wishes heaped upon me. When the driver gave me a seat in the stage, there was but one lady and her little daughter inside, and from my kindness to the child, I soon gained the respect and well wishes of the mother–for it is a well founded fact, that the passport to a mother's affections, is through the medium of a beloved child–hence, I felt secure in my further progress to the haven of my destination. Many of my friends, however, informed me, previous to my leaving, that my pass would avail me nothing after I had arrived at the river, as it was against the law to ferry slaves from a slave to a free state, unless under the eyes of their masters or guardians.

Our passage from Williamsport was one of pleasure and anticipated joy, until we arrived at Gaines' station, some 18 or 20 miles from Covington. Here the stage, belonging to Mr. G., was permitted to stop over night; and after the lady and child were ushered into the sitting room, I was conducted to the kitchen, where my supper was served up to me. To eat, however, was not my intention, acting upon the impulse of the "yankee" who informed king George, on being commanded to uncover before royalty, that *Americans* never bowed to any man—especially when they stood in *his kitchen*—whilst the master of the house seemed to say, as I cast my eyes towards the barroom, *"we don't allow niggers in here!"*

This, however, did not deter me from walking into the barroom, and drawing a seat to the fire. After a short time, Mr. Gaines, who had once before seen me, when the body servant of Major Charles Clarkson; began a series of questions, and counter-questions, as to who I was—where I belonged—and who was my master—thinking, and even charging me with being a runaway slave—having in my possession a forged pass—and that, if I were not apprehended before I reached the river, he, himself, would see that I should not escape to Ohio, without, at least, giving a more strict account of myself, than I had as yet. From me, he gained nothing—neither did his "quizzical leech" draw the blood of information from the stage driver, who was a friend of mine, and bore me on my journey at the instance of many of my friends, who stood accountable for my character and conduct to him, and to others.

Gaines, however, was not to be duped—and the next morning, when the stage started he despatched his "tools" through the woods, to head the team; and when I endeavored to cross the river, they were to apprehend me, and detain me, until his malignity was satisfied. But the Lord frustrated his intentions; and raised up friends for me in the persons of my fellow passenger and the driver, who informed me of their schemes, and projected a plan by which she, (God bless her) would insure me a safe passage to Cincinnati. This lady resided at that time in Newport, and the plan which she proposed was, that I should act in the capacity of her body servant, until she reached home, when she would send me to an old colored friend of hers, known as *"Uncle James Taylor,"* who had the command of the ferry, and see that I should be landed on the other side, unmolested. Accordingly we continued on our route until we reached the water's edge, when I was surprised and astounded; the very first man who met my eye was Major Carneal, who was so anxious to purchase me of Mr. Smith, on the day of my young mistress's marriage—but whom I refused to accept as a master—merely on the ground that I was one day to become *free*—not as a resident of a free state, but as a *slave*, living and learning among my fellow slaves. Here, a general system of *Indian warfare* took place, Major Carneal endeavoring to fasten his eyes upon me, and I, fearing that he should recognize me, dodging and ducking behind the head of the child, and the person of its mother. In my object of remaining unknown, I was successful, and with naught to mar my further progress, we reached the house of the kind lady in Newport. After spending a few moments here, she proceeded to put her scheme in practice, and giving a boy *"a bit,"* she despatched him with me to Old Uncle Jim, telling the boy to introduce me to him, as a particular friend of hers, whom she wished to transact some private and important business for her in Cincinnati. I was thus soon landed unquestioned and unmolested on the free shores of Ohio–beyond hearing of the overseer's lash–and beyond the oppression of the human panderer, who makes a filthy living of luxury, by bartering his own flesh and blood in a public mart. The off-spring of his own loins–the son of his own manhood–the daughter of his own blood, are dragged forth like cattle to the shambles, and sold like beasts of burden to the highest bidder.

Here, then, was freedom held out to me in all its bewitching forms. A life of slavery was behind–and a life of ease and liberty before me–but I scorned the boon and chose to obey the will of the Fates. I could not consistently sacrifice the confidence which Phillips had placed in me–and I felt fully assured that the hour of my deliverance had not yet come when I was to shake off my yoke of bondage, and proclaim my Emancipation to the world. I had delved for years–long and tedious years in slavery–and now, that I had touched upon a free soil, armed with a pass and signed by my master, authorizing my freedom to travel where I listed, I might have felt myself secure from the Shylocks of the Law, and laughed defiance at the administrators of Southern justice. But I craved not the aid of the laws of man. My liberation was to be *supernatural*–and effected through my own exertions. Hence, I cared not for the bright prospects which were then held out to me.

On arriving at Cincinnati, the first man whom I met, was a colored man, whom I had known at the South, and who had absconded from my master, Mr. Phillips. On seeing me, he immediately alarmed the citizens–stating that I belonged to a slave-trading Southerner, and that he felt confident that I was in search of *him.* This charge threw suspicion on me, as a kidnapper, and as such, I was arraigned before the mayor, the present former Judge, Isaac G. Burnett, a venerable and beloved citizen of Cincinnati–and there stood my trial. My pass was adduced, and I claimed that as a passport to freedom–but my intentions to return to the south on the call of my master, corroborated the circumstances against me, and not until I had a private conference with the mayor and a letter had been sent and replied to by Mr. Phillips, was the suspicion done away with in his mind; when I was honorably acquitted.

Whilst at Cincinnati, this honorable gentleman, together with many other friends, strongly urged me never to return to the South, but to fall in with their overtures, and they would see me safely landed in Canada. They regretted that one who placed such confidence in a slave-dealer's word–and refused so strongly to violate the authority of him whom I supposed was my master, as far as wealth gave him authority–should, for a longer period be made a subject for cruel treatment, and invidious distinction! But their kind wishes were cast aside, and as an obedient servant I chose to return to the home of Phillips. When the venerable Mr. Burnett saw that I was thus determined, he shook hands, and with watery eyes and a sorrowful tone of voice, he resigned me to my fate. Previous to leaving him, however, I remarked to him, having asked him if he thought he could again recognize me on meeting, that the day would come, after many years had elapsed, when I would become a free man–occupying a Barber's shop in Cincinnati, and claiming him as a regular customer.

Sixteen years since then have now elapsed and my prediction has been verified–my freedom has been achieved, and for the last five years the venerable old man has been a constant customer at my shop. The frosts of many winters are now scattered on his head–and he is fast verging to the land of Spirits. May the Almighty God sustain him and his amiable family to the last–and when their earthly career is run receive them and bless them in the world to come. For to the poor, he is a friend–and to all a beloved and respected citizen.

Accordingly, after the lapse of time, the letter of recall arrived. This letter contained instructions that I must throw away my pass and letters, which I had received from him, previously, and immediately wend my way homeward. Upon the commands of the letter, I immediately acted,–and embarking on board a boat, I was in the course of time, landed at Maysville. Here, before the boat had safely reached the shore, I promptly complied with the request of my master, and threw the pass and letters on the beach. This was merely done for the purpose of clearing myself of an act of *disobedience*,–but, as I had learned that these papers were of almost invaluable importance to me, and that they might materially aid me in my future freedom, as soon as I leaped on shore, I gathered them up once more and secured them about my person. I had now complied with his request, and my own desires; and feeling myself secure from all censure, I started with pleasure on my return to Paris. When I arrived in town, the first man whom I met was Major Throckmorton. He appeared glad to see me, but informed me that I had better secrete myself, as Phillips had threatened when he next got me, to inflict upon my bare back five hundred stripes. Of this, Phillips himself had informed me, stating that he had made the threat to shield himself. The Major did not know the understanding which existed between Phillips and myself, and consequently feared for my safety.–I thanked him for his kindness in warning me of the circumstance, but stated that I would go and see Mr. Phillips. Accordingly I bent my steps towards Phillips' room. The first question after shaking hands, and appearing overjoyed at again seeing me, was, whether I had obeyed him in throwing the pass and letters away. To this I replied that I had. This appeared to increase his confidence, and he informed me that I must now tell some plausible story, to screen him from all knowledge of my where-a-bouts, during my absence. To this I consented, although I felt my conscience check me at the mere idea of falsehood. But the ultimate good, bid fair to bury the present evil, and I chose for once to stoop to a little dissimulation.–Thus, Phillips was shielded in his iniquity, by one whom he claimed as his own–and it is thus that the slave-holders in general are shielded in crime and infamy, at the expense of even the soul and body of those whom their wealth holds as mere personal property. The gold of the rich, and the callous heart of the slave-dealer, make man, the image of God–a mere thing–an article to be pandered through the public mart, and sold to the highest bidder. His body is converted into a beast of burden–racked with toil, persecuted with stripes,[21] and as the red blood flows in streaks from the gashing wounds inflicted by the scourge, he is denied the existence of a soul and denied the rights of fellowship with his fellow-man. Can Heaven's vengeance long withstand his haughty arrogance of depraved mortality? Can God view unconcerned the bleeding pores of His own glorious likeness, lascerated and scourged by unfeeling fiends, and withhold his just indignation? No, his frown will come, and terrible will be his vengeance.

Here then my supernatural guide was again of advantage to my benighted soul.[22] My master, relying, as he thought, upon my rank ignorance, and upon my implicit confidence in him, imagined that his hypocrisy was a sufficient cloak for all his deep designs towards me. But, reckless soul–I knew his object too well. I knew, that upon the first opportunity it was his design to sell me;–I knew, too, in case of a sale, he would attempt a fraud, with regard to the $300 of mine, which he had in his possession; by forging a receipt, and imposing a belief upon my friends, that he had paid me ere he had sold me. But I said nothing. My tongue was struck dumb by the spirit, and I was compelled to abide the issue without a murmur. I was, however, permitted to advise with my friends, which I immediately concluded to do. But to cast the first hint to him that I was aware of his designs, was the farthest from my heart.–Hence, in the language of my spiritual guide, "thus far, and no farther, shalt thou come,"[23] I fortified my mind, and anxiously awaited the result. Phillips had again stated to me, that he designed taking a trip to the South, and informed me that I must hold myself in readiness to accompany him. This command I obeyed with so much eagerness, as to drive my master from the suspicions which he seemed to entertain towards my future plans. All went on as it should, and the rank hypocrisy which he so illy concealed, was daily becoming more and more apparent. Now, thought he, have I tested his confidence. He might have been free in Cincinnati, but his ignorance has driven him once more into the slave mart. He shall he sold–and as he is a valuable slave, he will command a high price, which with the three hundred dollars of his, I now hold in my possession, will recruit my fortune, and set me once more at ease.–But he little knew that that sale could never be consummated–that Billy Hayden was then in possession of his last earthly master, and that the genius of freedom stood ready to proclaim his deliverance from earthly bondage. His schemes were about to vanish, and he was shortly to be doomed to stand before the world in all the ignominy and shame he so richly merited.

Previous to our departure, however, I went to see my old friend Mr. Brent, whom I found in his store. I then told him of the villany of Phillips in his designs towards me. Mr. Brent seemed surprised at my narrative; yet his mind was partially prepared for such a crisis, from his former scrutiny of the man's conduct. He accordingly called me to speak with him more privately; and we retired by ourselves. He then made known to me that he had signed the note in my favor, and asked me if I could manage to keep it secure if he would relinquish it to my keeping. I replied that I thought I could; when he immediately transferred it to me. Before parting with him, however, we had a long conversation, in which I made known to him many of my plans of future action. With these he seemed to be highly pleased, and avowed that he had never before witnessed one of my race, who was to him so great a wonder as myself. He wished to know where I had picked up my information; but of this I was not capable to inform him. Hence, after a long time in private communion, I parted with the good old man, while the tears of sorrow trickled down my cheeks. I felt, on leaving him, as if I had parted from my father, for the acts of kindness which he had shown me, and which he had confirmed by endorsing the note and referring me to Mr. Postlewaite, of Natchez, cashier of the bank, where I could draw the money on sight of the note, had bound him to me with a tie, strong as the ligaments of my heart could bind a beloved object. God bless his memory–for it is a sweet and consoling reflection that he was one of my dearest friends in my captivity; and, in my freedom, I cannot be such an ingrate as to pass him by in silence. After leaving Mr. Brent, I immediately proceeded to a hatter's shop, where I procured a coon skin, and having carefully shaved the hair off, I sowed the note, together with Phillips' letters and his pass, safely within it, and having re-inclosed this in some old cloth and pieces of blanket, I sowed them all on the shoulder of my old coat between the lining and the cloth. This served a double purpose. By it, my shoulder was protected whilst pushing or pulling the boat, and in this place, although my trunks were searched, which I knew would be the case, my papers were secure. Thus equipped, I presented myself before my master, and awaited his orders for a departure.

In a few days we started,–and in the course of time landed again at Natchez. Here, I knew it was the design of Phillips to sell me, if possible. But still I entered no complaint, but was determined to serve no other earthly master. Near Bayou Sara, whither we went, there resided a fiend, (for I cannot call him man) named Sterling, who followed the avocation of *"negro-breaker."* This consisted in taking the raw slaves of the traders, and placing them in a field, with iron bands on their limbs, where they are made to work like beasts of burden.–This wretch who had several plantations, and who was notorious for his cruelty to the colored population, almost entirely subsisted upon their labor, whilst engaged in breaking them. I knew that in case I was sold, and refused to work, or even treated my purchaser with anything in the shape of impudence, that I would be passed over to this fiend, and treated more like a dog, than a human being. Hence, I concluded to abide patiently the ways of fate. After a few days my suspicions were confirmed. Phillips did indeed sell me to a Mr. Maxwell of Bayou Sara. This gentleman did not call on me for some days after, and during this time, Phillips had left the place, thinking when he returned, I should have been carried off by my purchaser. One day, however,

Mr. Maxwell came to the boat, and calling me to one side, he asked me how I would like to live with him? To this I replied, I could not tell, but if I belonged to him, I thought I would like it very well, as I had always found him a kind and indulgent master. He then informed me that he had purchased me of Mr. Phillips, and that having three stores in the place, and being compelled to spend most of his summers in the north, in consequence of his health, he needed just such a person as I was to take charge, and see that his business did not languish in his absence. He said he had some clerks, whom he did not think rendered him a strict account of the proceeds of the stores; he therefore wanted me, as I would be in their friendly notice through his influence, to correspond with him during his absence, and inform him of anything I might conceive to be not right. He further assured me that he had always heard me spoken of as an honest and upright man; whose word was as good as a bond, and that I was just the person, he would, of all things admire.

As he concluded, I fixed my eyes keenly upon him, and asked him, apparently unconscious, if he had indeed understood me to be upright and honest all my life?

He replied that he had.

"And do you believe it?" returned I.

"To be sure I do; and would stake my life upon your integrity."

"Then, sir," said I, "would you have me prove myself a villain and a liar in one day? You would have me, Mr. Maxwell, prove myself a hypocrite—you would have me gain the confidence of your clerks, with whom, as you say, I should share in their carousals; and whilst they were bestowing friendship on me, and placing their confidence in me, you would wish me to stab their reputation for honesty behind their backs. Sir, although a slave, I am not so base as to betray the first principles of humanity—and I would scorn to pursue such a course as you have pointed out. You are aware, too, that Phillips has pledged himself to free me as soon as I can raise $650, and, according to our agreement. *cannot sell me.*"

"But he has," said Mr. Maxwell, "and the bill of sale needs but the signatures."

"Which it shall never have," said I. "He now has $300 of my money, for which he has given his note, and I can very soon raise the remainder."

"But those $300 he has paid you long since—at least so he informed me."

"He did!" exclaimed I, in astonishment—"then, sir, all I have to say is, he informed of what was *false*—await until his return, and if I cannot arrange it so as to pay the full price of my freedom, and find him such a villain, I will willingly become your property. Till then I cannot act."

"All right," exclaimed Maxwell, shaking me warmly by the hand. "It shall be as you wish it. Meanwhile, good day."

He had expected the circumstances, when related to me, would fire me with rage, and in such a case Sterling's aid, who was present, promenading the levee with a long cow-hide, awaiting the issue, would be called upon to quell me; but having treated him so fairly and so much like my equal; my freedom, instead of offending him, had proved much in my favor; and I was permitted to enjoy my own way until Phillips' arrival.

In a few days he arrived. When the boat landed I was standing upon the wharf, and Mr. Maxwell, the gentleman who had purchased me was standing by my side. As Phillips came from the boat, he extended his hand cordially to me, and shaking mine warmly, he inquired how I got along. I told him very well; but circumstances had transpired since his departure for which I would wish him to account. He looked surprised, and asked me what they were. I then narrated to him all that had passed between Mr. Maxwell, and myself, and asked him if it was true, that he had indeed sold me. He laughingly replied, that some such occurrences had taken place but that the whole transaction was merely a joke between Maxwell and himself. I told him such jokes, I could not find it in my heart to relish, and referring him to our bargain, when I became his property, I told him that my term of servitude had expired.

"You are aware," said I, "that we were to maintain the relative positions of master and servant, so long as we could agree; but when either of us became dissatisfied, that bond was to be void." I now could agree to serve him no longer, as his course had destroyed all my confidence in him, and I could not consider myself bound to one whom I could not esteem.

"And again, sir, you have informed Mr. Maxwell that you have long since paid me the $300 which you were indebted to me, and for which you gave your note. This, you knew to be false, as your note is still in existence against you. All I now demand is, that you will return me the money, and we will part friends."

My language seemed to somewhat startle him, as he had no idea of losing so valuable a body servant as I had proved to be. Hence, he resorted to every kind of dissimulation, which it was possible for him to do, in order to gain my attendance on him on his return to Paris. He coaxed and cajoled,–and finally flattered so hard, that I agreed to go, but I expressly gave him to understand that I recognized myself as a free man, and that I would act in the capacity of a slave to no one. To this he made no reply, and I embarked with him on our passage up the river. It is true, I still continued to shave him every morning as usual, but further than this I claimed the privileges of a freeman, and refused to do all acts of servitude which I had hitherto done, paying my own passage to Paris.

Previous to leaving Bayou Sara, however, many of my friends came to me, and very generously offered to advance me the balance of the money, wherewith to purchase my freedom. I thanked them with gratitude for their sympathy for my distresses, but declined receiving their favors; from the fact that my deliverance was to work its way through some spiritual medium, backed by my own exertions. The hour, had not yet dawned upon me, but I felt assured of its swift approach.

With these feelings, and throwing myself upon what I deemed my rights,–

refusing to do the work of a slave, and devoting my time to my own amusements, we finally reached Paris. Hence, through the intervention of the spirit, I became fully satisfied that no mortal man could again purchase me.–This was strongly corroborated on our journey–where several wished to purchase me very much; among whom was Major Miner, but when I related to him my determination; and the understanding which existed between Phillips and myself, together with the means I had of freeing myself, they withdrew their desire, and refused to stand between me and my heart longing ends. Mr. Miner also informed me, that as soon as I had freed myself, if I would come to Natchez, and become a citizen of the place, I might depend upon any assistance which lay in his power to render me. To this I consented, and so after days, reaped the benefit, which his promise had held out to me. After we arrived in Paris, I went to the boarding house of Phillips, where I remained until towards night fell when I took my hat and bade Mr. Phillips "good night." He did not know what to make of this movement, and surprised as he was, he forebore to say anything. I remained away a few days, working with a friend in a Barber shop in the place, and during this time I saw nothing of Phillips. Finally he came to me, and asked me what I meant by such a course of conduct. I replied by asking him, if he did not remember what I had told him; that I would never again serve him in the capacity of a servant, nor would I enter the service of any mortal, unless assured of my wages, as was the right of every *freeman.* I also told him, if he was at leisure in the morning, I would call upon him, to know what he intended to do relative to the money, for which I held his note; –accordingly, he left me, and in the morning, I waited upon him. On demanding the money he told me to follow him to his room. This I did very willingly. When he had entered, he immediately locked the door, and going to his trunk, he took out a brace of pistols, and a bowie knife, and having examined them thoroughly, he laid them upon the table, at which I sat, and placed himself directly opposite me. Every muscle of his face was set in demoniac determination, and eyeing me attentively, as if he would have read my very soul, he deliberately informed me, that he owed me *nothing*–that a slave whilst in servitude, could command nothing of his master; that he and his, were the property of that master, and were at the disposal of his master, and that he was determined to *pay me nothing.* Fortified by the spirit, and not dreading the show of bravo, which he had exhibited, I informed him that I still held his note, and was determined by *some* process to collect the $300 which I loaned him. He then asked me for his note, which I refused to accede to. This, for awhile staggered him; and finding that I was not to be cozened by threats or falsehoods, he returned to his trunk and in a few moments counted me out the amount coming to me. After I had recounted it in his presence, in order to show him that I placed no confidence in his honesty, I gave him his note, and securing my money about my person, I took my hat, and very cordially bade him "good morning," leaving him to dispose of his note as he saw proper, and to return to his trunk his brace of "shooting irons," or turn them against his own head, as he saw fit; well assured that either would be much easier done, than frightening even a colored man, who knew himself to be fortified by a supernatural shield, and knowing his rights as a freeman, out of $300, of his hard earned wages.

Phillips did not call upon me for some days after the above occurrence; so that I concluded to go to *him*, hearing that he was determined to force me again into his service, to know his pleasure. He informed me that I was still his property, and commanded me to return to my duties. I recapitulated to him my determination of serving no mortal man, unless in the capacity of a freeman, and under wages; telling him at the same time, that it was upon the authority of his own agreement with me that I so acted. That he had promised when we could not agree, he would release me, and accept of my purchase money. That his own conduct had been such as to render it necessary for us to part—that he had betrayed confidence, and that I could never serve a master, in whom I had no confidence. A frown gathered upon his brow, but I heeded it not, and in the hight of his anger he informed me with an oath, that he would compel me to serve. This, I told him he could not do.

"And what," replied he, "would you do?"

"Choose death before I would serve *you*, or any other man in the capacity of a slave! What right have you to me? Who made me a slave? Was it He who placed us here in the great bond of brotherhood? Where was the first human soul made a marketable commodity? Surely it was not by the orders of God—nor by His word declared in revelation to mortal man in Holy Writ. All there recorded, goes to prove directly the reverse. Nor was it even in the Declaration of Independence, of your country. It is there plainly stated, that "all men are born free and equal," and have the same rights with one another. Whence, then, comes your authority? From the motto claimed by pirates and cut-throats—from the voice of panderers in human blood—from the blood-stained blade of him whose blows have filled Heaven with the cries of widows—the groans of oppressed humanity, and the wailing of almost frantic orphans. This is where your authority comes from, and I envy you not the very ELEVATED source of its coming. I envy you not your irreligious and unholy motto of action, that might makes right—those who know no better are free to groan in bondage as long as their minds are easy under their degraded yokes, but as for me, you will find me ready to shed the last drop which supports life, before I will serve either you, or any other dealer in the God-like attributes of man. Our fathers were first torn from their native country, and made beasts of burden at the shrine of wealth—were dubbed with the ignominious title of *slaves and things*—they left nothing else to us as a heritage—but I, for one, am determined to spurn the patrimony, and assume the rights, which nature and the God of nature designed, at my entrance into the world, I should—and for my support I appeal to God and the rights of man. God gave me means and the light, and by these I claim to be your equal."

By the time I concluded, there was quite a crowd of citizens gathered around me. Some of them were so incensed that a black man should thus address his master, that they raised the cry of "shoot him! shoot the d—d nigger!" But this alarmed me not. I turned deliberately upon him who had last uttered the cry, and baring my breast, asked who among them would be the executioner? You may shoot the body–but the soul belongs to God. The blush of shame mantled their cheeks, and many of my friends who were mixed in with them, seemed highly delighted with my course. Some of them asked me what I intended to do. "Do," repeated I, "I have both the means and the knowledge to travel by land or water–I have the money, and I am master of the English and French languages–you need not therefore fear for me becoming a pauper,–but a *freeman* I am determined to be!" They seemed utterly astonished at my determination; and seeing that nothing could be done to compel or wheedle me into the service of Phillips again, I was soon left standing "solitary and alone!" in all my glory.

I had for many years foreseen these trials and difficulties,–but I was warned of a safe deliverance from them all. There was, however, another dark cloud lowering in my horizon. I had been forewarned that at a certain period of my life, I was to be immured within a prison, and I now knew that the hour for that had arrived. I nerved myself for it, and felt assured that as I had outridden all my trials, through the Divine Providence of God, I would again come forth unscathed and free–triumphant over the combined efforts of my enemies. Nor was I doomed to be disappointed.

The declaration of my freedom, surprised many, even of my warmest friends, who had calculated that they were acquainted with all the events of my life. They had known me in Paris, for upwards of fourteen years, and had never heard me mention the circumstance of my approaching freedom before. Their astonishment therefore was great, when they saw me standing before those who had held me in bondage, and who still, as far as money held claims on human flesh, were entitled to the name of masters, and proclaiming as my own champion, my *rights* and *freedom* as a *man.* But others were not so easily to be thwarted. They feared that my example, unless punished exemplary, would arouse the ire of the other slaves, and endanger their future peace and authority. They, therefore, applied to Mr. Brent, my old friend, who was then Treasurer of the place, for his advice relative to my course.–Mr. Brent, with whom I was a great favorite, listened attentively to their complaints, and mildly informed them that they could do *nothing.* All that Billy Hayden has said, is true.–His knowledge he has gathered from some higher source than us, who refuse to educate the slave, and as he proclaims himself a free man, the easiest plan of conducting the matter to the satisfaction of all parties, will be for Phillips to take what he offers to him in fulfilment of his agreement, and sign his deed of emancipation. For rest assured, the bonds of slavery will never hold in bondage a spirit such as his!" The citizens listened with due deference to Mr. Brent, but were illy satisfied with his advice. They had ever been in the habit of witnessing the scourge applied to the back of a rebellious slave, until a meek spirit of surveilance was brought about. They longed for this course to be pursued towards me; but little did they know the heart with which they would tamper. I considered myself free–free, in the eyes of God and man–free, by all Laws human and Divine, and as such I was prepared to resent any indignity that might be offered me. I was surrounded by the shield of the spirit, and feared not the consequences, as my cause was that of Freedom and manhood–the two great gifts of an Almighty Power, who rules our destinies.

From the manner in which I spoke, and from what my friends, together with Mr. Brent told Phillips relative to me, he concluded that it would be necessary for him to appeal to stratagem and force. For this purpose, he drew up a sham Bill of Sale, and conveyed it over to a certain Christopher Keyser, better known as "Kit Keyser," who boarded with Mr. Throckmorton. After pursuing this course, he left the place, and I afterwards learned, he had also left the State. His object in this was, I expect to await until my arrest had been made, and I should be securely in the possession of Keyser. But here again, he was doomed to be disappointed. The spirit had armed me for the result and I feared not that it would speedily be righted. In order, then, to carry his object into effect, Keyser sent for me one morning stating that he wished to see me. I was ignorant of his intentions and immediately went to Mr. Timberlake's, whither he had removed.

On entering, I asked if he had sent for me.

He answered that he had.

I then desired to know his pleasure.

He informed me that he had purchased me from my master, and wished me to go and clean his shoes.

"Purchased me!" said I, "*You*, sir, cannot purchase me: I am a free man, and no power on Earth can compel me to play the part of the Slave any longer. And from my *master* too;–Sir, who is my master? Have you a Bill of Sale signed by the God of the Universe? If not, you have no Bill of Sale from the hands of my master. He alone I acknowledge as such–and He alone will I obey as such! Clean *your* shoes! thou audacious coxcomb![24] better were it that thou, in thy ill-gotten arrogance and assumption of power, which you know not how to use, should think of cleaning mine! for in the scale of honesty and morality, I look upon you as my inferior!–This is your first offence of the kind–let it be the last, you miserable puppy. I scorn you too much to meddle further with you," and turning to the other gentlemen who were present, and who were pleased to excess at my manly course, I bade them good morning, and retired, whilst the poor, chop-fallen Keyser knew not what to say. Thus things passed along a few days longer, when Dr. Willis Webb called on me and congratulated me on my independent course. I went again to Mr. Timberlake's, and saluting a saddler of my acquaintance, in the presence of Keyser, I asked him what he charged for making a pair of the largest sized saddle bags. He replied eight dollars. I then inquired, if he could have them done in a day.–He said he could; and I agreed to pay him his price, charging him not to disappoint me in the time, as I intended to go immediately to the Blue Lick Springs, and a day's delay would materially injure my future calculations.

I would here inform the reader that nothing was further from my mind than this. It was a bait thrown out to see how Keyser would bite. Nor was it thrown out in vain. Although the miscreant said nothing, yet I saw from the writhing of his soul he was struggling with assumed power and enmity. After making arrangements with the saddler, I proceeded to my old friend Carter Lightfoot's, who had at a former time been a partner in business with me, and telling him that the time of which I had so often warned him, was now at hand, and that I was compelled to go to jail, I then took the $450 which I had in money and stuck it in every hole and corner of his shop, where I knew it would be secure from the lynx eyes of the searchers of the Law; I then opened my trunk which was in his shop, and taking therefrom all my clothes, I consigned them to his care, until I should call for them. I then locked my trunk and hung the key above it, and having charged him to disclose nothing he knew of me–which he strictly promised me to fulfill,–I awaited in anxiety the issue of the evil which I knew was now to befall me. I moreover told him that I intended to go down to Timberlake's, and inquire the price of passage of the Springs–to engage a seat for myself, and then, tell the driver to stop at his shop in the morning for William Hayden. This I accordingly did to my own satisfaction; and arming myself with the aid of spiritual advice. I awaited the deadly enmity of Keyser, and the moment when the evil of which the spirit had forwarned me I should surmount, should come to pass. With a throbbing heart I awaited it, well convinced that I should come off triumphant.

At the appointed time, the stage drove up to the door of Carter Lightfoot, and I shortly appeared with my luggage. But I was well aware of what was to follow; and, as I expected, as I attempted to enter the stage, Keyser and his myrmidons rushed upon me, they having been watching my movements, and charging me with an attempt to leave the place as an absconding slave, they stated I must go and await the arrival of Mr. Phillips in jail. I replied very mildly that their will was my pleasure, and accompanying them, I was soon lodged in jail. I had remained here for three or four days, when, by inquiry, the people, with whom I was a great favorite, began to wish to know the where-a-bouts of Billy Hayden. This was soon answered by some of my friends, by the information, that I was confined in jail. Among those who most deeply sympathized with me, was Mrs. Throckmorton, whose children I used to befriend, together with those of Mrs. Timberlake, and the sons of whom were, for those acts of kindness, to release me from my confinement. But it will be necessary here, for the reader to understand the nature of the transactions and revelations I had made to Mrs. Timberlake, and, through her, to Mrs. Throckmorton.

In the year 1817, whilst keeping a small confectionary, I was in the habit of treating her children, and those of her friend, Mrs. Throckmorton, to sweetmeats, and advancing them money for all their juvenile wants. They remonstrated with me, asking me the reason I did so? I told them that I was sowing the seeds now in the shape of cents, which should, in the course of time, sprout to dollars–and the debt would be paid, not in filthy lucre, but by releasing me from a difficulty more essential than the wealth of all the south. "You will live, ladies," said I, "to see me, seven years from this, in the common jail; and one of your sons, I know not which, will be the means of my deliverance, which will be more than a sufficient recompense for all I may now bestow upon them. You may smile in incredulity–but such a state of things will come to pass, and you shall live to see the consummation of all that I have told you." They laughed heartily at the idea, but I felt fully convinced the words of the spirit would be fulfilled.

In jail I lingered for some six weeks, upon the rough fare of a common prisoner; at the expiration of this time, however, the influence of the spirit seemed to work upon the feelings of Mrs. Throckmorton, and after much uneasiness she was supposed to think that all was not right. She, therefore, acting under this influence, sent to the jail by her son Mordecai, one of the youths spoken of above, to know if I was well treated. I returned her an answer that I was not. After that, I was daily served from her own table, and I believe through her influence, received much kindness, which I would not otherwise have received from the Jailor. But still there was something which the spirit seemed to tell her was wanting, and it was indeed a long while before she could arrive at any means of ascertaining what it really was. Previous to this, let me here inform the reader, that I might have often freed myself, as I still reserved the written proofs of Phillips' villainy, signed by his own hand. But there was one thing which materially deterred me from so doing. Phillips was yet in the prime of life. He was looked up to by his aged and grey haired parents, as the prop of their declining years. They stood as it were, with one foot in the grave, and the other upon the brink; and was it my province to blast the reputation of this aged couple by an exposure of their son's conduct to me, and to others, in his absence? I could not think of it–I could not snatch the morsel of food from their lips, nor heap ignominy upon their heads, unless with the instructions of my guardian angel. But my good intentions, were by this spirit thwarted, as will appear in the sequel, and my own rights were to be vindicated unconcerned as to who suffered. Age and discrepency were to be blasted by the proofs–the tears of paternal and maternal grief were to be shed over the misdeeds of a son–and the withering curse of blasted reputation was to be attached to him, whose hypocrisy, concealed his tainted character. I shuddered at the issue, but it was the only one left me, and my counsel was, to avail myself of it.

Accordingly, the spirit working so powerfully upon Mrs. Throckmorton, she sent her son to me to inquire what was the matter, and what it was for, that I was really confined; as she could not believe it was for the alleged offence which general rumor assigned. At first, I hesitated to answer, but finally I requested the boy to go back to his mother, and ask her if she remembered seven years ago, when you were but a small boy, of a conversation I had with her and Mrs. Timberlake, relative to my reasons of relieving all the children's wants, of her and her friend. Ask her, if she remembers of my saying that *I* was sowing cents to reap the worth of dollars. *If* she does, she will know the reason why *I* am confined here. The boy immediately started, and *I* afterwards learned, delivered his errand as *I* had told him. Mrs. Throckmorton at first could not remember, and consequently she sent over for Mrs. Timberlake to come to her which she immediately did.

On entering, Mrs. Throckmorton immediately asked her, if she remembered Billy Hayden?

She said she did, and she had understood that he was now confined in jail in this place.

"He is," replied Mrs. Throckmorton; "but do you remember a conversation which he had with us seven years ago, when we remonstrated with him about surfeiting our children with candy, and furnishing them with money?"

The two old ladies sat to work to recollect the purport of my imprisonment. They remembered my many acts of kindness to their children, they remembered their remonstrance, and after computing the various ages of their children, they finally remembered the unconnected particles of the conversation I so much wished them to understand. They remembered that I had told them that seven years from that time, I should be imprisoned—that *I* was then sowing the seeds of gratitude, to be reaped thereafter in the bosom of their children; and they remembered too, that they had laughed and hooted at the idea; but now their computation just made it seven years, and *now* they felt was the time for their action. But how the knowledge could have arrived to me, was a question over which they long lingered, and could not solve. My conversation was plain—my imprisonment was now palpable; but how had *I* known it so long a time beforehand? This they could not divine. Surely the God of the universe had a hand in this. The ways of God are inscrutable[25]—He worketh his wisdom, and no man knoweth the extent of His power—He buildeth up the weak and destroyeth the mighty towers of the strong—He smileth on the oppressed, and smiteth with a heavy hand the oppressor—He protects the innocent, and brings to a debased position the children of vice. He enlightens the benighted, and dims the lamp of *I*ntelligence in the bosoms of the worldly wise. Thus, he had bestowed upon me a more than equal portion of His benign knowledge—led me through the labyrinths of slavery—elevated me to the rank of manhood—enabled me to bring to light villany, and to shield honesty. But how *I* had been enabled to predict this so many years before, was a matter which they, poor weak sighted mortals could not conceive. They fell short of scrutinizing the motives by which *I* was actuated, but they were fully convinced of one thing, (and this was the point to which *I* wished to bring them,) and that was, that my predictions had proved true—that *I* was now a prisoner, not for the alledged crime of attempting to escape, but to satiate a spirit of petty revenge, and they felt themselves called upon to use their exertions in my behalf.–God bless them, for in every station in life, and through every vicissitude. *I* ever found them endowed with the tender feelings of Christianity, and sympathy for the oppressed and down trodden. Nor did the contest rest with them. *It* seemed to become a bone of contention with the children, to know which had been appointed by the spirit to become the deliverer of his old friend; and amid tears of joy from the mothers, and high ambitious thoughts of the children, *I* was doomed to pass the day in solitude and gloom.

Accordingly, when Mr. Throckmorton came home, for he had been absent during the day, Mrs. Throckmorton called him into the parlor, and recapitulated all that had passed during his absence; asserting that she remembered the conversation–was grateful for my kindness, and that she felt that she was in duty bound to do something in my behalf. She therefore requested her husband to visit me in jail, and ascertain how she could serve me. Her husband hooted at all she said, and treated the whole matter as a thing of air. But Mrs. Throckmorton was not thus to be driven from her stand. She urged, that unless he came to me, she would, in person, come and see me, and learn my wishes. Hence, in order to appease her, Mr. Throckmorton came after tea, to the jail, and enquired for me. He appeared glad to see me, and after shaking hands with me, asked what was the nature of the "Cock and Bull story" his wife had been telling him of a conversation between us several years previous. I immediately narrated the circumstances to him, and concluded by telling him of the villany of Phillips. He appeared utterly astounded, and asked me if I could prove it. I told him I could. That I had written proofs from under Phillips' own hand, and showed him the letters and pass of Cincinnati memory. After he had read them, he ejaculated, "good God! who would have taken him to be such a scoundrel!"

He then asked me if I needed his assistance.

I told him that I would like it, and that I had the money to purchase myself.

He then pledged me his friendship, and assuring me I should not long stay in jail, he departed.

His wife was highly delighted when he informed her how matters stood, and exclaiming "she knew some villany was afloat," and entreated Mr. Throckmorton to lose no time in sifting the matter, and setting me at Liberty. To this he replied he would promptly see it attended to. Mrs. Throckmorton then communicated the result to Mrs. Timberlake, who appeared as much pleased to think that innocence should be righted, and guilt exposed as she herself, and the two kind hearted ladies wept tears of joy. They remembered me in distress, and their memory shall be revered by me through life–for they were indeed to me "friends in the hour of need."

In a few days Phillips arrived, but his reception was anything but a cordial one. His villany had been discovered, and the citizens could not find in their hearts any sympathy for one who could thus wantonly sacrifice all principles of honor and humanity. He saw however, that his scheme had failed, and that, although I was confined in prison, yet I was as much determined to serve no earthly master, as I was when I last conversed with him upon the subject. He did not appear to be fully prepared for this state of things, and was cogitating some other plan of enforcing servitude, when Mr. Throckmorton rallied him upon my freedom. "Free!" exclaimed Phillips, "do you think I would be foolish enough in the purchase of a slave, to enter into such a contract–or if I were that I would be fool enough to ever think of fulfilling it! If Billy is free, as you say, let him show the proofs to offset his word." "Phillips," replied Throckmorton, "it is all folly in your attempting to deceive us longer in this business. Your conduct is all known to us, and Billy Hayden has at this time, a free pass and two letters signed by you, which were sent to him whilst in Cincinnati." Phillips was thunderstruck. He had long since lived in hopes that these papers were destroyed, and he was now, for the first time, since my return to him, informed of their existence. The blush of shame mantled his cheeks, and muttering some horrid oaths, he said he would go down to the prison, and if the "d—d nigger had any such forged papers about him, he would off with his ears on the spot." Accordingly he came, and after being admitted by the jailor, he called me down stairs. I had heard of his threat, and I must confess I trembled somewhat for my safety, knowing the impetuous disposition of the man I had to deal with. When I had approached his person, he appeared glad to see me, and immediately held out his hand. I took it, and looking him keenly in the face, I could discover that fear prohibited him from taking any summary means of chastisement.

After a pause he asked me if I still had the pass and letters which he had given me.

To which I replied, that I had.

"Why, said he, I thought you informed me on your return, that you had thrown them away."

"And I told you the truth sir, I did indeed throw them away as we touched at Maysville. But think you, Mr. Phillips, I was ignorant of their future importance to me? If you do, you are much mistaken. I knew the course you would pursue with me, and I was determined that naught but death should separate me from the papers, consequently, as I leaped on shore, having obeyed your orders in throwing them away, I obeyed the orders of a higher power than you, in picking them up again, and reserving them. I have them now, and have showed them to some of my friends, who have kindly volunteered to use them to my advantage."

During this dialogue, the jailor, who was prompted by curiosity had been listening, and he had heard the question and answer, he rushed out to where my friends were standing, exclaiming "by Heavens, boys, Billy Hayden is free! I heard Phillips, myself, acknowledge that the pass and letters were genuine, and reprimand Billy for not destroying them."

When this was announced a general shout was raised, and Phillips finding he could do nothing with me, and the scorn of his former friends coming so hard upon him, he left the jail, and immediately went to Maysville. In leaving, however, he did not give orders for my liberation, but ever afterwards the doors of the prison were left open for the purpose of my escaping. It was a long while, and not until the jailor had become tired of my remaining, and my friends had advised and solicited me to leave, that I finally departed from my prison, and breathed again the breath of freedom, released from the shackles of bondage.

But my trials were not to stop here. Another act of villany, more hideous than the last was to be attempted in order to secure my remaining years in slavery. Several desperadoes were employed to visit my sleeping apartment, in the dead of night, and having gagged and bound me, to carry me off to some place where Phillips could again get possession of me and where he would have an opportunity of carrying me to the South, and selling me to the slave dealers. But their movements were not unknown to me. I foresaw the attempt—the intervention of friendship, and the safe deliverance which was for me in store. I therefore went to Lexington, hither the desperadoes followed me. There was, in the place, an old colored man, known as "Uncle Daniel." Upon this man, I used to lavish a great deal of loose change, which was of great advantage to him, in procuring him many little necessaries, which he otherwise would not have received. Often has he remonstrated with me upon the waste of my money, as he was pleased to term it, and asking the reason, why I did so, I told him, invariably that I was now paying him beforehand for an act of kindness, which he was appointed to perform for me in after days, and which no money could then purchase. The old man wept tears of joy, when I told him this, and raising his hands and eyes to heaven, he invoked its aid in enabling him to discharge his duty to me, in performing whatever act I might require.

For some nights after my release from prison in Paris, a servant of Phillips' who professed much friendship for me, but whose real object was to ferret out my future plans, and have them convoyed to his master, came to the house where I lodged, and slept with me. I had remarked, that he invariably left in the dead of night, leaving all the doors open. I was aware of his object, that it was to admit the kidnapping party, and was also aware of the time of the premeditated attempt and its consummation.

Accordingly, on the day appointed, I went to uncle Bob, a servant of widow Todd, and telling him that the hour had come, in which he was to aid me, requested him to come and sleep with me that night. To this he freely consented, and towards dusk we bent our steps towards the house. The emissaries of Phillips, I was fully assured had their lynx eyes upon us—but we pursued the even tenor of our way. On my way to Lexington, however, I passed the house of Castleman, to whom I immediately went, and after explaining to him the reason of my absconding from Phillips, I showed him the pass and papers. Castleman saw at once that I was free from blame, and that Phillips had proved himself a villain in the whole transaction. Mr. Castleman therefore extended to me his cordial friendship, but informed me that it was now too late, and that he could not be of any service to me at that time. We therefore shook hands and parted. On arriving at the house with uncle Bob, I told him the circumstance of the attempt of kidnapping me. He seemed startled–but I merely asked him to remain and watch, and that I would go to the pile of corn shucks which was in the field, and sleep there; and if any one come and asked for me, to tell them he knew nothing of me. This he promised, and at dead of night all I had told him proved true. On the succeeding morning, I turned my steps towards Lexington, which I reached in safety, and took lodging with Mr. Wickliffe, a tavern-keeper in the place, where I had often visited as Phillips' servant, and whom and his family had formed a friendship for me. On arriving there I was strongly invited to take dinner and tea with his own family, in order that they might have the news from the south. This invitation I accepted, and the servants being dismissed from the room, I was seated with the family of the landlord, and treated more as an equal than a slave. Here was a transition sure enough–a runaway, seated at the table with slaveholders, and engaged in a pleasant conversation.–O, ye powers! what various vicissitudes is man subjected to through life! Here, too, I again found my old friend uncle Daniel, who was a hostler with Mr. Wickliffe, and of whom I have above spoken. On meeting with him, and explaining how matters stood, through the superintendance of the spirit, I again escaped from slavery. The old man knew not what to think of it, and asked me what he was next to do? I told him that my absence would soon be observed from Paris, and that I would be advertised as a runaway. That I wished him to build me a sort of a room in the hay in the loft, and permit me to remain there, in the stable of Mr. Wickliffe, whom *I* had known long, from Mr. Phillips' recommendation to him, and whose good will I had secured. This, the old man promised faithfully to attend to, and I remained secreted in the stable nine days, living during the whole of that period, upon three cakes and the same number of pints of water. On the morning of the ninth, as I expected, hand Bills, bearing the signature of Keyser, who held the sham bill of sale, were circulated through the town, offering $50 reward for me, stating also, as I spoke and wrote the French and English fluently, I might possibly have a pass; but with a pass, or without one–dead or alive the reward would be paid for me on my delivery in Paris. Uncle Daniel, tearfully solicited to know what was next to be done. I told him to come to me at midnight, and I would leave by the back door of the stable and return to Paris. This he accordingly did, and travelling through the woods, I arrived at the half-way house, kept by Dr. Cochran, now of Louisville, in advance of the slave who was circulating the Bills for my apprehension. Here I made arrangements with the stage driver, to clean his horses and harness for my passage to Paris. Whilst I was engaged in this occupation the servant of Phillips, who was despatched with the Reward Bills passed the stable. I watched him closely until he was past, and discovered that his eye was directed to the lamp post before the door of the Inn. When he was past, and *I* had performed my work, *I* returned to the tavern, and looking at the lamp post, *I* discovered what had before escaped my observation, to wit: a Hand-Bill offering $50 Reward for Billy Hayden, dead or alive!" After awhile the stage was ready for starting, and the driver telling me to walk ahead a few miles, he would overtake me, and permit me to get in the stage. This *I* did, and in the course of a mile and a half, the stage overtook me. The only passengers which were in the stage, were two gentlemen from Philadelphia. The driver applied to them and asked them if they had any objections to my riding with them. They were very kind hearted men, and seemed glad of the opportunity, as they said of changing the conversation, accordingly *I* took my seat, and in due time we arrived at Paris. Some of my friends had previous to this warned me that Phillips had sworn to shoot me, when he next saw me, and entreated me not to go back, but *I* felt secure in the spirit, and fearlessly entered the town where he had arrived. As the stage dashed up to the door of Mr. Timberlake, *I* leaped upon the pavement, where many of my warmest friends were standing. As soon as they recognized me, they swarmed round me, shaking hands, and congratulating me on my return.

"And where have you been, Billy?" said they.

"Why, visiting my friends," returned I. "I am now free, and having some leisure moments, I thought I would profit by them and visit some of those whom I longed to see."

"And do you know," continued Squire Boon Ingles, "that there are now two Billy Haydens in town?"

I informed them, that I was not aware of the fact, and asked them where the second was.

"There!" answered they, pointing to a Bill for my apprehension.

I looked at it for some moments, and then turning to them, I said–"Poor Devil! He's some slave I suppose,"–"and pray is this Keyser the same impertinent puppy who boarded at Mr. Timberlake's when I left town?"

"The same," remarked they, bursting into a boisterous laugh.

"Then, indeed, I pity the poor wretch to serve so contemptible a miscreant as him."

"But, do you not recognize *yourself*, as the man there spoken of?" asked they.

"Me!" No, gentlemen, I am free! Free as any of you–and that Bill calls for a slave–a thing–an article of a negotiable nature!"

This brought from the by-standers, another round burst of merriment, much to the chagrin of Phillips, who stood present, and of whose appearance, *I* intentionally took no notice.

Mr. Timberlake's children now came forward, and clinging to me with childish affection, poured out their joy at my return, and informed me that their mother, who had heard of my arrival, wished to see me very much.

I sent Lady Timberlake word that I would call on her in the morning. I then bade my friends good morning, and wended my way to Mr. Lightfoot's. On my road thither, my friends poured to their doors shaking hands with me, and congratulating me on my courage in returning.

Among these, was my old friend Mr. Brent, who quietly asked me what I intended to do?

I informed him that the hour was nigh when I was to be pronounced free.

He wrung my hand warmly, and said, as the tears gathered in his eyes—"success attend you boy—may Heaven fulfill your dearest wishes."

The scene was too much for me, and the tears trickled down my cheeks, as I continued my walk to the house of my friend Lightfoot. When I arrived here, I found all things as I had left them, and my friend after warmly entreating me to be seated, recapitulated all that had transpired during my absence.—Here I remained until after tea-time, when I heard Phillips hail my friend, and ask if Billy Hayden was with him. He answered that he was. He told him to inform me that he wished to see me. I returned him as an answer that if his business was particular, he had as much time to wait upon me, as I had upon him. This answer being duly delivered, he returned to the Hotel, and about seven o'clock came to see me. He cordially extended his hand, which I took, and inquired after my health; I told him it was as good as I could expect. He wished to know why I had left town. I informed him that as a free man, I did not hold myself responsible to any man for where or when I might go or come. He strove so hard to get me again into his service, stating that if I would go with him once more to the South, that he would immediately liberate me on my return. But he strove in vain, for informing him that I would not take his word for a chew of tobacco, I peremptorily refused to accompany him.

"And you are determined to be free!" continued he.

"I am! and not only free in body but in mind. I promised you $600 for my liberty,"—and although I felt he was not entitled to the first cent of it, yet I would pay it in order to keep my word. I was now ready to pay $450, and would give him my note for the remainder.

Finding he could not accomplish the ends he had in view, he finally agreed to accept of it in the morning, stating that I was well aware it was a mere act of clemency on his part, as he could get $2000 for me in Atakapas.

"Provided, in all cases" replied I, that you had me there—but I am determined no wretch who barters in human blood, shall ever again have dominion over me in a slave market."

After he had left me, I went to Mr. Thomas C. Owens, an Attorney at Law, and informing him of the transaction, requested him to draw up the papers, and attend to my business for me. This he did, and in the morning, the deed of emancipation in my favor was signed and sealed, and I now stood before the world morally, religiously, and legally free! My own humble exertions had brought it all about, through the interposition of Divine Providence, and as the tears of joy bathed my swarthy cheeks, I offered up a heart-felt prayer to the Almighty God for my safe deliverance. In a few days the Deed was duly recorded in Court, and my name proclaimed to the assembled citizens, as a free and independent citizen of the land.—The reader can judge of my feelings, while *I assure* him that no language of mine can justly portray them.

After my liberation, I concluded to visit my old mistress at Georgetown. Since my boyhood, when she had made me kneel at her knee, with her own daughter, and raised her eyes to Heaven for blessings on us both, she had but seldom seen me. When I arrived at her house she did not know me, and it was a long while before I discovered myself to her. She had a partial recollection of the features, and as soon as I revealed myself to her she burst into tears, and throwing up her hands to Heaven, blessed the Lord, that she had seen the day of my deliverance. The servants were immediately called from the fields, and the house, although it was much earlier than the hour they were usually called, and after my mistress had made them acquainted with the high esteem she had for me, and held me up as a pattern of honesty and integrity to them, we sat down to a hearty and savory meal. At the house of my mistress, I staid but a short time, as I was then on my way to Louisville, to comply with the request of Mr. Miner, in becoming a citizen of that place. This gentleman had ever extended his kindness to me, and had even gone so far, as to procure for me a Bill of relief, from the Legislature of Mississippi. To this many of my friends objected, until ascertaining the standing of Mr. Miner, they finally waived their objections, and considered it wise in me to accede to the propositions made me by him. Accordingly after a short time, I embarked with Mr. Miner for Natchez, at $15 a month. This was the first occupation I had engaged in as a free man, and my heart throbbed violently, as I implored the aid of Heaven in upholding me, and thanked God for the many mercies extended to me.

After remaining in this place for the space of five years without hearing from my mother, I met with a gentleman direct from the place where she resided, and who informed me that she was very ill. I felt that the Lord had appointed me as her deliverer from bondage, and now that her declining years needed the prop of youth and the support of filial affection, I felt that the time had arrived, and that I must hasten on to her support. Accordingly, I began to make my preparations for my journey to Falmouth. Of this, however, I made known my intentions to none, but on the morning on which I started, I found that Mr. Brune, the agent of Mr. Miner, and who took a great interest in my welfare, was also going East. Under his protection, I therefore placed myself, and obeying his advice was enabled to get along very fairly. This gentleman was on his way to New York for goods; and he was anxious that I should accompany him; but I was forewarned to go no farther then the spirit of the Lord would permit. My poor mother was now ill, and I now felt that she might probably be within a few hours of the grave. Whose duty therefore, was it to prop her declining years? Was it not his who claimed the title of son? I felt that it was, and was determined that it should be performed.

Under this gentleman's guidance, things passed off very smoothly, and every one on the representations of Mr. Brune as to my character, and the object of my visit to the home of my childhood, looked upon me as an extraordinary individual, and treated me with all the due courtesy which is extended to the most exalted of another color. I was hailed as a *brother*, by all who heard my story. The first event of any interest which transpired after my leaving Natchez, was at Louisville, where on my friend Brune's representations as above spoken of, I met a gentleman who kept the stage tavern at Froststown, Maryland. This gentleman, as soon as he heard my tale of distress, and my filial devotion to my mother, immediately became deeply interested in my case, and giving me letters of introduction to his family, requested that I would, on all accounts, if I found my mother, call at his house on my return, and permit him to witness the mother of so obedient and affectionate a child–and if dead, he requested me to leave with him a spear of the grass from her grave as a memento of our meeting, and as a tribute of one, who, though born in slavery, and of a different race, could undertake so long and tedious a journey, to bathe the grave of a mother with the tears of a son so long absent. This I faithfully promised to fulfil, and in a short time, Mr. Brune and myself, departed for Wheeling. At this point, my friend was to leave me: and I felt that *I* was about to sever from one of the truest of God's noblemen, and the dearest friend *I* had ever found upon the face of the Earth. He is now in a distant country (Havre,) and he, who held him as a brother still lingers in the land of the living, many thousand miles away–with the wide waters of the ocean rolling between us. But wherever he may wend his way, the dearest prayers of his colored friend will follow–and hoping that God will sustain him in all his various vicissitudes through life, and in all his undertakings, I drop a tear to his memory, and bid him a heart-felt adieu!

When the hour of our parting arrived, my friend Brune came to me in company with a young gentleman, who had been a fellow passenger from Natchez, and with tears in his eyes bade me a cordial, yet a long good bye. My heart swells even at this late day, when the thoughts of that event come across me. Tears bathed my cheeks–and language failed to utter my gratitude and grief. He then turned and introduced me to the gentleman above spoken of, and related to him my history and my mission, requesting him at the same time to take charge of me as far as he went, and consider that all the kindness he had bestowed upon me, was the same as if he, himself, was the recipient thereof.

"Permit him not to be imposed upon," continued he, "by any, bearing a paler face, for a truer heart never beat in the bosom of any man, either in veneration of his God, or the world. But he has been raised a slave; and being so long subjected to the brutality of modern barbarism–and not permitted to avow his manhood, or his rights, his extreme modesty will not even now permit him to free himself by resenting the insults and impositions of such as he has been taught to look upon as his superiors. Take care of him, sir, and believe that while you are protecting him, you are lending your protection to

Wm. Brune, who never forgets a kindness. To your charge I now commit him–guard well your trust as you love God and your fellow man."

The gentleman faithfully pledged himself to see me safely to Washington, which promise he religiously observed. Mr. Brune thanked him, and kindly shaking me by the hand, turned sorrowfully away. We parted–and perhaps forever–but his memory is fresh in the bosom of the slave–and when the last trump shall summon all before the throne of Grace, I hope to see him crowned in glory on the right hand of a Righteous and Allwise Redeemer, and to this friend who protected me, may the Lord give his bounties and his blessings–richness and health, and a glorious eternity.

On my way to Falmouth, I again visited the house of Mr. Clay, and after a very flattering reception, I informed Lady Clay of my errand, and assured her that if my poor mother was dead, I should esteem it a great privilege to pluck from her grave some few spears of grass, and bear them with me to my own long home. This narration melted the heart of Mrs. Clay, and she burst into tears; and ere I left her, she made me promise her, that when I returned, I would stop at her house, and present her to the mother of such a son, assuring me, that although she stood high in the estimation of the world; yet she could not flatter herself that she had a child in whom she could place confidence to perform the same task for her. I assured her that I would, and hence departed.

We now took our course to Uniontown, at which place we received an acquisition to our company in the person of Mr. Stewart, who was bound for Washington city, having been elected to Congress from that district. Shortly after Mr. Stewart came into the stage, he inquired of my friend, who and what I was. The gentleman very affectionately repeated to him the story of my distress and the reason of my travelling. The narration so affected Mr. Stewart, as he was himself an orphan, and my attentions to him on the road during our passage, so pleased him, that he formed so strong an attachment for me, that he treated me as an equal, and even went so far as to call me brother.

When we arrived at Washington City, we stopped at the Stage Office, kept by Mr. Brown. Mr. Stewart strictly warned them to pay the same attention to me, after introducing me to them that they would to himself. Mr. Brown was himself absent, and the Bar tenders, after the departure of Mr. Stewart, neglected to comply with his request. Accordingly, the next morning, when he called on me and asked me how I fared, I told him. My words seemed to raise his ire, and with many apologies on the part of Mrs. Brown and her attendants, in justication of themselves, I was introduced. After his remonstrance, I was treated more like an equal than any thing else. Mr. Stewart informed them that I was an orphan Boy–that I was going on to Falmouth to purchase my mother by tears and entreaties, being penniless; or if I found her dead, to bathe her grave with the tears of filial affection, which but few whites would undertake to perform–that I had been kind to him,–and he considered an insult to me, more than one given to him, and if I could not receive the treatment of a gentleman from them, he would conduct me to where I could be treated as such. Mrs. Brown on the recapitulation of this, burst into tears and begged that all should be forgiven, and urged me on my return, if I found my mother alive, to be sure and stop with *her.* This I promised faithfully to perform, and after a few days sojourn I renewed my travels to Falmouth, in quest of my poor mother.

When my preparations were concluded, Mr. Stewart came to me, and before parting, he performed an act of kindness, for which he will ever be entitled to my gratitude. He went with me to the steam boat; and I having advanced him the money, he paid my passage to the captain, and after informing him of my intentions, he begged of the captain, as he valued *his* friendship, to treat me on the road as a gentleman. This the captain promised to perform, and with tears rolling from the pent up assylums of my eyes, I bade farewell to one of the kindest hearts that ever beat in the bosom of man.

On board of the boat I considered myself a perfect stranger; and the anxiety which I felt for the welfare of my mother–the uncertainty of her being longer numbered with the living, and the hopes of bearing with me in case of her death some slight memorial of her to my home in Natchez, whither I intended in such a case to return, kept me in a constant flood of tears. This attracted the attention of an old colored gentleman on board, by the name of Uncle Parish Green, who immediately approached me and kindly enquired the cause of my depression of spirits. I informed him that I was returning from a long absence to the home of my nativity, and that the uncertainty of my meeting my mother alive, gave me such uneasiness, and caused me to exhibit the weakness which he had witnessed. For awhile the old gentleman gazed at me in astonishment–telling me that I must surely be mistaken, as he had known me for a long time, though he could not call me by name, and that I was certainly some one of his neighbor's men. I replied to him that he had never seen me before, that I had been taken from my parents in infancy, and that I had not been in Belle Plains, where I was born, since that time.

"You born in Bell Plains!" exclaimed the old man, "and pray who *are* your parents?"

I informed him, that my mother's name was Alcy Shelton; and it was to her that I was now on a visit."

Uncle Parish looked at me wistfully for a few minutes, and bursting into tears, told me that he had been the play mate of my mother in infancy; that he had visited her a few weeks previous and found her well; but informed me that she had not to his knowledge, ever spoken of a son, who was absent. He then ran to the cabin, and called forth Mr. and Mrs. Fitzhugh, who had known my mother for many years, and for whom she had acted as midwife, when the young lady, their daughter, who was now travelling with them was born. When they came on deck, Uncle Parish, asked them if they had ever seen me. They unhesitatingly answered that they had, but where they could not then call to mind.

I reminded them that they were mistaken; that I was a perfect stranger to them, and was travelling to Falmouth, having purchased my own freedom, to see my mother, if living and free her from slavery—and if dead, to gather from her grave some few spears of grass, that I might keep as a memento of the spot where her body reposed. They then very anxiously inquired my mother's name, and when I told them that it was Alcy Shelton, the old lady raised her eyes to Heaven, and exclaimed:

"I knew it—her every feature is there! I would have known him, had I met him in New Orleans!"

The whole party were now bathed in tears, and the daughter having been called also on deck, I received their joint blessings and good wishes for the consummation of my filial devotedness.

On the road, Uncle Parish Green took particular interest in me, and pointed out to me many scenes, with which I had once been familiar, but which a long absence and the changes they had undergone, were but now indistinctly remembered. Among these was the spot where my father's cabin stood, and the house of his master, but none attracted my mind with much attention, until on rounding the point, my eyes fell upon the ruins of the home of my infancy. It was still a ruin, and whilst I gazed upon it, my heart throbbed, and my eyes were filled with tears. The past was before me, and I was choaked with gratitude to God, that there I had once been instrumental in saving from death a beloved brother and sister.

> "How dear to our hearts is the home of our childhood,
> When fond recollections recall them to view,"

and I praised God that I once more beheld it.

Nothing further of importance transpired until I arrived at Bell Plains, and I left the boat bewildered in mind, and shedding a copious flood of tears, as I thought of the probable fate of my mother.

Here the stage was awaiting us. My baggage had been taken from the boat, and placed in the boot of the stage. On inquiring of the driver, seeing that the inside of the stage was filled, I was informed that I could not go on to the place of my destination by that stage—that I must wait a return. I immediately went to the captain of the boat, and informed him, that I could not go, as the stage was full, and the driver refused to let me ride with him on the outside. The Captain therefore, hailed the stage and having examined the inside, informed the passengers and the driver that he was pledged to a gentleman of high standing and worth; that I should, by that stage, be taken to Fredericksburg—that it was optional with me to ride inside or out, as my name was the first on the way Bill; and that if they could not permit me to go, he had but to assure them the *stage* could not go. This had the desired effect, and after many vinegar looks, the driver consented to let me ride by his side. When I mounted the box, this august individual, closely drew his coat around him, and sheered off to the far side of the box, fearing no doubt that the touch of a colored man would contaminate him. But for this I cared not–my mind was too full of my poor mother, and her supposed death, to notice such trivial matters, and a surcharged heart found relief in a copious flood of tears. On passing the spot where the home of *my* infancy, and where the charred and blackened mass told me had once reared the humble cot that had sheltered me in youth was now visible, I could restrain my feelings no longer, but gave vent to them in loud sobs and many sighs. There was the spot where I first breathed the breath of Heaven's air–there the stream where I had in infancy sat and watched the rising of the two suns as I thought–there too, was the old apple tree, which when but a sappling, my mother has often taken her chair and leaning against which, she has entertained me with some juvenile tale, as she gave nourishment to my little sister. All, all was plain before me, as the noon day sun; and as the recollections through which I had passed flitted over of my mind, was it a wonder that I was unmanned, and made to feel as if indeed I were a child again? Perhaps now, the roundelays of innocence to which I had hearkened in my infancy, as they fell from the lips of a mother, were hushed in death–perhaps, that maternal eye which had so often shot forth sparks of joy as I told of some childish feat I had performed, had been closed and dimmed by the hand of the grim monster, and the hand which had smoothed my pillow, was nerveless and unstrung. Perchance, ere this the body had mouldered into dust–the worms had gorged and fattened upon her dear form, and the spirit had sought a habitation of rest in the mansions of the blest.[26] O, how I longed to unfold the reality of my fate, and if living to clasp a mother, once more to my fond bosom–to sooth her sorrows–to dry her tears, and to elate her heart with anticipations of freedom, and a happy home with me. These feelings crowded in quick succession upon me, rending the very chords of my heart, and opening every fountain of my soul. But I felt aware that God would uphold me in all my trials, as he had hitherto done; and I returned praises to His adorable name, as the tears trickled down my swarthy cheeks.

This burst of grief soon attracted the attention of the driver, who somewhat relinquishing his austere manner, enquired why I wept? I told him that I was now passing the scenes of my infancy,–that I had been born and raised upon the spot where that charred and blackened mass now presented itself; and that I could not gaze upon it but with the deepest feelings of reverence and regret. He seemed surprised, and told me that he had lived about the place all his life, but did not remember *me*; that I must be crazed; but that he knew me, having seen me somewhere before, but when or where, he could not at that moment tell. I informed him that he must be mistaken–that he had never seen me before, that I was a stranger in these parts; that I had been taken away in my infancy to the south. After a little conversation he politely enquired the name of my parents. I told him my mother's name was Alcy Shelton, and that my father's was James, a servant of Mr. Daniel. At the disclosure of this the driver dropped his lines, and seizing me by the hand, he warmly and affectionately welcomed me back to my long lost home. "My God!" said he, "why could I not before discover the likeness. Granny Alcy is my god-mother, but I knew nothing of her having a son in the south. He informed me that he would, if possible, like to drive through Falmouth, which was two miles out of the road, for the purpose of leaving me at my mother's door, but that the late fall of rain which had been, had rendered the road slippery and impracticable. That he would give the world to see the meeting between my mother and myself." Having made known who I was to the passengers, who were in the stage, and among whom were Mr., Mrs. and Miss Fitzhugh who had been made aware of the facts, as I have already stated on board the Boat, backed the driver in his desire, and solicited him, if possible, to go by the way of Falmouth. But it was found as the driver had anticipated, impassable—and after he had shown me the house where my father resided, and the path he generally chose in going and coming from the setting and examination of his traps, we held our way to Fredericksburgh, where we arrived at about one o'clock at night, on the 2d of July, 1828.

Here, he determined to become my Chaperoon himself. The driver delivered his team into the hands of the servants. He immediately led me into the bar room of Mr. Young, an old friend of his, and where I afterwards ascertained my mother had, a few days before been living, during the confinement of his wife, and taking me up to the light he asked Mr. Young if he knew me. The striking resemblance which I bore to my mother, prompted him immediately to answer that he did; and he seemed somewhat confounded when I informed him that he had never before seen me—that I was taken from that neighborhood when quite a child, and had come directly from Natchez on a visit to my mother, who was known as Alcy Shelton. The good old man, when he heard this, raised his eyes to Heaven and gave me his warmest blessing, thanking God that I had returned to relieve the anxieties of my mother, who was a general favorite with all the citizens of the place. In this prayer he was accompanied by Mrs. Young, who had been called to the bar room by the warm congratulations she heard going on, and never did, a poor soul feel his heart overflowing with happiness, more than I did at that moment. The mention of Natchez also brought to the room where I was, a great number of southern gentlemen from that place, and among whom were many of my customers and strongest friends. Their warm and zealous congratulations and joy at again seeing me, I will remember with gratitude to my dying day, and my own feelings, as a stranger in a strange land, meeting so unexpectedly with friends whom I so highly esteemed, I can never forget; even though years have passed away, it comes before me now as a green spot in my recollection.

I had here again to repeat to them the story of my travels and the reasons which prompted me to visit the scenes of my childhood—that it was for this purpose, and for this alone. When they had heard me through, the old folks again praised God that I had arrived to alleviate the bondage of my mother, and aid my brother and sister, who had married in the mean time, in order, that if my efforts were successful, all should again be rejoined, and constitute one family, devoted alone to God, and looking upon the past as so many trials which the Lord had strewn in our pathway, to teach us how much we are bound to thank and adore him. This sister I had always loved as the apple of my eye. It was she whom I had snatched from the burning building, and it was she, whom I felt almost as great an anxiety to unite with me in one family, together with her husband, as the release of our poor mother. The means were all that was needed to accomplish this mission, which I felt assured Heaven had designed, and which I felt, too, he would call up the means of consummating. As I before remarked there were present at Mr. Young's, many of my old friends from Natchez. These individuals had entered as Mr. Young was informing me of the anxieties of my relatives, and urging me to form such a family union, which was so desirable to Heaven and ourselves. They had heard me regret my want of means to do so, and they now generously stepped forward (God's name be praised) to alleviate my wants. Mr. Offord, of Georgetown, one who had been acquainted with me from my boyhood assured me, in the presence of his friends that I should not lack for the means of carrying my laudable desires into execution, and pulling a well filled wallet from his pocket, insisted that I should take from it as much as I myself thought it would require to consummate my wishes, and secure the freedom of my mother. Mr. Ballard, too, informed me to let money not stay me in my heart felt wish to free my mother. He told me to go to any person in the city, and purchase a wagon and a span of horses for their removal, and whatever else I needed, and to use his name with his free consent, as an endorser of my notes. To use his credit to any extent, but to be sure and remove my mother and sister, regardless of the expense. I thanked these gentlemen very kindly for their offers, but declined receiving their bounty unless I could not make my ends meet with my own exertions. After this, I retired to a private room with Mr. Young, who gave me a full and succinct account of my parent, and informed me where to find her. He bade me go to the Bridge, if I were anxious to go on, as it was a delightful moonlight night, and telling the keeper who I was, he would let me cross, and also put me upon the path to my mother's house. I determined to profit by his advice, and thanking him warmly for the interest he had taken in my affairs, I departed with a throbbing heart for my dear mother's abode. I felt that I was now treading the Land of my nativity, a free man—that I was the ambassador of a Heavenly Power, to alleviate the woes of a heart-stricken parent and furnish her also with the means of her *freedom* and a home, where her declining years should be supported, and her last sigh be registered in a son's heart. Where her least want should be tenderly administered to, and with these feelings, and with heart elate, I bent my steps towards her lonely dwelling, racked with anxiety and hope.

When I arrived at the bridge, all things were as Mr. Young had foretold me. The toll-gatherer, on ascertaining that I was the son of Alcy Shelton, immediately arose from his bed, and after a long conversation, during which he informed me, that my mother had been at his house the same evening and started for home, after night-fall, he opened the gates, and permitted me to pass. In parting from him, however, he informed me that as the road to my mother's house was difficult to find, he would advise me to stop with a colored man on the other side of the river, who was well acquainted with the road and whom he felt assured on hearing my story, would immediately accompany me. When I arrived at the house of this man, I found him wrapped soundly in sleep. Having awaked him, and informed him of my desires, he at first refused, but after a short time, with the offer of a half dollar being extended to him, he agreed to accompany me. Having therefore accoutred himself for the journey, which was but a short distance, we set out, and soon arrived at the door of my mother.

On rapping at the door, an old gentleman who was keeping my mother company, she being confined to her room by sickness, came, and demanded our business. I informed him that I was the bearer of a letter from Mrs. Shelton's son in the South to her. She immediately demanded that I might come in, which I hesitatingly did. As I entered, the old man held the light to my face, exclaiming;

"O, Alcy, if God ever gave you another son, this is him:–He is the very image of you, and has your voice, as nearly as two individuals can resemble each other in life."

My mother looked at me, from the pallet on which she was lying, and immediately asked if indeed I were her son?

I replied, by asking her if I looked like him?

She said she could not tell, but if I were, not to keep her in suspense.

I could stand it no longer, but catching her to my bosom, I exclaimed, "I am indeed your long lost son!"

After the first burst of affection had subsided with my mother, she sprang from the couch, and hastening to the door, she called to my sister to come over immediately. My sister having left her on the same evening, and fearing something was wrong, came running in her night clothes, accompanied by her husband. The scene that then ensued, I shall never forget, as my heart has never since been blessed with so much happiness. The next morning, my father was sent for, and after a recognition had taken place, I sat down with my mother and him at the table. There was none else present, and as I sat and witnessed the tears as they trickled down the cheeks of them both, and found a response with myself, I felt that the words of God had been fulfilled, and that one moment of my presence now added more to their happiness than many years had tended to give them previously. Thus was I again brought together with my family, and thus did the Lord prosper my actions as a son. All the praise be His.

My future plans were after a short time set about, and after much trouble and many trials, I achieved what my heart most panted for, the freedom of my mother. In this I was materially aided by the well wishes of many kind friends. After I had achieved her liberation, I accompanied her to the Court which was held in Stafford in order that I might witness the registering of her freedom. This was duly accomplished, and after she had received the certificate of the Court, that she was now a free and independent citizen of the land, she left the house to indulge in the feelings, which she fain would be relieved of by discharging the emotions of a surcharged heart. She retired from the Court House, and some time after I sought her behind the House, where she was pouring forth her tears of joy to an Almighty God, coupled with her prayers for the kind protection He bestowed upon her, and in upholding her through the severe trials which she had passed.

Never can I forget that scene! My mother, bathed in tears, and clutching the certificate of her release from bondage in her hand, as if it would leave her grasp, and praying to God to still shield her through life. My heart felt heavy as I witnessed her distresses–and my soul still felt elevated as I kissed from her cheeks all traces of her sorrow, and prepared to lead her from all her trials to a land of freedom and the home of a son.

After the freedom of my mother, finding that I could go no further at the present time by my own exertions, I accepted of the kind offers formerly held out by Mr. Ballard. On his credit I bought a horse and wagon, and having made all our hasty preparations, I took my mother and sister and bent our course to Natchez, where we arrived about the last of November, 1828.

But before parting with you, gentle reader, permit me to lay before you a few incidents which took place on my homeward passage. On starting from Falmouth, I carefully packed up my clothes in a trunk, and procuring an old ragged suit, the better to conceal my true motives, and appear more to advantage in the eyes of a sympathyzing people–for my funds were now run ashore, and my only hope of proceeding on my journey, was by begging. This suit was the one which I had assumed for the purpose of begging the freedom of my poor old mother, and in which I had proved successful; and I felt fully convinced I would also be successful in it in my second attempt–for I concluded that to cast away an old friend, who had stood by me in time of need, would be ill luck. But in order that the reader may the more readily conceive the appearance I made in these habiliments, *I* will endeavor, in my rude style, to draw a portrait of myself, for their satisfaction.

The pantaloons, which *I* wore, would have puzzled the wisest *m*agician of the east, to tell which was the original piece–so patched and repatched were they from waist-band to foot,–here stood out in bold relief, a large spot of Virginia linsey–there a half section of red flannel–here, a patch of home-made cloth, which appeared to have belonged to the nether garments of Mathusalem[27]–there, a portion of an old peticoat, which, no doubt Eve claimed the proprietorship of–and in fact from east to west–from north to south of those old pants–the leopard seemed their facsimile, and every spot and patch (which were almost as numerous as the sands of the sea,) assumed chamelion-like a different shade; whilst a thick coat of grease and tar added a gloss to them, which would put to blush the finest satin now worn by the most exquisite dandy, or City belle; and the coat!–Ye Gods! Joseph's was but a faint idea of the patch work, and variety of colors which decorated *my* back.[28] From black to green–from white to red–from olive to brown–from scarlet to claret–from yellow to crimson–from lake to blue, and in fact all these, with their innumerable shades added "*dignity*" to my looks (as the beggar would say) and acted as a mark of attraction to every passer by, and an open-sesame to the charity of all of whom I asked assistance–(for be it recollected that I was beggar generalissimo for a family of six besides myself and horses.) Nor was this the most remarkable feature of my habiliments. The hat! O, Jupiter, what a hat! Caesar wore his antique casque–Napoleon, his chapeaux–the "man wot eat the oysters," his ragged Beaver–but these were comfortable and comely, when compared to *my* head gear. *My hat* was an old wool, flat crowned *hat* (which had *once been a hat*) and which no doubt some old slave had thrown aside as a *nothing*–the brim fell over my eyes, and when I had pinched it into a three cornered cock, and decorated it with a sprig of green leaves at the different corners, you may well suppose that I resembled some scare-crow set in a field to protect the corn and grain of the farmer–nor was this resemblance lessened in my mind, when at every house we passed, the children ran from me, crying at the top of their lungs–"Lord! here comes the *rag man*;" and my family were rallied at all our stopping places for following such an object of commisseration and apathy.

On this journey I had many difficulties to surmount–many places at which we stopped, we were prohibited the privilege of remaining, owing to my uncouth appearance–but the Lord had extended his shield over me, and although we were compelled to encamp many a long and weary night by the road side, yet he still was with us, and protected us, as he did the children of Israel of old.[29] Yet *all* men were not thus hardened in heart–and in the capacity of a beggar, I was enabled to gather from the sympathizing people along the road, sufficient to support my family and the other inmates of the wagon, who had embarked with me for Natchez, and which consisted of two young ladies, and a young gentleman, who now reside in this city, (Nathaniel Belfour) who can at this day corroborate all which I have stated.

Nothing of importance transpired until we arrived at Washington, where Mr. and Mrs. Clay[30] then resided, (he being at that time, Secretary of State,) I immediately concluded to call upon her according to promise, and introduce my mother. This I did, and I felt fully satisfied with its beneficial results. When we arrived at her lodging, Mrs. Clay had not yet left her room, but on ascertaining that I, and my mother, had arrived, she instantly gave orders to admit my mother to her chamber. Here they were engaged in a long conversation, and in the course of time, she brought my mother to me, and gazing tenderly at me for a short time, congratulated her on having so affectionate a son. Her husband was then absent–but was expected home every hour, and we were strongly insisted upon to remain until his arrival; which owing to our want of time we were compelled to refuse. Mrs. Clay, however, for the purpose of inducing us, stated that if we would await his arrival, Mr. Clay would be happy, owing to the high opinion he, and his sons entertained for me, and knowing my filial regard for my parent, to furnish our scanty purse, and enable us to prosecute our journey to its end in comfort. But time pressed upon us—and we could not even avail ourselves of this kind and benevolent offer. When she found that all her importunities were in vain, she insisted upon our receiving from her a lot of provisions;—which consisted of a quantity of bread—a large and delicious ham—and a huge spicy cheese. This appeared to us a God-send, and lasted us for some weeks on our journey. Mrs. Clay when we parted, gazed alternately upon my mother and self, and as the tears trickled from her eyes, remarked:—

"Madam, you know not the treasure you have now in charge. You know not the value of your son. Were you *to hear my husband and sons, speak of him*, you might form some just estimate of his worth. Rest assured he is an individual of most surprising and unspeakable tenderness for his parents—and as I before told him, I have no child of whom I could expect the sacrifice which he has made for you."

Both she and my mother were bathed in tears—and offering up a prayer for our safe arrival at our destination, we parted, joyful indeed at the thoughts of God's will, and the kindness with which we met. If ever this Narrative should reach the eyes of my benefactress, I sincerely hope she will remember her kindness, and believe that it is still thought of with gratitude; and that she will not think it less worth as coming from the mouth of a poor creature, who groaned out thirty-six of his best years in bondage. May the Almighty protect her—and may all the pleasures and bounties, which He showers upon His people be her's—and when done with this world, may He accept her spirit among those of his own chosen band, is my sincere prayer.

On passing from the door of Mrs. Clay, we bent our steps to Georgetown, where my waggon had stopped;—owing to the sickness of my sister—yet, in looking back, we could discover Lady Clay, still standing in the door watching our steps, whilst beside her stood her old and faithful servant "*Letty*," and her daughter "*Nancy*," my old friends. She still looked, as in fact did all of them, as if they grieved for my inability to stay—and were blessing the mother, who was possessed of so kind a son. A long series of moons have passed since, but that scene is still fresh in my memory, and will follow me in greenness to my grave. The Lord's will be praised—for His goodness has followed me through every vicissitude, and blessed me with a fullness and richness of heart—which even now sustains and enervates me, at this late day.

On leaving Washington we wended our way smoothly until we reached the vicinity of Uniontown, when we met with an accident, from the breaking of our axle-tree. Yet the Lord was with us, and the misfortune happening before a kind neighbor's house, who was the proprietor of a Blacksmith shop, and having been informed of our circumstances, they very kindly and generously repaired the accident, and sent us on our journey rejoicing. But here, too, I was, in the appearance I bore, an object of apathy. My garb belied me—and they looked upon me as the *children* in all places did—a "rag-man;" but when my mother informed them that I was her son, and what I had suffered for her, the tune was generally changed, and I was cordially greeted with anxious inquiries, and benevolent wishes for my success.

Whilst the blacksmith was repairing our axle-tree, I accompanied my mother up to the residence of the mother of Mr. Stewart, the Congressman from Uniontown, of whom I have previously spoken—and whom I faithfully promised, if I passed that way to call upon. The meeting of the old folks, when she ascertained who I was, I could not withstand, and consequently sauntered away, to hide my tears from observation.—After a long conversation, Mrs. Stewart with tears in her eyes, requested my mother to await, and to induce me to remain until her son should arrive, whom she felt fully convinced would leave nothing undone to guaranty us in a comfortable and happy journey—but, as in the case of Mrs. Clay our time was urgent—and the old Ladies were compelled to part with each other, though with tears. After affectionate entreaties, Lady Stewart accompanied my mother to the end of the lane, in order to bid farewell to the family, which was some half mile distant from her residence. When she arrived, all were delighted to see her, and when I assure you that all equally regretted her departure—and tears were copiously shed on either side, I present to you but a faint idea of that meeting and parting—for if God ever implanted truth and honesty in the heart, which none can doubt—prayers and well wishes were freely exchanged at that humble wagon of the penniless and begging Ethiopian, who had thus reduced himself for his family's freedom, and his own affectionate regard for them.

Previous to this, however, I have neglected to mention one very important circumstance. The reader will remember that I have before mentioned a gentleman whom I met with, whilst in company with Mr. Brune, and who kept the stage office at Froststown, Maryland. This gentleman had strongly invited me in returning to call upon him, which I accordingly did. Here I remained with my family for a week, and I must say, that never was man and family treated more kindly than I was. Nothing appeared too much for him or his, to perform for me—and my request was all that was necessary to insure any service which lay in his power. I am sorry, I cannot now call him by name—but I feel assured the Lord still upholds him, if living—and if dead, that he has met a great and glorious reward for his kindness to a penniless boy, whose love of family had thrown him upon the wide bosom of a cold uncharitable world.

I had been in the habit, since I left Washington, of hailing the stage as it passed me, I ever being in advance of the wagon which bore my family, and inquiring if there were among the passengers any gentleman from the vicinity of my boyhood and acquaintance. This proved unsuccessful, until near Wheeling; when on my hail a gentleman answered, saying that he came from Paris, Kentucky. I immediately approached the coach, and gazed at the individual with feelings of joy. He proved to be an old acquaintance, and after eyeing me some time, for my scare-crow garb seemed a mystery to him, he asked–

"And who, pray, are you, that comes from Kentucky?"

"Why massa Huggard," replied I, "don't you remember me Mr. Brent's favorite,–Billy Hayden?"

"Impossible!" replied he.

"The same, sir, I assure you," replied I, "but my garb seems to belie me."

"My God! and is it so? and what in God's world has possessed you to wear such clothes?"

"Why, massa Jim, I'm begging now for a mother and sister, whom I have just rescued from bondage. The wagon which you passed, behind us, contains them, and we are bound for Natchez!"

"And are you really out of funds?"

"I am," replied I.

"Here then," said he, "is all the change I have at present; but at the next stopping place I will leave you some means to prosecute your journey," pitching out to me twenty-five cents.

I thanked him very kindly for his favor, and when I reached the place of stoppage, *I* very politely inquired if any money had been left there for me. Here, another difficulty occurred as the landlord and landlady refused to recognize me, or to give me the money until the arrival of the wagon, when my mother corroborated my statement, and claimed the funds.

The striking resemblance between myself and my mother convinced them; and after many apologies they handed me some five or six dollars, and filling our cargo with provisions, we again renewed our journey, rejoicing.

For this act of kindness on the part of Mr. Huggard, he has the sincere prayers of a faithful heart; and if unable to liquidate the debt in this world–rest assured that the same God who has upheld me through life, and who suffers not a sparrow to fall, without his knowledge, will treply reward him in a world to come.[31]

O, how good and glorious are the ways of a Divine Providence! He sustains the rich, whilst He extends a doubly protecting arm over the poor–He shields the monach, while he blesses and protects the subject–He turns all to love, where the heart rebels not, and he stands willing to pluck all to his protection who are willing to give up their hearts to Him.

The next incident of interest which transpired was when we arrived at Wheeling, Virginia. To the landlord of the stage office at this place, I had on my upward passage been introduced by my friend Mr. Brune, who hearing from his lips, a narrative of my history, strongly invited me to call on my return. At his house I accordingly stopped, and I must be permitted to say that his invitation at that time was faithfully repaid. As soon as we arrived at his house, and I had made known who I was, he took us to a colored family at the lower end of town, and after making arrangements with them for house-room and board–which he himself paid, and also furnishing us with provender for our horses, he left us comfortably situated. In the mean-time too, he secured for the balance of the family, save my mother and self, a passage on board a boat from that place to Maysville, whilst we were to proceed on our way to Maysville in our wagon. All that man could do–all that nature could possibly divine which belonged to man to perform for his neighbor was faithfully fulfilled, and religiously observed. The Lord had raised him up as a friend to me and to mine–for the Lord never yet according to Holy writ has seen his seed begging bread–nor the poor and righteous wanting in the affections and support of Christ. He had upheld me through the various trials and vexations of life–He had given me life–He had shielded me from all dangers, and though He placed difficulties, apparently insurmountable before me–yet He brought me forth in triumph and landed me safely upon the shores of faith, and the brink of Immortal love. Who, then, can fail to thank Him for all the kindness he bestows upon them in life–who can fail to consider that Christ himself, when he suffered crucifixion for a world, that they might be saved, would lead us safely through the fiery ordeal, and as he promised us on Earth, eventually lead us to the throne of Grace, to sup and rejoice with us in the presence of His Holy Father. Surely none–therefore, I can do naught but adore his holy name, and thank him for the innumerable blessings which he has showered upon me.

In Maysville, my mother met with a sister, whom she had not seen for a long time; and with whom she remained for some few days. This sister, she had not seen for at least forty years; but the result was not for me to witness. Those who have seen a meeting among the members of a family long separated, can fully appreciate the feelings which throb in their bosoms. The Lord had brought about a meeting, and the Lord alone could sympathize with those two aged females as they embraced each other with the tears of sisterly affection.

This was the last scene of interest which occurred until we arrived at Natchez, where, as I have before stated, we arrived in November, 1828.

Here we remained until 1835, when we removed to Cincinnati, where I now reside, and where in 1842, I buried the dear creature who had given me life, and watched over me with maternal affection, and here as a citizen I have felt the kindness of God in all my acts with my fellow men.

If any of my old friends see (and I am aware many of them will,) this narrative, my sincere hope is that the truths which I have herein stated will find a cordial response in their bosom, and having once paved the way they will again wish to hear more from their well wisher Billy Hayden.–In this I have not intended to wound the feelings of any–God knows I revere my friends, whilst I extend forgiveness to my enemies. My intentions have been to fulfill what I conceived to be a duty to myself, and my feelings toward my God, and my most earnest prayer shall be extended to Heaven in their behalf through life and in death—for they have travelled with me on Earth, and my desire is that we may all meet again in Heaven.

God's name be praised, for he has guided me safely through all the trials I have had to undergo through life, and aided me in my heart-felt wish and desire of obtaining a parent's freedom. Reluctantly, therefore, I bid you a heart-felt adieu for a short period. This hasty sketch, for it is my intention hereafter, to lay before you a more succinct history of the same, God willing, and your present liberality calling for it, is but the forerunner to prepare the way for what I conceive to be a final good.—Many of the most important incidents of my life are omitted, and many that would cause by a true and faithful narration, the hair to stand on end, for their cruelties have been but slightly winked at during this brief period. But I now, thank Heaven, enjoy the rights and immunities of a free citizen of your land—I enjoy the freedom of mind, body and soul, and can cast my eyes to Heaven, and exclaim, with my fellow mortals, "here Lord am I, and the treasures, tenfold increased, which thou hast given me." My mother, the saint over whom I so long held a son's faithful trust, I buried some years since in the Methodist Episcopal Burying Ground in this place. God bless her memory, for a son's tears now fall, in adverting again to her. As for myself, I am about to continue and lengthen out these memoirs, to be given to the public, if called for by them. Hoping, therefore, that the Almighty God may sustain us all through the various vicissitudes through life—that he may protect and watch over us in the hour of death, and finally save us, to partake of His richness in Heaven, is the sincere wish of your friend as he bids you a cordial and heart-felt ADIEU!

## WOMAN IN THE SLAVE WORLD

Woman! thy heart is love—thy form is grace,
Thy smile disarms the bloody hand of strife,
And beauty is enshrined upon thy face,
As gentle maiden, or as faithful wife.
The music and the melody of life;
A beam of mercy, sorrow's tear to dry,
To man with holy influences rife,
On Earth, thou art an angel of the sky.
Light from thine foot-prints shine, and glory from thine eye.

Winter prepares the embryo flowers of spring,
Among the leafless boughs the birds are mute
Again, that the more gladly they may sing;
The rose shall bloom again, the tendrils shoot
And branch in beauty, rich with golden fruit,
But blighted woman blossoms not again;
Dews may not cherish; sun-beams may not boot,
Her angel bowers she never shall regain,
Bright tears may pity shed, her sorrows are in vain.

The whitest robe most easily is stained,
The soft most readily the impression takes,
The acutest nerve most sensibly is pained,
The delicate machine, the soonest breaks;
The oak resists the storm, that ruin makes
Among the roses; in the finest mind
The reason slumbers when the fancy wakes,
The heart the most susceptible and kind,
To danger's most exposed–when mischief is designed.

Here how few gentle women then escape,
When all beneath the roses lucks the snare,
And wheresoever she her course may shape,
The influences of the earth and air,
Seduce, corrupt, and things themselves most fair,
Against the soft confider are combined;
No shield defends her, and no guardian care
Watches the varied workings of her mind,
By every impulse led, as Fancy is inclined.

Sees she the stars in Heaven, like angels, blaze,
In them she reads a history impure,
Or wanders she amid the forest's maze,
Within the solemn circle is a lure
For vestal virtue–who may then insure
The unheeding one against the poison'd wound,
Or if inflicted, who devise a cure;
It festers, gangrenes, till the whole is found
One pestilent disease–and leprosy unsound.

The pathway, how may she discover, where
The sun that rules the day is dark as night,
Amid the trackless waste how may she fare,
Where an impure Religion's meteor light,
The soul bewilders, and unnerves the sight.
And vice is worshipped, and the very shrine,
A place impure, and priestly fingers write,
Precepts unholy, that men deem divine,
To quench the unborrow'd lights, that in the spirit shine.

Alas! how wreck'd the promise of her birth!
In poison'd plants arise the ambrosial seeds.
She who might be the ornament of Earth,
A ruined temple overgrown with weeds,
A golden chamber, where the serpent feeds.
A rayless jewel, or a beamless star,
A silver cistern of unholy deeds,
The smile of gentle peace–the heart of war,
Impure idolatory the work of God to mar.

Yet she may pity claim, she never knew
The holy training of a law divine;
Nor the domestic right to nature true,
Nor love, nor truth that kindle on the shrine
Of a pure household–gods and men combine
To wreck and ruin–from a child a slave
Of sire and husband, who in chains confine,
And home–their Virtue's altar, is the grave–
The temple is a thrall from which no power can save.

Medicine may heal the body's deepest wound,
The spirit's gashes never close again;
For it, availing balsam is not found,
And for its fractures, ligatures are vain,
They knit not but incurable remain;
The leprous soul no leech may purify,
And no physician mitigate its pain,
No hand again may reinstate on high,
Palsied and bent to earth the native of the sky.

Can she be faithful? She who never knew
Love's rosy hopes, and its alternate fears?
Its fair varieties, forever new;
The sweet surprise, and the delicious tears,
As from one fountain flowing, in the ears
The melody of bliss, the blending heart,
The conscious smile that each to each endears,
The undisguised avowal without art,
The drama of true love wherein each plays a part.

The while the temple gates are open wide,
Seduction and to lawless love invite,
Beneath the shrine, her blushes she may hide,
Her creed may teach her that she acts aright,
A glory to her God, a faith to plight,
Or to his servants, holy men and pure,
United to these ministers of light,
Her endless happiness she will insure,
How may her virtue stand, or how result the lure.

Take from the groves, the vespers of delight,
The green leaves from the trees, the rose from spring,
The meek, the modest matron eye from night,
And from the birds, that sparkle and that sing,
The bells of music, and the rainbow wing,
But leave, oh! leave fond plighted love to youth!
Take that, you leave to wedlock but a sting
For mutual wounds, strife, jealousy, untruth,
The slave but deadly hate, the tyrant but untruth.

Oh! Jealousy is greedy as the grave
And as unpitying of its helpless prey;
Virtue availeth not, and may not save,
Though innocence may hold its spotless way,
Clear as the azure of an Hindoo day;
Man blackness sees, where there is not a speck,
And swears that Faith itself is gone astray,
She to the sword shall yield her slender neck,
And lie a headless trunk–beauty's degraded wreck.

## APPENDIX

After such exertions upon my part to free my mother, the reader would naturally wish to know what character, or in what estimation she was known, among her fellow beings in the neighborhood in which she resided. My mother was generally known throughout the country, as a midwife, and her success in her line of business, is attested in the following papers, together with her character for honesty, goodness, &c., &c., &c.

RECOMMENDATIONS

We the undersigned have known Mrs. Alcy Shelton, a woman of color, for twenty-five years past. She has practised midwifery with great success, and skill, and during the above mentioned period, she has not within our recollection met with any accident in her profession. We are indeed sorry to part with her, and her conduct and deportment has always been good. We can, however, with confidence, recommend her to the notice of ladies, wherever she may reside, &c., &c.

Susan C. Beale,

Mary F. Briggs,

S. J. Forbes,

Mary D. Buchanan,

Anna C. Gordon,

Elizabeth B. Vass,

Judith C. Corbin,

Hannah Leitch,

Jane Brooke,

Elizabeth S. Beckwith,

Susan S. Potts

Sept. 6th., 1828.

In addition to the foregoing, my mother received the following certificates of character, and skill in her profession, from Mrs. Esther T. Moncure, and from Dr. Carmichael and Lady, and which I beg leave to attach hereunto:

RECOMMENDATION OF MRS. MONCURE.

I have known the bearer, Alcy, for about 25 years, during which time, she has supported a most excellent character, and has been very successful in her profession as a midwife.

RECOMMENDATION OF DR. CARMICHAEL.

I have often met with Alcy, as a midwife for the last twenty years, in the neighboring towns of Falmouth, in the most respectable families. She may be safely trusted—always calling in medical aid in a proper time.

*James Carmichael.*

Fredericksburgh, Sept. 5th., 1829.

RECOMMENDATION OF DR. CARMICHAEL'S LADY.

This is to certify that Alcy Shelton has practiced midwifery for the last thirty years, with success, and that she in an honest and good woman.

*Elizabeth Carmichael.*

The above recommendations are not the trumped up certificates of the scum of the neighborhood, in order to impose upon the credulity of the reader, but are from the pens of the first families in the South. No one who knew Alcy Shelton, will for a moment hesitate to subscribe their testimony as to her honesty, and goodness of heart; and those upon whom she has been permitted to call, during the period of their confinement, have ever commended her for her kindness and attention. It is true that in order to attain her freedom, I was compelled to surmount barriers, which at first appeared to be almost impracticable; but I was laboring in the cause of my mother—one who was a favorite with all her acquaintances, and one whom to me was more than life itself. And what gentle reader, would be your feelings, as a son, if you were placed in similar circumstances. I anticipate your answer. Death to you would be a paradise, when compared to the thought of longer seeing your aged parent toiling in the bondage of Slavery—her toil worn limbs, hurried beyond their strength in the fulfillment of duties, dictated by a *master's will.* The tears of sorrow were hardening upon her wrinkled cheek—the fire of life was beginning to leave her eye; and the elasticity of youth, had long since departed from her step, and yet she was a slave—bound by laws, neither human nor divine, to fulfill whatever duty a master or a mistress, in their self-wisdom, or actuated by other motives, either of malice, or authority, should impose upon her. I was in the prime of my youth—the son of this aged sufferer. By my own exertions I had become a free man—and what course, let me ask, did humanity–the laws of God and nature, point out to me? Was it my duty to stand idly by, and witness the careworn struggles of an affectionate mother, without an effort for her freedom? No! I felt that such a course would blast my claims to humanity forever–I felt that unless I struck a blow for her freedom, I would be sacrificing all the feelings, which should bind a son in the ties of consanguinity and filial love to her who had given me existence, and protected me through childhood–that I was sacrificing the most heaven-born principles of Jehovah; and I concluded to strike fearlessly, and regardless of consequences. Acting under these impulses, I *did* strike, and struck too, effectually–so much so, that after surmounting all the difficulties thrown in my way, through the benign influence, and protection of the Almighty God, I succeeded in breaking her chains, and setting her free from the trammels of bondage, upon the broad basis of universal freedom, which acknowledges no distinction between the human family–drawing no line of demarkation between the sons of the north and south, between the tawny skin of the Ethiopian and the lily hue of the northern maiden. *All, all* are recognized as *free*, and as such, my mother was, through my exertions, enabled to proclaim her gratitude to God.

The reader will, no doubt, consider this as a digression from the subject, which should characterize this narrative; as indeed it is: but I feel well assured that he will pardon my indulgence, in a few filial reflections, guided by right, and approved of by Heaven; and hoping that such may be the case, I hasten to proceed to those papers, which will bear more directly upon myself, and at the same time confirm the premises laid down in the foregoing pages.

With this view I will unfold the pile of evidences and recommendations of character, and spread them before the reader in regular rotation; in order that he may know more fully, who and what he is, who has addressed himself to his understanding in the preceding narrative. I shall also claim the privilege, with the reader's permission, of making such comments as I may see proper, upon each gentleman's testimony, that I may thereby the more readily illustrate the matter.

The first, therefore, that I shall present to his observation, is the Deed of Emancipation, declaring me a free and independent citizen of the United States, entitled to rights and immunities of my fellow men. Yes that deed which consummated the object for which I toiled and struggled for many long and tedious years–for which my soul yearned–and for which I had so often prayed to God to bring within my grasp. My prayer was finally answered–and the health and strength which I was blest with, during my struggles, I was induced to look upon as blessings, showered upon me to accomplish my earthly purpose. But to the paper, which reads as follows:

Thomas Phillips'
Deed of Emancipation
to William Hayden.

This Indenture of Emancipation, made this second day of October, eighteen hundred and twenty-four: Witnesseth, that I, Thomas Phillips, of the town of Paris and State of Kentucky, do hereby emancipate, set free, and forever discharge from servitude of myself, my heirs, executors, administrators and assigns, a certain negro man slave, by the name of William Hayden, a barber, about thirty-five years of age, five feet ten or eleven inches high, and dark complexion.

Witness my hand and seal, the day and date above written.

(Signed,) Thomas Phillips.

Atteste:<br>
Henry Bridges,<br>
N. C. Marsh,<br>
Tho: C. Owings.

*Bourbon County Court, October Term*, 1824.

This Deed of Manumission from Thomas Phillips to William Hayden, was this day proven in open Court, by the oath of Thomas C. Owings and Nicholas C. Marsh, subscribing witnesses thereto, to be the act and deed of the said Phillips, and ordered to be recorded: Att. Thomas P. Smith, C.B.C.

State of Kentucky, ss.

I Thomas P. Smith, Clerk of the County Court of Bourbon, in the State aforesaid, do certify that the foregoing Deed of Manumission, from Thomas Phillips to William Haden, is truly copied from the record in my office. In testimony whereof, I have hereunto set my hand, and affixed the seal of said County, this fifth day of October, eighteen hundred and twenty-four, and in the 33d year of the commonwealth.

Thomas P. Smith, Clerk,<br>
By A. Chs. Dickerson, D.C.

I certify that the within Deed of Emancipation was received into my office, to be recorded, on the 16th day of January, 1826.

Woodson Wren, Clk.,<br>
By J. Greene, Dep. Clk.

State of Mississippi,<br>
Adams County.

I, Woodson Wren, Clerk of the County Court of said County, certify that the within Deed of Emancipation is a true transcript from the records of my Office.

Given under my hand, and the seal of office at the city of Natchez, this 20th day of February, 1826.

Woodson Wren, Clk.,<br>
By J. Greene, Dep. Clk.

This was the paper for which I had so long looked, with so much anxiety, and which when I received, I clutched to my bosom, with more true feelings of joy, than I would have done the immense wealth of the Mexican mines. It is true, many years elapsed, ere it came, but come it did, and when I knew it was really in my possession, and as I followed the traces of the hand that penned it, I felt that I was no longer a slave, but a representative of the Almighty God. I felt that I could now stand forth in my God-like attributes, and claim from my fellow men the rights and privileges which they themselves exercised. I looked upon the earth, and the beauties of nature, in a new light–

not that which fills the soul of the slave, as he witnesses the freedom of all around him, and shudders at his own chains, but as a human being—a being whose soul is God's and whose every aspiration is free to his will, alone: and I appreciated this change, my cheeks were suffused with tears, and in the fullness of my soul, I gave God the praise, and the glory of the great change which had been wrought in me.

Shortly after receiving the above deed of Emancipation, I prepared to conform with the request previously made of me, by Mr. Minor, of becoming a resident of Natchez, which in company with my mother and sister, I carried into effect. To facilitate this, and to show the kindness which he had formerly expressed for me, Mr. Minor procured for me, the following Bill of Relief, from the Legislature of Mississippi:

"AN ACT

*For the Relief of William Hayden and others.*

Sec. 1. Be it enacted by the Senate and House of Representatives, of the state of Mississippi, in General Assembly convened, That from and after the passage of this act, it shall, and may be lawful for William Hayden, James Miller, and Hannibal, free men of color, to reside within the limits of the state, any law to the contrary, notwithstanding: Provided, that the said William Hayden, James Miller, and Hannibal, do each and severally enter into bond, with good and sufficient securities, in the sum of five hundred dollars each, payable to the Governor, and his successors in office, conditioned for their good behavior and that they will not become a public charge.

Sec. 2. And be it further enacted that it shall be the duty of the Judge of Probate of the Countie's in which the said individuals may reside, to take and receive the bond, provided for in the first section of this Act, and file the same in the Clerk's Office of the Court over which he presides.

Sec. 3. And be it further enacted, that Peter Sewall, a free man of color, shall have leave to reside within the limits of this State, upon his entering into bond with good and sufficient security, in the sum of eight hundred dollars, payable to the Judge of Probate of the county of Wilkison, and his successors in office; conditioned for his good behavior, and that he will not become a public charge.

Ch. B. Green,
Speaker of the House of Representatives.
A. M. Scott, L't. Governor,
and speaker of the Senate.

Approved Feb. 14, 1828.
Gerard C. Brandon."

But I will not weary the reader with a multiplicity of papers which I might adduce as the testimony of my friends, relative to my character as a man and a christian, and whom in this little narrative, calls upon you for sympathy and support. Suffice it to say, that he holds letters of the strongest recommendation from the following gentlemen, who stand high for honor and integrity, and who move in the best society of their country:

Thomas C. Owings, *Paris, Ky.*
Francis A. Owen, H. Fooley, F. A. Owen. *Natchez.*
W. H. Richardson, *Lexington.*
W. P. Theobald, *Georgetown.*
Wm. Brune, *Natchez.*
W. O. Clarkson, *Covington.*
Thos. Phillips, *Paris.*
James Stockman, *Natchez.*
John C. Buckner, *Lexington.*

Rebecca Haden,
N. Falkner
John Branham,
Thomas H. Bradford,
W. Bower,
Lineal West,
M. H. Ferris,
John Shortridge,
Elijah Craig,
Woodson Wren,
and numerous others.

Hence, having satisfied the reader as to his honesty attested by the above named gentlemen, he only asks the privilege of inserting the following letters received from Mrs. Mary S. Smith, his young mistress, with whom he was raised, and with whom he received the blessings of her mother, and he will bid thee a God's blessing, and retire.

*Garrard County*, Oct. 16th., 1842.
MR. WILLIAM HAYDEN,

*Honored Sir:*–Your letter of September the 13th, came safe to hand a few days since–I was highly gratified to hear from you, as it is the first correct account I have had of you since you were at my house in Scott. I often think of you, William, and sometimes regret that I ever parted with you, thinking that you would have been of so great a benefit to me, in the absence of my husband, to have attended to his business. But, perhaps, it is all for the better–you were anxious to have your freedom, and would not have been satisfied without it. I hope that you are doing well, and have accumulated a handsome property. Knowing that you are very industrious and economical, I would of course come to such a conclusion. I would be pleased to hear from you more particularly,–whether you have a family–and of your situation, generally. I shall certainly expect a visit from you, as you have settled so near us. We are now boarding at Mr. George Moore's, in Garrard County, twelve miles north-west of Lancaster. I have not any of my children at home with me, at this time. I have a daughter married, and living in Lexington–and a son, married and located in Columbia, Missouri. He is a physician, and doing well in his profession. He is also a member of the Christian Church, and is very much devoted to the cause of Christ. My youngest daughter is now at school in Franklin, about three miles from Frankford. She is in her 15th year. I have but three children, and they are all professors of the Religion of Jesus, which is a great source of pleasure to me–they are comely, and possessed with good powers of mind. You requested me to give you some intelligence of my mother. She has gone to Missouri, and is living in Boon County, about three miles from Columbia. She lives with her youngest son, Joel, and has the most of her children near to her. She is very infirm, and has been afflicted for years. Mr. Smith, my youngest daughter and myself, went out last Fall, a year ago, and returned this Fall. Mother has resided in that State thirteen years. I think it is not such a country as has been represented. It is not like the rich part of Kentucky.

When you write let me know whether you are a follower of the Lord Jesus, for I view that of more importance than any thing on earth. We may live without it, but it is hard to die, unless we have a hope in the Saviour of sinners. But O, to think of dying a Christian's death, and meeting with our Heavenly Father and his Son Jesus Christ, and all the righteous who have gone before! O, how transporting the thought! It lifts my soul from earth to heaven!

I do not know whether the latter part of my letter will be interesting to you; but I do hope you have started in the heavenly race before this. But if you have not, let me entreat you not to delay. The wheel of time is rolling on, and we shall soon be laid in the dust. I will now close, by subscribing myself

Your friend & well-wisher until death. *Mary S. Smith.*

LETTER 2.

FROM THOMAS AND MARY S. SMITH.

*Lexington, May* 18th, 1843.

*Dear Sir.*–Yours of the 23d of April came safely to hand. We had been looking for you from Christmas until the time we received your letter, and felt a good deal disappointed in not seeing you. We are exceedingly sorry to learn by your letter of your bad health. This was wholly unexpected, as you have always appeared to be very healthy–but there is no certainty in this world, neither as to health nor life. We yet hope that you may recover. Whether, or not, we are much pleased to learn that you are ready to leave the world. This I deem of more importance than any thing else. You have done your duty, and feel, no doubt, a good conscience; you have obeyed your Lord, and have peace and comfort. How much better this than the world, especially to a sick man. Whether your time be long or short, I hope you will continue to trust in the Lord; and O, may your path be like that of the just, shining more and more, even unto the perfect day.

If you should get so, that you can come and see us, we shall be glad to see you at any time. You, no doubt, will take great care of yourself–keep from bad colds, and from every thing that would tend to promote your disease. Good nursing is a great thing for sick people, I hope this you will have. Let your mind be calm as possible, for this is good in sickness. It requires much patience to bear up. Remember, the scripture says, the sufferings of the present time are not worthy to be compared with the glory that shall be revealed in us–that all things work for good to them that love God, to those who are the called according to his purpose.[32]

As to your old mistress, she is yet living, I suppose. We heard she was as well as common, since I wrote you last. She lives in Boone County, Missouri, near Columbia the county seat. But if you can write, send it to me as you state in your letter, and I will direct it to her. She will be delighted to get a letter from you.–Write to Danville, as you have done, as soon as you can–Polly desires to be remembered to you. I subscribe myself.

Your well wisher, THOMAS SMITH.

O, William, I cannot let this letter be closed, without communicating a short epistle to you. I always respected you highly, but now I love you as a follower of our Lord and Saviour. Dear Brother, think of what our Saviour suffered for us–turn your eyes to Mount Calvary, and behold the bleeding Lamb of God. O, what love the father has bestowed upon a dying world. Is not that enough to make us love him, and try to serve him while we have breath. My dear William, if we should never meet again, I hope we shall meet in heaven. It would be a gratification to me, if you were near enough for me to visit you, and administer to your comfort, for good attention is a great thing in sickness. But I hope you will not suffer. For any thing we can do for you, you can command it. O, may God bless you, and give you strength to bear your afflictions as a Christian; and if it should please kind Providence to raise you, O, that you may live to His glory is the prayer of your devoted friend,

MARY S. SMITH.

Hence, the above letters will simply and faithfully show to the reader, the influence of a mother's early instructions. Little did I think, whilst kneeling at the feet of my old mistress, that as she laid her hand upon the head of her daughter and myself, and bade us love each other as brother and sister, that the feelings of those youthful days would cling to us through life, and that the warning voice of this very daughter, would strengthen me in my service of the Lord. O, the blessed influence a mother's blessing yields–it is a heavenly dew falling upon our paths, and bespangling them with flowers–or, if improperly yielded, it is a mildew which cankers and festers in the heart, making it a hell on earth. Would every mother pursue the course which was so affectionately adopted by my good old mistress,–were they to inculcate similar sentiments, what a paradise would this world be, to what it now is. The houses of infamy, penitentiaries and alms-houses, would be monuments of folly, and a spirit of brotherly love would supply their place, and sing their funeral dirge. For, I hold, that it is the early instructions of a mother that influences the world–that it is their precepts, and their examples that render us Christians, or worldly minded wretches. God in His goodness gave me the best of Christian's for a mistress, and her blessing has stamped upon my heart in indelible characters her christian precepts–they have been extended by her daughter, and I am happy. God in his mercy forever bless them.

## EDITORIAL NOTES TO *NARRATIVE OF WILLIAM HAYDEN*

1. God, the Supreme Being, the Lord, the Almighty.

2. John Dryden (1631–1700), *The Hind and the Panther*: "All, as they say, that glitters is not gold."

3. The apostle Paul (A.D. 10?–A.D. 67) was a first-century Jew, born in Tarsus in Cilicia (now Turkey). He changed from being an enemy of Christianity to being one of its leading missionaries.

4. This is possibly a reference to Herod Agrippa I, king of Judea from 41–44. He was the grandson of Herod the Great.

5. A revengeful, merciless Jewish moneylender in Shakespeare's *Merchant of Venice* (1600). Shylock attempted to exact the forfeit of a pound of flesh from Antonio's body.

6. Death, the Grim Reaper.

7. Fish.

8. Clean and sharpen.

9. Barber.

10. One of the seven archangels in Judaism and Christianity. In Luke 1, the sound of his trumpet declares the coming of the Messiah.

11. Croesus (?–circa 546 B.C.) was the last king of Lydia. He reigned from circa 560 B.C. until his death and was renowned for his great wealth. Golconda was a fortress and ruined city in southern India. The area was famous for its diamonds.

12. Exclamations of praise or adoration to the Lord or the Savior. See Matthew 21:9, "And the multitudes that went before, and that followed, cried, saying, Hosanna to the son of David: Blessed is he that cometh in the name of the Lord; Hosanna in the highest," and Mark 11:9–10, "And they that went before, and they that followed, cried, saying, Hosanna; Blessed is he that cometh in the name of the Lord: Blessed be the kingdom of our father David, that cometh in the name of the Lord: Hosanna in the highest."

13. A partial or complete state of unconsciousness.

14. One who gives great or undue attention to dress.

15. Hayden possibly means "swartrutter." Swartrutters were groups of men who wore black clothes and blackened their faces. These gangs were a threatening presence in the Netherlands during the sixteenth and seventeenth centuries.

16. Riches, according to Matthew 6:24. Milton, in *Paradise Lost*, used Mammon as the name of one of the fallen angels.

17. The Himalayas are the highest mountain system in the world.

18. A personal follower or subordinate official who executes orders with pity.

19. Shackled or otherwise confined in chains.

20. The auctioneer's gavel.

21. Welts caused by whipping.

22. Shrouded in darkness or ignorance.

23. Job 38:11.

24. Fool.

25. Hosea 14:9, "Who is wise, and he shall understand these things? Prudent, and he shall know them? For the ways of the Lord are right, and the just shall walk in them: but the transgressors shall fall therein."

26. Heaven.

27. Methuselah was one of the patriarchs who is said, in Genesis 5:27, to have lived 969 years.

28. Joseph was a Hebrew patriarch. His father, Jacob, gave him a "coat of many colors." His brothers became jealous and sold him to some Midianites, who sold him into Egypt (Genesis 30:23 and Genesis 39 to the end).

29. Old Testament Israelites.

30. Cassius Marcellus Clay (1810–1903) was a Kentucky politician and abolitionist. He served in the Kentucky legislature in 1835, 1837, and 1840, worked for Lincoln's election in 1860, and was a minister to Russia in 1861, 1862, and 1863–69. He was the founder of *The American*, an antislavery newspaper in Lexington, Kentucky. See Richardson, *Cassius Marcellus Clay.*

31. Matthew 10:29–31, "Are not two sparrows sold for a farthing? And one of them shall not fall on the ground without your Father. But the very hairs of your head are all numbered. Fear ye not therefore, ye are of more value than many sparrows."

32. Romans 8:18–19, "For I reckon that the sufferings of this present time are not worthy to be compared with the glory which shall be revealed in us. For the earnest expectation of the creature waiteth for the manifestation of the sons of God."